T0334724

JCMS Annual Review
of the European Union
in 2014

Edited by

Nathaniel Copsey
and
Tim Haughton

General Editors: Michelle Cini and Amy Verdun

WILEY
Blackwell

This edition first published 2015
© 2015 John Wiley & Sons Ltd except for editorial material and organization

Registered Office
John Wiley & Sons Ltd, The Atrium, Southern Gate, Chichester, West Sussex, PO19 8SQ, UK

Editorial Offices
350 Main Street, Malden, MA 02148--5020, USA
9600 Garsington Road, Oxford, OX4 2DQ, UK
The Atrium, Southern Gate, Chichester, West Sussex, PO19 8SQ, UK

For details of our global editorial offices, for customer services, and for information about how to apply for permission to reuse the copyright material in this book please see our website at www.wiley.com/wiley-blackwell.

The right of Nathaniel Copsey and Tim Haughton to be identified as the authors of the editorial material in this work has been asserted in accordance with the UK Copyright, Designs and Patents Act 1988.

All rights reserved. No part of this publication may be reproduced, stored in a retrieval system, or transmitted, in any form or by any means, electronic, mechanical, photocopying, recording or otherwise, except as permitted by the UK Copyright, Designs and Patents Act 1988, without the prior permission of the publisher.

Wiley also publishes its books in a variety of electronic formats. Some content that appears in print may not be available in electronic books.

Designations used by companies to distinguish their products are often claimed as trademarks. All brand names and product names used in this book are trade names, service marks, trademarks or registered trademarks of their respective owners. The publisher is not associated with any product or vendor mentioned in this book.

Limit of Liability/Disclaimer of Warranty: While the publisher and author(s) have used their best efforts in preparing this book, they make no representations or warranties with respect to the accuracy or completeness of the contents of this book and specifically disclaim any implied warranties of merchantability or fitness for a particular purpose. It is sold on the understanding that the publisher is not engaged in rendering professional services and neither the publisher nor the author shall be liable for damages arising herefrom. If professional advice or other expert assistance is required, the services of a competent professional should be sought.

Library of Congress Cataloging-in-Publication Data

ISBN 978-1-119-12082-7
ISSN 0021-9886 (print) 1468-5965 (online)

A catalogue record for this book is available from the British Library.

Set in 11/12.5 pt Times by Toppan Best-set Premedia Limited
Printed in Singapore

1   2015

CONTENTS

JCMS 2015 Volume 53 Annual Review pp. 1–5

DOI: 10.1111/jcms.12285

Editorial: 'As ye sow, so shall ye reap': the European Union in 2014

NATHANIEL COPSEY[1] and TIM HAUGHTON[2]
[1]Aston University. [2]University of Birmingham

Since we came into post as co-editors of the *JCMS Annual Review* in 2008, the European Union has been hit by what most observers, including the editors, described as a series of interlocking and seemingly intractable crises at home and abroad. Indeed, it has scarcely been possible to read an article or attend a seminar about the European Union over the past few years without the word 'crisis' appearing prominently.

Dictionary definitions of crisis vary widely, but generally refer to 'a time of intense difficulty' or perhaps 'a turning point'. We can therefore conclude that crises are supposed to be time-limited and should, at some point, draw to a conclusion, be it good or bad. For that reason, in taking stock of 2014, perhaps it may no longer be appropriate to talk about the European Union as being beset by crisis from within or crisis from without, but better rather to assess how the events of the past few years have changed the Union and shifted the boundaries of what we regard as 'normal'.

Much attention in recent times has focused on the acute 'crises' associated with the eurozone's woes, but there are deeper, chronic challenges associated with economic competitiveness, the limits of European integration, the linkage between the governed and political elites and demography that face the European Union, all of which are the culmination of long-standing and pre-existing trends (Copsey, 2015, pp. 215–22). Even some of the prominent turning points of recent times are better understood as a result of long-term trends, rather than bolts from the blue.

Without a doubt, the most serious and far-reaching of these turning points was in the Ukraine–Russia–EU triangular relationship that followed Russia's annexation of Crimea in March 2014. For the first time since the Second World War, the territory of one European country was militarily occupied and then formally incorporated into the territory of another. Indeed, Russia's actions posed a grave threat to the European integration project since the *raison d'être* of the EU, as a peace project, is precisely to preclude such acts on the European continent. The response of the EU was predictable: a package of economic and political sanctions. Time will tell if these are effective or not, although early indications suggested, however, that of far greater significance to Russia was the tumble in the oil price in late 2014 that threw its economy into recession.

It is easy to be wise in hindsight, but future historians will look back on the events of 2014 and wonder – in common with the collapse of Communism and the revolutions of 1989 – why almost no one predicted the ignominious fall of Viktor Yanukovych, the annexation of Crimea or the outbreak of civil war in Eastern Ukraine. The trends that led to the Ukrainian crisis were already well established. Three of these are of particular importance.

© 2015 The Author(s) JCMS: Journal of Common Market Studies © 2015 John Wiley & Sons Ltd, 9600 Garsington Road, Oxford OX4 2DQ, UK and 350 Main Street, Malden, MA 02148, USA

First among these, as Anand Menon (2014) argued in last year's *Annual Review*, was the well-documented and long-standing weakness of the EU in foreign affairs, which is primarily the result of the squabbling between Member States and the lack of 'classic' foreign policy tools that stems from its position as an international organization, rather that a state. A second long-standing weakness was the singularly ineffective European neighbourhood policy (ENP), launched with great fanfare by the Wider Europe Communication of 2003, that had sought to bring stability, good governance and prosperity to the neighbourhood with inadequate commitment, tools and resources. Since 2003, the neighbourhood, across an arc from Morocco in the south west to Belarus in the north east, has fallen victim to war and revolution while the EU has wrung its hands. A third long-standing trend is the mutual lack of understanding between Russia and the EU, which is accompanied by a lack of trust. On the Russian side, there is a sense that the EU is engaged in quasi-imperialistic expansion towards the east as part of an attempt to weaken the Russian state by surrounding it with hostile states. On the EU side, there is a fundamental naivety about Russia, and an inability to see things from a non-western perspective. More broadly, EU–Russia relations highlight the limits of globalization, which carries with it the appearance of superficial similarity while concealing much deeper differences behind the appearances of a shared 'global' culture.

While events in Ukraine took many by surprise, one of the other significant developments was dictated by the calendar. The 2014 European Parliament elections highlighted two underlining trends, one institutional and one of democratic linkage. In institutional terms, these elections marked the latest chapter in the turf war between institutions. During 2013 and 2014, the European Parliament (EP) took advantage of the open wording of the Lisbon Treaty[1] to grab additional powers for itself – in this case, the right to nominate the first 'elected' President of the European Commission in the form of the veteran Luxembourg Prime Minister Jean-Claude Juncker. Article 17 paragraph 7 of the Lisbon Treaty states:

> Taking into account the elections to the European Parliament and after having held the appropriate consultations, the European Council, acting by a qualified majority, shall propose to the European Parliament a candidate for President of the Commission. This candidate shall be elected by the European Parliament by a majority of its component members. (TEU, 2012, Article 17)

Reading this paragraph carefully, the intention of the treaty-makers appears to have been that, following the outcome of the elections to the EP, they would select (after bargaining among themselves and a decision requiring Qualified Majority Voting, if strictly necessary) a candidate whom they thought would be acceptable to the European Parliament, for its confirmation. The EP's reading of this article, however, was very different. It inferred that, following the German model, each party would put forward one 'leading candidate' (*Spitzenkandidat*, to follow the German political culture on which this reading was based) and that the *Spitzenkandidat* of the party that came first in the election would simply be confirmed by the European Council. As Desmond Dinan (2014) noted in last year's *Annual Review*, it was the EP's President Martin Schulz and its Secretary-General Klaus Welle who exploited the minor treaty change to bring about an institutional

---

[1] See Dinan in this volume.

© 2015 The Author(s) JCMS: Journal of Common Market Studies © 2015 John Wiley & Sons Ltd

realignment. The irony for Schulz, though, was that his ambition to become the next Commission President was thwarted when the Party of European Socialists, of which he was the *Spitzenkandidat*, won fewer seats than the European People's Party, leading to him holding the same post at the beginning of the year and at the end. *Plus ça change, plus c'est la même chose*, for Schulz at least.

The EP justified the *Spitzenkandidat* idea on the basis of improving democratic linkages and helping to restore some of the fraying ties between ordinary citizens and the political process. Although it would be wise not to read too much into the results of May's elections, the low turnout and the amount of voters who were mobilized enough to vote and cast their ballots for the National Front in France and the UK Independence Party underlined the strong feelings of frustration and disillusionment among a large slice of ordinary voters. Indeed, the EP elections confirmed that across Europe, from 'Athens to Zagreb and London to Ljubljana, long-established existing parties are losing their grip on the electorates' (Haughton and Deegan-Krause, 2014). We would be wise, however, not to overstate the case. Even in the EP elections in some countries, most notably in Central and Eastern Europe, many governing parties did win the elections. Nonetheless, the deeper problems of disillusionment and discontent are clear and becoming worse.

It was not just ties between voters and parties that appeared looser; there was also a weakening of bonds between citizens and their state. The year 2014 highlighted a rising tide of regional separatism, and its bed-fellow ethnic nationalism, in Scotland and Catalonia. Although the nationalist side was ultimately defeated by 55 per cent to 45 per cent in a referendum on Scottish independence in September, the closely fought campaign and the galvanization of voters by the Scottish National Party highlighted the fragility of the United Kingdom. Britain's experiences compared and contrasted with those of Spain, where an unofficial Catalonian independence referendum voted in favour of separation from the rest of the country just a few weeks later on 9 November 2014. Ethnic nationalism on the European continent is nothing new, and has arguably been on the rise since the early nineteenth century. What is new, however, is the sense that ever-smaller nation-states are viable in the context of a twenty-first century confederal European Union that provides many of the advantages of scale, scope and security previously vouchsafed by other unions.

The year was notable not just for the EP elections, but for a wider changing of the guard at the top of EU institutions. Not only did Juncker become Commission President and appoint a new team of Commissioners for the next five years, but also Donald Tusk was chosen as the new European Council President and Federica Mogherini as the new foreign policy chief. The choice of the three top post-holders was driven as usual by considerations of balance: political affiliation, gender, size and geographical location of their state, etc. It is too soon to pass judgements on them, but it is worth bearing in mind Juncker's quote, on coming into office, that his was the 'last chance' Commission.[2]

***

This is our seventh issue of the *JCMS AR* as editors. Although we have continued our policy of commissioning a number of special contributions from leading scholars in the field, we have changed the focus of some of the regular contributions and in consequence have recruited some new members to the team.

[2] *Le Monde*, 3 November 2014.

© 2015 The Author(s) JCMS: Journal of Common Market Studies © 2015 John Wiley & Sons Ltd

Separate contributions on the eurozone and non-eurozone countries make less and less sense with every passing year, as more and more countries adopt the single currency. Therefore, in place of the analysis of developments in the economies of Member States outside the eurozone, we commissioned Istvan Benczes and Balazs Szent-Ivanyi to examine broader trends in the European economy. The contributions focused on foreign policy have also been recalibrated to examine 'Europe as a Regional Actor' and 'Europe as a Global Actor'. We welcome aboard Karolina Pomorska and Sophie Vanhoonacker, who cover the latter theme. Furthermore, we are pleased to be able to reinstate a chapter on Legal Developments this year and thank Thomas Horsley for accepting our invitation to contribute. Last but not least, we welcome Charlotte Galpin, who has compiled the chronology.

We would like to express our thanks to the outgoing members of the regular team of contributors for all their efforts and for producing high-quality work over the past few years: Richard Connolly, Daniel Fiott, Amelia Hadfield and Fabian Neuner.

The European Parliament elections were one of the main events of the year, so we commissioned Sara Hobolt to examine and explain the results. Although nearly 30 per cent of the seats in the EP went to eurosceptic parties, she underlines the significant differences across the 28 Member States. She highlights that while the elections were the most 'European' to date, they also 'revealed deepening divisions in Europe, between the winners and the losers of economic integration, and between South and North and East and West'. She concludes by arguing: 'the elections highlight that Europeans are increasingly "divided in unity": they have been forced closer together, politically and economically, by the necessities of the eurozone crisis, yet this has only accentuated the lack of a common European outlook and the fragility of European solidarity'.

This year's *Annual Review* lecture is due to be delivered at the Council of European Studies conference in Paris in July. We are pleased to have secured Kathleen McNamara of Georgetown University, who touches on a vital yet often neglected theme in European politics: the importance of culture in shaping politics and attitudes. The EU's particular type of 'banal authority', she argues, suggests that 'any institutional fixes to improve EU democracy will need to work hand in hand with changes in the cultural infrastructure of European governance'.

Following three previous issues of the *Annual Review*, in which William Paterson (2011) examined Germany as a 'reluctant hegemon', Christian Lequesne (2013) explored the consequences of a new Socialist President in the Elysée and we examined Britain's EU referendum pledge (Copsey and Haughton, 2014), it seemed appropriate for this year's *Annual Review* to contain a contribution examining Italy and the European Union. Sonia Lucarelli's historical institutional analysis takes a long view on Italy and European integration since the 1950s and offers an analysis of the shifts in Italian attitudes towards the integration project in recent years 'from true love to disenchantment'.

In our final special contribution, David Phinnemore explores the argument made by several scholars in a number of significant accounts of the travails of the EU. To varying degrees, the books he reviews acknowledge the multiplicity of challenges – which the books invariably label as 'crises' – related to the eurozone, legitimacy, leadership, accountability, purpose and the democratic deficit. Phinnemore adds to this what he terms 'crises of (mis)understanding, of interdependence and of identity'. The books he reviews differ in terms of whether, how and to what extent the EU can continue to weather and overcome these challenges. Even the more optimistic accounts, however, acknowledge that 'serious rethinking and further reform are necessary'. We hope the contributions to this *Annual Review* will also provide food for thought for those rethinking the European Union.

We would like to thank all the contributors to this issue of the *JCMS AR* for their efforts and efficiency in producing such excellent copy within the usual tight time constraints. Finally, we would also like to thank the editors of the *JCMS*, Michelle Cini and Amy Verdun, for their continuing support.

References

Copsey, N. (2015) *Rethinking the European Union* (Basingstoke: Palgrave).
Copsey, N. and Haughton, T. (2014) 'Farewell Britannia? "Issue Capture" and the Politics of David Cameron's 2013 Referendum Pledge'. *JCMS*, Vol. 52. No. s1, pp. 74–89.
Dinan, D. (2014) 'Governance and Institutions: The Unrelenting Rise of the European Parliament'. *JCMS*, Vol. 52, No. s1, pp. 109–24.
Haughton, T. and Deegan-Krause, K. (2014) 'The Future (Probably) Lies East: Political Parties in Eastern and Western Europe', American Political Science Association's European Politics and Society Section Newsletter, Autumn, pp. 13–5.
Lequesne, C. (2013) 'A New Socialist President in the Elysée: Continuity and Change in French EU Politics'. *JCMS*, Vol. 51, No. s1, pp. 42–54.
Menon, A. (2014) 'The JCMS Annual Review Lecture: Divided and Declining? Europe in a Changing World', *JCMS*, Vol. 52, No. s1, pp. 5–24.
Paterson, W. (2011) 'The Reluctant Hegemon? Germany Moves Centre Stage in the European Union', *JCMS*, Vol. 49 No. s1, pp. 57–75.
Treaty on European Union (TEU). (2012) Available at: «http://eur-lex.europa.eu/legal-content/EN/ALL/?uri=CELEX:12012M/TXT».

© 2015 The Author(s) JCMS: Journal of Common Market Studies © 2015 John Wiley & Sons Ltd

JCMS 2015 Volume 53 Annual Review pp. 6–21   DOI: 10.1111/jcms.12264

The 2014 European Parliament Elections: Divided in Unity?*

SARA B. HOBOLT
London School of Economics and Political Science

Introduction

The winners of the 2014 European Parliament elections were eurosceptic parties, often found on the fringes of the political spectrum. Parties critical of, or even hostile to, the European Union topped the polls in France, the United Kingdom, Hungary, Denmark and Greece, gaining almost 30 per cent of the seats in the European Parliament. Does this eurosceptic surge indicate a rejection of the European project by a growing number of voters across Europe? Was support for these parties a sign that voters wanted less Union, or perhaps a different Union?

This contribution examines the context and outcome of the 2014 European elections. Previous elections to the European Parliament (EP) elections have generally been characterized by lacklustre and domestically focused campaigns and voter apathy, but two factors set these elections apart: they took place in the context of the worst economic crisis in post-war Europe and the political groups in the EP had for the first time nominated lead candidates to compete for the post of European Commission president. Many hoped that the increased saliency of European issues and the constitutional strengthening of the link between the EP ballot and the policy direction of the Commission would both mobilize voters to take part in the elections in greater numbers and encourage them to provide a democratic mandate for the future direction of the EU. The EP even put up large billboards in the run-up to the elections proclaiming 'This time it's different'.

Were these elections different? On the face of it very little changed. Turnout remained low at 42.6 per cent, government parties were the losers and smaller parties the winners, and the introduction of lead candidates seemed to have gone unnoticed by most citizens (see Hobolt, 2014a; Treib, 2014; Schmitt *et al.*, 2015a). Hence, the most European aspect of these elections was the fact that concerns about the EU, and its handling of the crisis, dominated the rhetoric in a number of countries and shaped vote choices. However, the findings of this study also show considerable variation not only in the electoral appeal of eurosceptic parties across countries, but also in the reasons for voters' support. Whereas the radical right parties performed well in Northern Europe, and to a lesser extent in Central and Eastern Europe (CEE), they gained only a handful of seats in the Member States that were recipients of a credit arrangement, or bailout, from the EU (Cyprus, Greece, Ireland, Portugal and Spain). In these debtor states, the critique of the EU was expressed by parties on the radical left instead.

* I would like to thank the *Annual Review* editors, Nathaniel Copsey and Tim Haughton, for very insightful comments on previous versions of this contribution.

© 2015 The Author(s) JCMS: Journal of Common Market Studies © 2015 John Wiley & Sons Ltd, 9600 Garsington Road, Oxford OX4 2DQ, UK and 350 Main Street, Malden, MA 02148, USA

The analysis of individual-level data from the 2014 European Election Studies (EES) reveals that support for leftist eurosceptic parties was not driven by a rejection of the European project, but by discontent with austerity policies and a desire for more European solidarity. In contrast, support for the anti-EU radical right in the north was more evidently motivated by an opposition to immigration and to transfers of funds to other Member States. 'Europe' thus played a more central role in these European elections than ever before, but the outcome also exposed deep divisions in opinions on the future of the European Union. Citizens who were most vulnerable in the economic downturn – the losers of globalization – were most likely to vote for eurosceptic parties. However, in the richer countries in the north, voters adversely affected by the crisis favoured *less* Union and closed borders, whereas similar voters in the south were calling for *more* European solidarity and integration. These contrasting narratives of how to solve the crisis are also evident in the national media coverage. The findings of this study thus highlight the challenges facing European politicians as they seek to find common solutions to the continent's problems.

This contribution proceeds as follows. First, it discusses the political and economic context of the 2014 EP elections and the national debate on the EU in the period leading up to the vote. Thereafter, it examines the support for eurosceptic parties and individual-level motivations, analysing a cross-national post-electoral survey. Finally, it discusses the broader implications of these elections for the future of the EU.

I. European Elections: No Longer Second-Order?

Elections to the EP ostensibly provide a unique opportunity for the citizens of the EU to shape the policies and the future of the Union. When direct elections to the EP were introduced in 1979, the hope was that this would enhance the democratic dimension of EU policy-making by creating a legislative chamber that was accountable to and representing voters' interests (Rittberger, 2005; Hix *et al.*, 2007). But rather than legitimizing the EU's authority, scholars and commentators alike have argued that the EP elections have failed to bring about the genuine electoral connection between voters and EU policy-makers that was hoped for. At the heart of the problem is the so-called 'second-order national election' nature of EP elections (Reif and Schmitt, 1980; van der Eijk and Franklin, 1996). According to the 'second-order election' explanation, voters treat EP elections as midterm elections. As a consequence, most voters simply do not care enough about these elections to even cast a vote. Turnout has declined in successive EP elections from 62 per cent in 1979 to just below 43 per cent in 2014.[1] Those who do turn out to vote tend to use their ballot to punish their national incumbent or vote on the basis of policy preferences relevant in a domestic policy space, rather than to decide on the issues facing the EU.

Numerous studies have shown that parties in national government are punished, particularly during the (national) midterm, and that larger parties are disadvantaged (see e.g. Marsh, 1998; Hix and Marsh, 2007). These patterns of behaviour are generally interpreted

---

[1] However, it is worth noting that this decline in average levels of turnout in EP elections can be largely accounted for by the changing composition of the EU electorate due to the multiple EU enlargements to countries often with lower turnout habits in general elections, especially in CEE (see Franklin, 2001).

© 2015 The Author(s) JCMS: Journal of Common Market Studies © 2015 John Wiley & Sons Ltd

as voters responding to the low-salience context of EP elections, and have led to the conclusion that European elections have largely failed in providing a strong democratic mandate for policy-making at the EU level. There were good reasons, however, to expect that the 2014 European Parliament elections would be different: less 'second-order national elections' and more truly European contests about the future direction of European integration. The reasons were two-fold: the introduction of 'lead candidates' for the position of Commission president and the eurozone crisis.

Starting with the institutional innovations, the EP took advantage of a constitutional change in the Lisbon Treaty's Article 17, which stated that the results of the EP elections should be 'taken into account' when selecting the next Commission president (see Dinan, 2014). To reinforce this link between the EP ballot and the selection of the Commission president, the major EP political groups decided for the first time to each rally behind a common lead candidate (*Spitzenkandidat* in German) for the post of the next President of the European Commission: Jean-Claude Juncker for the European People's Party (EPP); Martin Schulz for the Party of European Socialists (belonging to the Socialists & Democrats group); Guy Verhofstadt for the Alliance of Liberals and Democrats for Europe (ALDE), Ska Keller and José Bové for the European Green Party; and finally, Alexis Tsipras for the Party of the European Left. Thus, in theory at least, the 2014 EP elections allowed voters to give a mandate to a specific political platform for the EU's executive body, the Commission, since a vote for these parties was also a vote for one of the lead candidates as Commission president.[2] The Parliament's hope was that this would strengthen the European element in the campaigns, personalize the distant Brussels bureaucracy, and thereby increase interest and participation in European democracy (European Parliament, 2013; Hobolt, 2014a).

The second factor making these elections different from previous ones was the economic and political context. At the time of the elections in June 2014, the EU had been experiencing several years of severe economic crisis. The euro area's sovereign debt problems became increasingly evident in 2009 with the downgrading of government debt in many European states, particularly in the so-called 'GIIPS' countries (Greece, Ireland, Italy, Portugal and Spain). Concerns intensified in early 2010 and thereafter, leading the EU to implement a series of financial support measures such as the European Financial Stability Facility (subsequently the European Stability Mechanism).[3] These euro-rescue measures targeted at helping countries in a severe sovereign debt crisis came with strings attached, including government promises of fiscal austerity and structural reforms. A series of new legal instruments (the Six-Pack, the Two-Pack, the Macroeconomic Imbalances Procedure), new decision-making procedures (the European Semester) and a new inter-governmental treaty, the Fiscal Compact, were aimed at more tightly constraining national fiscal policy-making. The ongoing attempts to rescue countries on the brink of bankruptcy and avoid the collapse of the eurozone, and the more formal institutional changes to economic governance, were extensively covered in the national media across Europe. Section II looks at the coverage of Europe in the media and the shifting public mood.

---

[2] On the appointment of the new President of the Commission see Dinan's contribution to this volume.
[3] On eurozone governance see Hodson's contribution to this and previous issues of the *Annual Review*.

© 2015 The Author(s) JCMS: Journal of Common Market Studies © 2015 John Wiley & Sons Ltd

Table 1: Media Coverage of Who Bears the Main Responsibility for Solving the Crisis (%)

	Belgium	Finland	France	Germany	Italy	The Netherlands	Poland	Spain	UK
Euro group	44	57	60	37	35	60	26	22	53
EU/European Central Bank	29	19	15	18	34	16	50	35	30
Countries with sovereign debt problems	20	22	12	22	21	16	9	28	10
Countries without sovereign debt problems	1	0	6	13	5	3	11	14	3
IMF, banks and other lenders	6	2	7	10	5	5	4	1	4

Source: Reuters Institute (2014)
Note: Percent of articles on the crisis that mention an 'actor' with main responsibility for solving the crisis. Excludes 'none' and 'others'.

II. The Debate on Europe: Converging or Diverging?

As a consequence of the euro crisis, the EU issue became more salient in the national public sphere than ever before. This manifested itself in two ways. On the one hand, the public debate on the crisis was more 'Europeanized' than previously. Across Europe the national media debated similar issues, and European actors (such as Angela Merkel and José Manuel Barroso) were prominent in the domestic media landscapes (see Kriesi and Grande, 2014). On the other, domestic media coverage continued to be characterized by distinct national perspectives on the crisis, and the EP election campaigns were also dominated by national parties and national politicians.

Moreover, there were elements of the campaign that indicated an increasing divisiveness and disintegration, as the national discourses on the crisis diverged. Studies on how the euro crisis has been portrayed in the media have pointed to clear manifestations of a 'blame game', with different interpretations of who is to blame for the crisis (Hänska *et al.*, 2013; Reuters Institute, 2014). For instance, in Southern Europe, the hardship and unemployment of the euro crisis are often linked to the conditions associated with bailout agreements, attributed in part to Germany. In contrast, sections of the media in northern European countries, such as Germany and Finland, have argued that GIIPS countries have themselves to blame for the crisis. A large-scale study of media coverage of the euro crisis directed by Oxford Reuters Institute[4] provides insights into whom the national newspapers portrayed as 'bearing the main responsibility to solve the crisis' in the period between 2010 and 2012 (see Table 1). Interestingly, the national studies reveal a relatively convergent view that the European Union bears the main responsibility for solving the crisis – either the eurozone countries (44 per cent) or the EU as a whole (28 per cent). In some countries' media coverage, debtor countries themselves are also seen to bear the responsibility. That is a view found mainly in coverage in Finland, Germany and Belgium, and perhaps more surprisingly in Spain. A much smaller proportion of news coverage also points to 'creditor' countries as the main culprit, whereas the IMF, banks and other lenders are mentioned far less frequently (see Table 1).

[4] The 'Euro Crisis, Media Coverage, and Perceptions of Europe within the EU' project was directed by Oxford Reuters Institute. More than 10,000 articles from 40 newspapers in 9 countries were analysed in the project, between 2010 and 2012.

© 2015 The Author(s) JCMS: Journal of Common Market Studies © 2015 John Wiley & Sons Ltd

Studies of the media coverage in the years leading up to the 2014 elections thus point to an increasingly integrated Europeanized public sphere where the same European issues, European actors and EU responsibility appeared prominently in the news coverage across Member States. However, the national framing also remained dominant and the crisis was viewed from a distinct national perspective (see Kriesi and Grande, 2014; Reuters Institute, 2014).

Not surprisingly, the EU's response to the crisis also affected citizens' attitudes toward the European Union. Survey data show that citizens became increasingly aware of the euro crisis and more likely to hold the EU, rather than their national governments, responsible for the economic circumstances in their country in the period leading up to the 2014 elections (Cramme and Hobolt, 2014; Hobolt and Tilley, 2014; Hobolt, 2014b). At the same time, Eurobarometer data show there was a marked decline in trust in the European Union. Between the 2009 and 2014 elections, the percentage of people who 'tend to trust' the EU declined by 16 percentage points from 47 to 31 per cent, and similarly those who had a positive image of the EU declined from 45 to 35 per cent.[5] While trust in national governments also declined in the same period, this decline was less steep. But how did these developments in the institutional procedures, the campaigns and people's attitudes toward Europe translate into voting behaviour in the 2014 elections?

III. Voting Behaviour in the 2014 Elections

Given the rise in salience of European integration, and the strengthened link between the vote and executive politics in the EU, it was not unreasonable to expect that voters would be more motivated to turn out than in previous elections. While initial indications suggested a small increase in turnout, participation levels were in fact slightly below the 2009 level. Hence, although the EP was successful in ensuring that the lead candidate of the winning political group (EPP), Jean-Claude Juncker, eventually became Commission president, it is less obvious that the introduction of lead candidates made a substantial difference to voting behaviour. Evidence suggests that the lead candidates did have a mobilizing effect on the minority of voters who had knowledge of the candidates, especially in countries where they had campaigned (see Schmitt et al., 2015a). However, only a minority of Europeans were able to identify which political party the candidates belong to – only 19 and 17 per cent could link Juncker and Schulz, respectively, to their parties – and hence for the vast majority of citizens, these candidates made little difference (see also Hobolt, 2014a).

There was significant variation across the EU in levels of participation, as shown in Figure 1. Most of that variation can be explained by three factors that are not directly related to the European nature of the elections, namely compulsory voting rules, concurrent national elections and a relatively recent history of Communist rule. The most powerful predictor of turnout at European elections is compulsory voting (Belgium, Cyprus, Greece and Luxembourg) or a history of compulsory voting (Italy). It is well known that compulsory voting raises turnout, even when it is not strictly enforced, especially in low-salience elections (Franklin, 2001). A second factor is concurrent national elections that bring voters to the polls, such as the national and regional elections in Belgium and the

[5] See Eurobarometer surveys 2007–2014.

© 2015 The Author(s) JCMS: Journal of Common Market Studies © 2015 John Wiley & Sons Ltd

Figure 1: Turnout in the 2014 European Parliament Elections.

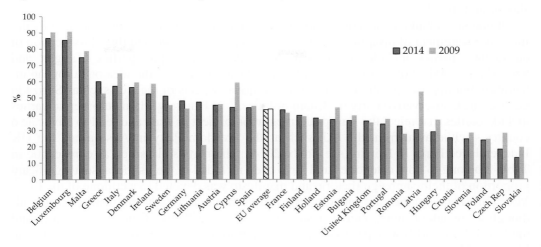

presidential elections in Lithuania (the latter helps explain the remarkable 21 percentage points increase in turnout compared to 2009). Finally, turnout in post-communist countries is significantly lower than in the rest of the Union. The may be due in part to general low levels of partisanship and political mobilization in these countries (Wessels and Franklin, 2009) and the fact that Europe is a less salient issue in CEE (Haughton, 2014; Haughton and Novotna, 2014).

While there was no great leap in participation levels, that is not to say that these elections were not distinctly more 'European' than in previous ones. At first glance, the outcome of the elections appears very similar to the 2009 elections: the centre-right EPP remained the largest party, but was also the elections' biggest loser as its seat share dropped from 36 to 29 per cent; it was followed closely by its centre-left rival, the Socialists & Democrats, with 25 per cent (the same as in 2009). The eighth European Parliament also includes the centrist ALDE group, with 9 per cent (down from 11 per cent in 2009), and the Greens, with 7 per cent of the seats (as in 2009). The clearest winners, however, were parties that belong to the groups more sceptical of the EU: on the right the European Conservatives and Reformists group (9 per cent, up from 7 in 2009) and the European Freedom and Direct Democracy group (6 per cent, up from 4); and on the left the United Left Group (7 per cent, up from 5) – as well as the 52 members (7 per cent, up from 4) who are not attached to any grouping.

The clearest indication that voters were more concerned about European issues was the surge in popularity for political parties that proposed radical reform of, or even exit from, the EU. The rise in the eurosceptic vote was therefore the message that dominated the headlines in the aftermath of the EP elections, and sent shock waves through domestic political systems. The most striking result was that radical right eurosceptic parties, which had never been in government, topped the polls in France, the UK and Denmark. This was not an isolated phenomenon. With the exception of Malta, all EU countries had a eurosceptic party gaining more than 2 per cent of the popular vote, although with considerable cross-national differences in their level of popularity. Overall, 220 of the EP's 751

© 2015 The Author(s) JCMS: Journal of Common Market Studies © 2015 John Wiley & Sons Ltd

members (MEPs) represented eurosceptic parties, accounting for 29 per cent of MEPs, as shown in Table 2.

Of course, not all eurosceptic parties are the same. Euroscepticism may be broadly defined as a sentiment of disapproval toward European integration, and this classification of eurosceptic parties includes both 'soft' and 'hard' eurosceptic parties (Taggart and Szczerbiak, 2004). Soft eurosceptic parties are those that accept the idea of European integration but oppose specific policies or institutional aspects of the EU, such as Syriza in Greece, the Conservative Party in Britain or Fidesz[6] in Hungary. Hard eurosceptic parties include parties that reject the European integration project as such and tend to advocate a country's withdrawal from the EU, such as the Freedom Party in Austria and the UK Independence Party in Britain (see Treib, 2014). The parties classified as eurosceptic in Table 2 belong to both categories and have been included in the list because a significant proportion of their campaign rhetoric and manifesto was devoted to a critique of the EU.[7] Most eurosceptic parties are found on the fringes of the left–right political spectrum, although a few adopt more centrist positions (such as the British Conservative Party and the Polish Law and Justice party) or reject any left–right classification (such as the Italian Five Star Movement).

While these parties share a critical, or even hostile, attitude to the European Union, they vary considerably in the nature of their position on the left–right spectrum and therefore also in their views on other issues, such as redistribution, immigration and civil liberties. The left–right positions also translate into differences in the critique of the EU. Right-wing criticism is traditionally centred on nationalism and thus opposition to the external threats to national sovereignty and of immigration (Mudde, 2007; Mair and Mudde, 1998). In contrast, the critique from left-wing parties of the EU is rooted in an anti-capitalist ideology and call for greater state intervention and redistribution both nationally and internationally. However, while much divides the radical right and the radical left, they share a eurosceptic, nationalist and often populist, rhetoric that cuts across traditional left–right alignments (Halikiopoulou et al., 2012). In the context of the 2014 EP elections, the concern about threats to national sovereignty and opposition to EU institutions and policies were shared by eurosceptic parties on both the right and the left, often combined with populist and anti-establishment rhetoric. However, the anti-immigration rhetoric was far more pronounced on the right (especially in Western Europe), while the anti-austerity rhetoric was more pronounced on the left.

As shown in Table 2, the majority of eurosceptic parties are found on the right, often on the far right. The popularity of radical right-wing eurosceptic parties is particularly pronounced in northern European creditor states: Austria, Denmark, the Netherlands, Finland and the UK: in other words, in the richer Member States that have generally benefited the most from the single market, but where there has also been a significant increase in social inequality (Copsey, 2015). The eurosceptic right also did very well in Italy and France, as well as in CEE, Bulgaria, Hungary, Latvia, Lithuania, Poland and Slovakia. Yet we also saw the success of radical left eurosceptic parties in a handful of

---

[6] Fidesz is unusual among eurosceptic parties, as it belongs to the pro-European EPP but its leader Victor Orbán's rhetoric has become increasingly hostile towards the EU (for example, he compared EU bureaucrats to Soviet apparatchiks). Orbán has described his position as 'eurorealist' rather than eurosceptic.

[7] The classification has been cross-referenced with expert judgements in the Chapel Hill Expert Survey, as well as other academic work on eurosceptic parties, notably Treib (2014).

© 2015 The Author(s) JCMS: Journal of Common Market Studies © 2015 John Wiley & Sons Ltd

Table 2: Eurosceptic Parties in the 2014 European Parliament elections

Country	Parties*	Eurosceptic Left vote %	MEPs	Eurosceptic Right vote %	MEPs
Austria	Freedom Party [R], EUstop [R], Coalition for another Europe [L]	2.1	0	22.5	4
Belgium	Vlaams Belang [R]; PTB-GO! [L]	2.0	0	4.3	1
Bulgaria	VMRO-BND/Bulgaria without Censorship [R]**, National Front [R], ATAKA [R]	-	-	16.7	2
Croatia	Croatian Party of Rights [R]	-	-	**	1
Cyprus	Progressive Party of Working People [L]; ELAM [R]	27.0	2	2.7	0
Czech Republic	Communist Party [L]; Party of Free Citizens [R]; Dawn of Direct Democracy [R]	11.0	3	8.4	1
Denmark	Danish People's Party [R]; People's Movement against the EU [L]	8.1	1	26.6	4
Estonia	Conservative People's Party of Estonia [R]	-	-	4.0	-
Finland	Finns Party [R]	-	-	12.9	2
France	National Front [R]; Left Front [L]; France Arise [R]	6.3	3	28.7	23
Germany	Alternative for Germany [R]; Left Party [L]; National Democratic Party [R]	7.4	7	8.1	8
Greece	Syriza [L]; Golden Dawn [R]; KKE [L]; ANEL [R]; Popular Orthodox Rally [R]	32.7	8	15.5	4
Hungary	Fidesz [R]; JOBBIK [R]	-	-	66.1	15
Ireland	Sinn Fein [L]	19.5	3	-	-
Italy	Five Star Movement [R]****; Northern League [R]; The Other Europe with Tsipras [L]	4.0	3	27.3	22
Latvia	National Alliance [R]; Union of Greens and Farmers [R]	-	-	22.5	2
Lithuania	Order and Justice [R]; LLRA [R]	-	-	22.3	3
Luxembourg	Alternative for Democratic Reform [R]	-	-	7.5	0
Malta	-	-	-	-	-
Netherlands	Freedom Party [R]; Socialist Party [L]; CU-SGP [R]	9.6	2	21.0	6
Poland	Law and Justice [R]; Congress of the New Right [R]; United Poland [R]; Right Wing of the Republic [R]	-	-	42.9	23
Portugal	United Democratic Coalition [L]; Left Bloc [L]	18.6	4	-	-
Romania	People's Party - Dan Diaconescu [L]; Greater Romania Party [R]	3.7	0	2.7	0
Slovakia	Ordinary People and Independent Personalities [R]; Nova [R]; Freedom and Solidarity [R]; Slovak National Party [R]	-	-	24.6	3
Slovenia	United Left [L]; Slovenian National Party [R]	5.5	0	4.0	0
Spain	United Left [L]; Podemos [L]; Peoples Decide [L]	20.1	12	-	-
Sweden	Sweden Democrats [R]; Left Party [L]	6.3	1	9.7	2
United Kingdom	UKIP [R]; Conservative Party [R]; Sinn Fein [L]; Democratic Unionist Party [R]	0.7	1	50.6	44
Total MEPs			50		170

Notes:
*Only parties with more than 2% of the national vote or 1 MEP have been included
**VMRO-BND formed a coalition with Bulgaria Without Censorship, a soft eurosceptic party, and other smaller parties, and their 2 MEPs joined the eurosceptic ECR Group.
***Croatian Party of Rights dr. Ante Starčević (HPS AS) formed an electoral alliance with three other parties. The HSP AS member sits in the ECR group, whereas the other coalition members sit in the EPP Group. The coalition got 41% of the votes.

countries. Interestingly, the eurosceptic left did well in the countries that experienced the most severe anti-austerity programmes and conditionality associated with their bailout packages, namely in Greece, Cyprus, Spain, Ireland and Portugal, where the parties polled an average of 24 per cent.

These voting data clearly demonstrate the heightened appeal of eurosceptic parties in the 2014 EP elections. Moreover, they point to important north–south and east–west differences: in the richer north, the radical right parties performed very well; in the poorer south-west (and Ireland), where the EU had imposed conditions of austerity and structural reform in return of credit, radical left parties did well, whereas there was a notable absence of radical right parties. In CEE, the eurosceptic parties on the right generally performed well, although voter apathy was more pronounced than vocal euroscepticism in this part of Europe (see Haughton and Novotna, 2014). These aggregate-level data, however, tell us less about the motivation of voters across Europe. In the next section, I analyse individual-level data to address the question of *why* eurosceptic parties were popular.

IV. Explaining the Eurosceptic Vote

What explains support for eurosceptic parties in the 2014 EP elections? As discussed above, the classic explanation for voting behaviour in European elections is the 'second-order national election' explanation (Reif and Schmitt, 1980, p. 9; see also van der Eijk and Franklin, 1996; Hix and Marsh, 2007). In comparison to first-order national elections, where the formation of a government is a primary objective, strategic consider-ations about party size and government performance matter less in second-order EP elections, and consequently voters are expected to vote more 'sincerely', focusing on ideological similarities. Moreover, voters may be motivated by a desire to punish national governments. Yet recent work on electoral behaviour in Europe has argued that the issue of European integration is becoming increasingly politicized, and this has meant that the issue of European integration matters more to voters (Tillman, 2004; De Vries, 2007; Hooghe and Marks, 2009). Studies of the 2004 and 2009 elections have shown that euroscepticism plays a considerable role in voters' decision to defect and abstain, but that this is conditioned by the politicization of the EU issue in the national political debate (Hobolt *et al.*, 2009; de Vries *et al.*, 2011; Hobolt and Spoon, 2012). Hence the extant lit-erature highlights three sets of factors which shape vote choices in EP elections: first, sin-cere ideological considerations, such as left–right and libertarian–authoritarian attitudes; second, dissatisfaction with the current (national) government and policy performance; and finally, attitudes that are specifically related to the European Union and European integration.

Electoral behaviour in EP elections is therefore often regarded as a 'protest vote': a protest against the incumbent national government or, indeed, against the direction of European integration. Since these elections remain 'second-order', they allow voters to express their dissatisfaction with the political establishment and policy performance with-out the constraints that voters feel when they are selecting a national government. Yet this does not render the elections insignificant. EP elections matter not only for policy-making in the EU, but also as barometers of citizens' preferences and as 'markers' in national pol-itics. In the context of an economic crisis in Europe, the fact that voters endorsed parties on the fringes of the political spectrum therefore seems unsurprising. But it still leaves several questions unanswered: if the rise of parties on the fringes was a protest vote, what were voters protesting against? How does this vary across Europe?

These questions can be addressed by analysing the EES 2014 – a post-election survey with representative samples in each of the 28 Member States (Schmitt *et al.*, 2015b).[8] This study allows us to examine the factors that motivated citizens to support eurosceptic parties across the EU. We examine support for both left-wing and right-wing eurosceptic parties by analysing responses to the EES question 'how probable is it that you will ever vote for this party?' on an 11-point scale. The distinct advantage of this question is that we are able to measure support for eurosceptic parties among *all* respondents and not just those who voted in the EP elections.[9] To examine the determinants of eurosceptic vote choice, we firstly measure individuals' socio-economic position by including a set of de-mographic variables (gender, age, education,[10] occupation[11] and unemployment) as well as a variable capturing individuals adversely affected by the crisis.[12] Second, we include a variable that captures individuals' ideological attitudes toward the government[13] and the economy.[14] Third, we capture ideology using questions on economic redistribution, immigration and combating crime versus civil liberties.[15] Finally, we include various questions that capture attitudes toward European integration[16] and EU policies on trans-national redistribution,[17] fiscal integration[18] and approval of EU performance dur-ing the crisis.[19] We also include a measure of (objective) knowledge of the European Union.[20]

Table 3 shows the results from a multi-level linear regression model of eurosceptic party support with random intercepts for political system.[21] I have run separate models for left- and right-wing eurosceptic parties (see Table 2) and for Western Europe – with more established party systems and longer democratic traditions – and post-Communist CEE, with less established party systems and lower salience of EU issues (Haughton, 2014; Haughton and Novotna, 2014). The results show both striking similarities and

[8] Approximately 1,100 respondents were interviewed in each EU member country, totalling 30,064 respondents. The EES 2014 was carried out by TNS Opinion between 30 May and 27 June 2014. All the interviews were carried out face to face. More information can be found here: http://eeshomepage.net/voter-study-2014/, where the EES questionnaire can also be found.

[9] I also ran the models with vote choice in EP elections as the dependent variable (1= Eurosceptic Left/ Eurosceptic Right party) and the same explanatory variables come out as significant in these models.

[10] Age of ending full-time education.

[11] Dummies for respondents in a working-class occupation (unskilled or skilled manual labour) and in a professional/ man-agerial position.

[12] Loss of income and/or loss of job in the household over the past 24 months.

[13] Disapproval of 'the government's record to date'.

[14] General economic situation over the next 12 months in country.

[15] Opposition to the redistribution of wealth from the rich to the poor in country; Opposition to a restrictive policy on im-migration; In favour of restricting privacy rights to combat crime

[16] Opposition to 'European unification'.

[17] Disagreement with the statement: 'In times of crisis, it is desirable for the [COUNTRY] to give financial help to another European Union Member State facing severe economic and financial difficulties.'

[18] Opposition to EU authority over the EU Member States' economic and budgetary policies.

[19] Disapproval of the actions of the EU during the last 12 months.

[20] A scale based on correct responses to six factual knowledge questions on the EU and the lead candidates.

[21] Estimating the models with country fixed-effects or clustered standard errors by country yields very similar results.

© 2015 The Author(s) JCMS: Journal of Common Market Studies © 2015 John Wiley & Sons Ltd

Table 3: Explaining the Eurosceptic Vote

	Eurosceptic Right						Eurosceptic Left				
	West			East			West			East	
	Coef	SE	Sig	Coef	SE	Sig	Coef	SE	Sig	Coef	SE
Female	−0.49	0.05	**	−0.12	0.06	**	0.05	0.06		−0.14	0.13
Age	−0.01	0.00	**	−0.02	0.00	**	−0.02	0.00	**	0.02	0.00 **
Education	−0.14	0.04	**	0.06	0.05		0.08	0.04		−0.38	0.11 **
Professional occupation	−0.18	0.09		−0.26	0.12	**	−0.36	0.11	**	−0.75	0.29 **
Working-class occupation	0.47	0.09	**	0.15	0.09		0.23	0.10	**	0.28	0.18
Unemployed	0.10	0.10		−0.18	0.10		0.09	0.10		0.53	0.23 **
Adversely affected by the crisis	0.09	0.04	**	0.07	0.04	**	0.10	0.04	**	0.26	0.07 **
EU knowledge	−0.04	0.02		0.14	0.03	**	0.15	0.02	**	−0.13	0.06 **
Government disapproval	0.19	0.03	**	−0.02	0.03		0.43	0.03	**	0.13	0.06 **
Economic pessimism	0.08	0.03	**	−0.08	0.04	**	−0.02	0.03		0.02	0.08
Anti-civil liberties	0.08	0.01	**	0.03	0.01	**	−0.04	0.01	**	0.04	0.02
Anti-redistribution (national)	0.09	0.01	**	0.01	0.01		−0.20	0.01	**	0.01	0.02
Anti−immigration	0.16	0.01	**	0.00	0.01		−0.11	0.01	**	−0.03	0.02
Anti-EU unification	0.10	0.01	**	0.02	0.01	**	0.00	0.01		0.03	0.02
EU performance disapproval	0.16	0.04	**	−0.13	0.04	**	0.17	0.04	**	0.17	0.08 **
Anti-EU redistribution	0.33	0.03	**	−0.09	0.03	**	−0.26	0.03	**	−0.17	0.07 **
Anti-EU fiscal integration	0.08	0.01	**	−0.01	0.01		0.01	0.01		−0.02	0.02
Constant	−0.84	0.27	**	2.92	0.35	**	4.58	0.33	**	1.85	0.57 **
N, groups	13,481			10,124			13,062			2285	

Note: Multi-level logistic regression of propensity to vote for Eurosceptic parties (see Table 2).
**p<0.05. Source: EES 2014

important differences across support for eurosceptic parties (left and right) and regions (west and CEE).

Starting with the similarities, we can see that people who are economically disadvantaged are more likely to support the eurosceptic parties: those in working-class occupations, the unemployed and those who have been adversely affected by the crisis. In other words, it is the 'losers' of European integration, and globalization, who are most attracted to eurosceptic parties – and there are a lot of them, as a result of the uneven distribution of the single market's benefits over the past 30 years (Copsey, 2015). It is also noteworthy that supporters of these parties are generally dissatisfied with the performance of both their national government and the European Union. This suggests that the eurosceptic vote is a classic protest against the political establishment among those who feel that that mainstream parties have let them down and those who have suffered most in the crisis.

Turning to the differences, we notice that the ideological motivations for supporting these parties vary considerably across party types and region. To illustrate the magnitude of these differences, Figure 2 shows the marginal effects (min–max) of each of the significant explanatory variables on eurosceptic party support (0-10). When it comes to left–right preferences, it is perhaps unsurprising that supporters of right-wing parties in the west are opposed to both redistribution and immigration, whereas support for left-wing eurosceptic parties in the west is driven by a contrasting set of attitudes, favouring

© 2015 The Author(s) JCMS: Journal of Common Market Studies © 2015 John Wiley & Sons Ltd

Figure 2: The Eurosceptic Voter.

a) Support for right-wing eurosceptic parties (west)

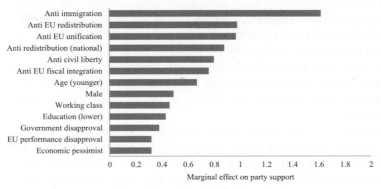

b) Support for right-wing eurosceptic parties (east)

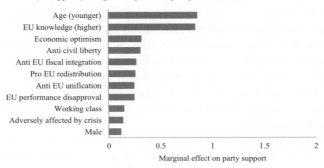

c) Support for left-wing eurosceptic parties (west)

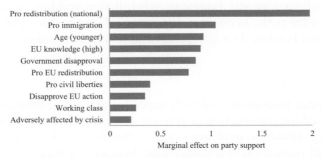

d) Support for left-wing eurosceptic parties (east)

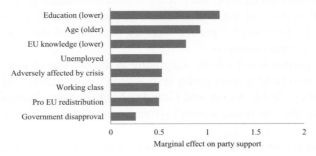

immigration and redistribution from rich to poor. In contrast, in CEE these ideological considerations were far less significant as a predictor of party support (see Figure 2b and 2d).[22] Figure 2a shows that anti-immigration attitudes were the most important driver of right-wing eurosceptic support, whereas Figure 2c shows that pro-redistribution attitudes were the key motivation behind left-wing eurosceptic support. This is of course also a reflection of the rhetoric and policy positions of these parties. Right-wing eurosceptic parties in the west have been able to successfully link their opposition to the EU to more salient concerns about immigration (from inside and outside the EU), whereas left-wing eurosceptic parties have related their critique of the EU policies to a more general anti-austerity platform.

Most interesting is the relationship between EU attitudes and the support for eurosceptic parties. One might have expected euroscepticism to be a key predictor of both right- and left-wing party support, given that a distinguishing feature of these parties is their critical position on European integration. However, that is not the case. We find a strong association between euroscepticism – opposition to European unification and opposition to specific EU policies – and supporters of right-wing eurosceptic parties in the west. However, general attitudes toward European integration are *not* a significant predictor of support for left-wing eurosceptic parties, such as Syriza and Podemos. If anything, supporters of these parties are more pro-European than mainstream party supporters. Moreover, they clearly favour greater financial transfers between EU Member States (a preference shared with supporters of right-wing eurosceptic parties in CEE). Supporters of left-wing eurosceptic parties in the west are also far more knowledgeable about the EU than the average voter.

Hence, far from being disengaged and anti-European, the findings suggest that the eurosceptic left-wing vote in the west is a call for a different Europe with greater solidarity and redistribution across and within European borders. Supporters of eurosceptic parties in the east also favour greater European redistribution and have a critical stance on the EU's handling of the crisis. In contrast, supporters of eurosceptic right-wing parties in the west favour closed borders, less integration and less redistribution.

Conclusion

Many inside the European institutions had high hopes for the 2014 European Parliament elections, as they marked the introduction of genuine contests between candidates for the Commission presidency. However, evidence suggests that these lead candidates were recognized by only a small proportion of the electorate. Instead of a contest between candidates with competing visions for Europe, the elections were dominated by national parties and the key 'European' feature of these elections was the success of parties that were highly critical of the EU. Eurosceptic parties won 29 per cent of the seats in the EP, and topped the polls in several countries.

The success of these parties is not wholly surprising in the context of a deep economic crisis for which the EU was held at least partly responsible by the media and by ordinary citizens (Hobolt and Tilley, 2014; Kriesi and Grande, 2014; Reuters Institute, 2014). In the period leading up to the elections, unemployment rates for the EU reached a post-

[22] But note that pro-redistribution attitudes are a significant predictor of left-wing eurosceptic party support also in CEE.

war high. The situation was particularly grave in the debtor states, such as Greece and Spain, where a quarter of the workforce was excluded from the labour market and youth unemployment was even higher. As a result of this crisis and policy measures adopted in response to the crisis, the EU was more salient than ever in the national media. Yet this Europeanized public debate was accompanied by distinct national narratives of the crisis and blame-shifting to the EU and other countries. In response, citizens become more critical of the EU, and trust in mainstream parties and national government also declined. This contribution has investigated whether the electoral success of eurosceptic parties on the fringes of the left–right spectrum is an expression of protest against national governments and parties, as the second-order election theory would predict, or whether voters cast their ballots with distinctly European questions in mind.

Of course, national and European politics are inherently intertwined, which makes it difficult to distinguish between 'national' and 'European' preferences. Nonetheless, our analysis of individual-level voting behaviour suggests that the success of eurosceptic parties was driven, at least in part, by distinctly European concerns, especially in Western Europe. First, we find that those individuals who were most vulnerable in the crisis were most likely to support eurosceptic parties. Our analysis shows that the support for eurosceptic parties was particularly high among those adversely affected by the crisis (the unemployed, the young, the manual workers and those who experience a reduction in income etc.). Second, the findings show that supporters of eurosceptic parties share a disapproval of both national government and the EU's performance during the crisis.

Importantly, however, our analysis also points to significant differences. In the richer north the far right generally performed better, driven by opposition to immigration as well as to closer EU integration and transfers of resources to other Member States. In contrast, support for the left-wing eurosceptic parties was most pronounced in the southern European countries that were hit hardest by the crisis and received credit from the EU and other lenders. Supporters of these parties were not averse to closer European integration and favoured a Europe of greater redistribution, across and within countries, and more open borders. Thus while disapproval of the EU's handling of the crisis seems to unite these voters of the left and the right, their vision for a better Europe is radically different.

Hence, the 2014 EP elections may well have been the most 'European' electoral contests to date, yet they also revealed deepening divisions in Europe, between the winners and the losers of economic integration and between south and north and east and west. The legitimacy of the European Union has always rested on the idea that it brought about greater prosperity for *all* its Member States rather than substantial redistribution between Member States. The euro crisis has called this basic premise into question not only due to the severity of the economic downturn but also because of the evident need for financial support, at least in the short term, for some Member States, especially poorer southern European countries, from the richer neighbours in the north (Copsey, 2015). The electoral appeal of eurosceptic parties in the north calling for *less* solidarity, contrasted with the demand for *more* solidarity by popular eurosceptic parties in the south, starkly illustrates the difficulty of establishing closer fiscal integration in the Union without further alienating a large group of voters.

The success of the eurosceptic parties is unlikely to transform policy-making in the European Parliament, where the pro-European centrist political groups continue to dominate. However, the results did send shock waves through a number of national political systems, by giving radical parties an important foothold and by signalling to governments

© 2015 The Author(s) JCMS: Journal of Common Market Studies © 2015 John Wiley & Sons Ltd

that many voters wanted a different direction for Europe. The fact that the visions for reform of the EU differ so radically across (and within) nations point to the challenges ahead
when it comes to finding common solutions for Europe. Rather than being 'united in diversity', as the EU's motto proclaims, the elections highlight that Europeans are increasingly
'divided in unity': they have been forced closer together, politically and economically, by
the necessities of the eurozone crisis, yet this has only accentuated the lack of a common
European outlook and the fragility of European solidarity.

References

Copsey, N. (2015) *Rethinking the European Union* (Basingstoke: Palgrave).
Cramme, O. and Hobolt, S.B. (eds) (2014) *Democratic Politics in a European Union under Stress*.
    (Oxford: Oxford University Press).
De Vries, C.E. (2007) 'Sleeping Giant: Fact or Fairytale? How European Integration Affects
    National Elections'. *European Union Politics,* Vol. 8, No. 3, pp. 363–85.
De Vries, C.E., van der Brug, W., van Egmond, M.H. and van der Eijk, C. (2011) 'Individual and
    Contextual Variation in EU Issue Voting: The Role of Political Information.' *Electoral Studies*,
    Vol. 30, No. 1, pp. 16–28.
Dinan, D. (2014) 'Governance and Institutions: The Unrelenting Rise of the European Parliament'.
    JCMS, Vol. 52, No. s1, pp. 109–24.
European Parliament (2013) The Power to Decide What Happens in Europe. Available at «http://
    www.europarl.europa.eu/news/en/news-room/content/20130905STO18723/html/The-power-to-
    decide-what-happens-in-Europe».
Franklin, M.N. (2001) 'How Structural Factors Cause Turnout Variations at European Parliament
    Elections.' *European Union Politics*, Vol. 2, No. 3, pp. 309–28.
Halikiopoulou, D., Nanou, K. and Vasilopoulou, S. (2012) 'The Paradox of Nationalism: The
    Common Denominator of Radical Right and Radical Left Euroscepticism'. *European Journal
    of Political Research*, Vol. 51, No. 4, pp. 504–39.
Haughton, T. (2014) 'Money, Margins and the Motors of Politics: the EU and the Development of
    Party Politics in Central and Eastern Europe'. *JCMS,* Vol. 52, No. 1, pp. 71–87.
Haughton, T. and Novotna, T. (2014) The European Elections in Central and Eastern EU States
    Illustrate that the Rise of Euroscepticism was Far from Uniform Across Europe. EUROPP
    blog, 29 May 2014. Available at «http://blogs.lse.ac.uk/europpblog/2014/05/29/the-european-
    elections-in-central-and-eastern-eu-states-illustrate-that-the-rise-of-euroscepticism-was-far-from-
    uniform-across-europe/».
Hix, S. and Marsh, M. (2007) 'Punishment or Protest? Understanding European Parliament elec-
    tions'. *The Journal of Politics,* Vol. 69, No. 2, pp. 495–510.
Hix, S., Noury, A. and Roland, G. (2007) *Democratic Politics in the European Parliament*
    (Cambridge: Cambridge University Press).
Hobolt, S.B. and Tilley, J. (2014) *Blaming Europe? Responsibility without Accountability in the
    European Union* (Oxford: Oxford University Press).
Hobolt, S.B. (2014a) 'A Vote for the President? The Role of *Spitzenkandidaten* in the 2014
    European Parliament Elections'. *Journal of European Public Policy*, Vol. 21, No. 10,
    pp. 1528–40.
Hobolt, S.B. (2014b) 'Public Attitudes towards the Euro Crisis'. In Cramme, O. and Hobolt, S.B.
    (eds). *Democratic Politics in a European Union Under Stress* (Oxford: Oxford University Press).
Hobolt, S.B. and Spoon, J-J. (2012) 'Motivating the European voter: parties, issues and campaigns in
    European Parliament elections.' *European Journal of Political Research,* Vol. 51, No. 6, pp. 701–27.

© 2015 The Author(s) JCMS: Journal of Common Market Studies © 2015 John Wiley & Sons Ltd

Hobolt, S.B., Spoon, J.-J. and Tilley, J. (2009) 'A Vote against Europe? Explaining Defection at the 1999 and 2004 European Parliament Elections'. *British Journal of Political Science,* Vol. 39, No. 1, pp. 93–115.

Hooghe, L. and Marks, G. (2009) 'Postfunctionalism, A Postfunctionalist Theory of European Integration: From Permissive Consensus to Constraining Dissensus', *British Journal of Political Science,* Vol. 39, No. 1, pp. 1–23.

Hänska, M., Keranen, O., Kyriakidou, M., Orsi, R., Paipais, V. and Radice, H. (2013) Euro Crisis in the Press. The Politics of Public Discourse in Europe. London School of Economics. Available at «http://blogs.lse.ac.uk/eurocrisispress/».

Kriesi, H. and Grande, E. (2014) 'Political Debate in a Polarizing Union'. In Cramme, O. and Hobolt, S.B. (eds). *Democratic Politics in a European Union Under Stress* (Oxford: Oxford University Press).

Mair, P. and Mudde, C. (1998) 'The Party Family and Its Study'. *Annual Review of Political Science*, Vol. 1, pp. 211–29.

Marsh, M. (1998) 'Testing the Second-order Election Model after Four European Elections'. *British Journal of Political Science*, Vol. 28, No. 4, pp. 591–607.

Mudde, C. (2007) *The Populist Radical Right in Europe* (Cambridge: Cambridge University Press).

Reif, K. and Schmitt, H. (1980) 'Nine Second-order National Elections – A Conceptual Framework for the Analysis of European Election Results'. *European Journal for Political Research*, Vol. 8, No. 1, pp. 3–44.

Reuters Institute (2014) The Euro Crisis, Media Coverage, and Perceptions of Europe within the EU'. Available at «http://reutersinstitute.politics.ox.ac.uk/publication/euro-crisis-media-coverage-and-perceptions-europe-within-eu».

Rittberger, B. (2005) *Building Europe's Parliament: Democratic Representation Beyond the Nation State* (Oxford: Oxford University Press).

Schmitt, H., Hobolt, S.B. and Popa, S.A. (2015a) 'Does Personalisation Increase Turnout? Spitzenkandidaten in the 2014 European Parliament Elections'. *European Union Politics,* forthcoming.

Schmitt, H., Hobolt, S.B., Popa, S.A. and Teperoglou, E. (2015b) 'European Parliament Election Study 2014, Voter Study'. GESIS Data Archive, Cologne. ZA5160 Data file Version 1.0.0, doi:10.4232/1.5160

Taggart, P. and Szczerbiak, A. (2004) 'Contemporary Euroscepticism in the Party Systems of the EU Candidate States of Central and Eastern Europe'. *European Journal of Political Research*, Vol. 43, No. 1, pp. 1–27.

Tillman, E.R. (2004). 'The European Union at the Ballot Box? European Integration and Voting Behavior in the New Member States'. *Comparative Political Studies*, Vol. 37, No. 5, pp. 590–610.

Treib, O. (2014) 'The Voter Says No, but Nobody Listens: Causes and Consequences of the Eurosceptic Vote in the 2014 European Elections'. *Journal of European Public Policy,* Vol. 21, No. 10, pp. 1541–54.

Van der Eijk, C. and Franklin, M. (1996) *Choosing Europe? The European Electorate and National Politics in the Face of Union.* (Ann Arbor, MI: University of Michigan Press).

Wessels, B. and Franklin, M.N. (2009) 'Turning Out or Turning Off: Do Mobilization and Attitudes Account for Turnout Differences between New and Established Member States at the 2004 EP Elections?'. *Journal of European Integration*, Vol. 31, No. 5, pp. 609–26.

© 2015 The Author(s) JCMS: Journal of Common Market Studies © 2015 John Wiley & Sons Ltd

JCMS 2015 Volume 53 Annual Review pp. 22–39   DOI: 10.1111/jcms.12276

JCMS Annual Review Lecture: Imagining Europe: The Cultural Foundations of EU Governance

KATHLEEN R. MCNAMARA
Georgetown University

Introduction

On 18 March 2015, more than ten thousand people from all corners of Europe crowded Frankfurt's Römerberg Square, chanting and waving handmade banners. Although the demonstration was peaceful, earlier in the day multiple police cars had been set on fire, and fights had broken out between activists and police. The occasion? The official inauguration of the long delayed, hideously expensive new European Central Bank building. Representatives of the Spanish political party Podemos and Greece's Syriza joined the anti-austerity protests, calling for an end, as one sign put it, to 'ECB Monetary Fascism'. Protesters were quoted as not just protesting against the European Central Bank (ECB) and the European Union's (EU) specific policies, however, but also asserting the need for just and fair treatment for their larger European community. One 30-year-old protester said: 'We can't always make cuts at poor people's expense and call them lazy Greeks, but we need to stand by in solidarity with them'.[1]

For those of us who have studied the European Union for decades, the visibility of the protests, the violence, the protester's explicit talk of European solidarity and the intense scrutiny of the actors being pilloried signals a startling change in the politics of the EU.[2] In the past, EU governance unfolded largely insulated from mass politics, marked by elite discussion rather than popular protests. Today, a profound transformation is at work. The opening of EU politics to public scrutiny and awareness is necessary for the EU to be a mature and legitimate political entity, but the supporting social foundation for EU governance will also need to change for this transformation to hold.

Scholars have long probed into how material and functional elements matter for the evolution of the EU, be they formal institutions, national preferences or economic forces. But we have spent much less time examining the cultural underpinnings of the EU's governance. A literature on identity and socialization has moved forward our understanding of individual conceptions of political identity. But we need to look to how broader cultural dynamics have shaped the EU's basic construction as legitimate political authority in order to fully understand the challenges the EU faces today.

---

[1] *Wall Street Journal*, 18 March 2015.

[2] I use the terms EU and Europe interchangeably, although the former is clearly a subset of the latter.

© 2015 The Author(s) JCMS: Journal of Common Market Studies © 2015 John Wiley & Sons Ltd, 9600 Garsington Road, Oxford OX4 2DQ, UK and 350 Main Street, Malden, MA 02148, USA

Specifically, I argue for attention to how everyday life helps construct the particular shared identities and broader cultural vocabulary for politics in the EU.[3] Today, life in Europe is repeatedly shaped by or imprinted with the EU, in symbols and practices sometimes obvious and at other times very much under the radar. Pick up an object such as a hair dryer or a cuddly plush toy and it will invariably have a small tag printed with a '€' logo (standing for *Communauté Européenne*), indicating the product meets EU safety standards. A family in the Netherlands with an ageing parent may now share their home with a healthcare worker from Romania, thanks to the European single market for labour that joins them together. German firms have recalculated their business plans in response to sanctions set by the EU in 2014 against Russia after Putin's interventions in Ukraine. In the Basque country, travellers now pass freely from France to Spain without showing any documents, a lone sign (depicting both Spanish and EU symbols) the only thing marking the move from one country to another. In these and many other ways, the EU is changing the basic foundations of day-to-day life for 'European citizens', and in the process subtly reframing as European those things, such as borders or safety standards or labour laws, that used to be solely understood as national political prerogatives. The consequences of EU symbols and practices even extend outside the boundaries of Europe, as the EU's foreign policies and its diplomats construct the EU as a sovereign actor among states, signing international treaties and sending ambassadors to foreign capitals.

EU programmes are important in themselves for quite down-to-earth reasons, as they create winners and losers and redistribute wealth and power. But they also engage latent social processes that create a backdrop for politics that profoundly shapes the path of governance. EU policies, both intentionally and unintentionally, have generated a vast array of symbols and practices that provide a vocabulary and toolkit for the accrual of power to the EU. As EU governance permeates through European life, a subtle, incremental building of layers of everyday symbols and practices – what I call its cultural infrastructure – has transformed peoples' lived experience. But, I argue, the particular ways in which this cultural backdrop has been fashioned imposes important limits on the EU's evolution as a legitimate authority. Just like nation-states, the EU has effectively used the tried and true political technologies of labelling, mapping and narrating to create social categories and classifications and make the European people governable (Scott, 1998). But the legitimation that is accrued through the EU's symbolic and practical activity is an unusual and relatively thin one, making it difficult to bring people together in collective responses to the stress and strife of crises such as the eurozone catastrophe.

Unlike the heavy-handed work done by nationalism to support the concentration of state power, the EU's cultural infrastructure is rooted in a specific type of banal authority, which navigates national loyalties while portraying the EU as complementary to, not in competition with, local identities. From the abstracted and generic iconography of the euro, to the labelling of the EU's foreign policy chief as the dizzyingly obscure 'High Representative of the Union for Foreign Affairs and Security Policy,' to the balancing done by the European passport's simultaneous joining of national and EU symbols, to the timid public architecture of Brussels and the cities of Frankfurt, Luxembourg, Strasbourg all serving as decentralized EU capitals, the symbols and practices generated by EU policies are often deracinated, purged of their associations with the powers of the

---

[3] This contribution draws on and develops the arguments made in McNamara (2015a).

© 2015 The Author(s) JCMS: Journal of Common Market Studies © 2015 John Wiley & Sons Ltd

nation-state. Instead of conveying a concentration of power and identity, the EU's symbols and practices are standardized into a seemingly unobjectionable blandness, metaphorically nested in Member States, even as a considerable amount of power and capacity is accruing to the EU. While effective in the short run, it may prove a fragile foundation going forward.

The construction of this cultural infrastructure is not only of historical or academic interest. Faced with the potential end to the 'permissive consensus' that previously underpinned the EU (Hooghe and Marks, 2009), the inherent limitations of the EU's particularly banal and tempered cultural infrastructure are now being sharply felt. Scholarship on comparative political development makes clear that dissent and struggle are nothing new for emergent political authorities (Fukuyama, 2011; Tilly, 1975). The protests at the new ECB building should therefore not surprise us. But the cultural infrastructure of governance of the EU, because of its particular banality and need to navigate robust national identities, may be poorly suited to support these struggles. Policy-makers, politicians, citizens and scholars need to come to grips with these new demands for a more politicized EU if they are to navigate forward to a legitimate and effectively functioning European Union.

This article proceeds as follows. I first situate the EU as a new emergent political form that has as one of its key challenges to establish itself as a taken-for-granted political authority, or to put it another way, as an unremarkable social fact. I then provide a brief empirical survey of the ways in which the EU is constructed through subtle, everyday cultural processes, noting the inherent fragility in that construction. Deracinated and banal, and gingerly navigating the nation-states, the cultural composition of the EU's legitimacy may not yet be enough to support the contestation that naturally comes with the deepening of political integration. In conclusion, I offer some thoughts on how to address these challenges by transitioning to a less deracinated and more emotive set of symbols and practices that allow for a more direct contestation over EU policies.

I. The Puzzle of the EU as an Emergent Political Authority

The EU is a new emergent political form, just as the Holy Roman Empire or the Hanseatic League or the modern nation-state all were at one point in time, and the EU likewise has its own trajectory of political development (Ruggie, 1993; Caporaso, 1996; Marks, 1997; Marks, 2012). Rather than seeing the EU only as an assemblage of laws and institutions designed to manage cross-border regulations over quotidian things like cheese or hair dryers, we should step back and consider the EU in terms of historical trends in governance, as a case of comparative political development (McNamara, 2015a, 2015b, 2015c; Börzel and Hosli, 2003; Börner and Eigmüller, 2015). When we see the EU in this way, as a new polity with claims on its 'citizens' and vice versa, it shines attention on the question of how its legitimate political authority is created (Copsey, 2015).

The indicators of this political authority range far and wide in the deep and intrusive ways that the EU increasingly and profoundly shapes public and private life throughout Europe. As a system of supranational governance has been built at the European level, the EU's membership has extended from the original six signatories of the 1957 Treaty of Rome to today's 28 Member States. EU institutions, administrative bodies, legislators, judges and policy-makers have come to do more and more of the work of governing over Europe as a whole. With the Single Market that has brought down barriers to trade and standardized rules for everything from electrical outlets to roaming tariffs on mobile

© 2015 The Author(s) JCMS: Journal of Common Market Studies © 2015 John Wiley & Sons Ltd

phones to financial reporting to public procurement rules (Egan, 2001; Egan, 2015; Kelemen, 2014), the single currency project (Matthijs and Blyth, 2015), and the extensive reach of European Court of Justice and its supremacy over national law (Stone Sweet, 2004, 2010; Schmidt and Kelemen, 2013), the EU has accrued much power and policy capacity in the economic realm. Non-economic areas such as social policy, citizenship, environmental policy, health policy, culture and entertainment, economic development and education have also been subject to collective European governance (Caporaso and Tarrow, 2009; Anderson, 2015; Shaw, 2008; Delreux, 2011, McNamara, 2015a). Importantly, however, although its policies indirectly redistribute wealth and opportunity, the EU does not have a formal system of direct taxing and spending, or debt creation at the European level, as is routine for all nation-states no matter how decentralized (McNamara, 2015c).

On the world stage, contrary to the conventional wisdom that the EU lacks foreign policy power, the EU signs treaties alongside sovereign states, negotiates in high-level talks such as those with the US and Iran over nuclear issues, litigates against nations such as China in the World Trade Organization, and has co-ordinated robust collective sanctions on Russia (Menon, 2014, 2015; Smith, 2011). In the military sphere, the EU has deployed troops, police forces and crisis management personnel to more than a dozen conflicts, and has taken over the responsibility for providing security in Bosnia-Herzegovina from the North Atlantic Treaty Organization (NATO) (Mérand, 2008; Norheim-Martinsen, 2013). However, the EU does not have its own European army under a hierarchical command, but rather networks the Member State militaries together for its limited joint EU actions.

Scholars, policy-makers and public figures have long wrestled with how to think about the question of the EU's legitimacy (Copsey, 2015, p. 73). Some have argued that a lack of direct democratic representation erodes the EU's legitimacy, while others argue that the EU should be seen as a case of entirely appropriate delegation from elected officials to EU bodies (Moravcsik, 2002), or that legitimacy varies depending on the fit between national government structures and the EU (Schmidt, 2006). Others have focused on the question of whether a European *demos* is possible, or in fact already emerging, and how to build in more space for democratic contestation (Mair, 2013; Schmidt and Kelemen, 2013).

I approach the question of the EU's legitimacy in a different way, by focusing on how political authority is socially constructed. Political authority can be conceptualized as the process of creating social control and compliance (Hurd, 1999). Legitimacy is present when a culturally accepted principle or value shores up the right of that political authority to rule. Legitimacy, in this telling, is a subtle form of power that rests in a political authority's ability to create consent for its governance while also appearing to transcend that particular political actor. 'Legitimacy', as Martha Finnemore has written, 'is by its nature a social and relational phenomenon' (Finnemore, 2009, p. 61). It cannot be assumed unilaterally, but must be conferred by others, and is dependent on the particular broader social setting to determine its content. The terms by which political legitimacy is established vary with historical context, as norms of dynastic rule legitimated European rulers for centuries but, beginning in the late eighteenth century, democratic sovereignty became the metric for legitimation (Bukovansky, 2002). A key part of the social foundation for legitimacy of any political entity lies in what I call the cultural infrastructure for governance, as I explain below.

© 2015 The Author(s) JCMS: Journal of Common Market Studies © 2015 John Wiley & Sons Ltd

II. Comparative Political Development and the EU

A Cultural Infrastructure For Governance

Scholars of comparative political development have pointed out that war has historically been an important crucible for the emergence of new political entities, as the need for security has overcome resistance to the concentration of power (Tilly, 1975, 1990). Economic logics also have long provided an incentive for scaled-up governance and new political institutions to support market development and trade (Spruyt, 1994). But in addition to these widely recognized security and economic drivers for political integration, underlying social processes must be marshalled for a new emergent political form to take hold and stabilize. Culture, as everyday symbols and practices, helps to constitute and naturalize what people view as the appropriate locus of political authority. Culture also helps to construct what Benedict Anderson termed an 'imagined community' to support that new authority (Anderson, 1993).[4] Yet the study of culture has largely taken a back seat to other logics in scholarship on the EU. To be sure, some scholars have integrated aspects of social logics into their accounts to parse the dynamics behind the EU's history (Stone Sweet *et al.*, 2001), while a newer literature on the EU has emphasized a social constructivist approach to symbolic representation, framing and ideas (McNamara, 1998; Christiansen *et al.*, 2001; Parsons, 2003; Checkel, 2007). But these approaches have tended to shy away from directly confronting the concept of culture, offering explanations that more narrowly focus on ideas and socialization rather than the larger social structures that surround actors and infuse meaning into their daily lives.[5] Thus they overlook the latent, taken-for-granted ways in which symbols and practices enable some type of politics, while constraining others. A more recent scholarly shift to an empirical focus on the work done through symbols and practices provides a new method of assessing the ways in which the social construction of the EU is occurring.

Culture has often been viewed by modern political scientists as a quagmire of intractable phenomena, or dismissed as a mask for other, more important, dynamics. On the other hand, some who have advocated for the role of culture have actually set back its study by approaching culture as unchanging, static and primordial. Samuel Huntington's 'Clash of Civilizations' thesis is one prominent example of this mistaken view of culture (Huntington, 1993). For Huntington, culture can be boiled down to an immutable religious affiliation. We are born into our culture, and die with our cultural identities intact. Much of the early work on political culture likewise understood nationalist identities of Kurds or Germans as part of the essential DNA of a citizen. But recent work in comparative politics and sociology has moved away from this view, arguing instead that culture and identities are continually constructed, dynamic and inherently contested (Thomas *et al.*, 1987; Sewell, 1995).

---

[4] Anderson defined imagined communities as cultural 'artefacts' that create a sense of 'deep, horizontal comradeship,' resting on a shared image of a limited, sovereign community even as its members will never meet or even know of each other (Anderson, 1993, pp. 6–7). They are invented, not given; 'distinguished not by their falsity/genuineness, but by the style in which they are imagined' (Anderson, 1993, p. 6).

[5] There are a few innovative studies that have argued for an explicit cultural approach, but these early studies tended to focus mostly on the malign effects and cynical calculations of actors promoting a 'European culture' as a way to mask the negative distributional impacts of European integration (Delanty, 1995; Shore, 2000). Recent work is closer to the approach I am arguing for here, emphasizing that culture is not under the control of any one actor but rather is the product of social interactions (Cram, 2001, 2009; Manners, 2011; Della Salla, 2010).

© 2015 The Author(s) JCMS: Journal of Common Market Studies © 2015 John Wiley & Sons Ltd

This newer literature on culture emphasizes its dynamic nature and offers a way of empirically demonstrating its causal impacts. Here, culture is defined as delineating a process of meaning making, shared among some particular group of people (Scott, 1985, 1998; Wedeen, 1999, 2002, 2008). We can think about meaning making as 'a social process through which people reproduce together the conditions of intelligibility that enable them to make sense of their worlds' (Wedeen, 2002, p. 717). Clifford Geertz's famous quote is helpful here: 'Believing, with Max Weber, that man is an animal suspended in webs of significance he himself has spun, I take culture to be those webs' (Geertz, 1973, p. 5). Throughout our day, whether it be in families, schools, terrorist cells, law offices or army units, we rely on a series of quotidian practices and symbols to stabilize our interactions. They are so prevalent that they become completely commonplace and taken for granted, unremarkable except perhaps when we move into a different setting and we are jolted into seeing all of the previously invisible rules and roles from our new perspective as an outsider. By seeing culture as practices of meaning making, we are able to probe into the ways in which actors are making their worlds intelligible and manageable (Wedeen, 2002, p. 720). This approach also opens up the potential to study more precisely the conflicts, cleavages and power involved in the construction of cultures, and how symbols can be used as resources in those conflicts (Swindler, 1986).

If cultures are not primordial and static but rather are the dynamic structures within which we interpret and make meaning of our worlds, then each of us also carries a unique cultural identity that is infused with the variety of all of these different experiences and commitments. We are not of one culture, but of many. This is very important, because if multiple identities can co-exist, it opens up the possibility that the creation of a European identity may not automatically be in a zero-sum battle between national and EU identities. Instead, those identities might be nested, parallel, hierarchical, conflicting, mutually exclusive or synergistic, to name but a few relationships. And they will be activated in different contexts, and with the prompting of different cultural symbols and practices.

Constructing an EU Polity Through Symbols and Practices

The historical experience of nation-states tells us that creating new political affinities is always an uphill battle. The construction of a new political community has always required a significant shift in citizens' vision of the appropriate polity: its scale, its membership, and its meaning. In many instances this shift occurs with coercion; in other instances it is more voluntary. But in all cases, it involves the creation of a perceived and experienced bond that can glue individuals together in a shared culture and shared identity. Motivated political elites have strategically attempted to create such shared identities, although never without pushback and reversals. They have been helped by the unintentional work done by the shifts in daily life brought about by the material impacts of various state-building policies.

Ambitious empirical work across a variety of historical cases has emphatically made this point (Weber, 1976). To note but one example, an astonishing study of the development of Scottish national sentiments based on the notion of the Highland traditions has likewise traced many of the purportedly 'ancient' Hibernian traditions (Scottish clans with distinct tartans made into kilts and so on) to a combination of creative hucksters in the early nineteenth century and romantic leanings on the part of various members of

© 2015 The Author(s) JCMS: Journal of Common Market Studies © 2015 John Wiley & Sons Ltd

Scottish society (Trevor-Roper, 1983). The creation of new national monuments and rituals, such as the Tomb of the Unknown Soldier, provided a sense of 'nationness' without specificity as to the particulars of who is, or is not, part of the community (Anderson, 1993, pp. 9–10). The development of the technology of the national census allowed the categorization and classification of this new group of citizens in a universal form while giving the state tools to extend its bureaucratic power (Loveman, 2005; Starr, 1987). Expressions of community, such as the museum and the map, were elevated to the national level and arts, artifacts and boundaries all become part of the larger project of the nation-state (Anderson, 1993). While the nation-state centralized and exerted control across a host of policy arenas, it also was an impressive 'symbolic accomplishment' (Bourdieu, 1984). These political and social technologies gave people a sense of community beyond their local villages and towns, forever changing the scale of polities.

The challenge for real-world actors, be they Eurocrats or national elites, attempting to establish the EU as a social fact is to make it seem unremarkable and natural, even as it may be actually quite novel and revolutionary. Bourdieu has called this the ability to 'construct the given' – that is, to make natural and unremarkable certain categories and actions that reinforce and legitimize political agency (Bourdieu, 1991, p. 170). For the EU, of course, the project is doubly hard as there are no analogs to the EU as a political form, and EU officials must be careful about not overtly mimicking the nation-state to avoid awkward confrontation over the EU's ultimate goals. Yet when successful, the EU is naturalized as an actor such that we don't even think about this process of actor creation, nor do we question the construction of an imagined community of European citizens, who must locate themselves inside this pervasive mental framework even absent a true European 'nation' or template for the EU's unique polity. Note that these processes of symbolic representation do not by themselves create unity, or loyalty, or emotional attachment. Instead, symbolic representation creates a unit, a vessel for discourse, reference and discussion. Agents may actively push back on the deployment of symbols—rejecting, resisting, subverting or creating counter-symbols. The blue and yellow EU flag may be viewed with approval when flying above a new economic development project in Croatia, but it might be trampled on by students in Greece protesting against economic austerity policies.

Culture as shared meaning is not only created through symbols, as discussed above, but also through practice. Practice—our day-to-day experiences and actions as humans —is what solidifies and makes real those constructions, or contradicts and inverts them (Wedeen, 2002; Pouliot, 2008). Europe can be represented as a borderless entity on the back of a euro note, but when a Dutch citizen at the Charles de Gaulle airport outside Paris joins with Italians and Poles in a line for 'EU Nationals' when entering France from the US it becomes part of that person's lived experience of what 'Europe' means, and eventually a taken-for-granted reality (McNamara, 2015a). In this view, instead of only considering what we think *about* (symbolic representation), we should also understand what we think *from* (Pouliot, 2008). Thinking 'from' a sense of European political identity is a much more powerful and ingrained dynamic than thinking 'about' political community and identity. In this view, crossing from France into Spain with no passport or experience of it as a border becomes a deeply engrained pattern of behaviour that changes the backdrop of discussion about European governance. Even if such practice does not make that governance unproblematic or uncontested, it changes the basic felt assumptions under which the discussion occurs.

© 2015 The Author(s) JCMS: Journal of Common Market Studies © 2015 John Wiley & Sons Ltd

III. The EU's Localized and Banal Authority

If I am right that the EU's legitimacy lies in part in the social processes that provide cultural or everyday naturalization of the shift in power toward Europe, then how has the EU accomplished this sleight of hand? Below I outline some of the symbols and practices that I argue build an implicit imagined European community, albeit one very different from what underpins the nation-state. A series of deliberate and surprisingly successful policy actions on the part of European officials have naturalized the EU, even as some attempts to create a sense of a unique European identity have been less successful. In addition, some EU policies targeted toward more material results have had important but unintentional cultural side effects, generating habits and representations that normalize the EU as a new emergent political form.

Navigating the Nation-State: Localizing Europe

The central difference between the EU's legitimation and the historic strategies of the nation-state is that the EU's cultural infrastructure must carefully navigate pre-existing loyalties and robust identities even as it creates a political community at the European level. The early nation-state symbolically asserted itself as supreme over long-standing political actors who sought to share its powers (Weber, 1976; Loveman, 2005). In contrast, the EU's efforts at labelling, mapping and narrating to naturalize Europe have sought instead to subtly recontextualize national symbols and practices so that they appear in a different light, taking on modified meanings that create space for a common – if not single – European identity. EU programmes and policies do not strip out national identities and associations, but rather reorient the EU's symbols and practices so that they are not necessarily viewed in opposition to long-standing national identities. For example, a EU programme officially anoints one or more European cities per year as the 'European Capital of Culture'. In so doing, the historical richness of a city such as Antwerp is projected outward into Europe as part of a shared cultural heritage, not one tied exclusively to Belgium (McNamara, 2015b). The goal is to resituate Member State affinities within a broader frame of Europe, allowing for both the universal (EU) and the local (Belgian), not replacing but complementing long-held identities. In this way, elements that are part of the daily national culture – that is, the symbols and practices that make meaning within the local political community – are reclassified from purely national, to national but simultaneously embedded within 'Europe'.

Multiple modes of symbolic representation and practice in the EU follow this logic. The primary language adopted by the EU for its legal actions uses the term 'EU directives' rather than calling the rules 'laws', a conscious decision to avoid direct conflict with sovereign nation-state but instead nesting the EU rules within the national rather than competing with it. While English is the overwhelmingly dominant language in practice across EU administrative offices, all of the 23 EU languages are celebrated as putatively equal in the official communications of the EU. While the euro's paper currency is standardized and uses only carefully abstracted, generic European images, each participating Member State issues its own euro coins with standard European imagery on one side and national symbols, such as the Brandenburg Gate or the Irish harp, on the other (McNamara, 2013). The national governments all use a standard EU passport design,

© 2015 The Author(s) JCMS: Journal of Common Market Studies © 2015 John Wiley & Sons Ltd

although the passports themselves are not actually issued by the EU. They use a common color (burgundy), with the EU name appearing in the national language (e.g. *Europese Unie*) at the top of the passport, but also with the national symbol and name, such as the Dutch royal coat of arms and *Koninkrijk Der Nederlanden*. So, we have both a deft co-optation and standardization of a core national symbol, the passport, while leaving control over passport issuance to the national authorities and setting the EU symbols side by side with the national ones.

A second way in which the EU has localized while categorizing its states together within the EU frame is by explicitly promoting 'universal', purportedly ahistorical, values that are widely shared among liberal democracies in the modern age. Making the EU centrally concerned with issues such as human rights, democracy and economic efficiency, in this view, therefore does not demarcate the EU as distinct or grounded in any particular national political culture (Soysal, 2002). Liberalism, with its emphasis on individual rights and its deep roots in western enlightenment thinking, is instead refashioned as universalism in this strategy. The motto of the EU, 'united in diversity', reflects this approach as it (paradoxically) stresses both commonality and a unified identity as well as diversity and pluralism. Some scholars have therefore argued that the EU should be understood not as a form of national identity but in terms of civic identity, in a departure from more traditional forms of ethnic or cultural identity (Sassatelli, 2002). The result is what some have termed a post-nationalist EU (Eriksen and Fossum, 2000). However, it is evident that the EU also appropriates quite traditional symbols and political technologies (passports, citizenship, paper money) and conventional expressions of state or national authority (Manners, 2011). The question is whether ideas such as 'united in diversity' can be made intrinsically meaningful despite their banality, or whether it is enough for the EU to function as an empty frame within which many multiple cultures flourish without eroding the whole.

These brief observations get to the point that Europe's cultural construction does not have the EU *replacing* pre-existing political authorities, as occurred with the historical rise of the nation-state. Tellingly, when the EU appropriates national symbols more directly, as with the failed effort at a European Constitution in 2005, it runs into trouble (Sternberg, 2013). EU policy-makers must instead find other ways to fit within the existing cultural context of the modern era of the nation-state, appropriating and reinventing national symbols, juxtaposing rather than confronting them. The EU and traditional national symbols co-exist, but policy-makers have attempted to frame them so as not to be in direct competition with each other, their effect additive and positive sum, not zero-sum. This creates a European space that does not depend on a unified, collective emotion or 'predisposed identity' nor one neatly bounded cultural community, but rather an 'assemblage of principles and their enactment,' such as democracy, progress, human rights and gender equality (Soysal, 2002, p. 281). The nation co-exists with the EU in this space, but it is resituated, reinterpreted, reimagined and no longer the sole legitimate authority.

Deracinating Europe

The EU's cultural infrastructure is notable for a second strategy, one that marks it as quite distinct from previous emergent political entities. That is the strategy of what I call deracination. The EU has been successful, in part, in legitimating itself because of the way in which it has portrayed a deracinated version of governance while pursuing the political technologies of labelling, mapping and narrating. It is no accident that the British press focuses on things like rules from Brussels on the size and shape of bananas, while sober central bankers rule over the euro and faceless lawyers in Luxembourg shape community law. For decades, the people of Europe dozed over the thought of the labyrinthine governance structure that is the EU, rather than contesting it. Indeed, blandness and integration by stealth is a long-standing EU tradition. The European Court of Justice succeeded in shifting legal power to the EU level in part because of the ability of law to serve as a 'mask' for politics, reducing revolutions in sovereignty to dry legalese, impenetrable and seemingly innocuous (Burley and Mattli, 1993). The euro was framed by policy-makers as simply a technocratic solution to dampen exchange rate variability within the single market, rather than the historic transfer of sovereignty it was (Jabko, 2006). This banality has its pluses and its minuses, as we shall see, but it is clearly part of how the EU has constructed itself as a political authority and social fact of remarkable tenacity. It has enabled the creation of a type of imagined community of Europeans who have taken on ways of thinking and acting within a new European governance scheme that, at the very least, creates a permissive consensus for the historic consolidation of power in Brussels in the decades following the 1958 Treaty of Rome. This 'banality by design' helps the EU to navigate the pre-existing and robust national communities by making the transfer of power seem like an unremarkable act of technocratic delegation.

Unsurprisingly, given this deracinated set of symbols and practices, the number of people who self-identify as European in interviews and polls is relatively low (Díez Medrano, 2003; Checkel and Katzenstein, 2009; Fligstein, 2008; Favell, 2008). People do not have the nationalist fervour or pride in themselves as citizens of the EU that they have as, for example, Swedes or Greeks. Yet, if my reading of the symbols and practices of EU governance is correct, displacing national identities is not what we should expect from the EU, as the labels, mental maps and narratives embodied in the EU's cultural infrastructure stresses complementarity of identities, not a single European identity. In daily life, EU citizens are inundated with subtle cues that privilege layering and blended identities, including the creation of a taken-for-granted Europeanness to match national and regional identities. So, instead of looking for the fervour of national identity as we traditionally think of it, we might look instead for evidence of what has been called 'banal nationalism' (Billig, 1995), translated into this new, non-state governance form – what I call 'banal authority.'

A key insight of this approach is that nationalism does not only arise in crisis and conflict, but that nations are reproduced on a daily basis, through banal and mundane ways, and it is those habits of mind and practice that underpin national identity (Billig, 1995). Those activities and representations that seem the most clichéd (flags and anthems, for example) matter, for they reproduce national identity in ways that prime populations for supporting their states in more emotional or difficult times, such as war. Established nations continually 'flag' or remind their populations of nationhood in a myriad of seemingly innocuous ways: 'this reminding is so familiar, so continual, that it is not consciously registered as reminding. The metonymic image of banal nationalism is not a flag which is being consciously waved with fervent passion; it is the flag hanging unnoticed on the public building' (Billig, 1995, p. 8). However, occasionally the symbolism becomes a subject of contestation, as when the former Czech president Václav Klaus

© 2015 The Author(s) JCMS: Journal of Common Market Studies © 2015 John Wiley & Sons Ltd

refused to fly the EU flag over the castle in Prague; his replacement, the more pro-EU Miloš Zeman, made the return of the blue and yellow flag one of his first official acts as president. The EU Member State embassies in Washington, DC fly the EU flag next to their national flags, an act unremarked upon even as it signals something remarkable about the sharing of political authority.

This concept of banal nationalism well captures the deracinated, 'under-the-radar' taken-for-granted rhetoric and practices that create Europe as a legitimate actor but reverberates back on individual identity in ways not captured in the polls (Cram, 2001, 2006). For example, the uncontroversial acceptance of a public EU entity, the Eurostat Agency, commissioning Eurobarometer polls that ask people whether they 'feel European' can be argued to have created a chain of representations and practices that creates and reinforces the concept of the EU as a legitimate actor and European as a legitimate category of identity. The work of seemingly mundane, technical bureaucrats and telephone polling agents does not excite the mind in the way that a national day of independence with fireworks and fervent anthem-singing might, but it may have important effects in creating the foundation for EU governance, by legitimating a range of statistical and information-gathering activities. Ironically, from this perspective, Eurobarometer is constructing European identity even as it is reporting its nonexistence. So, it is not the degree of felt or activated 'Europeanness' – although that is important in other contexts – that matters for this argument, but rather the normalization of the EU as a legitimate governor. We are clearly not in a situation where the EU has replaced national identity but the EU's cultural impact is real in the very particular type of 'banal' imagined community. Participation in this community involves both active dynamics ('imagine this!') and passive participation (unthinking repetition and habits of practice that reproduce Europeanness). Viewed this way, we might see the puzzle as not that there is so little European identity but rather that there is so much implicit, taken-for-granted Europeanness at work. It is both a strength and a weakness of the EU that it forges its imagined community with a particularly banal sense of nationalism – a rather bloodless, often highly technocratic, and usually quite quotidian sense of political authority – rather than impassioned, blood-racing heroism.

Conclusion: The Limits of the EU's Cultural Infrastructure for Governance?

What does Europe's particular type of banal authority mean for the future of the EU and its policies going forward from the eurozone crisis and beyond? Will it provide enough of a social foundation for dealing with the challenges ahead – be they economic malaise, insufficient democratic representation, xenophobia or societal exclusion? The legitimation that arises from the symbols and practices of the EU's imagined community has been constructed to support the rather stealthy consolidation of European political development, but is not necessarily well equipped to deal with the open political contestation inevitable in the EU as it evolves as an ever more significant source of governance. Deracinated and localized understandings of Europe, and citizens' places within it, are a weak foundation for the type of solidarity and sacrifices demanded in the face of Europe's economic, social and geopolitical challenges.

Those groups that are suffering disproportionately from the eurozone crisis are confronting the meaning of the EU in new ways. Its 'under-the-radar', taken-for-granted status has been swept aside by a new politicization of Europe – what the EU means, who it is for, and how it should be governed. The effects of the sovereign debt crisis that started with Greece in late 2009 continue to plague much of Southern Europe, while Northern EU states, most notably Germany, have seen their economic prospects only get rosier. The differing prescriptions for what to do to solve the crisis – with Germany in the person of chancellor Angela Merkel successfully demanding austerity and the cutting of public budgets and services – have made what was a sore point into a painful fault line across the EU states and their publics.

A key political challenge for the EU lies in the fact that the euro crisis has had such uneven effects across Europe's political community, with seemingly intractable youth unemployment soaring in the Mediterranean states while robust economic opportunities open up for new generations of Germans and other northern Europeans (Matthijs, 2014). Does the EU have the overall social solidarity and sense of political community to support the pooling and transfer of resources from the haves to the have-nots that the crisis seems to require (Copsey, 2015; McNamara, 2015c)?

The public debate has suggested there is little sense of collective belonging, even in circumstances where the richer states arguably gain the most from the continuation of the eurozone and the EU's larger economic integration. But despite this, the EU states together have pledged in the neighborhood of €1 trillion to keep the eurozone afloat and the Member States financially stable. European summits too numerous to count have been held, and a new layer of institutions, most prominently the European stability mechanism for back-up funding in times of crisis along with a European banking union, are being built at the EU level, further moving political authority up to the centre of the EU polity (Matthijs and Blyth, 2015; Howarth and Quaglia, 2014).[6] These moves have been grudgingly acquiesced to by the European public, if not embraced or even fully understood. I argue that they could not have been possible without the decades of slow accumulation of everyday symbols and practices that created a permissive consensus for such political developments. Indeed, the most effective and active actor in the eurozone crisis has been the ECB (European central bank), a relatively opaque and political independent body that has more in common with the EU legacy of deracinated, technocratic governance than with any new emergent sense of impassioned European political identity and solidarity. Yet as austerity policies continue to be the price paid by the laggard states for their debt issues, the close identification of those policies with 'Europe' is an association that is piercing the banal authority the EU has been built on and creating new challenges for legitimation, as evidenced by the Blockupy Frankfurt protests.

A second major area of challenge for the EU, however, goes far beyond any particular economic crisis. How can the EU improve overall democratic representation and citizens' participation in European-level politics, and what role do the symbols and practices of Europe play in creating a democratic culture to support it? My argument suggests that one way forward is to enhance democracy in the EU through less banality and more political contestation – but contestation of a healthy and inclusive kind. Because of the veneer of banality that the EU's symbols and practices create, the salience of EU issues for everyday citizens is low, and it is difficult for the 'mobilization of bias' to occur and drive debate and effective democratic participation (Schattschneider, 1960). Although it seems counter-intuitive, I argue that the EU needs more overt contestation and direct discussion

---

[6] See also Gren *et al.*'s contribution to this volume.

© 2015 The Author(s) JCMS: Journal of Common Market Studies © 2015 John Wiley & Sons Ltd

of its policies and debate over its leaders, a point made by other scholars from several different perspectives (Hix, 2008; Schmidt, 2006, 2009; Mair, 2013). The EU has profoundly shifted governance to the European level, even in those areas that formally were considered core state powers (Genschel and Jachtenfuchs, 2014). Conflict and contestation are the growing pains of any new polity, but they need to be directed into effective, legitimate and appropriate channels of representation and partisanship (Follesdal and Hix, 2006). What my account highlights is that the EU's cultural toolkit (Swindler, 1986) for this sort of contestation has been intentionally very limited.

There are some indications that we are moving in the direction of more open contestation, albeit with some important caveats. The 2014 European Parliament elections were much more publicly contested than any before in EU history, with wide coverage in national newspapers and various trans-European interest groups—from students to environmental activists to high-priced consultants—setting up websites and generating information relevant to their EU-wide constituencies.[7] Some small steps were made toward a true electoral contest for the European Commission president to replace Barroso as the second president since the Lisbon Treaty. A heavily promoted television debate, social networking and advertisements on various media all increased awareness of the European-level elections in ways not seen in previous years. But it was not to be the end of the EU's traditions of banality or deracination by any means. The voting result for the European Commission president was not legally binding, but only to be taken under advisement.[8] The ultimate choice of Jean-Claude Juncker, a Luxembourg prime minister and confirmed technocrat, to head the European Commission did not move the EU very far beyond its business as usual, even in a time of extraordinary tension over the euro crisis and the EU's future.

In the national settings, the shift in power to the EU has become more openly debated than ever before, as national electorates begin to move beyond their permissive consensus to something that is much messier but, in the long run, will produce a more robust version of democracy for Europe. Even David Cameron's promise to hold a referendum on British membership in the EU and the fervent denunciations of the UK Independence Party (UKIP) may, in the long run, prove an opening for a more transparent and pluralistic discussion of the pros and cons of EU governance. Radical anti-EU parties, such as the Danish People's Party, Beppe Grillo's Five Star Movement in Italy or the Golden Dawn in Greece, may not be exemplars of deliberative democracy, but the concerns they embody need a place in debates about the EU.

The argument I am making suggests that any institutional fixes to improve EU democracy will need to work hand-in-hand with changes in the cultural infrastructure for European governance. The meaning currently infused into the symbols and practices of life in Europe, as both directly and indirectly shaped by EU policies, is one that does not easily support overt democratic contestation over accrual of power to the EU. A shift will have to occur at every level of cultural experience in order to make this happen. In settled times, as Swindler points out, culture can directly influence political action by providing a tool kit or repertoire of social resources to construct strategies of action (Swindler, 1986). The symbols and practices of banal authority have done so remarkably well in the EU, creating a foundation for an extraordinary expansion of governance since World War II. Now, the unsettled

---

[7] On the 2014 European Parliament elections, see Hobolt's contribution to this volume.
[8] See Dinan's contribution to this volume.

© 2015 The Author(s) JCMS: Journal of Common Market Studies © 2015 John Wiley & Sons Ltd

times ahead will provide different opportunities for culture to shape outcomes. New cultural repertoires will need to arise to shape the meaning attached to the EU and increase the role of citizens and active political participation. Most importantly, the cultural strategies of deracination that support the EU need to be replaced with a more honest and open assessment of partisanship, and the winners and losers from various policies. Localization, or the careful symbolic balancing of local and state-level attachments and powers, will continue to be necessary. Thinking about the EU as a 'polity-in-the-making' (Copsey, 2015), or a 'coming together federalism' (Kelemen, 2014; Stepan, 1999) as a voluntary grouping of previously independent states, offers a template for the foundation of political culture that can live with the tension in levels of political authority implied by the EU.

My emphasis on the need for increased politicization and a more impassioned, less technocratic sense of European identity might make some readers very nervous. After all, nationalism was the cause of much injustice and bloodshed over the past century. Should we be worried about a new, more strident version of political identity being constructed at the European level? Efforts to create a European identity could support policies of social exclusion, military aggression and xenophobia. In the same way that Ernst Gellner (1983) viewed nationalism as a malign force historically, so writers such as Delanty (1995) and Shore (2000) see the EU's policies and dynamics as deeply pernicious. Delanty sees the 'European idea' as a 'totalising re-appropriation of forces that lie deep in European history' (Delanty, 1995, p. viii). He writes about the 'myth of Europe as a unifying and universalising project', linking it to the 'enforced and violent homogenisation' that occurred historically (Delanty, 1995, p. vii).

Although these are real and important concerns, my reading of the reality of the EU does not support these fears. The EU has some powerful symbolic and practical tools at its disposal; however, the process of authority construction is incomplete, lumpy and highly attenuated, varying across different EU national settings and social and economic groups, and can often be contradictory in its effects. There have been clear examples of xenophobic Europe, with anti-Muslim and anti-Semitic activities on the rise, but evidence also of an alternative type of political space, more peacefully overlapping and co-existing with national identity (Soysal, 2002). The idea of Europe as post-national, liberal enlightenment project is an underlying narrative, captured in the flashmobs playing the EU's informal anthem 'Ode to Joy' in Ukraine.[9] The EU is not a perfect liberal democracy and never will be. But the accomplishments of the EU over the postwar era indicate that it has been, on balance, a force for the common good that need not necessarily repeat the excesses of nationalism. The EU is an innovative political entity whose future is unknown, but the ways in which everyday symbols and practices have legitimated its political authority so far provide some clues as to where it has been, and where it might go.

References

Anderson, B. (1993) *Imagined Communities: Reflections on the Origins and Spread of Nationalism*, revised ed. (London: Verso).

Anderson, K. (2015) *Social Policy in the European Union* (Basingstoke: Palgrave Macmillan).

[9] *Express Tribune*, 31 March 2014.

© 2015 The Author(s) JCMS: Journal of Common Market Studies © 2015 John Wiley & Sons Ltd

Billig, M. (1995) *Banal Nationalism* (London: Sage Publications).

Börner, S. and Eigmüller, M. (eds) (2015) *European Integration, Processes of Change and the National Experience* (Basingstoke: Palgrave Macmillan).

Börzel, T. and Hosli, M.O. (2003) 'Brussels Between Bern and Berlin: Comparative Federalism Meets the European Union'. *Governance*, Vol. 16, No. 2, pp. 179–202.

Bourdieu, P. (1984) *Distinction: A Social Critique of the Judgment of Taste* (Cambridge, MA: Harvard University Press).

Bourdieu, P. (1991) *Language and Symbolic Power* (Cambridge: Harvard University Press).

Bukovansky, M. (2002) *Legitimacy and Power Politics: the American and French Revolutions in International Political Culture* (Princeton: Princeton University Press).

Burley, A-M, and Mattli, W. (1993) 'Europe Before the Court: A Political Theory of Legal Integration'. *International Organization*, Vol. 47, pp. 41–76.

Caporaso, J. A. (1996) 'The European Union and Forms of State: Westphalian, Regulatory or Post-Modern?'. *JCMS*, Vol. 34, No. 1, pp. 29–52.

Caporaso, J. A. and Tarrow, S. (2009) 'Polanyi in Brussels: Supranational Institutions and the Transnational Embedding of Markets'. *International Organization*, Vol. 63, No. 4, pp. 593–620.

Checkel, J. (ed.) (2007) *International Institutions and Socialization in Europe* (Cambridge: Cambridge University Press).

Checkel, J. and Katzenstein, P. (eds.) (2009) *European Identity* (New York: Cambridge University Press).

Christiansen, T., Jørgensen, K.E. and Wiener, A. (eds.) (2001) *The Social Construction of Europe* (London: Sage).

Copsey, N. (2015) *Rethinking the European Union* (London: Palgrave).

Cram, L. (2001) 'Imagining the Union: A Case of Banal Europeanism?'. In Wallace, H. (ed.), *Interlocking Dimensions of European Integration* (London: Palgrave).

Cram, L. (2006) 'Inventing the People: Civil Society Participation and the Enhabitation of the EU'. In Smismans, S. (ed.), *Civil Society & Legitimate European Governance* (London: Edward Elgar).

Cram, L. (2009) 'Introduction. Banal Europeanism: European Union Identity and National Identities in Synergy'. *Nations and Nationalism* Vol. 15, No. 1, pp. 101–8.

Delanty, G. (1995) *Inventing Europe: Ideas, Identity, Reality* (New York: St Martin's Press).

Della Salla, V. (2010) 'Political Myth, Mythology and the European Union'. *JCMS*, Vol. 48, No. 1, pp. 1–19.

Delreux, T. (2011) *The EU as International Environmental Negotiator* (Farnham: Ashgate).

Díez Medrano, J. (2003) *Framing Europe: Attitudes to European Integration in Germany, Spain, and the United Kingdom* (Princeton: Princeton University Press).

Egan, M. (2001) *Constructing a European Market: Standards, Regulation, and Governance* (Oxford: Oxford University Press).

Egan, M. (2015) *Single Markets: Economic Integration in Europe and the United States* (Oxford: Oxford University Press).

Eriksen, E.O. and Fossum, J.E. (2000) '*Post-National Integration*'. In Eriksen, E.O. and Fossum, J.E. (eds), *Democracy in the European Union* (London: Routledge).

Favell, A. (2008) *Eurostars and Eurocities: Free Movement and Mobility in an Integrating Europe* (Malden, MA: Blackwell).

Fligstein, N. (2008) *Euro-clash: The EU, European Identity, and the Future of Europe* (Oxford: Oxford University Press).

Finnemore, M. (2009) 'Legitimacy, Hypocrisy and the Social Structure of Unipolarity: Why Being a Unipole is Not All it is Cracked Up to Be'. *World Politics*, Vol. 61, No. 1, pp. 58–85.

Follesdal, A. and S. Hix (2006) 'Why There is a Democratic Deficit in the EU: A Response to Moravcsik'. *JCMS*, Vol. 44, No. 3, pp. 533–62.

Fukuyama, F. (2011) *The Origins of Political Order* (New York: Farrar, Straus and Giroux).

Geertz, C. (1973) *The Interpretation of Cultures: Selected Essays* (New York: Basic Books).

Gellner, E. (1983) *Nations and Nationalism* (Ithaca: Cornell University Press).

Genschel, P. and Jachtenfuchs, M. (eds.) (2014) *Beyond the Regulatory Polity? The European Integration of Core State Powers* (Oxford: Oxford University Press).

Hix, S. (2008) *What's Wrong with the EU and How to Fix It* (Cambridge: Polity Press).

Hooghe, L. and Marks, G. (2009) 'A Postfunctionalist Theory of European Integration: From Permissive Consensus to Constraining Dissensus'. *British Journal of Political Science*, Vol. 39, pp. 1–23.

Howarth, D. and Quaglia, L. (2014) 'The Steep Road to European Banking Union: Constructing the Single Resolution Mechanism'. *JCMS*, Vol. 52, No. s1, pp. 125–40.

Huntington, S. (1993) 'The Clash of Civilizations'. *Foreign Affairs* Vol. 72, No. 3, pp. 22–49.

Hurd, I. (1999). 'Legitimacy and Authority in International Politics'. *International Organization*, Vol. 53, No. 2, pp. 379–408.

Jabko, N. (2006) *Playing the Market: A Political Strategy for Uniting Europe, 1985–2005* (Ithaca: Cornell University Press).

Kelemen, R.D. (2014) 'Constructing the European Judiciary'. Paper prepared for LAPA Seminar, 24 March, Princeton University, Princeton, New Jersey.

Loveman, M. (2005) 'The Modern State and the Primitive Accumulation of Symbolic Power'. *American Journal of Sociology*, Vol. 110, No. 6, pp. 1651–83.

Mair, P. (2013) *Ruling the Void: the Hollowing-Out of Western Democracy* (London: Verso).

Manners, I. (2011) 'Symbolism in European Integration'. *Comparative European Politics* Vol. 9, pp. 243–68.

Marks, G. (1997) 'A Third Lens: Comparing European Integration and State Building'. In Klausen, J. and Tilly, L. (eds.) *European Integration in Social and Historical Perspective: 1850 to the Present* (Lanham: Rowman & Littlefield).

Marks, G. (2012) 'Europe and its Empires: From Rome to the European Union'. *JCMS* Vol. 50, No. 1, pp. 1–20.

Matthijs, M. (2014) 'Mediterranean Blues: The Crisis in Southern Europe'. *Journal of Democracy* Vol. 25, No. 1, pp. 101–15.

Matthijs, M. and Blyth, M. (eds.) (2015) *The Future of the Euro* (New York: Oxford University Press).

McNamara, K.R. (1998) *The Currency of Ideas: Monetary Politics in the European Union* (Ithaca: Cornell University Press).

McNamara, K.R. (2013) 'Imaginary Europe: The euro as symbol and practice'. In Moro, G. (ed.), *The Single Currency and European Citizenship* (London: Bloomsbury).

McNamara, K.R. (2015a) *The Politics of Everyday Europe: Constructing Authority in the European Union* (Oxford: Oxford University Press).

McNamara, K.R. (2015b) 'Building Culture: The Architecture and Geography of Governance in the European Union'. In Börner, S. and Eigmüller, M. (eds), *European Integration, Processes of Change and the National Experience* (London: Palgrave Macmillan).

McNamara, K.R. (2015c) 'Forgotten Embeddedness: History Lessons for the Euro'. In Matthijs, M. and Blyth, M. (eds), *The Future of the Euro* (New York: Oxford University Press).

Menon, A. (2014) 'The JCMS Annual Review Lecture: Divided and Declining? Europe in a Changing World'. *JCMS*, Vol. 52, No. s1, pp. 5–24.

Menon, A. (2015). 'Defence Policy and the European State: Insights from American Experience'. In King, D. and Le Gales, P. (eds.), *The Reconfiguration of the State in Europe* (Oxford: Oxford University Press).

Mérand, F. (2008) *European Defence Policy: Beyond the Nation State* (Oxford: Oxford University Press).

Moravcsik, A. (2002) 'In Defence of the Democratic Deficit: Reassessing Legitimacy in the European Union'. *JCMS*, Vol. 40, No. 4, pp. 603–24.

© 2015 The Author(s) JCMS: Journal of Common Market Studies © 2015 John Wiley & Sons Ltd

Norheim-Martinsen, P. (2013) *The European Union and Military Force Governance and Strategy* (Cambridge: Cambridge University Press).

Parsons, C. (2003) *A Certain Idea of Europe* (Ithaca: Cornell University Press).

Pouliot, V. (2008) 'The Logic of Practicality: A Theory'. *International Organization* Vol. 62, pp. 257–88.

Ruggie, J.G. (1993) 'Territoriality and Beyond: Problematizing Modernity in International Relations'. *International Organization* Vol. 47, No. 1, pp. 139–74.

Sassatelli, M. (2002) 'Imagined Europe: The Shaping of a European Cultural Identity through EU Cultural Policy'. *European Journal of Social Theory*, Vol. 5, No. 4, pp. 435–51.

Schattschneider, E.E. (1960) *The Semi-Sovereign People: A Realist's View of Democracy in America* (New York: Holt, Rinehart and Winston).

Schmidt, V. (2006) *Democracy in Europe: The EU and National Polities* (Oxford: Oxford University Press).

Schmidt, V. (2009) 'Re-Envisioning the European Union: Identity, Democracy, Economy'. *JCMS*, Vol. 47, No. s1, pp. 17–42.

Schmidt, S.K. and Kelemen, R.D. (eds) (2013) *The Power of the European Court of Justice* (London: Routledge).

Scott, J. (1985) *Weapons of the Weak: Everyday Forms of Peasant Resistance* (New Haven: Yale University Press).

Scott, J. (1998) *Seeing Like a State: How Certain Schemes to Improve the Human Condition Have Failed* (New Haven: Yale University Press).

Sewell, W.H. (1995) 'A Theory of Structure: Duality, Agency and Transformation'. *American Journal of Sociology*, Vol. 98, No. 1, pp. 1–29.

Shaw, J. (2008) *The Transformation of Citizenship in the European Union* (Cambridge: Cambridge University Press).

Shore, C. (2000) *Building Europe: The Cultural Politics of European Integration* (London: Routledge).

Smith, M.E. (2011) 'A Liberal Grand Strategy in a Realist World? Power, Purpose, and the EU's Changing Global Role'. *Journal of European Public Policy*, Vol. 18, No. 2, pp. 144–63.

Soysal, Y. (2002) 'Locating Europe', *European Societies*, Vol. 4, No. 3, September, pp. 265–84.

Spruyt, H. (1994) *The Sovereign State and Its Competitors* (Princeton: Princeton University Press).

Starr, P. (1987) 'The Sociology of Official Statistics'. In Alonso, W. and Starr, P. (eds), *The Politics of Numbers* (New York: Russell Sage).

Stepan, A. (1999) 'Federalism and Democracy: Beyond the US Model', *Journal of Democracy*, Vol. 10, No. 4, pp. 19–34.

Sternberg, C.S. (2013) *The Struggle for EU Legitimacy: Public Contestation 1950–2005* (Basingstoke: Palgrave MacMillan).

Stone Sweet, A. (2004) *The Judicial Construction of Europe* (Oxford: Oxford University Press).

Stone Sweet, A., Sandholtz, W. and Fligstein, N. (eds) (2001) *The Institutionalization of Europe* (Oxford: Oxford University Press).

Swindler, A. (1986) 'Culture in Action: Symbols and Strategies'. *American Sociological Review*, Vol. 51, No. 2, pp. 273–86.

Tilly, C. (ed.) (1975) *The Formation of National States in Western Europe* (Princeton: Princeton University Press).

Tilly, C. (1990) *Coercion, Capital, and European States, AD 990–1992* (Cambridge, MA: Blackwell Press).

Thomas, G.M., Meyer, J.W., Ramirez, F.O. and Boli, J. (1987) *Institutional Structure: Constituting State, Society and the Individual* (London: Sage).

Trevor-Roper, H. (1983) 'The Invention of Tradition: The Highland Tradition of Scotland'. In Hobsbawm, E.J. and Ranger, T.O. (eds), *The Invention of Tradition* (Cambridge: Cambridge University Press).

Weber, E. (1976) *Peasants into Frenchmen* (Palo Alto: Stanford University Press).

Wedeen, L. (1999) *Ambiguities of Domination: Politics, Rhetoric, and Symbols in Contemporary Syria* (Chicago: University of Chicago Press).

Wedeen, L. (2002) 'Conceptualizing Culture: Possibilities for Political Science'. *American Political Science Review*, Vol. 96, No. 4, pp. 713–28.

Wedeen, L. (2008) *Peripheral Visions: Publics, Power, and Performance in Yemen* (Chicago: University of Chicago Press).

JCMS 2015 Volume 53 Annual Review pp. 40–60   DOI: 10.1111/jcms.12274

Italy and the EU: From True Love to Disenchantment?*

SONIA LUCARELLI
University of Bologna

Introduction

As a founding member of the European Union, for a long time Italy was one of the foremost supporters of the integration process. Not only were some of the fundamental figures in the history of European integration (such as Alcide De Gasperi and Altiero Spinelli) Italians, but from the 1970s until the mid-1990s the country's support for the integration process and its participation in it was almost unfaltering. For many years no significant change occurred to this unchallenged europhilia, and a 'pro-integrationist paradigm' (Quaglia, 2007) tended to prevail whenever Italy expressed itself on European governance. Despite there having been no serious breach against a substantial pro-European policy (no empty chair policy or breach of European solidarity), what has changed since the early 1990s is the public discourse on Europe, the attitude of a part of the political elites, and the public's support for the European project. This trend was amplified during the 2000s, leading to the lowest recorded level of support for European integration.

In this respect, Italy is not different from other EU countries: for a long time, until the early 1990s, the integration process was a result of the national elites' wide scope for manoeuvre resulting from the 'permissive consensus' given by the national public's scant (if any) attention to European policies (Lindberg and Scheingold, 1970; Sbragia, 2001). Such a 'permissive consensus' turned into a 'constraining dissensus' when the debate on Europe became much wider and 'politicized', and political entrepreneurs mobilized themselves using the tension between relatively stable national identities and the European Union's rapid jurisdictional empowerment (Hooghe and Marks, 2009, p. 13).

However, such a general observation obscures important specificities of the Italian case, which can only be understood by looking at the interaction between domestic and international dynamics, as well as between elites and the larger public. Hence, the first aim of this contribution is to track the transformation of attitudes toward Europe in Italy over time, as well as the underlying path dependencies and turning points, and to provide an interpretative recollection of this transformation that draws on the international and domestic levels of analysis. The questions I seek to answer in this contribution are as follows: what are the main characteristics of Italy's relationship with the integration process? How have they remained stable or changed over time? What have been the driving forces of change? In order to respond to these questions, a loose historical institutionalist recollection of events

* I am indebted to Maurizio Carbone, Michela Ceccorulli, Furio Cerutti, Enrico Fassi, Marco Valigi and the editors of the *JCMS Annual Review*, Nathaniel Copsey and Tim Haughton, for their precious suggestions on an early draft, as well as to Ferdinando Nelli Feroci and Ettore Greco for interesting conversations on the topic. Needless to say, I remain solely responsible for any errors and omissions.

© 2015 The Author(s) JCMS: Journal of Common Market Studies © 2015 John Wiley & Sons Ltd, 9600 Garsington Road, Oxford OX4 2DQ, UK and 350 Main Street, Malden, MA 02148, USA

(Steinmo *et al.*, 1992) will be provided so as to make sense of the continuity and change resulting from the interaction between elites, civil society and institutions, and to show that change is not only a consequence – intended or not – of strategic actions filtered through perceptions and institutional constraints (Hay and Wincott, 1998, p. 955), but also of a transformation of loyalties and trust in politics and institutions at large.

The second aim of the contribution is to extrapolate from the above (nationally based) reconstruction the responses to a set of questions that have emerged in the broader literature on European attitudes toward the integration process. A first question here is about whether support for the integration process is always predominantly 'utilitarian' (based on interest in the costs and benefits of membership) rather than 'affective' (based on diffused and possibly emotional responses to the ideals of European integration) (Lindberg and Scheingold, 1970, p. 40), or are there other relevant reasons for support? Second, as far as support for integration is concerned, what relationship exists between elites and the wider public (Hooghe and Marks, 2005)? Third, is there a relationship between the specific historically developed understanding of national identity and support for European integration (Diez Medrano, 2003)? Finally, is it possible to talk of a diffused 'euroscepticism'?

In order to deal with these topics, the contribution proceeds through a historical recollection of (institutional, elite and public) attitudes toward the EU during the so-called 'First Republic' (1948–94) and 'Second Republic' (1994–), to show elements of change and continuity. It concludes by showing that, despite sharing similarities with other European cases, Italy's attitude toward the EU has deep national-specific roots in the following: (1) the way in which adherence to Europe was understood in the early days (which set a path dependency that lasted for a long time); (2) a specific feature of Italian political identity; (3) the domestic transformations of the political institutional context; and (4) the gradual delegitimation of politics and the transformation of national identity. In other words, the negative impact of the economic crisis – frequently considered the main reason for rising euroscepticism among Europeans – is only the latest in a long line of reasons why the Italians have passed from true love of European integration to disenchantment.

I. From Suspicion to True Love: The First Republic and Italy's Support for European Integration

It has frequently been claimed that Italy's support for European integration has been surprisingly high since the beginning. However, in reality, a significant shift in attitude occurred in the late 1960s and early 1970s, when the European integration project gained the support of most relevant political elites and the public. Hence, while we can affirm that some fundamental features of Italy's attitude toward the European project were set in the late 1940s, the origin of the so-called permissive consensus is to be found in the late 1960s. These phases will be presented in turn and a synthesis of the main features of attitudes during the First Republic will be provided at the end of this section.

1950s–1960s, the Founding Years: From Ideological (Dis)Affection to True Love

Italy's European choice emerged as early as 1947 when the Italian government, led by Alcide De Gasperi, signed the Marshall Plan. At that point, the choice for Europe had been made, and was intrinsically linked to a choice for the west (Croci, 2008). Also in this case (as always in Italy – see Brighi, 2013, pp. 5–6), Italy's foreign policy had a funda-mental domestic function. Anchoring Italy to the train of Europe and transatlantic rela-tions was the choice made by De Gasperi, Sforza and the governing political elite of the time to face the challenge of the country's reconstruction and modernization in the post-World War II period (Telò, 1996, p. 144ff). It also allowed for the recognition of the role played by the federalist movement in the fight against fascism and provided an element of internal political cohesion in a highly divided country (an attempt that would prove successful as early as the end of the 1960s). Moreover, the European choice also played a role in Italy's aspiration to regain the international status and legitimacy that had been lost with its defeat in the Second World War.

This choice initially split the political parties and public opinion: on the one hand, Christian Democracy (*Democrazia Cristiana*, DC) was in favour of the transatlantic and European course of Italy's foreign policy; on the other, the left (the Socialist Party, PSI, and the Communist Party, PCI) and the extreme right (*Movimento sociale italiano*, MSI) were against European integration (Conti and Verzichelli, 2005). Proposals for the creation of the European Coal and Steel Community and the European Defence Community were harshly criticized by exponents of the left (both PCI and PSI) as serving the interests of the US and Germany. Hence, the opposition was not against a unified Europe, but against a Europe that would exclude Russia and would play to the interests of the western powers (see Togliatti, 1951).

Very soon, however, support for European integration became a factor unifying most of the political elites and a fundamental component of the left's re-orientation (and at-tempt at re-legitimization). During the 1950s, in an attempt to create an alternative in Italy's foreign policy to transatlantic loyalty to the US (which opposed the PSI's entry into government in the early 1960s), after having distanced itself from the USSR, the PSI changed its attitude toward European integration, supported the Euratom and abstained on the vote for the EEC (European Economic Community) Treaty. Between the late 1960s and the 1970s, with the growing need to develop a more independent European way to communism, the PCI also gradually changed attitude, first by entering the European Parliament (1969) with its political representatives, and last by having its secretary Enrico Berlinguer, in February 1973, publicly call for a Europe that should be 'Western, democratic, independent and peaceful, neither anti-Soviet, nor anti-American' (Tomsic, 1976, p. 77). Furthermore, in the 1970s the PCI adhered to 'eurocommunism' and its secretary Enrico Berlinguer proposed the Italian '*Compromesso storico*'[1] with the other forces of Italian society and politics. A similar *conversione* to Europe occurred in the *Confindustria* (General Confederation of Italian Industry) (Petrini, 2005) and among the workers' trade unions (first those of Catholic and socialist inspiration, CISL and UIL; then the one closer to communist positions, CGIL) (Cruciani, 2007). It is interesting to note that, even though the integration process stemmed from an agreement between the Christian Democratic forces (three Catholic politicians had a leading role – Adenauer, De Gasperi and Schuman), since the beginning it had involved important figures from the left (Altiero Spinelli in first place) and, since the late 1960s, all the leftist

---

[1] The '*Compromesso storico*' was the process to bring the DC and PCI closer together following the Chilean putsch of 1973. The aim was to distance Italy from the Soviet Union and the 'red terrorism' that was terrorizing the country.

parties and more broadly social democratic forces, which saw the European project as a vehicle for social, economic and cultural modernization.

At the same time, during the first two decades, the integration process came to be an area of interest that went beyond the political elites to involve the wider public. While in 1948 the public was divided in two with respect to support for integration, by the end of the 1970s the percentage of supporters had very soon risen to represent around 80 per cent of the population, according to the available surveys and analyses (Isernia, 2008, p. 385). The 'Europeanization of Italian public opinion' (Ammendola and Isernia, 2005, p. 129) occurred between the early 1950s and 1970 and was largely due to a transformation in the east–west conflict, a changed attitude toward the USSR (after the 1956 and 1968 interventions in Hungary and Czechoslovakia), a more independent stance (vis-à-vis the US) on European integration and increased confidence in other European countries. Ammendola and Isernia (2005) have, interestingly, shown that it was the Europeanization of left-wing voters that contributed to the Communist Party's shift toward Europe, and not vice versa. The leftist electorate made its turn toward Europe before the left-wing parties and also functioned as a driving force behind the left's turnaround (particularly the PCI). The two authors signal that in 1948, according to available polls, only 50 per cent of Italians were in favour of a union of west European countries, while 21 per cent were undecided and 18 per cent against. In July 1970, however, as many as 78 per cent were in favour: part of the communist voters (28 per cent at the 1968 elections) had changed opinion before their party did (p. 129). All in all, Ammendola and Isernia (2005, p. 168) calculated that about 70 per cent of PCI voters would have considered changing political party had the PCI not come closer to Europeanism. As a matter of fact, by 1970, for left-wing voters too, Europe (and particularly some European states) had started to mean 'emancipation' from the persisting traditionalist ways of life of Italian society and 'modernization', rather than capitalist ideology (vs communism). In other words, it ceased to be framed as part of a west vs. east narrative (Isernia, 2008, pp. 400–1; Conti and Verzichelli, 2005, pp. 89–97). It is interesting to note the paradox: in the early 1970s Europe became attractive to the left as the locus of laicity and civil rights (as in the case of the debate on divorce in Italy), while for the very same reasons it more recently came to be criticized by the Christian Democrats.

The 1970s–Early 1990s: The Bipartisan Consensus

The 1970s opened two decades of bipartisan consensus for 'Europe'. With the changed attitude of the PCI, all the main political parties shared support for European integration, although with different arguments (Conti and Verzichelli, 2005). In the logic of the Cold War, the choice of camp was confirmed. It became an unchallenged part of Italy's foreign policy and – with very few exceptions – the federalist paradigm continued to prevail (Varsori, 2010, pp. 285–374; Bindi, 2011). The positive effects of being embedded in European institutions were particularly clear in the 1970s, when the severe crisis of the international economic system (with the end of the Bretton Woods regime and the 1973 and 1979 energy crises) and of the domestic political system (characterized by unstable governments, high inflation, public debt and unemployment, as well as the threat of domestic terrorism whose actions led to the kidnapping and killing of DC prime minister *in pectore*, Aldo Moro, in 1978) could lead the country into even more troubled waters.

© 2015 The Author(s) JCMS: Journal of Common Market Studies © 2015 John Wiley & Sons Ltd

Adherence to the European Monetary System (EMS) in 1979 was also a way to create external pressure for internal economic transformation, as well as a way to anchor Italy more closely to the western front. The choice was made very much by the political elites, despite some reluctance even among distinguished economists like Mario Monti and the governor of the Central Bank, Paolo Baffi (Ferrulli, 2009).

The argument of the necessary external constraints re-emerged in the early 1990s, in relation first to support for the creation of the euro and then to the decision to enter the first round of European monetary union (EMU). In the 1980s the Italian Central Bank, which, particularly under Governor Carlo Azeglio Ciampi, had become an important actor in Italy's European policy, was a great supporter of the use of external stimuli to solve some of the country's economic problems. Although there had been an economic recovery in the second half of the 1980s, the country's economy was still troubled by high and rising public expenditure, high public debt and high levels of tax evasion; these limits would have become unbearable with the completion of the single market and the possible creation of a common currency (supported by Commission President Jacques Delors). This led to a rapid implementation of the steps necessary to complete the single market and the lira's entrance into the EMS (Varsori, 2010, pp. 356–9). The next step was negotiation of the conditions for monetary union at the 1991 Intergovernmental Conference. In this context, Italy had to accept the five criteria of convergence agreed by France and Germany, but could obtain some flexibility in the implementation of parameters on the reduction of public debt and the establishment of phases to complete the monetary union (Dyson and Featherstone, 1996). By counting on the possibility to adjust through time, and possibly also on the fact that the criteria were not mentioned in the Maastricht Treaty (and could therefore be renegotiated), Italy was able to adopt the agreement (Bini Smaghi et al., 1994).

Contrary to what happened in other countries such as France (Lequesne, 2013), the decision did not provoke an immediate significant debate either in parliament or among the public (Varsori, 2010, pp. 370–1). Such a *permissive consensus* on the signing of Maastricht, however, would not persist in the long run. The challenge before the country was great, and the political elites were relying on the external constraints and stimulus to make a painful domestic transformation acceptable. However, they could not know that in 1992 watershed events would completely transform the country: the massive (and public) trials for corruption against many representatives of the political system, known as *Mani pulite* ('Clean Hands'), brought to light a deeply rooted system of corruption that led to the end of the First Republic.

As far as public opinion is concerned, the decades between 1970 and the early 1990s were years of high support (Eurobarometer data. For the years 1983–2011 see Figure 1 below), despite there being as yet little knowledge on the part of the public. Among the Italian public, these decades of economic and political difficulties, and acknowledgement of the inefficiencies of the political system (between 1972 and 1992 there were 21 governments, on average more than one per year),[2] produced distrust in the national institutions, but sufficient recognition of the importance of the European institutions (in 1985, 65 per cent thought the European Parliament important and 77 per cent thought that creating a United States of Europe would be a good idea).[3] Moreover, the EU continued to be considered important for its *transformational impact*, particularly as far as European inter-state relations are

---

[2] «http://www.governo.it/Governo/Governi/governi.html».
[3] Eurobarometer 24 – report available at «https://dbk.gesis.org/dbksearch/download.asp?id=9187».

© 2015 The Author(s) JCMS: Journal of Common Market Studies © 2015 John Wiley & Sons Ltd

Figure 1: Perceived benefits of EU membership.
Question 1: 'Taking everything into consideration, would you say that (your country) has on balance benefited or not from
being a member of the European Community/European Union?'.
Question 2: 'Generally speaking, do you think that (your country's) membership of the European Community/European Union
is …?' Replies for: 'a good thing'.
Source: Eurobarometer ("EU" includes the Member States on the date of the survey)

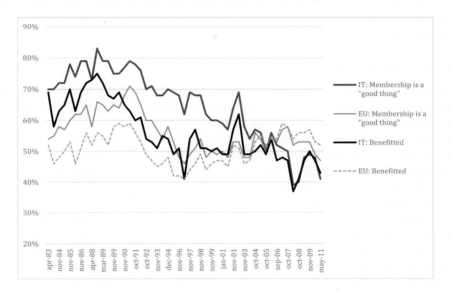

concerned. According to Standard Eurobarometer 27,[4] in 1987, 56 per cent of Italian respondents believed that the most important reason to 'feel European' was Europe's contribution to peaceful relations in Europe (the EU mean being 52 per cent),[5] while 46 per cent felt the most important reason was that it was possible to travel without difficulty (with a EU mean of 43 per cent) and 34 per cent put it down to the adventure of the formation of a United States of Europe (c.f. EU mean of 21 per cent). Only 14 per cent considered Europe a mere geographical fact (c.f. EU mean of 20 per cent). Moreover, membership was considered a good thing by a very high majority of Italians, with 83 per cent positive replies in 1974 and 1988 (Figure 1). Figure 1also shows that the Italians believed that membership was a good thing even when they did not believe that Italy had benefited from integration. This points to a support that was more 'affective' than 'utilitarian' (linked to the perception of material benefit), to use Lindbergh and Scheingold's (1970) distinction.

As for active participation in European democracy, the percentage of voters for the European Parliament never dipped below 80 per cent, far exceeding the European mean (85.65 per cent in 1979, 82.47 per cent in 1984 and 81.07 per cent in 1989).[6]

---

[4] Eurobarometer 27 – available at «http://ec.europa.eu/public_opinion/archives/eb/eb27/eb27_en.pdf». More than one response could be given.
[5] The figure was even higher in France (63 per cent).
[6] «http://www.ukpolitical.info/european-parliament-election-turnout.htm». However, it should be noted that, according to Art. 48 of the Italian Constitution, to vote is a 'civic duty' and from 1945 to 1993, by law any failure to vote had to be justified to the local municipality. This might have shaped the belief that voting is a 'duty' as well as a 'right'.

© 2015 The Author(s) JCMS: Journal of Common Market Studies © 2015 John Wiley & Sons Ltd

Summing up, we can say that there is a clear case of path dependency in Italy's attitude toward the EU: Italy's early steps in integration were to influence the subsequent years in a significant way. Initially a choice of camp in the logic of the Cold War, Europe soon become a source of internal cohesion. Three elements can be underlined as having highly characterized Italy's attitude toward the EU since the first phases of integration: Europe was regarded as a transformative force, a project for further integration and a source of civic identity. It is worth examining each of these in turn.

Europe as a Transformative Force

As we have seen, adherence to Europe was also driven by the belief that this would facilitate the modernization of the country. The belief in the need for a (positive) external constraint (*vincolo esterno*) to undertake such modernization was shared even more by the – traditionally very pro-European – bureaucratic and technical elites, who saw the requirements of integration as a necessary pressure on the national political elites. Because of its transformative power on Italy, support for European integration goes beyond the traditional utilitarian/affective typology present in the literature and points to a *projectual view of policy*, i.e. European integration is regarded as a polity-building instrument capable of reforming domestic politics in the interaction with Brussels. We can label this support as *political*. This type of support has been present also in other founding members, such as Germany (Paterson, 2011), but in Italy it has been enhanced by a very diffused self-representation of the country (that has never been overcome) as being less fit than others in the management of democratic politics, an attitude that has been captured in the expression 'Calimero syndrome'.[7] Within this self-representation, Italy suffered a 'fear of exclusion' (Sbragia, 2001, p. 93; Carbone and Quaglia, 2011) and for a long time Europe was presented and perceived as a necessity, in order for Italy not to be sidelined. In this, Italy is not dissimilar to newer Member States such as the Czech Republic, Slovakia and Slovenia (Haughton, 2009, 2010).

Europe as a Project of Further Integration

The legacy of Altiero Spinelli and the federalist movement was clear and tangible in Italy's European policy from the beginning. Despite being mostly reactive in its foreign policy (even including European policy), when proactive, Italy's European policy aimed to advance European integration (Bindi, 2011; Varsori, 2010). All in all, there were very few instances in which Italy's policy was more inspired by intergovernmentalism rather than supranationalism, and it was substantially 'acquiescent' with Europe even when that meant paying some national costs (Cotta, 2005).

Wide Support for European Integration and a Europeanized Italian Identity

The elites' 'acquiescent' attitude toward Europe was coupled with high public support for European integration. Such support, as we have seen, was linked to a general faith in the ability of European integration to transform (modernize and pacify) Europe ('political' support), to an appreciation of the benefits for the country ('utilitarian' support), but also

---

[7] *Calimero* is an Italian cartoon series about the life of a small black chick, the only one in a family of yellow chicks. Calimero complains about being black and excluded, so the 'Calimero complex' refers to the attitude of those who think the world is against them because they are the underdog.

© 2015 The Author(s) JCMS: Journal of Common Market Studies © 2015 John Wiley & Sons Ltd

to a diffused and emotional adherence to ideals of European integration ('affective' sup-port). What is specific about Italy is that such affection was the result of a growingly *Europeanized national identity*. What made the Europeanization of Italian identity take place in a relatively short time was the fact that Italian national identity had elements of weakness that the European layer of identity complemented. As a matter of fact, while the cultural/ascribed component of identity (linked to culture, history and language) had always been very strong, the civic/political component (that shapes the sense of belonging to a nation state and its institutions) was (and still is) much weaker (Della Loggia, 1998). The cultural component resisted the delegitimizing shock of fascism and the civil war that occurred in the country, while the civic component was severely weakened by these his-torical experiences. Hence, far from being exclusively a material and economic problem, the postwar reconstruction of the country was a fundamental moment of reflection over what Italy was and stood for in the newly defined international order: it was a question of identity. In this context, Europe had the function of externally legitimizing institutions that otherwise were not trusted. Thus, in the case of Italy, the relationship between na-tional and European identity is to be understood as one of inclusivity.[8]

These characteristics of Italy's European policy were to be challenged by significant changes at the international and domestic level at the beginning of the 1990s, to which I now turn.

II. The Second Republic: The End of Permissive Consensus

The end of the First Republic coincided with the opening of a new phase in Italy's attitude toward European integration. The seeds of the new season of contestation against Europe started in the early 1990s but were to bear fruit in the early 2000s. While the break with the permissive consensus occurred all over Europe and can be regarded as a by-product of deeper integration which brought the effects of European integration closer to the citizens (particularly through the completion of the single market and the introduction of the euro), the specific form of this transformation in attitudes are to be found in the country's domestic context.

Rising Contestation in the Early 1990s–2000s: The Seeds of Change

The end of the Cold War had very important repercussions for Europe and for Italy in par-ticular. Not only did the fall of the Berlin Wall create the momentum for a re-launch of the integration process and a new reflection on Europe's role in world politics, but it also af-fected Italy's internal political dynamics.

The signing of the Maastricht Treaty represented a fundamental shift in the EU's impact on its citizens' everyday lives. The level of public/intellectual attention to the EU rose significantly. For instance, in Italy the number of books published on European integration between 1990 and 1999 was double that of the previous decade.[9] Europe

---

[8] On the relationship between Italian and European identity, see Serricchio (2011). On European identity see, among others, Checkel and Katzenstein (2009); European Commission (2012); Lucarelli *et al.* (2011); Sanders *et al.* (2012).

[9] The number of books published in Italy with 'Europe' or 'European Community' or 'European Union' in the title in 1980–89 was 604; in 1990–99 was 1593; and in 2000–09 was 3334 (source: Catalogue of the Italian National Library in Florence, «http://opac.bncf.firenze.sbn.it/opac/c»).

© 2015 The Author(s) JCMS: Journal of Common Market Studies © 2015 John Wiley & Sons Ltd

could no longer be avoided and its rising complexity contributed to the development of a more articulated discourse on Europe rather than the simple expression of affective support (Conti and Verzichelli, 2005, p. 104). In particular, the creation of EMU was the first occasion for debate and the manifestation of some contestation against the integration process, not only in Italy but in Europe at large (Isernia, 2005, pp. 228–33).

However, in Italy popular affective support for the integration process continued to remain high throughout the 1990s (Figure 1), as did the Italians' self-identification as 'Italian and European': for all of the 1990s much more than half of the Italian respondents identified themselves as European as well as Italian, while the number regarding themselves as solely 'Italian' was much lower (under 35 per cent, less than the EU mean; see Figure 2).

A clear manifestation of persistently wide affective support for Europe (and also of the faith among the government and elite in Europe's *transformative power*) in the 1990s was the reaction to PM Prodi's 'tax for Europe' (December 1996), launched – to use a phrase of the time – in order to let 'Italy enter Europe' (i.e. satisfy the criteria to enter EMU). This opened debate among intellectuals and politicians, but did not cause substantial opposition from taxpayers. On the contrary, the Italians were willing to pay the costs owing to the possible positive effects on the country (which explains why in these years we can see a stronger sense of Italian identity and a stronger sense of European identity – Figure 2). The Eurobarometer data confirm this claim: Italy was a country in which support for EMU was so high that between 1995 and 1997 the mean percentage of Italians in favour of a single European currency was 74 per cent.[10] This level of support was not only far above the EU mean (50 per cent), but also above the mean in France (57 per cent) and way above the mean in Germany (37 per cent).

So did nothing change in the public attitude toward Europe? We can identify three things that did change that would influence the public discourse on Europe in subsequent years: the creation of conditions for EMU that, in the long run, would make the EU a tangible presence in its citizens' lives (as seen above), the further delegitimation of the political system, and a relevant transformation in the structure of the Italian party system. Let us focus attention on the last two factors.

In Italy, the end of the Cold War created the momentum to deal with long-term deficiencies in the political system, which brought to the end of the so-called First Republic. The origin was the abovementioned *Mani Pulite* operation and the revealing of a deep-rooted system of corruption known as *Tangentopoli* ('Bribesville'). The internal turmoil that *Tangentopoli* brought about made the process of internal adaptation impossible to implement and postponed the problem of internal reforms, creating structural problems and long-term negative effects at the moment the new currency was adopted. Not only that, the massive trials followed closely by the media (some trials were shown on television) had important effects: a further delegitimation of the political system; a reinforced image of a 'Cinderella Italy' that needed an internal clearance and an external controller; the crisis of some of the old political parties and the emergence of new political forces. *Tangentopoli* gave rise to anti-political sentiments but also to the hope that the system could be changed thanks to a clear-out by the courts and the appearance of new faces in politics. According to data from Transparency International, in terms of perceived

[10] «http://ec.europa.eu/public_opinion/cf/showchart_column.cfm?keyID=200&nationID=16,6,3,8, &startdate = 1995.12&enddate = 1997.11»

© 2015 The Author(s) JCMS: Journal of Common Market Studies © 2015 John Wiley & Sons Ltd

Figure 2: The Identity of Italians: European and National Sentiments.

Question: 'Do you see yourself as…?' '(Nationality) only', '(Nationality) and European', 'European and (Nationality)', 'European only'.

Source: Eurobarometer.

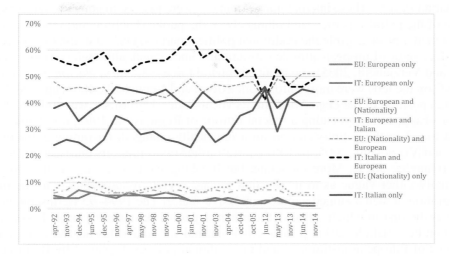

corruption in 1995 Italy ranked 33rd out of the 41 countries included in the sample.[11] This also explains the low trust in Italian institutions in 1997: 29 per cent according to Eurobarometer data. The same Eurobarometer showed a much higher trust in European institutions (63 per cent).[12]

Moreover, *Tangentopoli* led to a redefinition of the political system, the dissolution of the DC and the PSI as unitary political parties (1994) and the appearance of new political formations. The most significant of the latter were the *Lega Nord* (Northern League) and *Forza Italia* (FI).[13] The *Lega Nord* – the union of a set of local 'Legas' that had started to spring up in the 1980s, with a federalist and at times separatist agenda – entered parliament with 8.6 per cent of the votes in 1992 and since then has become an important player in Italian politics. The second highly relevant new entry on the Italian party landscape was FI, the centre-right political formation launched by businessman Silvio Berlusconi, which entered parliament in 1994 as the most-voted-for Italian party (21 per cent of votes) and went on to become the leading political force in four governments.[14] Meanwhile, in 1991 the PCI had been transformed into the *Partito democratico della sinistra* (Democratic Party of the Left, PDS; further re-named in 1998 as *Democratici di sinistra*, Democrats of the Left, DS and in 2007 as Partito Democratico, Democratic Party, PD), and the *Partito di Rifondazione Comunista* (Communist Refoundation Party, PRC) was created

[11] «https://www.transparency.org/files/content/tool/1995_CPI_EN.pdf».

[12] Eurobarometer 48 – Variables report: «http://isysweb.gesis.org/isysnative/RjpcaHRkb2NzXHNob3J0Y3V0LnBkZlxlY19jYlxaQTI5NTlfY2RiLnBkZg==/ZA2959_cdb.pdf#xml=http://isysweb.gesis.org/isysquery/irl51b5/18/hilite»

[13] As is common in the Italian system, both the *Lega Nord* and *Forza Italia* have changed their names during their lifetime. For an analysis of the evolution of the Italian political system in the past 20 years, see Newell and Carbone (2015).

[14] Berlusconi led four governments: May 1994–January 1995; June 2001–April 2005; April 2005–May 2006; and May 2008–November 2011.

on its left: the largest communist party in Europe had ceased to exist as a unitary party. This transformation was completed with the adoption of a new electoral law (known as 'Mattarellum', 1993–2005), which substituted the proportional system with a 75 per cent majoritarian system. These internal transformations were to have major consequences in the attitude of the political parties, and ultimately of the public (Fabbrini and Piattoni, 2008).

As a matter of fact, while the traditional political parties (DS/PD in the first place) kept their affective pro-European attitude substantially unchanged, although with more nuance (Conti and Verzichelli, 2005), the more peripheral forces (*Alleanza Nazionale* on the right and PRC on the left) were more eurosceptic (Conti and Verzichelli, 2005, pp. 108–9). The utilitarian position of the *Lega Nord* and its vocal leader, Ugo Bossi, was emblematic. Initially pro-European (advocating a federal Europe of Regions), in 1998, following a transformed mood in the country, its position drastically changed, becoming anti-European (Conti and Verzichelli, 2005, p. 106) before further reinforcing its euroscepticism in the 2000s (Quaglia, 2011). More moderate, but breaking with the past, was the attitude of FI. Initially rather vague as to its position toward specific issues relative to the process of integration, it then assumed a more aggressive stance. The 1994–95 Berlusconi government was the first in which 'none of the member parties belonged to major European political families' (Bindi, 2011, p. 56). Also unusual for Italian history was the manifest ignorance of European institutions and international politics displayed by Berlusconi.

It is likely that the newer political leaders were not trained by party schools and were not affected by the legacy of the pro-European political culture developed in the country in the previous years; this allowed these new political formations to adopt a utilitarian or 'strategic' form of euroscepticism (juxtaposed with the 'ideological' euroscepticism of the left in the early years of integration). More traditional right-wing political forces, on the contrary, started to gradually become more eurosceptic the more the EU was associated with non-traditional/laic social values.[15]

Euroscepticism, more than in the party manifestoes (Quaglia, 2011; Conti and Verzichelli, 2005), emerged in the parties' attitude in public debate, which is what influences the public most. In this respect, even though on the basis of its manifestos one would not consider FI a eurosceptic party (Quaglia, 2011, p. 35), Berlusconi's communicative style on Europe as well as his (uneven but present) eurosceptic attitude was echoed in the media system (Rowinski, 2013). Given all the above transformations, it is clear the 1990s created the conditions for the wider declining support for the EU in the 2000s.

The Early 2000s–2014: Disillusionment

The 2000s were crucial years for the fate of the European Union and Italy's attitude toward the integration process. The decade was opened by the 2001 terrorist attacks on the Twin Towers in New York and the subsequent invasion of Iraq by the US-led coalition, which sparked a new phase of international politics and a new season of (more tense) transatlantic relations. In Europe, the introduction of the euro in 2002 was followed by difficulties in some countries and a significant effort by the EU to cope with both the

---

[15] In this respect the Catholics' criticism in the mid-2000s of the draft constitutions for lacking reference to Europe's Christian roots, as well as the European Parliament's rejection of the Commissioner *in pectore* Buttiglione for his reference to homosexuals as sinners, are emblematic.

process of enlargement and treaty reform. The wide enlargement of 2004 (followed by the smaller ones in 2007 and 2013), the failure of the EU constitutional treaty in 2005 and the signing and entry into force of the Lisbon Treaty (2007/9) were all important events in the EU's life that were debated in the Member States to an unprecedented extent. However, the biggest troubles for Europe have arisen since 2008, when the economic crisis threatened not just the European economies but also European solidarity. Moreover, during the long years of economic crisis (still persisting at the time of writing in 2015), Europe's credibility has been questioned by the weak stance of its foreign policy as well as by friction among the Member States on relevant policy areas such as the control of illegal migration. This time, for the first time in its history, the EU even made the front page of the main European newspapers and anti-European sentiments rose nearly everywhere.

The Italian political system also underwent important changes, which had a significant impact on Italy's attitude toward Europe. The first novelty was the stability of governments, which resulted in seven years of Berlusconi's centre-right coalition government in the first decade of the twenty-first century (2001–05; 2008–11), with a two-year parenthesis for a centre-left Prodi government (May 2006–May 2008), also including the PRC and the Radical Party. This allowed Berlusconi's style to impose itself and significantly affect public debate in the country, as well as the image of the country abroad (Croci and Lucarelli, 2010). FI's attitude toward Europe was composite (due to different internal positions) and incoherent (due to ad hoc instrumental choices made by Berlusconi, see Quaglia, 2011, p. 44). However, all in all Berlusconi sent frequent messages of delegitimation of the European institutions and introduced to the Italian public debate on Italy's foreign policy a reference to Italy's national interest that had been largely 'absent from foreign policy rhetoric throughout Italy's republican history – [as] it had always been taken for granted that Italy's national interest coincided with Europe's interest' (Carbone, 2009, p. 98). Further effects of the Berlusconi years (in government or in opposition) were a significant worsening of the tones of political confrontation and a substantial personalized division of the country between supporters and adversaries of 'Il Cavaliere' (Berlusconi's epithet), let alone direct attacks on state institutions. As the newly elected prime minister, in 1994, he declared on a TV show that 'The *Mani Pulite* judges should be arrested; they are a criminal conspiracy (*associazione a delinquere*) with a licence to kill that aims to overthrow the democratic order'.[16] Moreover, the parliament was delegitimized in the eyes of the people due to its failure to deal with Mr Berlusconi's conflict of interests. Another institution that soon came to be attacked in an unprecedented manner during the 2000s was the presidency of the Republic, under the Europeanist (and former communist) Giorgio Napolitano (2006–15), who was even accused of organizing 'with Europe' the premature end of the fourth Berlusconi government in 2011. In terms of political action, the Berlusconi governments (also due to the moderating presence of the former Christian Democrats in the ruling coalition) did not substantially change Italy's European policy but introduced elements of contestation against the undisputed virtues of Europe's positive transformative power and (at least temporarily) opposed some European policies, such as the 2001 disagreement on the European arrest warrant and the debate on the stability and growth pact in 2003 (Quaglia, 2011). In

---

[16] *Sgarbi quotidiani*, Canale 5, 16 September 1994.

© 2015 The Author(s) JCMS: Journal of Common Market Studies © 2015 John Wiley & Sons Ltd

Berlusconi, these elements of contestation were combined with a rhetorical style, a dele-gitimation of institutions, a populist attitude and the definition of an Italian interest be-yond Europe. Perhaps the major blow inflicted by the Berlusconi cabinet on the credibility of the European institutions happened at the beginning of 2002, when the euro was introduced as the circulating currency in the participating countries. The government declined not only to emphasize the importance of this event, but also to exert any control on the effective exchange rate between the lira and euro. While the legal rate was 1,936:1, many shopkeepers set the new prices at 1,000:1, thus contributing to the generalized and accurate perception that the euro led to higher prices (Jones, 2009). The comparison between perceived and real inflation made by the national statistics agency (ISTAT) revealed that the former was much higher than the latter (Del Giovane and Sabbatini, 2009), and this affected the image not only of the new currency but also of the integration process as such, unleashing a long-lasting wave of resentment against the euro and the EU.

All these elements were to play an important role in the attitude of the public toward the political system in general and the EU in particular. When the economic crisis arrived, a further layer of concern arose – more directly tangible for the Italians, who had already started to perceive the effects of the euro and the European constraints in 2002. Mean-while, the performance of the fourth Berlusconi government and of the political system as such had so detached the Italians from politics that when the technical government led by Mario Monti took office in 2011, 80 per cent of the Italians supported the new prime minister and only 5 per cent declared that they still trusted the political parties.[17] Yet the very high expectations of the ability of the Monti government 'to save Italy' were not met with tangible results as far as ameliorating the living conditions of the Italians was concerned. The government ended by asking for further sacrifices in the name of Europe, echoing a request that the Italians had received in 1990 (with the euro tax) and that had not led to the perception of better living conditions. This increased the distance from the European economic troika, which came to represent the EU in the public debate. The troika and Germany became the object of fierce criticism on the part of an ever more (right-wing) eurocritical press and loud populist voices. The *Lega Nord* exacerbated its eurosceptic stance and, after a scandal in 2011 that involved its leader and other key figures in the party, it attempted to gain new legitimacy and support by pleasing the anti-political sentiments of the population. In a significant shift, under the new leader Matteo Salvini, the enemy was no longer the Italian unitary state but Europe, the euro and Europe's migration policy. These critical positions granted the *Lega* 4 per cent of the votes at the 2013 national elections and 6 per cent at the European elections.

However, the movement that benefited the most from anti-political sentiments, and that contributed to furthering them, was the *Movimento Cinque Stelle* (Five Star Move-ment, M5S). Founded in 2009 from groups led by former showman Beppe Grillo, the movement gained ground among those dissatisfied with politics thanks to a light populist agenda grounded on the idea of introducing elements of direct democracy through the web and public manifestations such as the 'V-Days'.[18] The movement rapidly gained

---

[17] Demos opinion poll, November 2011 – «http://demos.it/a00652.php».
[18] V-Day (named by the M5S *Vaffanculo-day* – 'Fuck You Day') is a public mobilization to express dissatisfaction with politics that was launched in 2007.

© 2015 The Author(s) JCMS: Journal of Common Market Studies © 2015 John Wiley & Sons Ltd

ground, launching a violent attack on domestic and European institutions. The success of the movement (which got 25 per cent of votes at the 2013 national elections and 21 per cent in the 2014 EP election) helped to further exacerbate the tone of the debate on Europe.

The economic crisis, although not being the *cause* of euroscepticism, radicalized anti-European ideological positions both on the right and left. The right-wing party *Fratelli d'Italia* (Brothers of Italy) created in 2012, taking up the legacy of *Alleanza Nazionale*, participated in the 2013 and 2014 elections with a nationalist agenda critical of the EU's economic policy, the EU's inability to cope with illegal immigration and European support for same-sex marriages, and supporting a withdrawal from the euro. The party got only 2 per cent at the 2013 national elections, so it represents a minority of the electorate. Supportive of a more federal Europe but critical of the EU's economic policy, the left-wing party *Sinistra Ecologia e Libertà* (SEL), which ran with the list of Alexis Tsipras – the leader of the Greek left-wing anti-austerity *Syriza* party – in the 2014 European elections, got 4 per cent.[19] Interestingly, also critical of the EU's economic policy of rigour are the trade unions, in particular the leftist CGIL and FIOM.

The net result of the domestic political transformations, of the economic crisis and its instrumentalization by the political forces and of the disenchantment toward politics in general has brought about a significant change in the Italian public's attitude toward the EU. A few figures can describe the magnitude of the change.

In the 2000s, trust in European institutions decreased to unprecedented levels (23 per cent in 2013, with a loss of 28 percentage points in the 2003–14 period). Trust in national institutions also negatively registered a reduction of 10 percentage points in the same period (from 27 per cent to 17 per cent).[20] This is by far the greatest loss of trust in the EU, and one of the few cases in which the loss of trust is both in the EU and in domestic institutions (Figure 3).

Also, the traditional Italian affective support for Europe that had characterized the First Republic changed. Looking at Figure 1, we can appreciate that this attitude started to change in the early 2000s. Until 2001 the level of appreciation remained above 60 per cent; it then started to decline to the low levels of 2008, when only 37 per cent of Italian respondents considered EU membership 'a good thing'.[21] Moreover, Figure 1 also shows that until the early 2000s the overall evaluation of Italy's membership in the EU was higher than the alleged benefits, confirming the idea of a not purely instrumental appreciation of the EU among the Italians. On the contrary, in the years 2009–10, more Italians believed that Italy had benefited from integration than those who stated a general appreciation of the integration process: for a significant section of those interviewed, Europe was no longer a value in itself, nor a source of benefits for Italy. Even if we look at the support and appreciation for specific EU policies, the scenario is not much rosier. In 2014, respondents to the Standard Eurobarometer 82 depicted a completely changed scenario with respect to the support for the euro registered in the mid-1990s: only 54 per cent were in favour

---

[19] See Hobolt's contribution to this volume.
[20] «http://ec.europa.eu/public_opinion/cf/showtable.cfm?keyID=2193&nationID=1,6,3,8,9,10, &startdate = 2003.11&enddate = 2014.11».
[21] «http://ec.europa.eu/public_opinion/cf/showchart_line.cfm?keyID=5&nationID=16,8, &startdate = 1973.09&enddate = 2011.05#fcExportDiv».

© 2015 The Author(s) JCMS: Journal of Common Market Studies © 2015 John Wiley & Sons Ltd

Figure 3: Trust in EU Institutions and National Government 2003–14.
Question: 'For each of the following institutions, please tell me if you tend to trust it or tend not to trust it? "The European Union" and "national government"'.
Source: Eurobarometer.

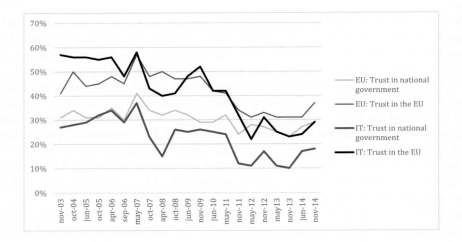

(c.f. the EU mean of 56 per cent and the eurozone mean of 67 per cent), 32 per cent against and 14 per cent undecided ('don't know'). The level of support was by far the lowest among the EU founding members and if we compare it with the 1990s figures, there has been a loss of 20 percentage points.

Another feature of attitudes until the end of the 1990s was that the percentage of those expressing they felt both 'Italian and European' was higher than those considering themselves only Italian (Figure 2). On the contrary, in the 2000s the number of those expressing they felt 'national and European' diminished more than the EU mean. The same decline also occurred as far as appreciation of membership of the EU is concerned. After the 2014 European elections only 35 per cent (the EU mean being 51 per cent) said EU membership is 'a good thing': the second lowest percentage in the EU after the Czechs (27 per cent).[22]

Italy is also the country that had the greatest reduction in turnout at the European elections, with a steady decline from the 85.65 per cent of voters in 1979 to the 60 per cent of 2014 (with a loss of 25.65 percentage points from 1979). This reduction is higher than the reduction in electoral turnover at the national parliamentary elections.[23]

Summing up, in the early 1990s, after at least two decades of undisputed support for the integration process, Italian public support for European integration gradually started to fade. In relative terms (with comparison to prior positions), the data reveal a higher decrease in affection for Europe with respect to the citizens of the other founding Member States. The main factors in the origin of this further, more relevant than ever, acceleration of disenchantment toward the EU seem to have been the deepening of integration; the

[22] «http://www.europarl.europa.eu/pdf/eurobarometre/2014/post/post_2014_survey_analitical_overview_en.pdf».
[23] For the Chamber of Deputies, turnout was 90.6 per cent in 1979; 86.3 in 1994; 81.2 in 2004; and 72.5 in 2013. See «http://elezionistorico.interno.it/index.php?tpel=C».

© 2015 The Author(s) JCMS: Journal of Common Market Studies © 2015 John Wiley & Sons Ltd

further transformation of the Italian party system and the role of the 'new parties'; and, only lastly, the economic crisis.

Deepening of Integration

The introduction of the euro in 2002 occurred in the political conditions described above and with a substantially unchanged economic system with respect to the limits that the Italian negotiators acknowledged at Maastricht. With the introduction of the common currency and the constant reference in public debate to the need to satisfy the Maastricht criteria, Europe became a more tangible reality in Europeans' everyday lives. In the case of Italy, this general effect was coupled with an additional problem relative to the widespread perception among citizens that the new currency had brought higher inflation.

The Role of the Political Parties

As we have seen, in the mid-1990s, some of the political parties began to adopt a utilitarian approach to the EU, supporting it or criticizing it on the basis of a strategic calculus (FI and *Lega* first of all). In this scenario, the centre-left (DS/PD) remained the bulwark of an attachment to the EU that was both affective and 'political', while over time – and particularly since the 2000s – the sceptical FI and *Lega* and new political parties raised their voices more against the EU. This eventually produced a distinction between a continued *in primis* ideological attitude toward the EU (DS/PD on the one – supportive – side; PRC, SEL or *Fratelli d'Italia* on the other – critical – side) and a utilitarian/strategic attitude (FI, M5S, *Lega*). The role played by the utilitarian forces and their anti-European rhetoric, as well as their delegitimation of political institutions at different levels, has helped to further antagonize the Italian public with respect to European institutions. Among the critical parties, however, those who have had the most damaging impact on public attitudes toward the EU have been those ontologically adverse to the EU, who do not differentiate between the *policies* of these European institutions and the EU as such (*Lega*, M5S, *Fratelli d'Italia*).

The Economic Crisis

Europe's inability to cope with the crisis quickly and effectively weakened the EU's credibility. Moreover, the policy of rigour chosen by the EU, in line with the Maastricht Treaty and in response to Germany's concerns, was quickly presented by a variety of political actors as a constraint that impeded rather than contributed to overcoming the crisis. Hence EMU, originally considered to be a positive *vincolo esterno*, did not produce the expected reforms (due to Tangentopoli and to the failures of subsequent governments to make them in the 1990s), deprived Italy of the main instrument that had historically been used to deal with its economic crises – currency devaluation (and consequent inflation) – and has started to be regarded as a negative constraint.

Can we conclude that we are looking at a former europhoric country that has become anti-European? This allegation would not be consistent with the data available for several reasons: the position of the political parties, the entity of dissatisfaction and the target of the dissatisfaction.

© 2015 The Author(s) JCMS: Journal of Common Market Studies © 2015 John Wiley & Sons Ltd

Looking at the electoral manifestos of the European elections in the 2000s (see Conti and Memoli, 2012), we can affirm that with the exception of the *Lega Nord* and M5S, most of the political spectrum has continued to diversify its positions, with rising attention to Europe from one election to the next. Moreover, while it is true that the campaign for the 2014 election for the European Parliament was characterized by rising eurosceptic tones (particularly by the *Lega*, M5S and *Fratelli d'Italia*), several critical parties have adopted a position of criticism of *this Europe* but not of Europe *tout court* (e.g. the left-wing party *Sinistra Ecologia e Libertà*). Eventually, in 2014, the centre-left PD, which had confirmed its strong Europeanism of both affective and political types, won the elections with 41 per cent of the votes. Such a victory cannot be attributed to the PD's European policy, but rather to the 'campaign of hope' launched by the PD's new leader, Matteo Renzi. However, it means that the electors also appreciated the position assumed by the party, of a proud Europeanist Italy eager to set things straight in order to be able to make its voice heard in a united Europe. The elite surveys conducted by the research project INTUNE in 2007 and 2009 confirm the idea that the political parties (with the partial exception of the *Lega*) have maintained a high level of support for common European policies – from foreign policy to a unitary fiscal system and social security (De Giorgi and Verzichelli, 2012). We can conclude that Italy's position can best be described as what Taggart and Szczerbiak (2002) call 'soft euroscepticism', which implies dissent on a number of policy areas but does not put into question Italy's membership in the EU. More broadly, Italian party politics is characterized more by a severe form of 'poliscepticism' (scepticism with respect to politics) than by the victory of euroscepticism.

Indeed, the target of dissatisfaction seems to be more *the political system* as such than the EU in particular. For instance, looking at the data on abstention from the last three European elections, we notice that the most popular answer was a 'lack of trust in/dissatisfaction with politics in general' and that respectively 30 per cent, 37 per cent and 29 per cent of Italian respondents did not vote for this reason. This percentage was higher than the EU mean and much higher than the tendency in the founding Member States.[24] Moreover, during the 2000s the number of those not having a specific opinion on the EU rose to unprecedented levels (38 per cent in 2013). Finally, Italy's lack of trust in politics is probably to be regarded in connection with a high perception of corruption in the country (the highest in Europe according to Transparency International).[25] This seems to point to a significant portion of the population that, more than being for or against, are 'agnostic' and disappointed with national and European institutions alike.

III. Conclusions: Toward a More Politicized (and Less Ideological) Debate on Europe?

The founding years of integration had a long-term legacy on Italy's European policy. The interpretation of Europe as a transformative force and the choice of the western camp, the

[24] See Flash EB 162 Post European elections 2004 survey («http://ec.europa.eu/public_opinion/flash/FL162en.pdf»); Special Eurobarometer 320 Post elections Surveys («http://www.europarl.europa.eu/pdf/eurobarometre/28_07/EB71.3_post-electoral_final_report_EN.pdf»); Post-election Survey 2014 («http://www.europarl.europa.eu/pdf/eurobarometre/2014/post/post_2014_survey_analitical_overview_en.pdf»).
[25] Transparency International Index of Perceived Corruption 2014, available at: «http://www.transparency.org/cpi2014/results».

© 2015 The Author(s) JCMS: Journal of Common Market Studies © 2015 John Wiley & Sons Ltd

preference for a federal Europe and the marriage between a strong Italian cultural identity and a possible European civic identity were elements that characterized Italy's attitude to Europe. These characteristics have not substantially changed, and the euro-western choice has never been seriously contested (nobody has asked for a referendum on membership, as in the UK). What has changed is the way in which Europe is perceived in terms of a source of political identity and public trust.

The turning point in this attitude was the end of the Cold War, not only because of what it represented in terms of the changed international environment but also due to the deepening of the integration process that the event caused and its domestic implications. In the case of Italy, the end of bipolarism created the space for a significant transformation in the institutional system and political landscape. Not only that, the chain of transmission of traditional europhile political values provided by the traditional political parties was interrupted by the creation of new parties with no particular affiliation to the European tradition that were, all in all, critical of the pre-existent political systems (domestic and European alike). New stakeholders emerged with a more critical stance toward European integration and the public debate on Europe changed significantly. This change transformed Italy from (one of) the most enthusiastic supporters of European integration as a source of intrinsic values to a more moderate supporter.

This transformation in Italy's attitude toward the integration process is interesting not only in itself, but also for what it says on the broader debates about the integration process.

In the first place, the Italian case shows the close link that exists between a country's European policy and the domestic concerns of the leading elites. The use of Europe as a *transformative force* of the domestic environment was a consolidated characteristic of Italy's European policy and led to unexpected consequences at crucial moments when, for domestic reasons, it could not work as planned (as in the implementation of the monetary union). Then in the Second Republic, with a significant change in the political system, Europe started to be portrayed as a limit rather than a resource.

Second, the Italian case showed that the traditional utilitarian/affective typology of support of European integration is insufficient. To capture a support derived from the above mentioned faith in the transformative power of Europe (and in a low faith in Italy's own capabilities), one needs to add a third type of support: 'political'. The latter and affective support prevailed in the First Republic, while they were challenged by more utilitarian attitudes (of the elites and public) during the Second Republic.

Third, the Italian case seems to prove Lindberg and Scheingold's (1970) expectation that affective support for an institution develops before (or at least contemporaneously to) specific/utilitarian support. For a long time, the Italians' support for Europe was very high and higher than the perceived benefits of integration for their country. This gradually (but not radically) changed when people started to more directly perceive the (negative) impact of Europe on their daily lives.

Fourth, the Italian case shows that public and political elites' attitudes toward Europe are in dynamic interaction and not in direct causality with each other. Not only did the political parties first set the terms of Europeanism in the early days, but they were then trapped by the public's Europeanist attitude and counted on it to grant internal transformation. More recently, the appearance of eurosceptic political parties, together with their blaming Europe during the economic crisis, has further changed the terms of the public debate and also given rise to negative evaluations of the impact of Europe on Italy among the public.

Fifth, in terms of political identity, the Italian case shows that European identity is a *process* (more than an entity), which is very nationally contingent. If we were to express an evaluation of the Italians' European identity today, rather than talking of less European identity, we would do better to talk of a different European identity – less ideal, but probably more politically concrete. It is also an identity of choice, more than before.

Finally, the Italian case shows that we need to be careful in labelling critical stances toward Europe as euroscepticism. In the case of Italy, indeed there are eurosceptic forces, but simply talking of high levels of euroscepticism is misleading. What characterizes the debate is greater consciousness of how European integration might create costly constraints, understanding the limits of an unfinished polity, and disenchantment toward politics regardless of the level of governance. This implies that Europe as a dream has made way for an image of Europe as a political space in which different views compete in a context of uneven power. This does not point to a dramatic change, but to a politically relevant one. Equally, it does not point to a negative element, but perhaps to a more mature, less ideological and more conscious political debate on Europe, where alternative political views of Europe are compared. However, it might even point to a much less conscious opposition to the EU, which is linked not to alternative political projects but to an overall disaffection toward politics. The little knowledge of the EU and its institutions in the country, the persisting low level of coverage of European issues in the media, the inward-looking attitude of Italian political elites and the country's inability to fully profit from European integration (not least by using the financial support provided by the EU, which gets lost due to Italian inefficiencies) are elements of concern.

Yet there is space for concern in Europe at large. Neo-functionalists expected that once the elite-driven process of integration left room for a wider politicization and involvement of the public, there would be pressure for further integration as a result of growing demands for centrally provided services (as was the case during the consolidation of the nation state). In reality, at the moment, the growing involvement of the public, coupled with a transformation of the leading elites in several countries and their instrumental use of European politics in the domestic debates, is producing negative consequences in terms of support for further integration. Where this will lead is an open question, whose answer will depend to a large extent on the ability of (as-yet-unseen) farsighted elites to provide tangible answers, legitimizing discourses (Schmidt, 2009), trustable institutions and a renewed, politically 'dreamable' project. There is no other way out of the dilemma: it is only by facing (and winning) the challenge of politicization that the EU can become a fully fledged polity.

References

Ammendola, T. and Isernia, P. (2005) *'L'Europa vista dagli italiani: i primi vent'anni'*. In Cotta, M., Isernia, P. and Verzichelli, L. (eds).

Bindi, F. (2011) *Italy and the European Union* (Washington D.C.: Brookings Institution Press).

Bini Smaghi, L., Padoa-Schioppa, T. and Papadia, F. (1994) The Transition to EMU in the Maastricht Treaty, *Princeton Essays in International Finance*, No. 194. Available at «http://www.princeton.edu/~ies/IES_Essays/E194.pdf».

© 2015 The Author(s) JCMS: Journal of Common Market Studies © 2015 John Wiley & Sons Ltd

Brighi, E. (2013) *Foreign Policy, Domestic Politics and International Relations: The Case of Italy* (London and New York: Routledge).

Carbone, M. (2009) 'Italy in the European Union, between Prodi and Berlusconi'. *The International Spectator: Italian Journal of International Affairs*, Vol. 44, No. 3, pp. 97–115.

Carbone, M. and Quaglia, L. (2011) 'Italy and the EU: Seeking Visibility, Fearing Exclusion'. In Carbone, M. (ed.) *Italy in the Post-Cold War Order: Adaptation, Bipartisanship and Visibility* (Lanham: Lexington Books).

Checkel, J. T. and Katzenstein, P. J. (2009) *European Identity* (Cambridge: Cambridge University Press).

Conti, N. and Memoli, V. (2012) '*L'Europa secondo i partiti: vincolo, scelta o opportunitá?*'. In Bellucci and Conti, N. (eds). Gli Italiani e l'Europa. Opinione pubblica, élite olitiche e media (Rome: Carocci)

Conti, N. and Verzichelli, L. (2005) '*La dimensione europea del discorso politico in Italia: un'analisi diacronica delle preferenze partitiche (1950-2001)*'. In Cotta, M., Isernia, P. and Verzichelli, L. (eds).

Cotta, M. (2005) '*Élite, politiche nazionali e costruzione della 'polity' europea. Il caso italiano in prospettiva comparata*'. In Cotta, M., Isernia, P. and Verzichelli, L. (eds).

Cotta, M., Isernia, P. and Verzichelli, L. (eds) (2005) *L'Europa in Italia* (Bologna: Il Mulino).

Croci, O. (2008) 'Not a Zero-Sum Game: Atlanticism and Europeanism in Italian Foreign Policy'. *The International Spectator*, Vol. 43, No. 4, pp. 137–55.

Croci, O. and Lucarelli, S. (eds) (2010) 'Italy in the Eyes of European and Transatlantic Allies'. Special issue of *Modern Italy*, 15 March.

Cruciani, S. (2007) *L'Europa delle sinistre. La nascita del Mercato comune europeo attraverso i casi francese e italiano (1955–1957)* (Rome: Carocci).

De Giorgi, E. and Verzichelli, L. (2012) 'Classe politica e integrazione europea: segnali di crisis?' In Bellucci, P. and Conti, N. (eds) *Gli italiani e l'Europa. Opinione pubblica, élite politiche e media* (Rome: Carocci).

Del Giovane, P. and Sabbatini, R. (2009) 'Euro, inflazione e inflazione percepita'. In XXI Secolo (Rome: Treccani). Available at: «http://www.treccani.it/enciclopedia/inflazione-e-inflazione-percepita-euro_%28XXI_Secolo%29/».

Diez Medrano, J. (2003) *Framing Europe: Attitudes to European Integration in Germany, Spain, and the United Kingdom* (Princeton: Princeton University Press).

Dyson, K. and Featherstone, K. (1996) 'Italy and EMU as "*Vincolo Esterno*": Empowering the Technocrats, Transforming the State'. *South European Politics and Society*, Vol. 1, No. 2, pp. 272–99.

European Commission (2012) 'The Development of European Identity/Identities: Unfinished Business. A Policy Review.' Available at «http://ec.europa.eu/research/social-sciences/pdf/policy_reviews/development-of-european-identity-identities_en.pdf».

Fabbrini, S. and Piattoni, S. (2008) 'Italy in the EU'. In Fabbrini, S. and Piattoni, S. (eds) *Italy in the European Union: Redefining National Interest in a Compound Polity* (Lanham: Rowman & Littlefield).

Ferrulli S. (2009) 'L'Italia e l'ingresso nello SME: vincoli e opportunità di una scelta difficile'. *Il Ponte*, May 2009. Available at: «http://www.ilponterivista.com/article_view.php?intId=78#_ftnref4».

Della Loggia, G. (1998) *L'Identità italiana* (Bologna: il Mulino).

Isernia, P. (2008) 'Present at the Creation: Italian Mass Support for European Integration in the Formative Years'. *European Journal of Political Research*, Vol. 47, pp. 383–410.

Jones, E. (2009) 'Italy and the Euro in the Global Economic Crisis'. *The International Spectator*, Vol. 44, No. 4, pp. 93–103.

Haughton, T. (2009) 'For Business, for Pleasure or for Necessity? The Czech Republic's Choices for Europe'. *Europe-Asia Studies*, Vol. 61, No. 8, pp. 1371–92.

Haughton, T. (2010) 'Vulnerabilities, Accession Hangovers and the Presidency Role: Explaining New EU Member States' Choices for Europe'. CES Central & Eastern Europe Working Paper, Series No. 68. Available at «http://aei.pitt.edu/14473/».

Hay, C. and Wincott, D. (1998) 'Structure, Agency and Historical Institutionalism'. *Political Studies*, Vol. 46, No. 5, pp. 951–57.

Hooghe, L. and Marks, G. (2005) 'Calculation, Community and Cues. Public Opinion on European Integration'. *European Union Politics*, Vol. 6, No. 4, pp. 419–43.

Hooghe, L. and Marks, G. (2009) 'A Postfunctionalist Theory of European Integration: From Permissive Consensus to Constraining Dissensus', *British Journal of Political Studies*, Vol. 39, pp. 1–23.

Lequesne, C. (2013), 'A New Socialist President in the Elysée: Continuity and Change in French EU Politics', *JCMS*, Vol. 51, No. s1, pp. 42–54.

Lindberg, L. and Scheingold, S. (1970) *Europe's Would-be Polity* (Englewood Cliffs, NJ: Prentice-Hall).

Lucarelli, S., Cerutti, F. and Schmidt, V. (eds) (2011) *Debating Political Identity and Legitimacy in the European Union: Interdisciplinary Views* (London and New York: Routledge).

Newell, J.L. and Carbone, M. (2015) 'The Italian Political System in the Last Twenty Years: Change, Adaptation or Unfinished Transition?' Special Issue of *Contemporary Italian Politics*, Vol. 7, No. 1.

Paterson, W.E. (2011) 'The Reluctant Hegemon? Germany Moves Centre Stage in the European Union'. *JCMS*, Vol. 49, No. s1, pp. 57–75.

Petrini, F. (2005) *Il liberalismo a una dimensione. La Confindustria e l'integrazione europea 1947–1957* (Rome: Franco Angeli).

Quaglia, L. (2007) 'The role of Italy in the European Union: Between Continuity and Change'. *Journal of Southern Europe and the Balkans*, Vol. 9, No. 2, pp. 133–48.

Quaglia, L. (2011) 'The Ebb and Flow of Euroscepticism in Italy'. *South European Society and Politics*, Vol. 16, No. 1, pp. 31–50.

Rowinski, P.(2013) 'Euroscepticism in the Berlusconi and Murdoch Press'. In Charles, A. (ed.) *Media/Democracy: A Comparative Study* (Newcastle upon Tyne: Cambridge Scholars Publishing).

Sanders, D., Magalhaes, P. and Toka, G. (eds) (2012) *Citizens and the European Polity: Mass Attitudes Towards the European and National Polities* (Oxford: Oxford University Press).

Sbragia, A. (2001) 'Italy Pays for Europe: Political Leadership, Political Choice and Institutional Adaptation'. In Green Cowles, M., Caporaso, J. and Risse, T. (eds) *Transforming Europe: Europeanization and Domestic Change* (Ithaca: Cornell University Press).

Schmidt, V.A. (2009) 'Re-Envisioning the European Union: Identity, Democracy, Economy'. *JCMS*, Vol. 47, No. s1, pp. 17–42.

Serricchio, F. (2011) *Perchè gli italiani diventano euroscettici* (Pisa: Pisa University Press).

Steinmo, T., Thelen, K. and Longstreth, F. (eds) (1992) *Structuring Politics: Historical Institutionalism in Comparative Analysis* (Cambridge: Cambridge University Press).

Taggart P. and Szczerbiak, A. (2002) *The Party Politics of Euroscepticism in EU Member and Candidate States*, SEI Working Paper No 51/ Opposing Europe Research Network Working Paper No 6 (Brighton: Sussex European Institute).

Telò, M. (1996) 'L'Italia nel processo di costruzione europea'. In Barbagallo, F. (ed.), *Storia dell'Italia repubblicana: L'Italia nella crisi mondiale. L'ultimo ventennio*, Vol. 3 (Turin: Einaudi).

Togliatti, P. (1951) 'Fermiamo la mano ai nemici della pace!'. *l'Unità*, 25 September. Available at «http://archivio.unita.it/esploso.php?dd=25&mm=09&yy=1951&ed».

Tomsic, G. (ed.) (1976) *Berlinguer, discorsi 1969-1976* (Rome: Sarmi).

Varsori, A. (2010) *La cenerentola d'Europa? L'Italia e l'integrazione europea dal 1947 a oggi* (Soveria Mannelli: Rubbettino).

© 2015 The Author(s) JCMS: Journal of Common Market Studies © 2015 John Wiley & Sons Ltd

JCMS 2015 Volume 53 Annual Review pp. 61–74   DOI: 10.1111/jcms.12267

Crisis-Ridden, Battered and Bruised: Time to Give Up on the EU?

DAVID PHINNEMORE
Queen's University Belfast

Rethinking the Union of Europe Post-Crisis: Has Integration Gone Too Far?, by G. Majone (Cambridge: Cambridge University Press, 2014, ISBN 9781107694798); viii + 370 pp., £21.99 pb.

The European Council and the Council: New Intergovernmentalism and Institutional Change, by U. Puetter (Oxford: Oxford University Press, 2014, ISBN 9780198716242); xiv + 265 pp., £55.00 hb.

Why Europe Matters: The Case for the European Union, by J. McCormick (London: Palgrave, 2013, ISBN 9781137016874); xiv + 198 pp., £14.99 pb.

Unhappy Union: How the Euro Crisis – and Europe – Can be Fixed, by J. Peet and A. LaGuardia (London: Economist Books, *2014*, ISBN 978-1610394499); xvi + 220 pp., £20.00 pb.

Rethinking the European Union, by N. Copsey (London: Palgrave, 2014, ISBN 9781137341662); xii + 260 pp., £28.99 pb.

European integration, as George Ross noted in his study of the European Union (EU) and its crises, 'has never been an easy process', and the EU in particular has been especially 'crisis-prone' (Ross, 2011, pp. 1 and 7). With first the financial crisis of 2008, and then recession and the near fracturing of the eurozone, much of the past decade has seen the EU faced with its most sustained and testing period of crisis. Not only has the future of monetary union and the euro been put in serious doubt, but commentators and politicians have seriously questioned whether the EU would actually survive this latest set of crises. For many, the past five years have seen the EU, or at least the eurozone, fighting for its survival. Not since the eurosclerosis and europessimism of the 1970s has there been such a sustained mood of undoubted and, for some, existential crisis.

The seemingly relentless sense and reality of crisis appeared to begin to abate in 2014. References to the euro's imminent demise and the eurozone's impending break-up no longer fed media headlines, even if doubts soon intensified about whether Greece, under the Syriza-led government that took office in January 2015, would remain part of it. EU leaders ceased invoking notions of an existential crisis and scaled

© 2015 The Author(s) JCMS: Journal of Common Market Studies © 2015 John Wiley & Sons Ltd, 9600 Garsington Road, Oxford OX4 2DQ, UK and 350 Main Street, Malden, MA 02148, USA

back their calls for closer integration of at least the eurozone. Bold steps to establish banking union, fiscal union and economic union to save the eurozone and the EU seemed, for many observers, to be no longer necessary. The apparent, yet qualified, success of responses to the crisis – whether the European Stability Mechanism (ESM), the Fiscal Compact Treaty or the pledge of the President of the European Central Bank (ECB), Mario Draghi, in August 2012 to do 'whatever it takes' to save the euro – appeared to have brought an end to the mood of impending doom regarding the future of the EU. For many observers and commentators, however, any sense of crisis receding needs to be tempered. Whereas in Ireland and Portugal post-bailout austerity-based reforms appear, at the time of writing, to be bearing fruit, Greece remains in crisis and the prospect of 'Grexit' rather than receding is no longer regarded as unacceptable and to be avoided at all costs. Moreover, containing and resolving the eurozone crisis is a question of addressing not only immediate causes, notably sovereign debt, but also the structural shortcomings of, and indeed flaws in, the design of the eurozone and the wider process of economic and monetary union (EMU). Furthermore, crisis can not only beget new crises but also expose or intensify existing crises. And this is certainly the view of some of the more provocative assessments of the EU produced in recent years. For Zielonka, the EU's days as the primary focus for, and vehicle of, European integration are numbered; the EU is destined to become 'toothless and useless' (Zielonka, 2014, p. 106).

The books under review here each, albeit to varying degrees, accept that the EU has recently been experiencing – and in many respects continues to experience – a multiplicity of crises. The eurozone crisis has been the most potent and energy-sapping. Pre-dating it, yet also exacerbated by it, are crises of legitimacy, leadership, accountability, purpose and democratic deficit. To this may be added crises of (mis)understanding, of interdependence and of identity. Whether, how and to what extent the EU can continue to weather and overcome these crises is where the books differ. For Majone, the future is very bleak. The other authors are, rightly, less pessimistic. The EU has its flaws, but as even the eurozone crisis has shown, it can act and adapt. The issue for Copsey, Peet and LaGuardia and McCormick is that some serious rethinking and further reform are necessary.

Peet and LaGuardia focus on the eurozone crisis, a crisis to which *The Economist*, for which both authors write, has dedicated considerable editorial space and not an insignificant number of characteristically provocative front covers (which the book conveniently reproduces). For Peet and LaGuardia, the euro, in the face of the financial storm caused by the collapse of subprime mortgages in the United States and the ensuing credit crunch, 'turned out to be a flimsy umbrella that flopped over in the wind and dragged away many of the weaker economies [and] led to the worst economic crisis in Europe since the end of the second world war' (p. xi). The crisis was so bad that 'Europe became the world's basket case', with 'Europhiles and Eurosceptics alike' exhibiting a growing belief that the euro had 'undermined, and may yet destroy the European Union' (p. xii).

Readers of *Unhappy Union* looking for a lively account of the eurozone crisis delivered in a punchy journalistic style will not be disappointed. The authors chart key developments in the crisis, working through the events that culminated in bailouts for Greece, Ireland and Portugal and the establishment of the ESM and the adoption of the Fiscal Compact Treaty, and also place the crisis in the broader context of the EU's development. Consequently, they highlight both the institutional design flaws of EMU and the euro and reflect on key turning points in the crisis and its significance for the balance of power in the EU. The analysis is well presented and will also be familiar to those who followed the crisis: 2012 was a key year, with Angela Merkel's commitment to keeping Greece in the euro and Draghi's 'whatever it takes' announcement in August – 'Draghi's great bluff' (p. xv); the crisis firmly established Germany as the predominant power in the EU; and the whole saga exposed tensions between eurozone 'ins' and 'outs', notably the United Kingdom.

Peet and LaGuardia also explore what the eurozone crisis reveals about the EU more generally covering the EU's crisis of legitimacy, its democratic deficit, the short-termism of EU leaders and their limited capacity to solve the eurozone crisis and address its economic and political fallout. The crisis has, however, demonstrated resolve: '[EU] leaders have shown they will act to avoid imminent shipwreck. This means a sudden catastrophic default and currency redenomination is improbable' (p. 175). They are probably right; the EU has moved into calmer waters and shown that it can, however cumbersomely and laboriously, address at least some of the symptoms and causes of the crisis. However, despite the apparent calm, further episodes in the crisis cannot be ruled out. Indeed, *Unhappy Union* anticipates further crisis: banks remain 'wobbly' despite new supervisory mechanisms; the ECB's bluff could be called if and when doubts about its commitment to intervene intensify; the legal status of Outright Monetary Transactions continues to be challenged; and economic stagnation persists, with growth slow and unemployment high. Moreover, there are important political challenges facing the EU. Two in particular are highlighted: the increased popular disaffection with the EU that has led to increased support for, and promoted by, anti-EU and anti-immigration parties;[1] and the possibility of a UK exit from the EU. All these are perfectly sound observations.

The fact that the EU has very much 'muddled through' the eurozone crisis offers little hope to *Unhappy Union*'s authors that EU leaders – 'not proven to be endowed with long-term vision' (p. 177) – will ever pursue a bolder, radical transformation of the EU into a more integrated political and economic union. So, 'the best that can probably be hoped for is that the eurozone lurches from one crisis-induced reform to another', a state of affairs that will be 'unnecessarily costly and painful, but might somehow lead to a more coherent and workable system' (p. 177). The alternative is that the EU runs the risk that 'one or all of its members lose the will to preserve the single currency, and perhaps the wider project' (p. 177). The first scenario, given the past experiences as well as the more recent history of the EU, seems the more likely, and Peet and LaGuardia appear to accept this, offering a number of suggestions for reform. Some relate specifically to the eurozone and include greater risk-sharing, a speedier restructuring of problematic sovereign debt, an element of fiscal union in the form of a 'European fund' that could issue bonds, effective banking union and a more courageous ECB willing to loosen monetary policy. Other proposals look more widely: the EU should enhance the role of national parliaments by increasing their scrutiny roles and allowing them to veto or modify EU legislation; national MPs could also be brought together to oversee EU-level decisions regarding bailouts, for

---

[1] See Hobolt's contribution to this volume.

example; a leaner and 'fitter' Commission should also be pursued; and Germany should assume a clear leadership role.

Whether the reforms proposed would be sufficient to 'fix' the euro crisis and 'Europe', as *Unhappy Union*'s subtitle suggests, is open to question. The discussion of solutions is brief, and how far the institutional reforms – long-established propositions from *The Economist* – would really equip the EU to address the challenges associated with the future of the eurozone is far from clear. The EU's capacity to generate effective political leadership remains a problem – simply reducing the size of the Commission, potentially downgrading the European Parliament (EP) and giving national parliamentarians greater opportunities to block EU-level activity would contribute little; these proposals appear to reflect more a political agenda sceptical of certain supranational institutions as opposed to a coherent reform project. Moreover, how likely is it that national parliaments already struggling to use existing powers to provide effective scrutiny of the EU and its activities will be able to adapt practices and cultures to take on additional powers? And how does an even more courageous independent ECB sit with the concerns about reducing the EU's crisis of legitimacy? The ideas are nevertheless contributions to a much-needed debate. And for Peet and LaGuardia, this is a debate about the future of the EU, not a Europe without the EU. The EU, despite its flaws, has its value. Its contribution to supporting peace among its members for more than six decades is noted – and in the light of the Ukraine crisis, this should not be forgotten. Yet the EU is in need of leadership both on the eurozone and on selling the added value of integration: 'something of great value may… be lost through carelessness or timidity' on the part of EU leaders. They 'fear undoing European integration, but dare not promote it either' (p. 179).

If EU leaders were minded to make the case for the EU more forcibly, they could usefully prepare themselves by studying McCormick's *Why Europe Matters*, a self-proclaimed antidote to the 'toxic stew of pessimism, denial hesitancy, myth and scepticism' in which 'discussion of Europe is mired' (p. 7). And the book certainly delivers in so far as it presents a forcibly argued defence of, and case for, the EU. In doing so McCormick provides a valuable corrective to many of the misinformed and often ignorant positions present in media and popular discussions of the EU; in turn, his highly readable account of Europe as peacemaker, marketplace, democracy, community, political model and global player challenges and often lays bare core assumptions of hard and soft eurosceptics alike. Running throughout the narrative is McCormick's frustration, no doubt shared by many readers, with the state of knowledge about the EU. For him, '[i]t is hard to think of a public debate that has been both so consequential and yet so abundantly plagued by misinformation' (p. 7). How true.

For some readers, McCormick's analysis may come across as that of a starry-eyed euro-idealist. He does though state his case for the EU well, seeing the crisis glass half-full as opposed to half-empty. The EU does have its problems, and these extend beyond the eurozone crisis. And there may well have been a 'cacophony of woe emanating from the euro zone which has, in turn, fed off and been given new energy by a damaging combination of indifference and inattention' (p. 146). However, there is quite rightly no reason to abandon either the euro or integration. The EU matters. Neither the EU's dissolution nor a rollback of integration – McCormick's first two options for exiting the current malaise – is either a viable or a desirable option. Nor is 'stagnation' – a continuation of the 'muddling through' approach that has so characterized the EU's response to the

© 2015 The Author(s) JCMS: Journal of Common Market Studies © 2015 John Wiley & Sons Ltd

eurozone crisis. Equally undesirable and unrealistic – and here McCormick's pragmatism and understanding of the politics of integration come through – is the 'federal' option of a European superstate. Instead, he settles for 'a programme of informed and sensible reform' (p. 9) that will see the EU emerge as an identifiable 'confederal' entity.

For McCormick, the 'confederal option' of 'a group of sovereign states with a central authority deriving its powers from those states, and citizens linked to the central authority through the states in which they live' (p. 28) has the advantage of 'locking in the best of what the EU has achieved, providing a label by which Europeans might better understand and measure the work of the EU, assuaging the fears of those who oppose further integration, and minimizing opportunities for the works of the EU to be misrepresented' (p. 150). However, simply conceptualizing the EU as a confederation cannot – and must not – in any way be regarded as a panacea for the EU's ills. These ills need to be recognized, which McCormick does. So, the EU has to: engage its citizens; reform its institutions to make them more democratic, more transparent and more efficient; be more responsive; complete unfinished business; and simplify and adjust the division of competences between the Member States and the supranational level. Much can be achieved by proceeding pragmatically, by drawing breath and by 'deepening rather than widening, allowing the European project to settle, allowing time for its flaws to be worked out in a considered fashion unpolluted by scepticism, pessimism, myths, misunderstandings and crises' (p. 151).

McCormick points to the Laeken Declaration of 2001 as a blueprint for how the EU might proceed. Much maligned, Laeken was supposed to 'mark a decisive step towards a simpler Union, one that is stronger in the pursuit of its essential objectives and more present in the world' (Council of the European Union, 2001: point 3) and launch a debate on how the EU's institutions could be brought closer to its citizens and how the EU should engage with a fast-changing globalized world. Such challenges still exist, and many of the questions set out in the Laeken Declaration still need to be answered. Re-engaging with Laeken – or, better still, a revised set of questions reflecting the challenges and issues highlighted by McCormick and the other volumes under review – could be a useful exercise, particularly if second time around a genuine and informed 'future of Europe' debate could be generated. Organizing such a debate would be a major challenge, not least because Member States, the key interlocutors between citizens and the supranational level, are notoriously disinclined, if at all able, to generate debate on European integration. An informed debate needs to be had in the EU if it is to re-establish itself as an entity and process that enjoys broad popular support.

Neither Majone nor Copsey, both of whom set about 'rethinking' the EU in the light of the eurozone crisis, explicitly share McCormick's interest in revisiting the Laeken Declaration. Neither mentions it. Given Majone's analysis, there would probably be little point, for essentially European integration has simply gone too far and it is time to revert to a 'club of clubs' (p. 321). Post-crisis Europe therefore needs greater flexibility in terms of its political organization; it needs to be something other than European integration as 'a simple linear extrapolation of the traditional nation state model' (p. 321). Indeed, for Majone, there is a need to question 'the very nature and the aims of the integration process' (p. 316). And this is not merely a consequence of the eurozone crisis, but rather of the fundamentally flawed design of the EU and nature of EU-based integration. The EU's 'collective leadership' *modus operandi* is severely limited in what it can achieve,

© 2015 The Author(s) JCMS: Journal of Common Market Studies © 2015 John Wiley & Sons Ltd

and the 'total absence of the traditional government-opposition dialectic' – a major problem for the EU, as Copsey also notes – means that 'nobody can claim to govern the EU' (p. 14). Moreover, the EU has long suffered from a significant mismatch between what it promises and what it has delivered. The failure of monetary union to deliver the anticipated economic benefits is particularly serious: its visibility is much greater and its effects are much more widely felt than anything previously. The political consequences of a failure therefore threaten to be far more significant.

For Majone, the EU, whose 'ever-widening and deepening integration process has proved impotent to arrest the decline of Europe's economy relative to its major competitors' (p. 16), needs to be fundamentally reconsidered. His challenging analysis, elements of which will be familiar to readers of his earlier works (e.g. Majone, 2009), is therefore less a focus on the most recent period of eurozone-dominated crisis, more a forthright and trenchant criticism of the way in which the EU is structured and has evolved and of significant elements of academic analysis (notably neofunctionalism). He does not, though, question the idea of integration *per se*; he does, however, question the method. A key point is that EU leaders operate within a prevailing political culture of 'total optimism' concerning the EU and further integration, and so 'the long-term consequences [of their action] are heavily discounted or altogether ignored' (p. 61). They are therefore generally unprepared for crisis, having failed to agree contingency plans. For Majone, the eurozone crisis, having moved the EU from 'total optimism to catastrophism' (p. 70), confirms this all too well, and integrationist leaders within the EU, especially Germany, come in for strong criticism for always assuming that the solution to any crisis lies in 'more Europe'.

That the history of the EU has been based on an optimistic view of the potential benefits of integration is hard to dispute. Whether the optimism has been total, however, is highly questionable, as is the assertion that the feasibility of projects has always been ignored. Few if any developments in the history of the EU have been pursued without considerable debate, contestation and negotiation, at least at governmental levels. A convincing case that, for example, successive UK governments since 1973 have succumbed to a political culture of 'total optimism' in further EU-based integration simply cannot be made. A similar argument can be made for most other Member States. Majone nevertheless makes an important point in bemoaning the lack of detailed analysis and assessment of the results of integration. Few comprehensive assessments have been attempted, let alone made. However, to suggest that a European-level process is flawed because results may have fallen short of optimistic expectations and assumed promises is to ignore the regular failures of national-level politics. How many political parties or politicians that enter power regularly deliver in full on their electoral or government programme promises?

Majone's critique of the EU's democratic deficit – moving increasingly to a 'democratic default', and in the case of monetary union with democratic input 'almost totally absent' – is more compelling. His solution – a 'radical transformation of the present system, or a drastic limitation of the powers delegated to the European levels' (p. 193) – would, however, appear to have little prospect of being pursued, given the political commitment to the EU that the overwhelming majority of Member State governments have to the process. Even the UK government's recent balance of competences review concluded that, fundamentally, the balance between what Member States and the EU do – at least as far as the UK as a non-eurozone member is concerned – is broadly supported and seen as appropriate. Moreover, in the light of the criticisms raised in several of the books under review here, it is questionable whether sufficient leadership exists for such a process of transformation, just as the leadership to pursue more ambitious forms of deeper EU integration is evidently lacking.

Majone's solution to what he sees as the flaws inherent in the EU as a model for integration is to abandon the open-ended commitment to 'ever closer union' and instead establish a 'finite political goal' for integration; base integration on 'cooperative cooperation' (p. 269) as opposed to excessive harmonization; and pursue integration through a 'Europe of clubs' (p. 116) organized around functional tasks, with larger-scale projects being pursued only if there is clear evidence of support, for example through a super-majority in national parliaments. The role of the EU would be to monitor co-operation rather than pursue its own unilinear development towards a grander European version of the nation state. The focus should be on greater recognition and accommodation of Europe's diversity. Closer eurozone integration is therefore dismissed, just as, with considerable force, is 'more Europe' generally.

This is all highly provocative, and intentionally so. Majone's fierce criticism of EU integration raises important questions about how far integration has progressed and the form it has taken. This is a very thought-provoking and intellectually stimulating book and Majone's diagnosis of the problems and challenges facing European integration should not be ignored. Important questions are raised. However, one cannot but help thinking that some of the core claims are overstated. Majone talks of a 'race towards deeper integration' (p. 303). Europe over the past 60 years has certainly experienced a process of deepening integration, but to view it as a 'race' is to ignore the piecemeal manner in which it has been achieved, the hard bargaining and negotiation that has been necessary and the more federalist and integrationist ambitions that have been dashed along the way. There are serious problems with the eurozone's 'one-size-fits-all' monetary policy and the design of monetary union more generally; but the history of the EU is one of seeking to address and resolve problems that integration has raised and incrementally adapt the EU accordingly. This has generally worked to date, and the fact that the EU has emerged from the eurozone crisis essentially intact, if battered, bruised and weary, suggests that the model remains durable and broadly supported, at least at the elite level. Even at the popular level, Eurobarometer polls consistently reveal marginally greater trust in the EU compared to national parliaments and governments (European Commission, 2004, p. 8). This is not to dispute in any way the need for reform, or the pressing need to address the EU's legitimacy and democratic deficits. Insights and ideas can be taken from Majone's analysis, but there appears little need to take up his call to effectively return to the drawing board with how integration is pursued, abandoning the EU as we know it, and pursue integration in a radically difficult manner. Moreover, one has to question how feasible this would be politically. The appetite – as with the case of full-blown political union – simply does not exist. Furthermore, the whole case tends to ignore the increasingly differentiated nature of EU-based integration; the flexibility that Majone is calling for partly exists already, and there is scope for more, provided fundamental principles are not compromised.

Like Majone, Copsey offers a far more detailed analysis than McCormick of the challenges facing the EU. He also presages his remarks by stressing that the gravity of the challenges should not be underestimated. The recent travails of the eurozone and the 'Great Recession' that went before have not only been crises in themselves, but have also exacerbated a range of 'underlying social, economic and political problems [that have]

© 2015 The Author(s) JCMS: Journal of Common Market Studies © 2015 John Wiley & Sons Ltd

been mounting for decades' (p. 2). In addition, the eurozone crisis has confirmed the 'apparent powerlessness of the EU's collective leadership' (p. 5) to do anything more than shore up the euro. If anything, recession and crisis have weakened the EU more than is commonly recognized and brought to the fore 'a sense of intractability, failure and loss of purpose and general drift that [has] challenged and undermined much of what has been understood and written about the EU and European integration' (p. 214). *Rethinking the European Union* provides a well-argued reminder that, even as it appears to be putting the darkest days of the eurozone crisis behind it, the EU is still faced with significant challenges that need to be addressed if it is to survive as a purposeful contributor to economic, political and social development in Europe.

Copsey explores four specific challenges in detail. The first concerns the question of who actually identifies with the EU. The answer, beyond a broadly enthusiastic elite, is relatively few people. At best there is a grudging popular acceptance of the EU by a generally apathetic majority. Whether this will be sufficient to sustain the EU is rightly questioned, particularly as integration and its costs and benefits become increasingly contested. Second, there is the related issue of the EU's popular legitimacy. Here Copsey notes the EU's long-standing democratic deficit, yet is quick to point out that it is less severe than its most ardent critics maintain and that democracy has its shortcomings at the level of Member States as well. He also makes the important point that the situation is exacerbated by the culture of consensus-building in the EU which tends to deny voters real choices. Compounding matters is the elite-determined response to the eurozone crisis which has seen austerity imposed without popular approval. Consequently, and here Copsey and Majone concur, the EU has arguably reached the limit of what it can legitimately do, at least in the absence of explicit popular endorsement. A key question is how the EU should set about securing such endorsement.

The third challenge concerns solidarity and the winners and losers in the EU. Once again, European integration disproportionately favours elites, with Copsey suggesting that only 17–20 per cent of Europeans benefit from the EU's predominantly market-based integration. Any notion of fairness is seriously undermined. So, to establish any sense of solidarity, the EU needs to move beyond market-based integration as its ideological basis. The fourth challenge – sustainability – has two dimensions: internally, the EU's economic model; externally, the EU's global role. On the former, the case is made for sustaining 'European capitalism' – the social market economy – with its mix of capitalism, social protection and market regulation. It is not to blame for the EU's economic ills. What is needed, however, is job creation, and here Copsey stresses the need to complete the unfinished business of the liberalization of services and deregulation of labour markets. Lessons are to be learnt from the German experience with its Agenda 2010 and Hartz reforms. On the EU's global role, what is lacking is a grand strategy and EU relevance in the face of new global players. At present, the role and influence of the EU is less than the sum of its 28 Member States, and so Europe risks fading into global irrelevance.

Like Majone, Copsey is strong on identifying and diagnosing problems and challenges. Whereas Majone very much sees the EU glass as half-empty at best, Copsey is rightly more positive, having at least some faith in the proven durability of the established structures. However, as he also notes, the need for change has to be recognized, and this has to be accompanied by greater regard for the future. Short-termism needs to be overcome and more strategic thinking needs to be deployed. If socio-economic decline is to be addressed, reform is needed across the EU, and not just in the bailout states – Greece, Cyprus, Portugal and Ireland – or those that have struggled – e.g. Spain and Italy – to service and reduce their sovereign debt. Copsey points particularly to France, which still has to come to terms with globalization and reform and can presumably act as a model for reform elsewhere. It is in the context of the dynamics of economic reform that *Rethinking the European Union* provides one of its most interesting observations on the EU. The southern Member States, having joined the EU without the same level of pre-accession conditionality as the central and eastern European states, are not only seeing their comparative economic advantage eroded by globalization, but, having failed to engage to the same degree in reforms in response to globalization, are being challenged in terms of their relative economic standing by the likes of Slovakia, Slovenia, Estonia and the Czech Republic, who are all set to overtake Portugal and Greece in terms of per capita GDP in 2015 (p. 221). This has political as well as economic significance for the relative standing of individual Member States within the EU and heralds an end to the era of 'old' and 'new' Member States; it should result in a further re-calibration of the north–south/reformist–laggard/liberal–protectionist camps into which the Member States are ostensibly divided, and in each case to the benefit of the reformist discourse.

Copsey details a range of additional changes that are required. Among these is the need to re-balance the theory and practice of EU integration with less emphasis on markets and consumers and more on the EU's values and on people as citizens. Also needed is a better understanding of the EU. Here Copsey rightly bemoans the 'wilful ignorance of Brussels and its workings', especially among national politicians, civil servants and judges: '[a]fter nearly sixty years of the European project, it [is] surely time for national institutions to catch up with Europe's political reality as a polity-in-the-making' (p. 220). To this should be added the point that governments and electorates need to accept and promote national and EU levels of policy-making as being part of the same evolving 'European' political system.

Copsey's diagnosis of Europe's problems and his calls for change are well made and are followed by a concluding, albeit unfortunately rather brief, discussion of the 'choices' Europe has to make. Three are identified: a 'new project, narrative or vision for Europe'; the means to deliver effectively at national and EU level; and a decision on how far the 'new project' will extend. For the first, historical narratives of peace and prosperity need to be supplemented with a narrative of 'European values' and of 'unity in strength', and a shared sense of a 'common purpose' for the EU. A range of ideas are floated: addressing Europe's ageing population, increasing economic productivity, increasing labour market participation, and ensuring long-term investment in energy and power generation, research and development, education and training. In order for this to be done, a debate needs to be had on the model of free markets the EU will promote. In terms of delivery, Copsey is brief, pointing to the need for political will and robust and modernized institutions well resourced financially and in terms of human capital. On the delineation of the EU's borders, he is briefer and inconclusive; essentially a case of 'time will tell'. The conclusion to this ambitious book, with its authoritative discussion of issues, informed analysis of where the EU is and attempt to 'rethink' the EU, unfortunately rather tails off.

That the EU needs a 'new project, narrative or vision for Europe' is hard to dispute; the EU has to re-assert its sense of purpose. Copsey's call raises the question, however, of who in the EU can – and should – provide the necessary leadership. Few informed

© 2015 The Author(s) JCMS: Journal of Common Market Studies © 2015 John Wiley & Sons Ltd

observers can deny that Member State governments must take a leading role here. They are not only the key drivers of integration, but they continue to be the primary means through which citizens, increasingly affected by integration, involve themselves in the process. Institutionally considerable responsibility lies with the European Council, now firmly established as the dominant forum for decisions – and in some cases brakes – on further integration. The eurozone crisis has demonstrated as much: members of the European Council gathered on no fewer than 26 occasions in 2010–13; those from eurozone Member States attended a further ten 'Euro Summit' meetings. And it was these gatherings that either agreed or paved the way politically for the establishment of the European Financial Stability Facility, for the bailouts of Ireland, Greece and Portugal, for the creation of the ESM and for the adoption of the Fiscal Compact Treaty.

It would be wrong to assume, however, that the eurozone was the making of the European Council. Successive rounds of treaty reforms since the early 1990s have not only formalized but also reinforced its role as the body initially charged with providing the EU with 'the necessary impetus for its development' and defining its 'general political guidelines' (Article D TEU, Maastricht). References to other specific responsibilities now permeate the texts of the EU's constitutive treaties. The Treaty of Lisbon's formal designation of the European Council as an EU 'institution' was therefore, presentationally at least, little more than a belated recognition of its central role in the life of the EU. Where the Treaty of Lisbon went further than previous treaties was in investing in the European Council responsibility for providing 'the general political *directions* and *priorities*' of the EU (Article 13 TEU, Lisbon) and providing it with the institutional means to sustain the predominant position it had assumed. With the heads of government and state now 'electing' their own full-time President of the European Council to 'drive forward its work', providing the President with dedicated administrative support and formally meeting more regularly, the way has been paved for greater continuity and coherence in the work of the European Council. Meetings would also become smaller and presumably more focused, with the High Representative for Foreign Affairs and Security Policy participating as opposed to, by default, all Member State foreign ministers.

The evolution of the European Council over the past two decades and more is ably and thoroughly charted in *The European Council and the Council*: *New Intergovernmentalism and Institutional Change*. Here Puetter offers a comprehensive review of the European Council's roles, structures and working methods and demonstrates effectively how this originally unintended body that initially operated informally and outside the institutional structures of the European Communities has evolved into the EU's 'new centre of political gravity' (chapter 3). Puetter explores in detail how the European Council's internal organization has been 'geared towards increasing its capacity to generate consensus over policy' (p. 145) and how its working methods have become more formalized and focused on substantial policy debates, with meetings being more 'issue-driven' and the European Council conclusions increasingly providing 'a key instrument for exercising leadership' (p. 135).

Puetter's central argument is that this evolution is part of a wider process of 'new intergovernmentalism' that has the Council and European Council as the predominant institutions in the EU. Within this new intergovernmentalism, the Council retains its historic position at the heart of EU decision-making, but this traditional understanding of the Council has to be qualified, not least through accommodation of the greater role that the

European Council now has and plays and the increasing co-legislative responsibilities that successive rounds of treaty reform have bestowed on the EP. While the EP's status as a co-legislator is almost universally presented as a clear challenge to the assumption that the Council is the EU's prime legislative institution, the new intergovernmentalism thesis is sustained by reference to the changing role of the EU, which Puetter presents as one of increased intergovernmental policy co-ordination and declining traditional community method-based law-making. Such a shift is reflected in changes to how the Council operates and how it relates to, and interacts with, the European Council.

As with his discussion of how the European Council has operated and now operates with its post-Lisbon structures, Puetter provides a highly insightful, empirically rich, original and well-researched analysis of three key Council formations – the Economic and Financial Affairs Council (ECOFIN), the Foreign Affairs Council (FAC) and Employment, Social Policy, Health and Consumer Affairs – and their working methods, as well as the informal Eurogroup and a number of expert committees and working groups. In doing so, the book provides a highly valuable addition to the existing, relatively and surprisingly sparse, literature on the Council and non-community method-based decision-making in the EU, particularly where new arrangements such as the replacement of the rotating Council Presidency with dedicated chairs of meetings (i.e. High Representative in the FAC, and the Presidency of the Eurogroup) are concerned.

While undoubtedly informative and perceptive in its analysis of the changes that the European Council and Council have experienced in the post-Maastricht period, the book is less convincing, in its purported contribution to how European integration should be understood and theorized. This stems from key assumptions underpinning the study and claims about the existence of a 'new intergovernmentalism' and the utility of a new conceptual framework of 'deliberative intergovernmentalism' for understanding the contemporary nature of EU policy-making. The first of Puetter's key assumptions is that the EU is facing 'an integration paradox'. This is presented as the Member States since the early 1990s, fearful of the 'irreversible dismantling of national sovereignty', having 'insisted on strictly limiting further transfers of ultimate decision-making powers to supranational actors' yet at the same time being 'equally eager to expand the scope of EU policy-making activities significantly so as to include all core areas of national sovereignty such as economic governance, foreign affairs and defence, welfare state policies, and [justice and home affairs]' (p. 8).[2] One might question how 'eager' the Member States have actually been to expand 'all' areas, and also whether there is actually a 'paradox' here.

A second key assumption is that the Maastricht Treaty 'marks the constitution of a particular logic of integration to which all subsequent treaties have subscribed… [K]ey decisions at Maastricht and beyond concerning the broader institutional architecture of the Union, and notably the new areas of activity, have played a pivotal role in informing the emergence of a new intergovernmentalism in EU policy-making and a related process of profound institutional change that is concentrated around the European Council and Council' (p. 7). That there has been a significant expansion of EU activities and 'profound institutional change' in the EU cannot be disputed. The areas of EU activity have

---

[2] Later the 'integration paradox' is presented slightly differently as the institutional dilemma represented by the increasing clash between 'the conviction that stronger EU-level action is the precondition for resolving today's fundamental policy challenges' and 'insistence on ultimate national sovereignty' (p. 30).

© 2015 The Author(s) JCMS: Journal of Common Market Studies © 2015 John Wiley & Sons Ltd

obviously expanded to include, most notably, monetary union and a single currency; a common foreign and security policy; and the area of freedom, security and justice. And the EU's institutional architecture today, particularly with the ECB and the European External Action Service, is more densely populated than it was in the early 1990s. Furthermore, the distribution of powers and responsibilities has clearly shifted, primarily to the benefit of the EP. However, to claim that this is an essentially post-Maastricht phenomenon and to present the Maastricht Treaty as a 'watershed' moment tends to overlook the extent to which it codified and built on existing integration dynamics within and around the then European Communities, including the direction of EMU and extra-EC activities in the area of justice and home affairs (JHA).

Puetter is correct to stress a shift in the post-Maastricht era from legislative activity to intergovernmental policy co-ordination and responsibility for implementation being vested in the decentralized resources of the Member States as opposed to the Commission, particularly where the new areas of activity that Puetter discusses in detail are concerned. Here the analysis is particularly persuasive. However, whether this is tantamount to the EU being characterized by a 'new' intergovernmentalism is open to question. Legislative activity has continued elsewhere, as has the exercise of power by both established and more recently created supranational bodies, notably the ECB. Also, whether the consequential 'implementation failure', policy ineffectiveness and 'easy' defection from EU-level policy objectives were, as claimed, 'an intended feature of the post-Maastricht EU' (p. 4) must be challenged. Not all Member States have been content with the tendency to eschew supranational policy-making and the community method in favour of the lowest common denominator of intergovernmental policy co-ordination. Moreover, as the case of JHA – detailed consideration of which is not provided – clearly shows, the focus on intergovernmentalism was intended to be transitional. Hence the communitarization through the Treaty of Amsterdam of much of the EU's pillar three activities caused little surprise, particularly in light of the difficulties that early post-Maastricht efforts at intergovernmental policy co-ordination had faced. A number of limited opt-out/opt-in arrangements had to be agreed for Denmark, Ireland and the United Kingdom, but the broad consensus was on communitarization. Similarly, with the Treaty of Lisbon, the bulk of the Member States supported the effective communitarization of residual pillar three activities and the extension of the Court of Justice's jurisdiction, delayed until 2014 only at the insistence of the United Kingdom. More generally, it has often been the case with the EC/EU that new policies have been introduced through intergovernmental co-operation only to be subsequently institutionalized and – as Schimmelfennig has already noted in his assessment of 'new intergovernmentalism' as advanced by Puetter and co-authors elsewhere (see Bickerton et al., 2014) – all these policies are 'governed less intergovernmentally now than in the pre-Maastricht era' (Schimmelfennig, 2015, p. 4). Hence, 'new intergovernmentalism' is much 'better understood as an issue-specific approach focusing on a particular set of [non-regulatory] policies … or 'core state' powers' with many of its features appearing to 'fit well to such policies … [but] they neither define the post-Maastricht era in general nor neatly coincide with the pre-/post-Maastricht temporal divide' (Schimmelfennig, 2015, p. 1). The same argument can be applied to Puetter's volume under review here.

This is not to deny the increasing role of the European Council in the EU, the centrality of the Council to decision-making or policy co-ordination, the fact that community method-based decision-making no longer dominates decision-making in the EU or that

© 2015 The Author(s) JCMS: Journal of Common Market Studies © 2015 John Wiley & Sons Ltd

Member State governments generally demonstrate a reflex preference for retaining control over policy-making despite accepting arguments for more collective and co-ordinated action in the face of significant policy challenges. This has been evident in recent years in many of the various challenging debates on how to respond to developments in the eurozone crisis. And with EU leaders being obliged to resort to extra-EU mechanisms, notably the Fiscal Compact Treaty, to achieve their goals, considerable force is given to Puetter's argument for the preference to avoid investing new powers in the supranational institutions and reverting to community method-based policy-making. Indeed, Puetter's analysis of the Fiscal Compact Treaty is compelling. And he does acknowledge the roles that supranational actors have been granted in this latest example of a preference for an essential intergovernmentally dominated response. However, whether the full set of claims for a 'new' distinctive intergovernmentalism can actually be sustained is arguably overstated. In addition to the observations above, it also tends to downplay the support that has existed among at least some Member States for more supranationally oriented reforms regarding banking, fiscal and even economic union – even if banking union so far is a lot more intergovernmental than some hoped for – and the fact that moves beyond intergovernmental policy co-ordination cannot be ruled out.

A final comment on *The European Council and the Council* relates to 'deliberative intergovernmentalism', Puetter's 'umbrella term' for an analytical framework 'which holds that the EU's dependency on permanent consensus generation among Member State governments in day-to-day policy-making … determines intergovernmental decision-making'. It predicts that 'institutional engineering will occur in all spheres of European Council and Council decision-making' (p. 5). This is all demonstrated in detail based on a set of theoretically grounded – but equally, empirically deducible – propositions in regard to a selection of policy areas. The latter is important since the claims Puetter is making about deliberative intergovernmentalism relate only to the EU's 'new areas of activity'; there are considerable areas of more supranational EU activity and certain Council activity where the case for deliberative intergovernmentalism is not being advanced. This important caveat to Puetter's analysis and argument should not be overlooked.

Although not its purpose, *The European Council and the Council* does show how, in part at least, the EU institutionally has been responding to the eurozone crisis, and reveals the continuously evolving nature and structures of the two institutions covered. Their flexibility and adaptability will provide some comfort to those who maintain the EU is able to adjust in the face of crisis and survive. Advocates of supranationalism and those nostalgic for the heyday of community-method domination of EC policy-making will be dismayed, however, at yet further well-documented evidence of sustained and increasingly institutionalized intergovernmentalism within the EU.

Whether this intergovernmentalism enhances the EU's capacity to take up the reform challenges set out by the authors of the other volumes under review here remains to be seen. There will be doubters. Boldness and decisiveness and the setting aside of short-term political considerations in favour of longer-term principles and the interests of the EU, its citizens and integration have not always been the hallmarks of responses to the eurozone crisis or indeed other previous crises and challenges. A tendency towards muddling through is the norm in the EU and is likely, on the basis of evidence to date, and as Peet and LaGuardia argue, to remain so despite the urgings of McCormick and

© 2015 The Author(s) JCMS: Journal of Common Market Studies © 2015 John Wiley & Sons Ltd

others for the EU to be bolder and more decisive. Puetter's stress on deliberative intergovernmentalism and consensus-building also conspires against swift and ambitious action. Yet, used effectively, a more deliberative response can have its advantages, providing opportunities to reflect, consider and take informed decisions. It also provides scope – regrettably often ignored – to engage wider interests in the process of formulating responses. The challenge for the EU is to take those opportunities and use that scope.

It will need to if the underlying problems challenges identified by Copsey in particular are to be addressed, and in a manner that does not exacerbate the EU's existing democratic and legitimacy deficits. These have become critical and further attempts to deepen integration significantly without effective public consultation and endorsement are likely not only to fail, but also to undermine irreversibly the prospect of embedding broad popular support for the EU. For such a consultation to take place, honest assessments of the EU and integration are essential. What unites each of the volumes under review is their informed reflections on the state of the EU and the manifold problems and challenges it faces. They demonstrate quite clearly that the eurozone crisis is not the only crisis facing the EU, and even its resolution – far from an assured outcome – will not see an end to crisis. Yet the persistence of crisis is no reason to abandon either integration or the EU. There is demonstrable resilience and a capacity to respond in the EU, even if crisis responses may often seem, and are, sub-optimal and tardy. While Majone would not be alone in assuming otherwise, Copsey, McCormick, Peet and LaGuardia all at least hope, if not believe, that the EU can adapt further to address the crises facing it. It goes without saying that moving the EU into a settled, supported and sustained future requires the complex range of problems diagnosed here to be addressed. A key question is whether the EU in its current or a reformed state has the capacity to do so. Its resilience through crisis to date suggests it probably does.

References

Bickerton, C.J., Hodson, D. and Puetter, U. (2014) 'The New Intergovernmentalism: European Integration in the Post-Maastricht Era'. *JCMS*, Vol. 53 No. 4, pp. 703–22.

Council of the European Union (2001) *Presidency Conclusions – European Council Meeting in Laeken, 14 and 15 December 2001*, SN/300/1/01 REV 1, Brussels. Available at «www.consilium.europa.eu/uedocs/cms_data/docs/pressdata/en/ec/68827.pdf».

European Commission (2004) Standard Eurobarometer 82 (Brussels: European Commission). Available at «http://ec.europa.eu/public_opinion/archives/eb/eb82/eb82_first_en.pdf».

Majone, G. (2009) *Europe as a Would-be World Power: The EU at Fifty* (Cambridge: Cambridge University Press).

Ross, G. (2011) *The European Union and its Crises: Through the Eyes of the Brussels Elite* (Basingstoke: Palgrave).

Schimmelfennig, F. (2015) 'What's the News in 'New Intergovernmentalism'? A Critique of Bickerton, Hodson and Puetter', *JCMS*, Vol. 53 No. 4, pp. 723–30.

Zielonka, J. (2014) *Is the EU Doomed?* (Cambridge: Polity Press).

© 2015 The Author(s) JCMS: Journal of Common Market Studies © 2015 John Wiley & Sons Ltd

JCMS 2015 Volume 53 Annual Review pp. 75–82   DOI: 10.1111/jcms.12268

The Fifth Greek Presidency of the Council of the European Union: The Most Unlikely Captain?

GEORGE KYRIS
University of Birmingham

> In the last three years my country has been seriously challenged, Europe was also challenged. Some were predicting the so-called 'Grexit'… Some were predicting that the euro itself would not make it either. We proved them wrong, Europe worked, our Union has problems but is also has the capacity to solve those problems and go ahead.
>
> Greek Prime Minister Antonis Samaras, 2 July 2014

In April 2003, the signing of the Treaty of EU accession of 12 European countries in the shadow of the Athenian Acropolis marked one of the most significant milestones in European integration and a memorable moment of the then fourth Greek Presidency of the Council of the EU. The Athens Declaration, which was adopted during the event, reiterated the EU's 'determination to put an end to centuries of conflict and to transcend former divisions on [the] continent'. At the same time, the host, Greek PM Costas Simitis, was one of the many European leaders to underline the importance of the global role of the EU, which had become even more obvious given international developments, not least the Iraq War which had started two months earlier. A joyous Greece took pride in hosting such a celebration for a union which concluded its largest ever enlargement and the reconnection of the continent in the aftermath of the Cold War.

When Greece reassumed the presidency of the Council of the EU 11 years later, things could not have been more different. The EU was much more introverted in comparison and Greece a far less prominent, let alone joyous, member. The most important reason for those changes was the eurozone crisis, which started in 2009 and became the longest lasting crisis the EU has ever faced in its history. Given this, the EU was now less preoccupied by its international role and more with internal issues, not least the crisis and its major economic and political implications. In this regard, the fifth Greek presidency adopted a boat as its symbol and branded its term the 'common quest' of the EU and Greece, the country at the very heart of the eurozone crisis. At the same time, however, Greece was the country that personified not only the crisis, but also the increasingly awkward relationship between European citizens and 'Brussels'. In this regard, this contribution reviews the fifth Greek presidency, a presidency set against perhaps the most politically charged environment of recent times. After an introduction to the context of the presidency and its programme, the analysis turns to different priorities and concludes by drawing on more general comments on the role of the institution of the presidency in the 'post-Lisbon' era as well as the future of relations between Greece and the EU.

© 2015 The Author(s) JCMS: Journal of Common Market Studies © 2015 John Wiley & Sons Ltd, 9600 Garsington Road, Oxford OX4 2DQ, UK and 350 Main Street, Malden, MA 02148, USA

I. The Big Eurozone Storm

In January 2014, four years had passed since the outbreak of the greatest crisis in the history of the EU, and that of Greece in particular. The country was at the centre of the eurozone 'storm', which had seen its economy and political life shattered to pieces. The austerity policies that had come with the bailout agreements between Greece and the EU/International Monetary Fund (IMF), and what was perceived as increasing EU interference in domestic affairs, had put the relationship between the two sides to its most difficult test: on joining the eurozone in 2001, 51 per cent of Greeks had a positive image of the EU (European Commission 2001); by the time Greece undertook the presidency in 2014, the positive image of the EU had reached an all-time low of 16 per cent, which was also the lowest across all the Member States (European Commission 2014a). These attitudes also meant sweeping changes in the political scene, where the once dominant centre-right New Democracy and the centre-left Panhellenic Socialist Movement (PASOK) had haemorrhaged support in the wake of the EU's bailout agreements and had been forced to form a coalition government for the first time in history. What is more, this was not a particularly popular coalition: anti-bailout parties and especially the leftist Syriza had seen their support increasing. Last but not least, the crisis has also witnessed the growth of the extreme-right Golden Dawn.

Against this background of domestic instability and tension, the Greek presidency's 'voyage' did not start with the best omens but, instead, with a good deal of scepticism. For example, a series of European media outlets, such as *Der Spiegel*, *La Republica* and the *Guardian*, underlined the challenging economic and social context, which cast doubt on the ability of the country to complete such a mission.[1] A few days before undertaking the presidency, Ireland became the first of the four crisis-hit eurozone countries to exit its bailout. This only served to highlight how far Greece remained from its own exit. Greece, with all its problems, did seem to be the most unlikely 'captain' at the helm of the Council in such a challenging period. Interestingly, previous presidencies had also come at critical conjunctions to 'test' Greece: the first ever presidency came in 1983 just two years after joining and provided a test of the ability to undertake member responsibilities, while the latest one in 2003 came shortly after the country joined the eurozone (Dimitrakopoulos and Passas, 2004).

II. Principles and Objectives of the Presidency

With a relatively limited budget and staff, the Greek presidency was guided by three main principles, which revealed a deep concern with the political and social aspects of European integration.[2] First of all, the presidency focused on enhancing civic and society engagement in the EU, through policies and initiatives in response to everyday problems, concerns and insecurities of European citizens. A closely related principle was the reinforcement of the EU's democratic legitimacy and accountability, along with 'building up collectivity and solidarity links among Member States'.[3] These latter priorities can be seen as a response to the debate on the so-called 'democratic deficit' of the EU, which obtained new momentum also because of the eurozone crisis and rising euroscepticism

---

[1] «http://www.kathimerini.gr/64171/article/epikairothta/ellada/epifylaktika-gia-thn-ellhnikh-proedria-ta-die8nh-mmebr».
[2] «http://gr2014.eu/eu-presidency/the-greek-presidency/programme-and-priorities».
[3] «http://gr2014.eu/eu-presidency/the-greek-presidency/programme-and-priorities».

© 2015 The Author(s) JCMS: Journal of Common Market Studies © 2015 John Wiley & Sons Ltd

and the potential impact that this could have had on the upcoming European Parliament (EP) elections in June 2014. Last but not least, and perhaps in a more pragmatic tone, the Greek presidency principles also included deepening the EU, and especially economic and monetary union (EMU), by promoting policies and actions to remedy and restore initial deficiencies in the euro-area architecture that the recent crisis had unveiled. The more specific policy priorities of the presidency were organized around three main themes: (1) further European integration, especially in the eurozone; (2) jobs–growth–cohesion; and (3) migration–borders–mobility. Though these priorities were constrained by the Trio Presidency programme agreed between Lithuania, Ireland and Greece,[4] the latter also managed to introduce a horizontal focus on maritime policies as a unique element of its programme.

III. Sailing Out of the Crisis?

Generating growth and improving economic governance seemed to bridge the priorities of Greece as a Member State and the EU as whole in the eyes of Greek officials involved in the presidency.[5] Indeed, the programme of the Greek presidency focused a lot on further integration of both the EU and the troublesome eurozone. This too was linked to the development of the eurozone and the so-called banking union[6] as overarching objectives of the Trio Presidency dossier, which, as the last country, Greece undertook to finalize. During 2013 the Council had agreed a general approach towards a single resolution mechanism (SRM), aimed at complementing the single supervisory mechanism (SSM) and dealing with the finance and restructure of failing credit institutions in Member States that are part of the banking union. As a result, the deal between the Council and the EP in 2014 can be seen as an important achievement of the Greek presidency. This is because negotiations on the SRM had been controversial for a long time, with a series of members raising objections to the institutional, legal and political aspects of the mechanism; while the Greek presidency itself also found it difficult to compromise with the EP, which among others objected to some of the decision-making and implementation processes (European Parliament, 2014; see also Howarth and Quaglia, 2014). In the words of the then Greek finance minister Gikas Hardouvelis, the SRM 'substantially completed the building up of the banking union, which constitutes one of the most challenging goals towards economic and financial integration, since the adoption of the common currency'.[7] Indeed, the SRM can be seen as an important step towards banking union, allowing participating states to take decisions about failing credit institutions in a more co-ordinated and effective manner than before. The agreement of Member States on the Single European Fund just before the end of the Greek presidency term, as an essential part of the SRM, was also important in this context.

As for the area of growth–jobs–cohesion, the Council adopted a recommendation on the Quality Framework for Traineeships, which opened with a direct reference to how 'young people have been hit particularly hard during the crisis' (Council of the European Union, 2014b) but was not criticism-free, as many stakeholders asserted that the recommendation

---

[4] «http://eu2013.ie/ireland-and-the-presidency/about-the-presidency/trioprogrammeirelandlithuaniaandgreece/».
[5] *Euractiv*, 21 February 2013.
[6] See also Howarth and Quaglia (2014).
[7] «http://www.neurope.eu/article/last-ecofin-under-greek-presidency-mission-accomplished».

© 2015 The Author(s) JCMS: Journal of Common Market Studies © 2015 John Wiley & Sons Ltd

did not ensure quality work and access to social protection.[8] The Council also agreed an increase in support to small and medium-sized enterprises (SMEs) and many events were organized in Athens aimed at increasing awareness and access to EU funding, such as the 'Growth Enhancing Access to Finance for Research and Innovation' conference. Lastly, quite important progress was made in the Digital Agenda for Europe and the presidency also organized events, such as the 'Eskills for Jobs 2014' conference, that showed support for the Commission's campaign of the same name. This prioritization of growth and cohesion underlined the presidency's focus on combining economic development with social policies, but this was not a particularly Greek element. Not too dissimilarly to the advancement of eurozone integration discussed so far, this was in line with the main objective of the Trio Presidency programme; indeed, the Lithuanian presidency was branded as one 'for a credible, *growing* [my emphasis] and open Europe' (see also Vilpišauskas, 2014) while the Irish presidency called 'for stability, jobs and growth' (see also Laffan, 2014). This emphasis followed a trend of recent EU presidencies, given that since 2007 Trio programmes have increasingly focused on growth and internal affairs, often at the expense of external priorities.

IV. The Troubled Waters of Justice and Home Affairs

The Greek presidency also sought to address migration–borders–mobility, a triptych of issues quite close to home that also relates to the programme's cross-theme focus on maritime policies. This indeed reflected Greece's special maritime status and Europe's increasing challenges related to immigration,[9] particularly from the Middle East and North Africa. This, in combination with other factors like the eurozone crisis, sparked an increasingly poisonous public debate and the rising popularity of extreme groups, such as Golden Dawn in Greece, as well as attacks on immigrants. At the same time the October 2013 shipwreck in Lampedusa, Italy, which resulted in the death of more than 360 immigrants,[10] and the similarly unprecedented shipwreck near the Greek island of Farmakonissi, with 11 immigrant victims, only a few days after Greece began its presidency underlined in the bleakest way the importance of immigration for the south and the EU more generally.

In perhaps the most important development in this regard, the June 2014 General Affairs Council adopted the Maritime Security Strategy (MSS), subsequently endorsed by the European Council, which outlined maritime security principles and objectives, interests, risks and threats. Based on those, the strategy identified areas of implementation to strengthen the EU's response, including external action, maritime awareness, surveillance and information sharing, capability development, risk management and research, innovation, education and training (Council of the EU, 2014b). The Italian presidency,[11] which followed Greece, was tasked with drafting action plans for the strategy. In this regard, and as with many issues on the agenda of presidencies, Greeks worked on the MSS after the suggestion of the Council and on the basis of the joint

[8]«http://www.youthforum.org/pressrelease/joint-letter-condemning-council-recommendation-on-quality-framework-for-traineeships/».
[9] See Monar's contribution to this volume.
[10] See also Monar (2014).
[11] See Carbone's contribution to this volume.

© 2015 The Author(s) JCMS: Journal of Common Market Studies © 2015 John Wiley & Sons Ltd

communication of the Commission and the High Representative (European Commission, 2014b), also with the extensive involvement of the Greek Commissioner for Maritime Affairs and Fisheries Maria Damanaki. But this is not to undermine the opportunity that the Greek presidency, its focus on maritime policies and the challenges in the Mediterranean provided for reflection on the issue. Indeed, Greek PM Samaras underlined that the sea is an 'integral part' of the country's European identity[12] and that prioritizing maritime policies was also dictated by the national interests of the country, which has a very significant place in international shipping and the longest coastline across the EU.[13]

Indeed, the Greek presidency's keenness on maritime issues goes beyond the MSS and is also important for exploring co-operation between the Greek and Italian presidencies – a 'happy coincidence' according to the then Greek Deputy PM and Foreign Minister Evangelos Venizelos (Hellenic Republic, 2014). Greece set the agenda for maritime affairs and immigration in close co-operation with Italy and together they declared 2014 the 'Year of the Mediterranean' for the presidency of the Council of the EU. But beyond Italy and maritime affairs, strictly speaking, the Greek presidency provided a new impetus for the promotion of a 'political south': when taking up the presidency, Greece, along with Italy and Spain, launched a grouping of Mediterranean countries, which also included Portugal, France, Malta and Cyprus. In close co-operation with the Union for the Mediterranean, this informal grouping of foreign ministers met many times to promote the Mediterranean agenda in EU policies and discuss common issues such as migration.

Lastly, the Greek presidency and the Council announced post-Stockholm strategic guidelines for justice and home affairs (JHA), which were agreed by the European Council in June 2014. These focused on better links between internal and external policies and relations with third countries, the transposition, implementation and consolidation of the legal instruments and policy measures in place, the protection of fundamental rights, dealing with migration, asylum and borders policy. Besides this, the Council also decided to expand the tasks of the European Police College (CEPOL) to include law enforcement agencies beyond police. The Greek presidency did not manage to conclude the long and controversial discussion on data protection and a partial general approach on a Regulation was reached at the very last JHA Council meeting, with the Italian presidency taking over the effort to find a compromised solution on the controversial one-stop-shop principle, which calls for disputes between citizens and firms to be dealt by the national authority of the state in which the firm is based.

V. Of Solidarity, Accountability and Legitimacy

Of the Greek presidency programme, what is left to assess is the priority of reinforcing the EU's democratic legitimacy and accountability, along with building up the collectivity and solidarity between Member States. In terms of the accountability of the presidency itself, the report from Transparency International suggested that Greece failed to provide information on the budget of its term and this meant it was impossible to hold it

---

[12] «http://www.amna.gr/english/articleview.php?id=5000».
[13] «http://www.primeminister.gov.gr/2014/07/01/12876».

© 2015 The Author(s) JCMS: Journal of Common Market Studies © 2015 John Wiley & Sons Ltd

accountable. As far as EU policy development regarding accountability during the Greek presidency is concerned, the report commented positively on the general prioritization of anti-corruption issues and, more specifically, the finalization of negotiations on a directive to reduce corruption in the financing of European political parties and therefore enhance their accountability. Elsewhere, the report regretted the relative neglect of dossiers such as the Joint Transparency Register, which would make the process through which the Council is lobbied and decides more accountable (Transparency International, 2014).

In terms of building up collective solidarity and links between the Member States, the Council adopted new rules on the European Solidarity Fund as well as rules and procedures for the implementation of the 'solidarity clause', which provides for EU help when a member is victim of a terrorist attack or disaster. The Greek PM argued that these actions showed the importance the presidency placed on the principle of solidarity.[14] But in other policy developments there was also an extra emphasis on 'solidarity'. For example, the MSS outlined above included references to solidarity when Member States face extraordinary challenges and this was of particular importance because of the geostrategic position of Greece, where officials often called for more help in dealing with maritime challenges, particularly immigration.[15] Not too dissimilarly, the Regulation establishing rules for the surveillance of the external sea borders also included specific 'solidarity' mechanisms for the assistance of a state that faces an urgent situation at its border (European Parliament and Council, 2014), which was particularly important for Greece given the challenges of immigration from the east and the south.

Finally, the EP elections in June 2014 are significant for the legitimacy of the EU in the eyes of European citizens. As expected, the results were marked by the often resounding victory of parties with strongly eurosceptic platforms – the most prominent examples being the UK Independence Party and *Front National* in France.[16] But, interestingly, Greece saw the leftist Syriza claiming victory for the first time by advocating a break with previous EU-promoted policies of austerity as a response to the financial crisis. This wave of euroscepticism throughout Europe, combined with the decreasing turnout of voters (despite hopes for the opposite), certainly did not put the heated debate on the EU's democratic deficit to sleep.

Conclusion: Destination Unknown

As with many recent presidencies, the changes introduced by the Treaty of Lisbon were reflected in the case of Greece. We saw before how the new 'trio' system (in place since 2007 and formally introduced by the Lisbon Treaty) meant that priorities like the advancement of the banking union were part of an 18-month programme. This can be seen as contributing to continuity and consistency, a main objective of the Lisbon Treaty. At the same time, the trio system has limited the ability of individual presidencies to promote their separate aims - maritime policies or the introduction of the 'Mediterranean Group' in the Greek presidency might appear to be an exception – but it is also important to underline the close co-operation between Greece and Italy and other southern countries in this regard and what this tells us about the significance of synergies in the post-Lisbon presidency

[14] «http://www.gr2014.eu/sites/default/files/PM%20Antonis%20Samaras%20on%20Greek%20EU%20Presidency%20Achieve
ments%20%20%20%20%20June%2016%202014-1.pdf».

[15] «http://www.ekathimerini.com/4dcgi/_w_articles_wsite1_1_19/07/2014_541531».

[16] See Hobolt's contribution to this volume.

© 2015 The Author(s) JCMS: Journal of Common Market Studies © 2015 John Wiley & Sons Ltd

system. Changes from the Lisbon Treaty might also partially explain external relations issues as the most obvious gap during the Greek presidency term. While presidency officials declared an early appetite to deal with policies such as enlargement, external issues were downplayed. This was also true for the Trio Presidency programme, which focused more on internal issues of the EU, which had become far more pressing given the eurozone crisis. But the institutional reforms brought by the Lisbon Treaty, such as the introduction of the High Representative post as a chair of the Foreign Affairs Council, also seem to have decreased the relevance and leverage of the rotating presidency in foreign policy. For example, the crisis in Ukraine did not attract the attention of the presidency, possibly because of the relatively close ties between Greece and Russia, and was dealt with more by the then High Representative Catherine Ashton and her team. But Lisbon Treaty reforms might have also saved the Greek 'face' in some respects. Dinan (2011) has argued that the permanent presidency of the European Council might be a much better solution than a rotating PM who faces troubles at home, and this can be certainly said for the Greek presidency and PM Samaras, who enjoyed very little popularity and was actually ousted a few months after the end of the Greek term.

Every presidency can be seen as an opportunity for a state to promote its credibility as an EU member. In the case of the fifth Greek presidency this was even more pressing, given how the status of the country had been undermined in recent years due to the economic crisis. As a result, and as with every presidency conclusion, the Greek assessment of its term was positive, suggesting that 'together, we've sailed further' (Greek Presidency, 2014) and that the country was 'back to normal'[17] and 'Europe works' too.[18] Previous Greek Presidencies have been assessed as having varied degrees of success (Blavoukos and Pagoulatos, 2003) and this fifth presidency seems to have done rather well as far as its programme is concerned, but not much in terms of changing the difficult situation of the country or indeed the EU in itself. Indeed, the months that followed disproved the presidency's conclusions in the most spectacular way. Not only did the eurosceptic flavour of the EP elections cast doubts over whether Europe really 'works', but fresh elections in Greece in early 2015 with the anti-austerity party Syriza forming the resultant government and its head-on conflict with EU partners revived speculation about 'Grexit' and undermined in the most obvious way the return of Greece to 'normality'. Only a few months after the conclusion of their 'common quest', the destination for both Greece and the EU remains alarmingly unknown.

References

Blavoukos, S. and Pagoulatos, G. (2003) 'A Medium Country's Middle-of-the-Road Success: The 2003 Greek Presidency of the European Union'. *South European Society and Politics*, Vol. 8, No. 3, pp. 147–64.

Council of the European Union (2014a) Council recommendation on a Quality Framework for Traineeships. Available at «https://www.consilium.europa.eu/uedocs/cms_data/docs/pressdata/en/lsa/141424.pdf». [Accessed on 23 April 2015]

Council of the European Union (2014b) European Union Maritime Strategy. Available at «http://ec.europa.eu/maritimeaffairs/policy/maritime-security/index_en.htm». [Accessed on 23 April 2015]

Dimitrakopoulos, D.G. and Passas, A.G. (2004) 'The Greek Presidency: In the Shadow of War'. *JCMS*, Vol. 42, No. s1, pp. 43–6.

[17] «http://www.euractiv.com/sections/eu-priorities-2020/greece-closes-eu-presidency-says-country-back-normal-303191».

[18] «http://www.euractiv.com/video/europe-works-says-greek-pm-antonis-samaras-307676».

© 2015 The Author(s) JCMS: Journal of Common Market Studies © 2015 John Wiley & Sons Ltd

Dinan, D. (2011) 'Governance and Institutions: Implementing the Lisbon Treaty in the Shadow of the Euro Crisis'. *JCMS*, Vol. 49, No. s1, pp. 103–21.

European Commission (2001) Eurobarometer, Report Number 55. Available at «http://ec.europa.eu/public_opinion/archives/eb/eb55/eb55_en.pdf». [Accessed on 23 April 2015]

European Commission (2014a) Standard Eurobarometer 82. Available at «http://ec.europa.eu/public_opinion/archives/eb/eb82/eb82_en.htm». [Accessed on 23 April 2015]

European Commission (2014b) Joint Communication to the European Parliament and the Council for an open and secure global maritime domain: elements for a European Union maritime security strategy. JOIN (2014) 9. Available at «http://eur-lex.europa.eu/legal-content/EN/TXT/?uri=CELEX:52014JC0009». [Accessed on 23 April 2015]

European Parliament (2014) Letter of the Committee on Economic and Monetary Affairs to the Greek Presidency of the EU. Available at «http://www.europarl.europa.eu/document/activities/cont/201401/20140116ATT77594/20140116ATT77594EN.pdf». [Accessed on 23 April 2015]

European Parliament and the Council (2014) Regulation (EU) no 656/2014 of the European Parliament and of the Council of establishing rules for the surveillance of the external sea borders in the context of operational cooperation coordinated by the European Agency for the Management of Operational Cooperation at the External Borders of the Member States of the European Union. Available at «http://eur-lex.europa.eu/legal-content/EN/TXT/?uri=uriserv:OJ.L_.2014.189.01.0093.01.ENG». [Accessed on 23 April 2015]

Greek Presidency (2014) Greek Presidency Scoreboard. Available at «http://www.gr2014.eu/sites/default/files/Scoreboard_New_Eng.pdf». [Accessed on 23 April 2015]

Hellenic Republic (2014) Deputy Prime Minister and Foreign Minister Venizelos' intervention at the European Parliament's Foreign Affairs Committee (AFET) regarding Maritime Security (Strasbourg, 14 April 2014). Available at «http://www.mfa.gr/en/current-affairs/top-story/deputy-prime-minister-and-foreign-minister-venizelos-intervention-at-the-european-parliaments-foreign-affairs-committee-afet-regarding-maritime-security-strasbourg-14-april-2014.html». [Accessed on 23 April 2013]

Howarth, D. and Quaglia, L. (2014) 'The Steep Road to European Banking Union: Constructing the Single Resolution Mechanism'. *JCMS*, Vol. 52, No. s1, pp. 125–40.

Laffan, B. (2014) 'In the Shadow of Austerity: Ireland's Seventh Presidency of the European Union'. *JCMS*, Vol. 52, No. s1, pp. 90–8.

Monar, J. (2014) 'Justice and Home Affairs'. *JCMS*, Vol. 52, No. s1, pp. 141–56.

Transparency International (2014) *'EU Presidency Anti-corruption Scorecard'*.

Vilpišauskas, R. (2014) 'Lithuania's EU Council Presidency: Negotiating Finances, Dealing with Geopolitics'. *JCMS*, Vol. 52, No. s1, pp. 99–108.

© 2015 The Author(s) JCMS: Journal of Common Market Studies © 2015 John Wiley & Sons Ltd

JCMS 2015 Volume 53 Annual Review pp. 83–92　　　　　　　　　　DOI: 10.1111/jcms.12273

Beyond the Telemachus complex: courses, discourses and the 2014 Italian Presidency of the Council of the European Union[*]

MAURIZIO CARBONE
University of Glasgow

Our generation has the duty of rediscovering itself as Telemachus and being worthy heirs of the [European Union's] founding fathers
(Matteo Renzi, Strasbourg, 2 July 2014)

Introduction

When Matteo Renzi appeared for the first time in the European Parliament in July 2014, he did not sound like Italy's Prime Minister presenting the priorities of the rotating presidency of the Council of the European Union (1 July–31 December 2014), but like someone who was proposing a new vision for a different Europe. In a speech loaded with passion and literary allusions, before an attentive audience, he urged Europe to 'find its soul again' and invited 'the current generation to rediscover itself as Telemachus', taking into account the lessons of the founding fathers while attempting to navigate autonomously.[1] Considering his ambitious reformist agenda at home and the extraordinary performance of his *Partito Democratico* (Democratic Party, PD) at the May 2014 European elections, he raised hopes significantly, in spite of some potential drawbacks: first, about the transferability of his leadership style to the European context;[2] second, about what a post-Lisbon Treaty rotating presidency could actually achieve in six months. In fact, this contribution demonstrates that the rather high expectations were largely unmet: the 2014 Italian presidency may have at best contributed to partially changing the discourse, but it failed to alter the course of the European Union. Renzi's assertiveness produced results at home, at least in terms of popular support, but did not have the same effect at the EU level, where his inexperience showed on many occasions and even backfired.

[*] I am very grateful to the *JCMS Annual Review* editors, Nathaniel Copsey and Tim Haughton, and to Mark Gilbert, Erik Jones, Gianfranco Pasquino, Simona Piattoni and Luca Verzichelli for their valuable comments. This article was completed during my research leave (January–May 2015) spent at the University of Bologna and at the Johns Hopkins University Bologna Center, for which I want to thank respectively Sonia Lucarelli and Filippo Andreatta, and Mike Plummer.
[1] *Corriere della Sera*, 4 July 2014. Renzi took inspiration from a book published by psychologist Massimo Recalcati (2013), who argued that, contrary to Oedipus, Telemachus waited for his father's return not to challenge him but to be supported in re-establishing order in Ithaca.
[2] Renzi was dubbed *rottamatore* ('scrapper') for the aggressive methods he used in his attempts to transform Italy's economic and political institutions and get rid of existing political elites. On his leadership style and an early assessment of his government see Bordignon (2014) and CIRCaP (2015).

© 2015 The Author(s) JCMS: Journal of Common Market Studies © 2015 John Wiley & Sons Ltd, 9600 Garsington Road, Oxford OX4 2DQ, UK and 350 Main Street, Malden, MA 02148, USA

I. Change Italy to Change Europe?

Existing analyses of the presidency of the Council of the European Union tend to focus on two broad, interlinked issues. A first group of scholars is interested in the behaviour of different Member States when they are at the helm of the EU, and more specifically whether they abuse their privileged position. The general assumption is that they should seek to promote the common good, in line with the accepted norms of neutrality, consensus-building and effectiveness; moreover, the changes introduced by the Treaty of Lisbon, particularly the institutionalization of the trio, have placed more constraints on their freedom (Niemann and Mak, 2010; Alexandrova and Timmermans, 2013). Nevertheless, and this is the alternative view, rotating presidencies may still seek to promote their national priorities (Elgström, 2003; Tallberg, 2004). This also entails that initiatives could be framed and presented as European problems, benefiting the whole EU rather than a part (Alexandrova and Timmermans, 2013). To achieve their goals, national governments often seek to turn the EU presidency into a national concern and invoke a sort of national truce with domestic opposition forces (Johansson *et al*., 2012). A second strand of the literature looks at the performance of rotating presidencies. The focus in this case is on their ability to implement the programme, deal with unexpected events and crises and achieve consensual agreements. With the functions of business manager and mediator becoming more prominent, the room for launching new political initiatives seems greatly diminished (Quaglia and Moxon-Browne, 2006), though not completely absent.

In fact, Matteo Renzi, who in February 2014 had replaced Enrico Letta in a sort of old-style party coup to become Italy's youngest Prime Minister ever, conceived the rotating presidency primarily as a powerful platform to change the course of the EU. But to do so, he had first to establish his legitimacy domestically and then enhance his credibility internationally.[3] Thus, as he took over as Italy's Prime Minister, he announced a number of institutional and economic reforms, to be launched within 100 days, with the aim of stimulating an economy struggling to emerge from a decade of zero nominal growth (Carbone and Newell, 2013). Rather than using the EU as a lever (i.e. *vincolo esterno*) to pass unpopular reforms, as done by previous leaders (Fabbrini and Piattoni, 2008; Carbone and Quaglia, 2011), he maintained that Italy necessitated structural reforms because it was in the best interest of its citizens. This ambitious agenda paid off at the May 2014 elections for the European Parliament, where the ruling PD took 40.8 percent of votes – the best result ever for a party of the Italian centre-left. This remarkable result, in counter-tendency with most countries where eurosceptic parties had recorded significant gains, not only enhanced his legitimacy at home but also boosted his profile internationally, making him the rising star of the centre-left in Europe and possibly the right person to challenge the soft hegemony of Angela Merkel (Nicolaidis, 2014).

Initially, most of Renzi's attention was absorbed by institutional reforms, whereas economic reforms were slow to appear on the public agenda. Eventually, when it became clear that the economic indicators were not improving and the country was slipping into recession, the Renzi government passed a controversial reform of the sclerotic labour market, making it easier for companies to hire and fire people, and adopted new

---

[3] *La Stampa*, 4 July 2014; *Corriere della Sera*, 9 August 2014.

© 2015 The Author(s) JCMS: Journal of Common Market Studies © 2015 John Wiley & Sons Ltd

expansionary measures, including a diminution of social security contributions for newly hired workers, a reduction of local business taxes and a permanent bonus for low-income families – measures compensated by cuts in government spending, particularly at the sub-national level.[4] The new deadline for completing the reform package, extended from 100 to 1000 days, reflected the ambition of the new agenda but was also an indication of the fact that Renzi had underestimated the size of the task, particularly in terms of the resistance of political parties (including his own) and trade unions (Carbone and Newell, 2013). It was certainly a response to criticism that he was more adept at announcing than passing reforms. The adoption of these measures, however, came halfway through the European semester, probably when he had already squandered much political capital, as we will see in the next section.[5]

II. A Fresh Start for Europe?

The Italian presidency commenced on 1 July 2014 but had received a significant boost from the European Council held at the end of June, under the Greek presidency. In that context, together with France and other countries run by centre-left leaders, Italy obtained a promise for more flexibility in the EU's Stability and Growth Pact (SGP) in return for its support of Jean-Claude Junker's nomination as president of the European Commission.[6] Flexibility figured prominently in Renzi's speech before the European Parliament on 2 July 2014, where he stated that both the economic crisis and the ensuing austerity measures had generated a general disillusionment with the European project – and the rise of anti-EU parties were to bear testimony to this. Renzi chose not to present the priorities of the Italian presidency, dubbed 'A fresh start for Europe' (Italia, 2014a), but it was clear that attention would focus on economic growth, migration and external relations.[7] Meanwhile, a major stumbling block had emerged: the complicated institutional transition.[8]

Controversies Over Top Posts

With the selection of Juncker as president of the European Commission, two other senior posts needed to be filled: president of the European Council and High Representative for Foreign Affairs and Security Policy. A solution was not easy, in that geographical, gender, party and small–large state balances would have to be taken into account. The failure to reach a compromise at the 16 July 2014 European Council not only threw into disarray plans to complete the composition of the European Commission by mid-August, but also represented a major blow for Italy.[9] Renzi's initial proposal of Federica Mogherini, then Italian minister for foreign affairs, met significant resistance from various leaders, mainly in central and eastern Europe, who thought she was inexperienced and too lenient towards Russia.[10] It may be possible that France's support for Mogherini in return for Italy's

---

[4] *Financial Times*, 9 August 2014; *International New York Times*, 19 November 2014.
[5] *The Economist*, 13 September 2014; *Il Sole-24 Ore*, 17 September 2014.
[6] *The Guardian*, 17 June 2014; *European Voice*, 3 July 2014.
[7] *Euractiv*, 3 July 2014; *Corriere della Sera*, 3 July 2014; *Il Sole-24 Ore*, 3 July 2014.
[8] See Dinan's contribution to this volume.
[9] *European Voice*, 17 July 2014; 18 September 2014.
[10] *The Guardian*, 18 July 2014.

© 2015 The Author(s) JCMS: Journal of Common Market Studies © 2015 John Wiley & Sons Ltd

support for their finance minister Pierre Moscovici's nomination as a commissioner helped, yet the solution to the impasse was primarily due to the deal-making skills of Herman Van Rompuy and the logics of the grand coalition. The emergence of Donald Tusk as candidate for president of the European Council, endorsed by the UK and Germany,[11] was sufficient to both relax opposition against Mogherini and guarantee the co-operation of the European People's Party (EPP) with the Party of European Socialists (PES).[12] Tusk and Mogherini were officially nominated at the European Council on 30 August 2014, so that the institutional transition could be completed on time. Claiming that Mogherini's appointment represented a 'sad day for Europe'[13] is certainly an exaggeration, yet the campaign to place her at the top of Europe's external relations portfolio irritated many leaders in Europe, who saw in it Renzi's bid for an assertion of prestige in the EU.[14]

Paths to Economic Growth

The central focus of the Italian presidency was economic growth.[15] In opposition to the German-dominated narrative of fiscal rectitude and austerity, Italy positioned itself as the champion of a flexible interpretation of the Stability and Growth Pact, in a way that could encourage public investment: 'without stability there is no growth, and without growth there is no stability' was the refrain heard on many occasions. The view was that EU Member States should be given some leeway if they made structural reforms in areas such as pensions, health care, and workers' rights. Yet Italy's proposal of a golden rule excluding, in part or in full, money spent for growth-enhancing purposes from deficit calculations failed to gain support.[16] The European Fund for Strategic Investment (EFSI), presented by Juncker and briefly discussed at the European Council of 18 December 2014, was claimed as the most tangible result of the Italian presidency. Building on €21 billion in EU seed money (€16 billion from the EU's budget and €5 billion from the European Investment Bank) that should allow the EIB to raise funds in private capital markets to be then invested in high-risk and unfunded projects worth an estimated €315 billion, the EFSI received mixed reactions: for some it was 'an ambitious and new way to boost… investment without creating new debt'; for others it looked more like 'a conjuring trick than a credible financial engineering operation'.[17] Where Italy achieved more concrete results is on taxation and banking issues: automatic exchange of information between tax authorities must include more forms of income such as share dividends and insurance payments; new amendments to the parent-subsidiary directive were adopted to close tax loopholes exploited by multinationals; detailed rules governing the EU's bank resolution mechanism, with France and German banks paying the bulk of the contributions to the resolution fund, were agreed upon; inter-change fees for credit and debit cards were capped; and a deal on combating money laundering was signed.[18]

[11] *Financial Times*, 1 September 2014.
[12] *Financial Times*, 27 August 2014; *European Voice*, 4 September 2014.
[13] *Le Monde*, 28 August 2014.
[14] *EUobserver*, 17 July 2014; *Corriere della Sera*, 9 August 2014.
[15] See Hobolt's contribution to this volume.
[16] *International New York Times*, 5 July 2014; *Il Sole-24 Ore*, 5 January 2015.
[17] *Financial Times*, 1 December *2014*; *La Stampa*, 19 December 2014. See also *Financial Times*, 25 November 2014; 26 November 2014.
[18] *European Voice*, 29 December 2014.

Risks of International Migration

Following the October 2013 Lampedusa tragedy (when more than 300 people drowned), Italy launched Mare Nostrum, a search-and-rescue operation patrolling the Mediterranean for ships in distress, which in the space of a year rescued an estimated 150,000 people.[19] Nevertheless, this operation became the object of daily tensions, with opposition parties pointing to the high financial cost borne solely by Italy (€9 million a month) and the potential unintended consequences (arrivals soared since its adoption, the view being that migrants would embark on difficult trips knowing that they would be saved at sea). Various Italian governments had tried, unsuccessfully, to persuade other Member States of the need to take a common approach and share the burden of increased migration flows.[20] The 2014 rotating presidency was seen as a propitious opportunity to change the existing state of affairs: to use Renzi's words, a 'Europe that … turns its back when there are dead bodies in the sea cannot call itself civilised'.[21] The adoption of Joint Operation Triton in August 2014, to be co-ordinated by Frontex, was enthusiastically saluted in official discourse as a success of the Italian presidency (Sannino, 2015). A number of doubts, however, were raised across Europe, particularly by human rights organizations, when it became clear that Mare Nostrum would be simultaneously terminated. In fact, not only was Triton's budget significantly lower (about €3 million a month) than Mare Nostrum's, but its scope was limited to patrolling the sea only up to 30 miles from the coast – the idea was to place more burden on North African countries for operations in their own waters.[22] Pessimistic predictions about increased risks for migrants to perish at sea eventually became a reality when, in the early months of 2015, it became known that thousands of people had died while attempting to sail to Italy.[23]

Challenges in External Relations

A number of important debates took place, and some decisions were made, in the second part of 2014, but only in a few cases is it possible to see Italy's mark on them. In the case of the Russia–Ukraine crisis, the Italian presidency was not perceived as a neutral player seeking compromise solutions – with the exception of a meeting between Vladimir Putin and Petro Poroshenko facilitated in the context of the ASEM summit in Milan on 17 October – but more as attempting to block escalations of sanctions against Russia.[24] The reason behind this behaviour – at least for detractors – was that of seeking to promote its national interest in the energy and agriculture sectors, though not very successfully. In fact, no additional funding was agreed for those exporters, particularly from Italy, who were penalized by sanctions against Russia; moreover, Putin announced that the South Stream pipeline, strongly supported by all Italian governments since its conception, would not be built.[25]

---

[19] See Monar's contribution to this and the previous volume of the *Annual Review*.

[20] *Financial Times*, 10 July 2014; *European Voice*, 23 October 2014.

[21] *Financial Times*, 9 July 2014.

[22] *The Guardian*, 27 October 2014; 31 October 2014; *International New York Times*, 5 November 2014.

[23] *La Stampa*, 3 January 2015.

[24] *Financial Times*, 14 July 2014; *Corriere della Sera*, 19 December 2014; *Il Fatto Quotidiano*, 11 Janaury 2015.

[25] *European Voice*, 29 December 2014. Limited results were also achieved in the area of external trade: the Italian presidency consistently stressed the importance of the Transatlantic Trade and Investment Partnership (TTIP), yet it managed to obtain only the declassification of documents, rather than acceleration in the negotiations (*Euractiv*, 9 October 2014; *Financial Times*, 24 November 2014; *Il Fatto Quotidiano*, 11 January 2015).

© 2015 The Author(s) JCMS: Journal of Common Market Studies © 2015 John Wiley & Sons Ltd

By contrast, the Italian presidency could claim some success in the adoption of a common position on the climate change and energy package ahead of the international summit held in Peru in December 2014. Following tense negotiations with concessions made to several countries (e.g. Denmark, Ireland, Poland, Spain and the UK), EU leaders pledged to reduce carbon emissions and increase energy efficiency and sustainability, but also inserted a controversial clause to revert to the issue after the UN summit in Paris in March 2015.[26] Moroever, Italy was instrumental in the compromise found between the Council and the European Parliament on genetically modified organisms (GMOs): Member States would have the right to ban GMOs in their own territory while maintaining an EU-wide system of authorization (Battistella, 2015).[27] But one of the most important blows to the Italian presidency was the failure to reach an agreement on making 'made-in' labelling mandatory. The European Parliament had already endorsed a proposal stating that all products should reveal their country of origin, which would result in improved product safety and reduced counterfeiting. By contrast, EU Member States were divided, with countries in southern Europe (e.g. France, Italy and Spain) lamenting diminished export opportunities for their manufacturers, and countries in northern Europe (e.g. UK and Germany) complaining about a potential loss of profit for large retailers. No agreement was reached, and for that the Renzi government was harshly criticized at home.[28]

III. A Missed Opportunity?

Assessing the performance of any rotating presidency is not an easy task, not least because it is difficult to establish fair terms of comparison. First, if we look at initial expectations, the outcome looks rather thin, with no significant political initiative being launched. Renzi himself conceded that the Italian presidency should not be evaluated only in terms of concrete results, but against the (alleged) paradigm shift on economic growth: the focus of the European Union would no longer be solely on fiscal discipline, but also on investment and employment. But if for undersecretary Gozi (2014, p. 1) this change of discourse 'represented the most important achievement of the Italian Presidency', for more neutral observers 'the sacrosanct battles on economic growth, employment and the flexibility of the European rules and pacts have been taken no further than a noisy festival of words'.[29] Second, if we compare it with previous Italian experiences in the same position, the 2014 presidency is not an outlier. It would probably fare worse in relation to the ones run by the Craxi government in 1985 and the Andreotti government in 1990, which respectively played a pivotal role in the creation of the single market and set the foundations for the creation of the single currency. It would certainly fare better in relation to the one run by the Berlusconi government in 2003, which failed to achieve a compromise on the Reform Treaty and took positions which were often at odds with all other

---

[26] *European Voice*, 29 October 2014; *Euractiv*, 15 December 2014.

[27] *European Voice*, 27 October 2014. A case where the Italian presidency performed well was in facilitating an agreement to regulate the use of plastic bags: Commissioner Timmermans indicated that the European Commission would withdraw its proposal in response to diffuse resistance, but eventually was obliged to back down and admitted that he could not stand on the way for a compromise.

[28] *Il Sole-24 Ore*, 5 December 2014.

[29] *Il Sole-24 Ore*, 5 January 2015.

© 2015 The Author(s) JCMS: Journal of Common Market Studies © 2015 John Wiley & Sons Ltd

EU Member States (Fabbrini and Piattoni, 2008; Quaglia and Moxon-Browne, 2006). Third, if we look at its behaviour in office, it sought to elevate some national priorities to the EU level, for instance on economic governance and migration (more successfully) and on agriculture and 'made-in' labelling (less successfully). In the case of Mogherini's appointment, Renzi used a vast amount of political capital, to no obvious advantage for Italy (Gramaglia, 2014).[30] Interestingly, the UK and France were given two portfolios in the new European Commission – respectively, financial services and economic affairs – which seemed more in line with their national priorities.[31]

Thus, had Renzi not raised the expectation bar so high, the Italian presidency would probably have received similar ratings to the ones that preceded it, particularly those following the adoption of the Treaty of Lisbon: 'with neither praise nor blame'.[32] While at the beginning his intention was to use the rotating presidency as a platform to change Europe, at the end Renzi conceded that 'Italy's contribution to the European Union is not here [as holder of the rotating presidency] but at home'.[33]

There may be some extenuating circumstances for this mediocre performance. The first concerns the fact that it fell at the intersection of a period characterized by power struggles and bad timing – though periods of fluidity provide capable leaders with opportunities to shape agendas. For several weeks the Italian presidency did not have interlocutors because of the prolonged institutional transition. Moreover, it had to face the redefinition of alliances between parties within the European Parliament and, probably more significantly, a number of tensions between EU Member States: some involved the emphasis on flexibility over austerity; others concerned the degree of Europeanization in migration policy; yet others related to the more or less antagonistic stance to take against Russia.

The second extenuating circumstance refers to the consequence of the installation of a new executive in Italy a few months before the start of the European semester. In fact, Renzi decided to change the strategy designed by his predecessor – who had transformed the weak Ministry of Community Policies (responsible solely for the downloading phase in Europeanization processes) into a more powerful Ministry for European Affairs (also in charge of the uploading phase) (Bindi, 2011) – with the view to maintaining tight control over the EU file, to be handled by an undersecretary directly from the Prime Minister's Office. This centralization of power – reinforced by the fact that prominent ministers for Foreign Policy (Emma Bonino) and for European Affairs (Enzo Moavero Milanesi) were replaced with more loyal figures (respectively Federica Mogherini, eventually substituted with Paolo Gentiloni, and Sandro Gozi) – made co-operation between Rome and the Italian Representation in Brussels less than smooth.

It could thus be claimed that in the second semester of 2014 there were two Italian presidencies at work. On the one hand there was the 'political' presidency (personified by Renzi and Gozi), which was colourful and aggressive. It was characterized by a

---

[30] Some have judged this outcome more positively, at least from Renzi's perspective. First, he could sell it as a triumph domestically, claiming that he secured one of the most prestigious posts in the EU. Second, he would be free to battle with the European Commission on issues more directly linked to Italy's national interest, leaving Italy's appointee out of these attacks (*The Guardian*, 1 September 2014).

[31] *Il Sole-24 Ore*, 26 July 2014.

[32] *Corriere della Sera*, 19 December 2014; *Il Sole-24 Ore*, 5 January 2015.

[33] *La Stampa*, 14 January 2015.

© 2015 The Author(s) JCMS: Journal of Common Market Studies © 2015 John Wiley & Sons Ltd

muscular attitude towards the European Commission, considered excessively bureaucratic and too powerful (Bonvicini, 2014),[34] and by an ambiguous preference for an intergovernmental European Union: it was often stated that important decisions must remain in the hands of national leaders, yet minimal attempts were made to team up with other EU Member States (with the occasional exception of France).[35] Incidentally, Italy was the first of a trio which included Latvia and Luxembourg, but it never sought to significantly engage with them in the definition of priorities (nor did it feel constrained by it). On the other hand, there was the 'bureaucratic' presidency (co-ordinated by the Italian Representation in Brussels, particularly Ambassador Stefano Sannino), which was grey and defensive: for some it performed routine duties impeccably,[36] for others it often improvised and failed to provide direction.[37] Interestingly, one of the most challenging tasks for the 'bureaucratic' presidency was to cover for the attacks launched by the 'political' presidency on EU supranational institutions. Paradoxically, the main challenge faced by the Italian presidency may have been Renzi himself: certain daredevil methods that appeared to work domestically did not seem appropriate in the EU context.[38]

Conclusion

When Matteo Renzi returned to the European Parliament in January 2015 to review the achievements of the Italian presidency (Italia, 2014b) before a distracted and almost empty room (with the exception of highly critical opposition parties from Italy), he soberly acknowledged that changing the course of the European Union proved more complicated than he had expected. Of course it is an exaggeration to conclude, using an image from one of *The Economist*'s cover pages, that Renzi's – and Italy's – contribution to the sinking EU boat was just that of eating an ice-cream,[39] but it cannot be denied that results were far below expectations. The personality of the Prime Minister may obfuscate evaluations. In fact, little space in public debates was given to specific policy areas – for instance, environmental policy, where a number of successes could be claimed. While Renzi's assertiveness has been considered an asset in domestic politics, it did not work that well in Europe, where achieving a positive outcome requires the formulation of a focused agenda and the patience to engage with other EU governments and supranational institutions in a constructive dialogue. From the EU's point of view, the main achievement of the Italian presidency was that of partially changing the discourse on economic growth, with more focus on flexibility and investment than only austerity. Nevertheless,

---

[34] One of the most visible examples is Renzi's decision to make public a strictly confidential letter sent by the European Commission demanding an explanation for Italy's 2015 budget (together with a threat to reveal the costs of European institutions). For Renzi it was a response to citizen demands for transparency, while for President Barroso it risked further undermining trust in the European Union (*European Voice*, 23 October 2014; *The Economist*, 26 October 2014). The reaction of President Junker should be read along similar lines: he responded to Renzi's harsh criticism of the European Commission by saying that he was not 'the chairman of a gang of bureaucrats' (*EUobserver*, 5 November 2014).

[35] This could have been a deliberate choice. In the words of the minister of the economy Pier Carlo Padoan: 'I am opposed to strategies based on the concept of an alliance with this or that EU Member States: an alliance with someone is always also an alliance against someone else. Instead, we need to move forward in a united way, patiently and tenaciously building conditions of mutual trust'. *Il Sole-24 Ore*, 28 December 2014.

[36] *Il Sole-24 Ore*, 5 January 2015.

[37] *L'Espresso*, 15 January 2015.

[38] *La Stampa*, 9 July 2014.

[39] *The Economist*, 30 August 2014.

© 2015 The Author(s) JCMS: Journal of Common Market Studies © 2015 John Wiley & Sons Ltd

it should be noted that this partial shift had already started in the first semester of 2014 under the Greek presidency,[40] and that concrete results (for instance, the implementation of the Juncker plan) would start materializing only in 2015. From Italy's perspective, the two alleged successes, most notably the appointment of Federica Mogherini as High Representative for Foreign and Security Policy and the adoption of Triton to control migration flows, have in retrospect proven questionable. In sum, in its six-month term as president of the Council of Ministers of the European Union, Italy did not engage reverse gear because it was not able to engage forward gear – but at least the car did not veer into the oncoming traffic or off the road.[41]

References

Alexandrova, P. and Timmermans, A. (2013) 'National Interest versus the Common Good: The Presidency in European Council Agenda Setting'. *European Journal of Political Research*, Vol. 52, pp. 316–38.

Battistella, D. (2015) 'Ambiente e clima, i risultati del Semestre di Presidenza italiana'. *Europae*, 4 January.

Bindi, F. (2011) *Italy and the European Union* (Washington: Brookings Institutions Press).

Bonvicini, G. (2014) 'Semestre breve, sfortunato e limitato'. *AffarInternazionali*, 26 December.

Bordignon, F. (2014) 'Matteo Renzi: A "Leftist Berlusconi" for the Italian Democratic Party?'. *South European Society and Politics*, Vol. 19, No. 1, pp. 1–23.

Carbone, M. and Newell, J.L. (2013) 'Unlocking Italy?'. *Contemporary Italian Politics*, Vol. 7, No. 3, pp. 203–4.

Carbone, M. and Quaglia, L. (2011) 'Italy and the EU: Seeking Visibility, Fearing Exclusion'. In M. Carbone (ed.), *Italy in the Post-Cold War Order: Adaptation, Bipartisanship, Visibility* (Lanham: Lexington Books).

CIRCaP (2015). 'Buon compleanno, Renzi – il primo anno di governo – Rapporto CIRCaP sul Governo Italiano'. Research note, University of Siena, 20 February.

Elgström, O. (ed.) (2003) *European Union Council Presidencies. A Comparative Perspective*, London: Routledge.

Fabbrini, S. and Piattoni, S. (eds) (2008) *Italy in the EU. Redefining National Interest in a Compound Polity* (Lanham: Rowman & Littlefield).

Gozi, S. (2014) 'I frutti del semestre di presidenza europea'. *AffarInternazionali*, 26 December.

Gramaglia, G. (2014) 'Renzi vince, l'Europa chissà'. *AffarInternazionali*, 31 August.

Italia (2014a). Europe: a Fresh Start, Programme of the Italian Presidency of the Council of the European Union, 1 July to 31 December 2014. Available at «italia2014.eu».

Italia (2014b). Six-month Italian Presidency of the Council of the European Union: Summary Report (July-December 2014). Available at «italia2014.eu».

Johansson, K.M., Langdal, F. and von Sydow, G. (2012) 'The Domestic Politics of European Union Presidencies: The Case of Sweden'. *Government and Opposition*, Vol. 47, No. 2, pp. 206–27.

Nicolaidis, K. (2014) 'Merkel and Renzi are the partners who can reshape Europe'. *Financial Times*, 3 July.

[40] See Kyris's contribution to this volume.

[41] *Il Sole-24 Ore*, 5 January 2015.

© 2015 The Author(s) JCMS: Journal of Common Market Studies © 2015 John Wiley & Sons Ltd

Niemann, A. and Mak, J. (2010) '(How) Do Norms Guide Presidency Behaviour in EU Negotiations?'. *Journal of European Public Policy*, Vol. 17, No. 5, pp. 727–42.

Quaglia, L. and Moxon-Browne, E. (2006) 'What Makes a Good EU Presidency? Italy and Ireland Compared'. *JCMS*, Vol. 44, No. 2, pp. 349–68.

Recalcati, M. (2013) *Il complesso di Telemaco. Genitori e figli dopo il tramonto del padre*. Bologna: Feltrinelli.

Sannino, S. (2015) 'Gli otto punti di forza del semestre italiano', *ISPI Commentary*, 12 Janaury.

Tallberg, J. (2004) 'The Power of the Presidency: Brokerage, Efficiency and Distribution in EU Negotiations'. *JCMS*, Vol. 42, No. 5, pp. 999–1022.

© 2015 The Author(s) JCMS: Journal of Common Market Studies © 2015 John Wiley & Sons Ltd

JCMS 2015 Volume 53 Annual Review pp. 93–107
DOI: 10.1111/jcms.12262

Governance and Institutions: The Year of the *Spitzenkandidaten*

DESMOND DINAN
George Mason University

Introduction

In terms of institutional change, the year 2014 resembled that of 2009. Elections for the European Parliament (EP) took place in May 2014 and June 2009, as they had in each of the previous five years since the introduction of direct elections in 1979. The beginning of a new parliamentary term, including a turnover in membership, a reconfiguration of political groups and important leadership changes, is a major event in the EU's institutional existence. So, too, is the appointment of a new Commission, which follows the European Parliament elections. For the first time, under the terms of the newly implemented Lisbon Treaty, in 2009 the EU acquired a standing President of the European Council and a High Representative of the Union for Foreign Affairs and Security Policy. The election of a new European Council President and the appointment of a new High Representative in 2014, successors to the inaugural officeholders, were also noteworthy events.

Yet the similarities between 2009 and 2014 obscure a number of profound differences in the political life of the EU. By 2014, the eurozone crisis had exacted a high toll (Copsey, 2015). The EU seemed more fractious than ever, with yawning gaps between the euro-ins, pre-ins, and forever-outs; between net contributors to and net beneficiaries from the budget; between governments insisting on strict austerity in return for financial assistance and governments reeling from severe cutbacks; between a seemingly hegemonic Germany and the other countries; between an increasingly prickly United Kingdom and its partners. As a result of economic and political pressures between 2009 and 2014, the EU had assumed a different character. Economic governance was stronger,[1] but political bonds were weaker. The Community method seemed in retreat and intergovernmentalism in the ascendant. Institutionally, the European Council had come to the fore.

The events of 2009–14 were bound to affect public attitudes towards the EU. Disillusionment with national governments, let alone with supranational governance, inevitably soared. Anti-establishment political parties flourished, united across the political spectrum in their opposition to the EU. The circumstances could hardly have been worse for the elections of 2014, especially as EU leaders desperately wanted to reverse the continuous decline in voter turnout since 1979. This time (2014) risked being different in ways that could further damage the European Parliament's image. The European Parliament's leadership resolved to make the 2014 elections different instead in ways that would challenge euroscepticism and increase voter turnout (European Parliament, 2014a).[2] As noted in last year's *Annual Review* (Dinan, 2014), the main plank of their

---

[1] See Hodson's contribution to this and previous volumes of the *Annual Review*.

[2] For more on the elections see Hobolt's contribution to this volume.

© 2015 The Author(s) JCMS: Journal of Common Market Studies © 2015 John Wiley & Sons Ltd, 9600 Garsington Road, Oxford OX4 2DQ, UK and 350 Main Street, Malden, MA 02148, USA

approach was to link the conduct and outcome of the European Parliament elections to the election of the Commission President. Based on its interpretation of the relevant provisions of the Lisbon Treaty, the European Parliament insisted that the European Council nominate as Commission President the candidate of the European political party that won the largest number of seats in the elections, or of a coalition of parties that could command a majority in the European Parliament. The European Parliament would then elect that candidate as Commission President.

The European Parliament's goal was not just to increase voter turnout. More profoundly, the European Parliament sought to strengthen the legitimacy of the EU by strengthening the legitimacy of the Commission President and, indirectly, that of the entire Commission. The European Parliament also sought to bolster parliamentarianism in the EU by tying the European Parliament elections to the election of the Commission President, the head of the EU's executive body. In sum, the European Parliament was attempting to inject an additional dose of partisan politics into the EU as a means of tackling the chronic democratic deficit, something which scholars such as Simon Hix had long advocated (Hix, 2008). In the process, the European Parliament confronted the European Council, which hitherto had a free hand in nominating the Commission President.

How different would things really be this time? Would the turnout in the European Parliament elections finally increase? Would the European Council acquiesce in the European Parliament's ploy? If so, would the Commission and the Commission President enjoy greater political legitimacy? Would the office of the Commission presidency, and the new Commission President, be strengthened? How consequential would the institutional innovation prove to be? These were key questions for EU governance in 2014, though definitive answers to most of them would not be known for some time.

1. Electing the Commission President

Most of the European political parties chose their candidates for Commission President in early 2014. European Parliament President Martin Schulz, a main architect of what came to be called the *Spitzenkandidaten* (lead candidate) procedure, was elected unopposed by the Party of European Socialists (PES) (PES, 2014). The European People's Party (EPP) elected Jean-Claude Juncker, the former Prime Minister (PM) of Luxembourg, who defeated the only other contender, Internal Market Commissioner Michel Barnier, by 382 to 245 votes (EPP, 2014). The Alliance of Liberals and Democrats for Europe (ALDE) struggled to choose between former Belgian PM Guy Verhofstadt, leader of the party group in the European Parliament, and Commissioner Olli Rehn. Verhofstadt and Rehn finally reached an accord, which the party endorsed, whereby 'the two candidates [would] jointly lead the campaign, on an equal footing ... [but] Verhofstadt [would] be the ALDE Party's candidate for Commission President ...' (ALDE, 2014a, 2014b). With Schulz having being elected unopposed and Rehn and Verhofstadt having struck a deal, the EPP seized the moral high ground, claiming that 'In nominating [its] candidate ... the EPP was the only major European political party to have implemented a process which was open, transparent, competitive and democratic' (EPP, 2014).

Thus began a political campaign unprecedented in the history of the EU. Picking up steam in April and May, the *Spitzenkandidaten* crisscrossed Europe, giving interviews, attending rallies, buttonholing pedestrians and participating in a number of televised (and webcast) debates. Given that the EPP and the PES were far ahead of ALDE in

© 2015 The Author(s) JCMS: Journal of Common Market Studies © 2015 John Wiley & Sons Ltd, 9600 Garsington Road, Oxford OX4 2DQ, UK and 350 Main Street, Malden, MA 02148, USA

the aggregate of seats in the national parliaments and in the European Parliament, the campaign boiled down to a contest between Juncker and Schulz. 'Let's be clear about this', Juncker declared in mid-March, 'one of us will get the job'.[3]

It remained uncertain whether the European Council would go along with Juncker's assessment. In the meantime, the *Spitzenkandidaten* faced the rigours of an EU-wide campaign, with all of its geographical, cultural and linguistic challenges:

> One of the biggest difficulties facing both Schulz and Juncker is boosting their profile across the bloc. That entails ... holding impassioned speeches in foreign languages. ... Juncker visited 32 cities in 18 EU countries on his two-month-long campaign trail, from Helsinki to Madrid, Cyprus to Ireland. He gave 27 press conferences and over 300 interviews. Most of the time, he traveled in a blue bus emblazoned with a 'Juncker for President' slogan but covered the longer distances in a chartered plane ... Schulz had an even busier schedule. The campaign proved to be a journey through European cultures that must on occasion have left the candidates not entirely sure in which city they'd woken up. ....'[4]

The *Spitzenkandidaten* were conspicuous by their absence in one big Member State: the UK. Under PM David Cameron's leadership, the Conservative Party had left the EPP in 2009, forming instead the eurosceptic European Conservatives and Reformists group. Accordingly, Juncker had little incentive to campaign in Britain. Although the Labour Party belonged to the PES, for domestic political reasons party leader Ed Miliband did not support the euro-federalist Schulz, who was not welcome in the UK either. Here was another example of British exceptionalism.

Spirited though it was, the campaign failed to excite public opinion throughout the EU. The European Parliament elections continued to be organized and waged largely along national lines. Only in Germany did the *Spitzenkandidaten* seem to generate much interest, perhaps because of Schulz's prominence in Germany's Social Democratic Party (SPD) and Juncker's frequent media appearances there over the years, especially since the onset of the eurozone crisis. The two leading candidates had two lively debates on German television in the fortnight before the elections, broadcast at prime time. They sparred over prescriptions for economic growth and the social cost of austerity, without breaking with the German-inspired orthodoxy of fiscal rectitude in response to mounting public debts. Schulz took aim at Luxembourg's extravagant use of tax breaks to attract international business, a practice that flourished under Juncker's long premiership.

None of this seemed to affect voter behaviour or turnout in any significant way. In elections marked by a decline in overall support for the three centrist parties, the EPP's share of the vote dropped from 36 per cent in 2009 to 29.4 per cent, which nonetheless gave the EPP more seats (221) than the PES (191), whose percentage of the vote held steady (25.4 per cent). The biggest disappointment for the European Parliament's leadership was that voter turnout again declined, however slightly, from 43 per cent in 2009 to 42.6 per cent (European Parliament, 2014b). Whatever else, the *Spitzenkandidaten* procedure had failed to bring more voters to the polls, proving Schulz wrong when he declared confidently in mid-March that the '[e]lection turnout will increase. The competition between myself and Juncker will help to ensure that'.[5]

---

[3] *Spiegel International*, 19 March 2014.
[4] *Spiegel International*, 20 May 2014.
[5] *Spiegel International*, 19 March 2014.

© 2015 The Author(s) JCMS: Journal of Common Market Studies © 2015 John Wiley & Sons Ltd, 9600 Garsington Road, Oxford OX4 2DQ, UK and 350 Main Street, Malden, MA 02148, USA

It was the European Council's prerogative to nominate the Commission President, 'taking into account the elections to the European Parliament' (Treaty on European Union, Article 17.7). Nominating the Commission President has never been easy for national leaders. Verhofstadt, the ALDE candidate, had himself been a victim, in 2004, of bickering within the European Council over who would become President, when UK PM Tony Blair blocked his candidacy. Juncker had been mentioned at the time as a possible candidate, but had taken his hat out of the ring, preferring to remain in Luxembourg. Though he was confident that otherwise he could have become Commission President, Juncker might also have been blocked by Blair or another national leader. In the event, José Manuel Barroso got the job.

Of the national leaders, Cameron was the most obdurate in opposing Juncker and the *Spitzenkandidaten* procedure. Though ostensibly both Cameron and Juncker belonged to the centre-right, Juncker was still to the left of Cameron. More to the point, Juncker's ardent Euro-federalism was anathema to Cameron (Copsey and Haughton, 2014). With the UK Independence Party gaining ground at home, supporting Juncker could have cost Cameron and the Conservatives dearly. Demonizing Juncker, by contrast, was an easy way for Cameron to score points with British eurosceptics. Similarly, Cameron opposed the *Spitzenkandidaten* procedure because it privileged the supranational European Parliament, which he disliked and ardent eurosceptics despised, over the intergovernmental European Council.

Displaying remarkable institutional agility, the European Parliament moved quickly after the elections to lock the new procedure in place. Almost immediately, Juncker and Schulz agreed that Juncker, as the candidate of the winning party, was now the sole candidate for Commission President. Soon afterward, the Conference of Presidents of the European Parliament, including the party group leaders and the European Parliament President (Schulz), endorsed Juncker and wrote accordingly to the European Council, which had scheduled an informal summit that evening (27 May) in Brussels.[6] At the summit, Cameron and a handful of other national leaders expressed their opposition to Juncker and resentment of the European Parliament's assertiveness. Rather than rush to judgment, the national leaders agreed to open formal consultations between the European Council and the European Parliament, as called for in the Treaty, giving European Council President Herman Van Rompuy a mandate to act on their behalf (European Council, 2014a). The European Council would make a definitive decision at its regular end-of-semester meeting on 26–27 June.

Cameron may have thought that he could block Juncker by exercising a veto in the European Council. Although national leaders had been able, since the implementation of the Nice Treaty in 2003, to nominate the Commission President by a qualified majority vote, a quest for consensus remained the norm. Even so, Cameron attempted to bolster his position by forming an anti-Juncker coalition. Few national leaders were enthusiastic about Juncker, but most – regardless of political affiliation – were willing to accept him, in deference to the *Spitzenkandidaten* procedure. A few remained strongly opposed, or so it seemed to Cameron. Chief among them was German Chancellor Angela Merkel, the most influential member of the European Council.

In fact, Merkel was equivocal. Like Cameron, she disagreed with Juncker's politics, which appeared to be more social democratic than Christian democratic. She disliked some of the positions that Juncker had taken during the eurozone crisis, especially when he flirted with the idea of Eurobonds, which, Merkel believed, would punish Germany

[6] *Agence Europe*, 28 May 2014.

© 2015 The Author(s) JCMS: Journal of Common Market Studies © 2015 John Wiley & Sons Ltd, 9600 Garsington Road, Oxford OX4 2DQ, UK and 350 Main Street, Malden, MA 02148, USA

with higher borrowing costs and reward profligate eurozone countries with lower borrowing costs. Merkel had gone along with French President Nicolas Sarkozy in blocking Juncker from being elected the European Council's first President, in 2009, which Juncker bitterly resented.

Yet there were limits to how far Merkel would or could go to stand in Juncker's way. Merkel's Christian Democratic Union (CDU), after all, was a leading constituent member of the EPP. As Europe's most prominent Christian Democrat, Merkel herself was complicit in Juncker's selection as the EPP's *Spitzenkandidat*. Even the SPD, in coalition with the CDU, supported Juncker's nomination, because it supported the new procedure. Merkel might have wished that Juncker would withdraw, but she was not about to cause an institutional crisis by forging a blocking minority in the European Council against him.

By the time that the European Council met at the end of June, the EPP, the PES and ALDE had rallied behind Juncker. The deal between the EPP and the PES reportedly included Juncker's commitment to appoint Schulz as Commission First Vice-President (VP), although it was far from certain that German's coalition government would nominate Schulz to the Commission.[7] As Merkel pointed out, the CDU had won many more votes than the SPD in the European Parliament elections. On 23 June, shortly before the European Council met in Brussels, the executive board of the CDU unanimously voted for Germany's current Commissioner to stay on for a second term, thus taking Schulz out of the running.[8] For its part, ALDE had hoped that if the EPP and the PES failed to reach agreement in support of Juncker or Schulz, Vehofstadt might instead become the Commission President candidate. Seeing that this would not happen, ALDE threw its support behind Juncker. Accordingly, Van Rompuy was able to report to the European Council that Juncker most likely had the necessary votes in the European Parliament to be elected Commission President.

The emergence of the pro-Juncker juggernaut failed to deter Cameron. Although by now unequivocally behind Juncker, Merkel feared that a crushing defeat for Cameron in the European Council would increase the UK's largely self-imposed alienation from the EU. The best solution would have been for Cameron to back down gracefully; to accept the inevitability of Juncker's nomination and let the matter drop. Instead, much to the dismay of Van Rompuy, who tried valiantly to smooth things over, Cameron insisted on holding a vote. The result was humiliating for Cameron. Not only was he resoundingly defeated, but the only other leader to vote against Juncker was Hungarian PM and EPP member Viktor Orbán, one of the least popular members of the European Council because of his undisguised authoritarian tendencies.

The European Council offered Cameron some political cover. At his insistence, the summit conclusion's stated that:

> The UK raised some concerns related to the future development of the EU. These concerns will need to be addressed. In this context, the European Council noted that the concept of ever closer union allows for different paths of integration for different countries, allowing those that want to deepen integration to move ahead, while respecting the wish of those who do not want to deepen any further. Once the new European Commission is effectively in place, the European Council will consider the process for the appointment

---

[7] *Spiegel International*, 7 June 2014.

[8] *EurActiv*, 25 June 2014.

© 2015 The Author(s) JCMS: Journal of Common Market Studies © 2015 John Wiley & Sons Ltd, 9600 Garsington Road, Oxford OX4 2DQ, UK and 350 Main Street, Malden, MA 02148, USA

of the President of the European Commission for the future, respecting the European Treaties (European Council, 2014b).

Despite these soothing words, Cameron did not retreat in his post-summit press conference: '[L]et me be absolutely clear, this is a bad day for Europe. It risks undermining the position of national governments. It risks undermining the power of national parliaments and it hands new power to the European Parliament' (Cameron, 2014). Whether or not it was a bad day for Europe, arguably, it was a bad day for Britain in the EU.

Following the drama in the European Council, the vote in the European Parliament, on July 14, was anti-climactic: 422 for Juncker, 250 against and 47 abstaining (European Parliament, 2014c). Nevertheless, it was an historic occasion for the EU. According to Schulz, 'the European Council and the European Parliament have together … [ushered] in a new democratic era … by establishing a new constitutional procedure, which did not necessitate a revision of the treaties' (European Parliament, 2014d). The success of the new procedure nevertheless rested on an expansive interpretation of the existing treaties.

The Juncker Commission, the High Representative and the European Council President

President-elect Juncker was a well-known quantity, with widespread EU experience. Having been a PM for eighteen years (1995–2013), Juncker had attended countless meetings of the European Council and had twice presided over the body in the pre-Lisbon era. During that time, Juncker had seen the EU expand from 15 to 28 countries, and with it the Commission expand from 15 to 28 members. He had served alongside four Commission Presidents (Jacques Santer, 1995–9; Manuel Marin, who was interim President briefly in 1999; Romano Prodi, 1999–2004; and Barroso, 2004–14). He had also dealt extensively with the European Parliament.

Coming from a small country and being a euro-federalist, Juncker favoured a strong Commission presidency and a strong Commission. Having seen first-hand the European Council's rise to prominence during the eurozone crisis, Juncker was critical of the Commission's relative decline. If appointed Commission President, he reportedly told the EPP in June 2014, he would not simply become the secretary-general of the European Council.[9] No wonder that Juncker called his administration 'the last chance Commission'.[10] He would use the office of the presidency, now strengthened by the *Spitzenkandidaten* procedure, to stand up to national leaders and become a chief agenda-setter for the EU. Earlier, while explaining why he might not have been a good European Council President, Juncker observed that 'I see myself as a driving force rather than a follower'.[11]

His ability to become a driving force as Commission President would depend not only on the authority that he would derive from the office itself, but also on his acumen, ability, political skills, sensitivity to national and other key interests and relationship with leading actors, especially in the European Council. Within the Commission, Juncker's *chef de cabinet* would be crucial for Juncker's success. Juncker's choice of Martin Selmayr, a

[9] *Agence Europe*, 12 June 2014.
[10] *EurActiv*, 22 October 2014.
[11] *Spiegel International*, 24 January 2011.

© 2015 The Author(s) JCMS: Journal of Common Market Studies © 2015 John Wiley & Sons Ltd, 9600 Garsington Road, Oxford OX4 2DQ, UK and 350 Main Street, Malden, MA 02148, USA

hard-charging former *chef de cabinet* to an outgoing Commission vice-president, sent a clear message within the Berlaymont.

Prevailing circumstance would matter as much as personal factors and personnel decisions (Tömmel, 2013). For all his ambition, the EU's plight in 2014 did not appear conducive to ever closer union. Nor did Juncker's relations with key national leaders seem especially close. He and Cameron would have to find a *modus vivendi*, and as President Juncker would want to help the UK stay in the EU. More important were Juncker's relations with Merkel and French President François Hollande, which were merely workmanlike. It was difficult to imagine Merkel, Hollande and Juncker forming a triumvirate to forge closer political and economic integration along the lines of the famous Kohl–Mitterrand–Delors triumvirate of the late 1980s.

The strength of Juncker's Commission would depend in large part on the quality of the other Commissioners and the allocation of responsibilities among them. Juncker had no control over who national governments nominated as Commissioner, though he tried to exert some influence, urging especially that governments pay attention to gender (he hoped to exceed or at least equal the number of women – nine – in the outgoing Barroso Commission). But nominations to the Commission are generally in the gift of national leaders, one of whom, Slovenia's outgoing PM Alenka Bratušek, bestowed the gift upon herself.

The only commissionership in play among national governments was that of the High Representative (HR) for Foreign Affairs and Security Policy, who also serves as a Commission VP, and whose selection – for reasons of intra-EU regional balance, as well as national, party political, ideological, and gender balance – was bound up with that of the European Council President. After much back-and-forth, brokered by Van Rompuy, national leaders agreed to appoint Federica Mogherini, then Foreign Minister of Italy, to become HR/VP, and elected Polish PM Donald Tusk to become President of the European Council for the period 1 December 2014 to 31 May 2017 (European Council, 2014c).

Both Juncker and Mogherini come from founding countries, one small and one large. Tusk balanced this by coming from a new, large country. Juncker and Tusk are EPP; Mogherini is PES. Mogherini was reputedly soft on Russia; Tusk was quite the opposite. As European Council President, Tusk would preside also over the Eurozone Summit (meetings of the leaders of countries in the eurozone), despite coming from a country that is not a eurozone member. Yet the frequency of Eurozone Summit meetings had declined dramatically since mid-2012, partly because the eurozone crisis seemed to have ebbed and partly because Sarkozy, architect of the Eurozone Summit, had left office (the Eurozone Summit met only once in 2014). Known as a political scrapper rather than a conciliator, and enjoying Merkel's strong support, it looked as if Tusk would be a very different kind of European Council President than the reserved Van Rompuy. Even so, the European Council presidency is tightly constrained by its brokerage role and by its incumbent's separation from national political office.

Mogherini's relative inexperience as a Foreign Minister fuelled speculation that key national leaders did not want a political heavyweight to succeed Baroness Ashton as HR/VP. Perhaps not coincidentally, Ashton herself had been criticized for inexperience at the time of her appointment and for never having mastered the job (Barber, 2010). Given that the European External Action Service (EEAS), which Ashton had trouble

© 2015 The Author(s) JCMS: Journal of Common Market Studies © 2015 John Wiley & Sons Ltd, 9600 Garsington Road, Oxford OX4 2DQ, UK and 350 Main Street, Malden, MA 02148, USA

setting up and which Mogherini would have to lead, 'is a huge bureaucracy, which must be managed well if it is to be effective', a veteran Brussels insider saw Mogherini's 'lack of managerial experience [as] her key weakness' (Gros, 2014).

Mogherini shared a common trait with the other Commissioners-designate: most came from the top ranks of national politics. Indeed, Juncker's proposed Commission had more former PMs than any of its predecessors. Here, again, Britain was an outlier. Far from nominating a senior politician, Cameron nominated Lord Hill, Leader of the House of Lords and a former junior minister. Although Hill could turn out to be a fine Commissioner, his nomination left many Brussels-watchers scratching their heads.

National governments pay close attention to the allocation of portfolios among Commissioners. Commission Presidents have acquired more independence in carrying out this task over the years, but governments still lobby for 'their' Commissioners to receive weighty portfolios. As well as having to deal with pushy national governments, Juncker faced the challenge of having too many Commissioners chasing too few relevant responsibilities. By common consent, having one Commissioner per country resulted in a Commission that was too cumbersome, but this organizing principle had become sacrosanct following Ireland's initial rejection of the Lisbon Treaty (O'Brennan, 2008).

Juncker dealt with the dilemmas of national pressure for key portfolios, notably from the big countries, and the Commission's large size by establishing a matrix system. Apart from the HR/VP, Juncker appointed six VPs, all from small countries, three of whom had been PM. In general, Juncker gave them responsibility for broad policy fields rather than for specific portfolios, which he allocated among the other Commissioners-designate. Bowing to political realities, Juncker gave the choice portfolios to the Commissioners-designate from the big countries. As is often the case, the allocation of portfolios was sometimes controversial. For instance, France reportedly lobbied for, and Germany against, giving former French Finance Minister Pierre Moscovici the Economic and Financial Affairs portfolio. France wanted Moscovici to have a prestigious portfolio, covering a policy area of great national sensitivity; Germany objected to having a Commissioner for Economic and Financial Affairs who had failed, as a national Finance Minister, to submit a single budget that conformed to EU rules.[12]

Germany was assuaged to some extent by an important innovation in the Juncker Commission, whereby four of the VPs would lead 'project teams, steering and coordinating the work of a number of Commissioners'. This was intended to 'ensure a dynamic interaction of all Members of the College, breaking down silos and moving away from static structures' (Commission, 2014a). It might also act as a check against politically powerful Commissioners. Thus, Moscovici would be part of the team for 'A Deeper and Fairer Economic and Monetary Union' under Valdis Dombrovskis, Vice-President for the Euro and Social Dialogue, a no-nonsense deficit hawk from Latvia. (Germany's Commissioner was given the portfolio of Digital Economy and Society, as part of the Digital Single Market team under Commission VP Andrus Ansip, from Estonia.)

The various project teams encompassed overlapping sets of Commissioners. In addition to being part of the EMU project team, for instance, Moscovici would be part of two other project teams: Jobs, Growth and Investment and the Digital Single Market. Together with all the other Commissioners, he would work with the VP for Budget and

---

[12] *Spiegel International*, 3 September 2014.

© 2015 The Author(s) JCMS: Journal of Common Market Studies © 2015 John Wiley & Sons Ltd, 9600 Garsington Road, Oxford OX4 2DQ, UK and 350 Main Street, Malden, MA 02148, USA

Human Resources. The matrix system extended as well to Mogherini's sprawling external relations responsibilities. The HR/VP would 'be responsible for the project of "A Stronger Global Actor", helping steer all of the Commission's external relations activities … in particular [the work] of the Commissioners for European Neighbourhood Policy and Enlargement Negotiations; Trade; International Cooperation and Development; and Humanitarian Aid and Crisis Management' (European Commission, 2014a). Further emphasizing the HR/VP's closer ties to the Commission, Juncker asked that Mogherini move her office and cabinet from the EEAS headquarters across Rond-point Schuman (the Schuman roundabout in the heart of the EU district) to the Commission's headquarters in the Berlaymont (European Commission, 2014b).

Juncker chose former Dutch Foreign Minister Frans Timmermans as the Commission's 'First VP', to 'act as the right-hand of the President', with responsibility for Better Regulation, Inter-Institutional Relations, the Rule of Law and the Charter of Fundamental Rights (European Commission, 2014a). Juncker won near-universal praise for appointing the younger, more charismatic, centre-left Timmermans, who was to work with all Commissioners, but particularly closely with the Commissioner for Justice, Consumers and Gender Equality and the Commissioner for Migration and Home Affairs (European Commission, 2014a).

The Commission has been promoting 'Better Regulation' since 2002, in an effort to simplify and strengthen the regulatory environment (European Commission, 2006, p. 6). It has been an uphill task. In view of the importance of better regulation for the success of the EU's 'core business' – the internal market and the related common policies (Schrefler *et al.*, 2014) – and for countering caricatures of the Brussels bureaucracy, giving Timmermans this responsibility sent a powerful signal about the Juncker Commission's priorities. In his mission letter to Timmermans, Juncker noted that 'Respect for the principles of subsidiarity, proportionality and better regulation will be at the core of the work of the new Commission. … When we act, we will always look for the most efficient and least burdensome approach. … I will therefore pay particular attention to your opinion … before including any new initiative in the Commission Work Programme or putting it on the agenda of the College' (European Commission, 2014c).

The proposed College needed to win the approval of the European Parliament, based on hearings of the Commissioners-designate in the relevant parliamentary committees. Such hearings were far from novel, having first taken place in 1999 for the Prodi Commission. The hearings had developed over time into opportunities less for substantive exchanges with Commissioners-designate than for grandstanding on the part of MEPs and jousting between political groups. It was not unusual for MEPs in committee hearings to give the Commissioners-designate a hard time, or even to vote against particular nominees, thereby making their positions untenable.

Philippe Lamberts, co-chair of the Group of the Greens/European Free Alliance, complained that Juncker's allocation of portfolios 'seemed like an exercise in political satire, matching all the candidates to the policy portfolios for which they were least suited' (Lamberts, 2014). Trying to score a political point, Lamberts was referring to a number of Commissioners-designate who would be subject to particular scrutiny. Apart from Moscovici, these included Miguel Arias Cañete, the Commissioner-designate for Climate Action and Energy, who had long-standing connections to the oil industry, and Tibor Navracsics, the Commissioner-designate for Education, Culture, Youth and Citizenship, a former Foreign Minister in Hungary's increasingly illiberal government. As a British

© 2015 The Author(s) JCMS: Journal of Common Market Studies © 2015 John Wiley & Sons Ltd, 9600 Garsington Road, Oxford OX4 2DQ, UK and 350 Main Street, Malden, MA 02148, USA

Conservative and the Commissioner-designate for financial services, a portfolio for which his government had lobbied, Hill would also come under special scrutiny.

The much-vaunted 'grand coalition' of the EPP, PES, and ALDE, in support of the Juncker Commission, threatened to break down during the hearings as members of the EPP went after Moscovici (PES) and members of the PES went after Arias Cañete and Navracsics (both EPP). Coming from a party outside the coalition, Hill was especially exposed to MEPs' attacks. Indeed, he was obliged to provide written responses to 23 supplementary questions and return for a second hearing before the Economic and Monetary Affairs Committee (ECON), which eventually voted to approve him. The extent of inter-party bickering over the vulnerable EPP and PES Commissioners-designate demonstrated the frustration of some MEPs with the seemingly excessive bipartisanship in support of Juncker. But there was a limit to how far partisanship over the approval of Commissioners-designate could go. Moscovici, Arias Cañete and Navracsics were protected by the political equivalent of mutually assured destruction: if the EPP voted against Moscovici, the PES would vote against Arias Cañete and Navracsics. The Greens characterized this as an EPP–PES 'non-aggression pact'.[13]

Not surprisingly, the sole European Parliament 'scalp' during the hearings – the one Commissioner-designate who received a negative committee vote – was ALDE member Bratušek, the former Slovenian PM, who was unpopular for putting herself forward for the job and who performed poorly at her hearing to head the Energy Union project team. After some resistance, Bratušek agreed to step down. The EPP and PES advocated replacing her with a prominent Slovenian MEP and PES member. Understandably, ALDE objected. The Slovenian government, which alone was responsible for replacing Bratušek, nominated Violeta Bulc, a recent arrival on the national political stage, who affiliated with ALDE.

Not wanting to appoint Bulc as a VP, Juncker reallocated portfolios, naming Maroš Šefčovič of Slovakia – who had already been approved by the European Parliament as Commissioner-designate for Transport – VP for Energy Union, and giving Bulc the Transport portfolio. This necessitated hearings for Bulc and Šefčovič before the relevant committees, which took place in Strasbourg, where the European Parliament was in plenary session, on the evening of 20 October. That paved the way for the European Parliament as a whole to vote on the proposed Juncker Commission on 22 October.

Addressing the European Parliament just before the vote, Juncker announced other changes in the allocation of portfolios in response to the European Parliament hearings. The most noteworthy was to take Citizenship away from the controversial Hungarian nominee and give it to the Commissioner in charge of Migration and Home Affairs, who would work closely on this matter with the Commissioner for Justice and Consumers. Nevertheless Juncker was careful 'to reiterate my confidence and trust in Tibor Navracsics, who performed excellently in his hearing and demonstrated a strong European commitment' (European Commission, 2014d).

The European Parliament duly voted to approve the Juncker Commission by a sizeable majority: 423 in favour; 209 against; 67 abstaining. Addressing the European Parliament shortly after the vote, Juncker noted that having 'a majority of around 400 … [would] allow us to work over the coming five years'.[14] Not that the Commission needed a parliamentary majority in order to stay in office, in the same way that most national

---

[13] *Agence Europe*, 1 October 2014.

[14] *Agence Europe*, 23 October 2014.

© 2015 The Author(s) JCMS: Journal of Common Market Studies © 2015 John Wiley & Sons Ltd, 9600 Garsington Road, Oxford OX4 2DQ, UK and 350 Main Street, Malden, MA 02148, USA

governments did: the Commission's legislative proposals would certainly need majority support, but – depending on the subject matter – would likely divide MEPs along left–right lines, regardless of there having been a grand coalition in support of the Commission's appointment. In drafting new legislative proposals, which Timmermans soon announced would be fewer than in previous years, the Commission would doubtless take into account the strength and positions of the European Parliament political groups, just as previous Commissions had. The main difference this time was the large number of anti-system MEPs, who would likely oppose most Commission proposals.

The extent to which the Commission could work, and work well, over the next five years depended more on its internal coherence than on support in the European Parliament. Once again, Juncker proclaimed after the European Parliament vote of 22 October that his Commission 'will be a real team … [it] will … work differently … Not through silo mentalities, clusters, and portfolio frontiers, but as a collegiate, political body'.[15] Yet there was no guarantee that the matrix system would function as Juncker hoped; that Commissioners from the big countries would accept the team leadership of Commissioners from smaller countries; that all of the Commissioners would accept the President's highly centralized management style, under the direction of Juncker's powerful *chef de cabinet* and the Commission's Secretary-General; or that First VP Timmermans could possibly carry out all of his official responsibilities. Nor could Juncker change political realities that have always impeded the Commission's freedom of action. It was one thing for him to proclaim that the HR/VP should 'no longer [be] thwarted by the Foreign Ministers of the Member States and I will ensure this does not happen'; it was quite another for the Foreign Ministers to oblige (Juncker, 2014).

Perhaps the greatest threat to the Juncker Commission came in the form of 'LuxLeaks' – the public release on 6 November of an investigation by an international consortium of journalists into the tax advantages of more than 300 multinational companies based in Luxembourg, which reopened the controversy about Juncker that had surfaced during the election campaign (ICIJ, 2014). Predictably, eurosceptic MEPs called for a vote of censure. Equally predictably, the European Parliament establishment rallied around Juncker, and the vote fell far short of the required two-thirds majority (European Parliament, 2014e). But that was not the end of the matter. Green MEPs, with the support of some PES and even EPP members, pressed for the European Parliament to set up a committee of inquiry into the revelations.[16] Regardless of the manoeuvrings within the European Parliament, LuxLeaks overshadowed the launch of the Juncker Commission and threatened to erode confidence in and ultimately political support for the Commission President – within the College itself, in the European Parliament and among national leaders.

Conclusion

With respect to the EU's institutional development, the significance of 2014 lies in the election of Commission President Jean-Claude Juncker by the European Parliament, based on competition in the earlier European Parliament elections between candidates of the main European political parties and on the European Council's nomination of the

[15] *Agence Europe*, 23 October 2014.

[16] *EurActiv*, 3 December 2014.

© 2015 The Author(s) JCMS: Journal of Common Market Studies © 2015 John Wiley & Sons Ltd, 9600 Garsington Road, Oxford OX4 2DQ, UK and 350 Main Street, Malden, MA 02148, USA

leading candidate following the elections. The new system for electing the Commission President rested on an interpretation of the Lisbon Treaty pushed by the European Parliament and resisted by some national leaders lest it tie the hands of the European Council. Here was another example in EU institutional history of the European Parliament's assertiveness and innovativeness. More revealing for EU governance, however, was the role of the European parties. National leaders are not just heads of government and of national parties; most are also leading members of European parties, notably the EPP, PES and ALDE. Having gone along as European party leaders with the *Spitzenkandidaten* procedure, they could not or would not reverse course in the European Council.

A more fundamental question is what the new system portends for EU governance. In theory, it strengthens the legitimacy of the office of the Commission presidency, but does it strengthen the Commission President? After all, successive treaty changes since Maastricht have strengthened the Commission presidency, but successive Commission Presidents have not been especially influential or powerful. In the past, much depended on who the European Council selected; much now depends on who the EPP and the PES select as their *Spitzenkandidaten*. The story so far is revealing. Throughout EU history, national leaders have mostly selected senior national politicians (more recently PMs). Juncker, the EPP candidate in 2014, is exactly the kind of politician who would have emerged (and almost did, in 2004) as the European Council's nominee. Schulz, the PES candidate, was different. As someone who had spent his entire career in EU rather than national politics, and become European Parliament President, Schulz was well placed to win the PES nomination but would never have been nominated by the European Council under the old system. This is not to say that Schulz had the makings of a successful Commission President, only that the new system opens the office to leading EU politicians beyond those in national government, although the universe of such politicians is still relatively small.

The greater legitimacy of the Commission presidency rests on the link between the *Spitzenkandidaten* and the European Parliament elections. The potential weakness of that link, all too evident in 2014, is low voter turnout and low awareness throughout the EU of the candidates and of the relationship between the elections and the selection of the Commission President. If voter turnout does not improve appreciably in 2019, and if the next crop of *Spitzenkandidaten* once more campaigns zealously but without exciting much public interest, how will the stronger legitimacy of the presidency translate into stronger influence for the President, regardless of that person's ability and prevailing circumstances? Will accomplished politicians who have the potential to become effective Commission Presidents want to put themselves through a grueling, albeit short, election campaign if voter interest and turnout remain low? Will government ministers, especially PMs, be obliged (legally or politically) to step down if they become *Spitzenkandidaten* and are campaigning for Commission President (an issue that did not arise in 2014)? The real test of the new system will come in 2019, or even 2024 (despite the European Council's commitment to review the system before the next European Parliament elections, national leaders cannot put the genie back in the bottle, even if they are willing to try). From the vantage point of 2014, it seemed fair to say that the new system will not necessarily help to produce stronger Presidents.

Regardless of how Juncker came to office, having a new Commission President, and having a new HR/VP and a new European Council President, were noteworthy institutional events in 2014. Two other developments merit mention. One is the switch, on 1

© 2015 The Author(s) JCMS: Journal of Common Market Studies © 2015 John Wiley & Sons Ltd, 9600 Garsington Road, Oxford OX4 2DQ, UK and 350 Main Street, Malden, MA 02148, USA

November, under the terms of the Lisbon Treaty, to a new system of voting in the Council, whereby a qualified majority consists of at least 55 per cent of countries (currently 15) representing at least 65 per cent of total EU population (European Council, 2014). The impact of the new system, in terms of national influence and decision outcomes, will not be apparent for some time, and a preference for consensus will likely remain the norm. The other concerns the European Parliament presidency, for which a new two-and-a-half year term began on 1 July, when the European Parliament started its new term. MEPs made history by re-electing Schulz (European Parliament, 2014f). Having failed to become Commission President, one of the main architects of the *Spitzenkandidaten* procedure had the considerable consolation of keeping his old job. He managed to do so because of a long-standing agreement between the EPP and the PES to alternate the presidency between them during each European Parliament term. According to this arrangement, which other political groups and some members of the EPP and PES disliked, the position should have gone to the EPP on 1 July, but Schulz succeeded in reversing the rotation so that he could stand as President for the first half of the term. Thanks to the EPP–PES alliance, Schulz won 409 out of 612 valid votes cast. Thus, the would-be Commission President became the once-again European Parliament President. Though he did not secure the job he wanted, Schulz at least had the satisfaction of shepherding the success of the *Spitzenkandidaten* procedure, which he and the European Parliament championed.

References

ALDE (2014a) Agreement between Olli Rehn and Guy Verhofstadt—statement by ALDE Party President, 20 January. Available at «http://www.aldeparty.eu/en/press-releases/agreement-between-olli-rehn-guy-verhofstadt-statement-alde-party-president».

ALDE (2014b) Guy Verhofstadt and Olli Rehn to lead joint European election campaign, 1 February. Available at «http://www.aldeparty.eu/en/news/guy-verhofstadt-and-olli-rehn-lead-joint-european-election-campaign».

Barber, T. (2010) 'The Appointments of Herman van Rompuy and Catherine Ashton'. *JCMS*, Vol. 48, No. s1, pp. 55–67.

Cameron, D. (2014) European Council June 2014: David Cameron's Speech, 24 June. Available at «https://www.gov.uk/government/speeches/european-council-june-2014-david-camerons-speech».

Copsey, N. (2015) *Rethinking the European Union* (London: Palgrave).

Copsey, N. and Haughton, T. (2014) 'Farewell Britannia? "Issue Capture" and the Politics of David Cameron's 2013 EU Referendum Pledge'. *JCMS*, Vol. 52, No. s1, pp. 74–89.

Council (2014) Qualified Majority: A New Rule from 1 November 2014. Available at «http://www.consilium.europa.eu/en/council-eu/voting-system/qualified-majority/».

Dinan, D. (2014) 'Governance and Institutions: The Unrelenting Rise of the European Parliament'. *JCMS*, Vol. 52, No. s1, pp. 109–24.

European Commission (2006) Better Regulation Simply Explained (Luxembourg: Office for Official Publications of the European Communities).

European Commission (2014a) Press Release, "Memo," 10 September. Available at «http://europa.eu/rapid/press-release_MEMO-14-523_en.htm».

European Commission (2014b) President Juncker's Mission Letter to Federica Mogherini, 1 November. Available at «http://ec.europa.eu/commission/sites/cwt/files/commissioner_mission_letters/mogherini_en.pdf».

© 2015 The Author(s) JCMS: Journal of Common Market Studies © 2015 John Wiley & Sons Ltd, 9600 Garsington Road, Oxford OX4 2DQ, UK and 350 Main Street, Malden, MA 02148, USA

European Commission (2014c) President Juncker's Mission Letter to Frans Timmermans, 1 November. Available at « http://ec.europa.eu/commission/sites/cwt/files/commissioner_mission_letters/timmermans_en.pdf».

European Commission (2014d) Jean-Claude Juncker: Setting Europe in Motion: Speech before the European Parliament, 22 October. Available at «http://ec.europa.eu/transport/newsletters/2014/10-24/articles/junckers_speech_en.htm».

European Council (2014a) Remarks by President Herman Van Rompuy following the informal dinner of Heads of State or Government, Brussels, 27 May. Available at «http://www.consilium.europa.eu/en/meetings/european-council/2014/05/27/».

European Council (2014b) European Council 26/27 June 2014 Conclusions, Brussels, 27 June 2014. Available at «http://www.consilium.europa.eu/uedocs/cms_Data/docs/pressdata/en/ec/143478.pdf».

European Council (2014c) Special Meeting of the European Council (30 August 2014) Conclusions, Brussels, 30 2014c. Available at «http://www.consilium.europa.eu/uedocs/cms_data/docs/pressdata/en/ec/144538.pdf».

European Parliament (2014a) This Time It's Different: Act, React, Impact, available at «http://www.europarl.europa.eu/news/en/top-stories/content/20130902TST18451/html/Act-React-Impact». accessed 30 March 2015.

European Parliament (2014b) Results of the 2014 European Elections, 1 July. Available at «http://www.europarl.europa.eu/elections2014-results/en/election-results-2014.html».

European Parliament (2014c) Parliament Elects Jean-Claude Juncker as Commission President, 15 July. Available at «http://www.elections2014.eu/en/news-room/content/20140714IPR52341/html/Parliament-elects-Jean-Claude-Juncker-as-Commission-President».

European Parliament (2014d) Speech to the European Council by Martin Schulz, President of the European Parliament, 23 October. Available at «http://www.europarl.europa.eu/the-president/en/press/press_release_speeches/speeches/speeches-2014/speeches-2014-october/html/speech-to-the-european-council-by-martin-schulz--president-of-the-european-parliament».

European Parliament (2014e) Motion of Censure against the Commission Rejected by a Large Majority, 27 November. Available at «http://www.europarl.europa.eu/news/en/news-room/content/20141121IPR79864/html/Motion-of-censure-against-the-Commission-rejected-by-a-large-majority».

European Parliament (2014f) Martin Schulz Reelected President of the European Parliament, 1 July 2014. Available at «http://www.europarl.europa.eu/news/en/news-room/content/20140630IPR51020/html/Martin-Schulz-re-elected-President-of-the-European-Parliament».

EPP (2014) Jean-Claude Juncker Elected as EPP Candidate for President of the European Commission, 7 March. Available at «http://www.epp.eu/jean-claude-juncker-elected-epp-candidate-president-european-commission».

Gros, D. (2014) 'The Government Europe Deserves?' *Project Syndicate*, 16 September. Available at «https://www.project-syndicate.org/commentary/daniel-gros-examines-the-eu-s-new-leadership-and-sees-trouble-ahead-for-efforts-at-further-integration».

Hix, S. (2008) *What's Wrong With the EU and How to Fix It* (Cambridge: Polity Press).

ICIJ (2014). Luxembourg Leaks: Global Companies' Secrets Exposed. Available at «http://www.icij.org/project/luxembourg-leaks». accessed 30 March 2015.

Juncker, J-C. (2014) New Start for Europe: My Agenda for Jobs, Growth, Fairness and Democratic Change, speech to the EP, Strasbourg, 15 July. Available at «http://ec.europa.eu/priorities/docs/pg_en.pdf».

Lamberts, P. (2014) 'Jean-Claude Juncker's Pack of Jokers Invites a Reshuffle', *Financial Times*, 30 September.

O'Brennan, J. (2008) 'Ireland and the Lisbon Treaty: *Quo Vadis?*' CEPS Policy Brief, No. 176, October.

PES (2014) 'First PES Common Candidate: Martin Schulz', 1 March. Available at «http://www.pes.eu/candidate».

Schrefler, L., Renda, A. and Pelkmans, J. (2014) What Can the Better Regulation Commissioner do for the EU? CEPS Commentary, 29 September. Available at «http://www.ceps.eu/system/files/LS%20et%20al%20Commission%20Priorities%20Regulation.pdf».

Tömmel, I. (2013) 'The Presidents of the European Commission: Transactional or Transforming Leaders?' *JCMS*, Vol. 51, No. 4, pp. 789–805.

© 2015 The Author(s) JCMS: Journal of Common Market Studies © 2015 John Wiley & Sons Ltd, 9600 Garsington Road, Oxford OX4 2DQ, UK and 350 Main Street, Malden, MA 02148, USA

JCMS 2015 Volume 53 Annual Review pp. 108–127   DOI: 10.1111/jcms.12265

'The Court Hereby Rules...' – Legal Developments in EU Fundamental Rights Protection

THOMAS HORSLEY
University of Liverpool

Introduction

Two years have elapsed since the publication of the last survey of legal developments in this *Review* (Amtenbrink, 2013). Back then, the spotlight was on 'make or break' reforms to eurozone governance and financial market supervision – and the Court of Justice's role in policing the constitutionality of new policy instruments in both areas. The intervening period is marked by a degree of continuity with respect to both the focus of Union activity and the institutional role of the Court of Justice. As before, the EU institutions and Member State governments continue to wrestle with the legacy of the eurozone crisis. The Court of Justice too remains at the centre of ongoing efforts to reform further eurozone governance and financial market supervision. During 2015, the Grand Chamber of the Court will deliver its eagerly anticipated verdict on the constitutionality of the European Central Bank's controversial system for Outright Monetary Transfers – a likely subject for review in next year's *Legal Developments* contribution.[1]

The enduring legacy of the eurozone crisis has not, however, extinguished scope for innovation in other key fields of Union activity. A survey of contributions to this Journal illustrates clearly the breadth of Union policy-making in recent years. Across all areas of European Union activity EU law, and the Court of Justice in particular, continues to play an important role in managing European integration. In 2014, the Court (sitting as a Full Court or Grand Chamber) delivered a total of 48 decisions – another busy, but not record, year for the Luxembourg Court.[2] Surprisingly perhaps, only one decision dealt directly with reforms to economic governance and financial market supervision.[3] The remaining judgments from the upper tiers of the Court addressed a diverse array of other substantive and institutional matters. Aside from the usual, unremarkable body of repeat decisions and infringement actions against Member States, the Court was requested to rule, inter alia, on the definition of 'human embryos' in EU law;[4] the application of EU social welfare instruments to surrogacy arrangements;[5] the notion of 'parody' in intellectual property law;[6] and the standing rights of natural and legal persons before the Court.[7]

---

[1] *Gauweiler and Others* (C-62/14) (pending).

[2] Statistics from InfoCuria http://curia.europa.eu/juris/recherche.jsf?language=en (accessed 28 March 2015).

[3] *United Kingdom v Parliament and Council* (*Short Selling*) (C-270/12) EU:C:2014:18.

[4] *International Stem Cell Corporation* (C-364/13) EU:C:2014:2451.

[5] *C.D. v S.T* (C-167/12) EU:C:2014:169.

[6] *Deckmyn and Vrijheidsfonds VZW v Vandersteen and Others* (C-201/13) EU:C:2014:2132.

[7] *Inuit Tapiriit Kanatami and Others v Parliament and Council* (C-583/11) EU:C:2013:625.

© 2015 The Author(s) JCMS: Journal of Common Market Studies © 2015 John Wiley & Sons Ltd, 9600 Garsington Road, Oxford OX4 2DQ, UK and 350 Main Street, Malden, MA 02148, USA

Following past practice, this contribution surveys some of the choice judicial highlights of the previous year. The selection of decisions is thematic and designed to bring together a range of the most significant legal developments from a cross-section of Union activity. At the request of the editors, account will also be taken of important judgments delivered during 2013 to fill the gap in analysis of legal developments in last year's *Annual Review*. Section I briefly assesses the Court's end-of-year bombshell: Opinion 2/13 on the Draft Agreement on EU accession to the European Convention on Human Rights (ECHR).[8] Section II explores two key judgments in the field of EU data protection, including the much-discussed ruling in *Google Spain* on the so-called 'right to be forgotten'.[9] Thereafter, Section III looks back to 2013 and the landmark decisions in *Akerberg Fransson* and *Melloni* on the scope of application of the EU Charter of Fundamental Rights (EUCFR).[10] Finally, attention turns in Section IV to consideration of subtle, but potentially significant, evolutions in the jurisprudence on EU citizenship rights.

Fundamental rights protection is the theme that unites the case law examined in this contribution. In isolation, the selected judicial highlights from 2013 and 2014 illuminate particular points of advancement, refinement and fracture in the legal framework governing the protection of fundamental rights across a range of EU policy areas. In their broader guise, the individual Grand Chamber judgments also offer a renewed restatement of the nature and profound impact of judicial power in EU integration.

I. Opinion 2/13: Judicial Self-Interest or Faithful Adherence to the Treaties?

The first part of this contribution considers what is undoubtedly the legal highlight of the previous year: Opinion 2/13 on the Draft Agreement on the accession of the EU to the ECHR. On 18 December 2014, the Court of Justice, sitting as a Full Court, delivered its verdict on the compatibility of that agreement with the EU Treaties. In a surprise verdict to many observers, the Court concluded that the Draft Agreement was not compatible with key provisions of the Treaties. The Court's call to try again (again)[11] leaves the process for EU accession to the ECHR – now expressly mandated by the Treaty – in serious difficulty. The Court's lengthy Opinion, together with the accompanying, rich analysis provided by Advocate General Juliane Kokott, cannot be adequately critiqued within the scope of this contribution. Rather, this section simply sketches out, and offers some initial reflections on, principal aspects of this important judicial milestone.[12]

Background to the Draft Agreement

The Draft Agreement has its origins in the EU's post-Lisbon constitutional architecture. Art 6(2) TEU, in particular, provides that the 'Union shall accede to the European Convention for the Protection of Human Rights and Fundamental Freedoms'. That formal

---

[8] Opinion of the Court (Opinion 2/13) EU:C:2014:2454.

[9] *Google Spain SL and Google Inc. v Agencia Española de Protección de Datos (AEPD) and Costeja González* (C-131/12) EU:C:2014:317.

[10] *Åklagaren v Åkerberg Fransson* (C-617/10) EU:C:2013:105 and *Melloni v Ministerio Fiscal* (399/11) EU:C:2013:107.

[11] The Court derailed ECHR accession in Opinion 2/94 EU:C:1996:140 on the grounds of a lack of competence in the Treaties.

[12] For a fuller reaction, see e.g., Editorial (2015) 'The EU's Accession to the ECHR – a "NO" from the ECJ!'. *Common Market Law Review*, Vol. 52, No. 1, pp. 1–15.

© 2015 The Author(s) JCMS: Journal of Common Market Studies © 2015 John Wiley & Sons Ltd

commitment on the part of the Member States at Lisbon addresses earlier judicial concerns regarding the Union's competence to accede to the Convention. It also expresses a collective intention to complement the Union's own increasingly developed fundamental rights framework through the introduction of a new system of external control.

Negotiations for accession opened in June 2010 with the Commission designated by the Council as EU negotiator. The resulting Draft Agreement was concluded in April 2013 and comprises a package of measures that contracting parties agreed were necessary to secure accession.[13] Essentially, the relevant instruments tackle two particularly important legal issues. First, the Draft Agreement seeks to provide for the Union's admission to the ECHR as a 'non-State' party to the Convention. Second, it established a set of institutional and procedural mechanisms to govern interactions between the Union institutions (and the Court of Justice, in particular), Member States, non-Member State parties to the Convention and the European Court of Human Rights (ECtHR) in connection with disputes engaging Union law. As the Court's Opinion indicates, the Commission and the Member States were in broad agreement that the Draft Agreement package was compatible with the EU Treaties overall.[14]

The Court's Assessment in Opinion 2/13

The political wind behind the Draft Agreement had little impact on the Court's own approach. On the one hand, the Court's Opinion is clear that, as a matter of principle, Union law is open to ECHR accession. Further, the Court also acknowledged that, as a result of accession, 'the EU and its institutions, including the Court of Justice, would be subject to the control mechanism provided for by the ECHR and, in particular, to the decisions and the judgments of the ECtHR'.[15] On the other hand, however, the Court of Justice took issue with the specific terms of the Draft Agreement, prompting its finding of incompatibility with the EU Treaties. In short, the Full Court was not satisfied that the Agreement sufficiently safeguarded the unique characteristics and autonomous character of EU law. Furthermore, it also considered key aspects of the institutional and procedural machinery envisaged by the Agreement incompatible with the Treaty framework governing ECHR accession. The Opinion identifies seven particular points of conflict under five distinct headings. The paragraphs that follow offer a summary of the Court's main findings.

The Court's opening objections to the Draft Agreement concern the specific characteristics of Union law and its autonomy.[16] Under that heading, the Court pointed first to the absence in the Agreement of a mechanism to coordinate the competence of contracting parties to trade up the level of rights protection under the ECHR, pursuant to Art 53 ECHR, with the demands of Art 53 EUCFR.[17] It also expressed concern at the Draft Agreement's failure to recognize fully the fundamental importance of the principle of 'mutual trust' that, in the Court's view, uniquely binds the Member States in their relations to one another as regards the protection of EU fundamental rights.[18] Finally, the Court held that the Draft Agreement failed to make provision to govern the relationship

---

[13] Opinion of the Court (Opinion 2/13) EU:C:2014:2454 at para. 48.
[14] At para. 109.
[15] At para. 181.
[16] At paras 179–200.
[17] At para. 189.
[18] At para. 194.

between the preliminary reference procedure under Art 267 TFEU and the 'opt-in' system for advisory opinions under Protocol 16 ECHR.[19]

The second overarching ground of objection concerned Art 344 TFEU. That provision provides that Member States undertake not to submit disputes involving the interpretation or application of the Treaties to any method of settlement other than those provided for internally by the Treaties. Art 3 of Protocol No. 8 on EU Accession to the ECHR states expressly that the accession agreement must not affect that provision. The Full Court was not satisfied that the Draft Agreement complied with the demands of Art 344 TFEU. In particular, it ruled that Art 5 of the Agreement did not exclude the possibility that the EU or its Member States might submit an application to the ECtHR, pursuant to Art 33 ECHR, involving the interpretation or application of Union law.[20] In its view, the existence of such a possibility was not only contrary to Art 344 TFEU, but also 'goes against the very nature of EU law, which… requires that relations between the Member States be governed by EU law to the exclusion, if EU law so requires, of any other law'.[21]

On its third and fourth grounds of review, the Court of Justice critiqued the detail of the two procedural mechanisms established by the Draft Agreement. The first of these mechanisms, the 'co-respondent' procedure, was introduced in order to enable the EU or a Member State to become a party to proceedings before the ECtHR in certain circumstances. Where the EU acts as 'co-respondent,' a second mechanism, the 'prior involvement procedure', grants the Court of Justice a prior right to assess the compatibility of provisions of Union law with rights defined in the ECHR in instances where it has not yet done so. The Court found aspects of both procedures problematic in Opinion 2/13. Among other things, it objected to the fact that, under both mechanisms, the ECtHR enjoyed potential scope to adjudicate on the interpretation of EU law.[22] By way of illustration, the Court pointed out that the Draft Agreement empowered the ECtHR to determine whether the Court of Justice had already given a ruling on the same question(s) of law at issue in proceedings before it.[23]

Finally, the Court's Opinion declared the Draft Agreement incompatible with the EU Treaties on the basis of its inclusion of substantive policy fields that fall outwith the scope of its own jurisdiction.[24] Under that Agreement, the ECtHR would enjoy jurisdiction to rule on the compatibility of measures falling within the Common Foreign and Security Policy (Title V TEU) with ECHR rights. Art 24(1) TEU places significant restrictions on the Court of Justice's own jurisdiction in that field.

Initial Reflections on Opinion 2/13

The Court's review of the Draft Agreement is open to competing interpretations. Being generous to the Court, it is possible to argue Opinion 2/13 simply gives effect to the Member States' agreed position with respect to the terms of accession. While Art 6(2) TEU expresses a clear commitment that the Union 'shall accede' to the Convention, that

---

[19] At para. 199.
[20] At para. 207.
[21] At para. 212.
[22] At para. 224 and para. 246 respectively.
[23] At para. 240.
[24] At paras 249–257.

© 2015 The Author(s) JCMS: Journal of Common Market Studies © 2015 John Wiley & Sons Ltd

provision and the accompanying Protocol impose restrictive conditions on accession. Those conditions speak directly to the five headline sets of objections outlined above. Specifically, Art 6(2) TEU and Protocol No. 8 EU expressly provide that the accession agreement must preserve the 'specific characteristics of the EU and EU law'; ensure that accession 'does not affect the competences of the EU or the powers of its institutions'; and not interfere with the demands of Art 344 TFEU. Thus, on one view at least, responsibility for the Court's finding of incompatibility in Opinion 2/13 rests in part with the Member States themselves. Member States ought to have pushed harder to secure less onerous 'internal' conditionality at Lisbon.

However, it is equally possible and, it is argued, rather more accurate to assert that Opinion 2/13 is informed by a considerable degree of judicial self-interest. As one leading legal Editorial reaction puts it,

> the Opinion of the Court… appears to reflect a somewhat formalistic and sometimes uncooperative attitude in defence of its own powers vis-à-vis the European Court of Human Rights.[25]

There is indeed little evidence of any 'pro-accession' spirit in the Court's reasoning. The glue that binds the Opinion together is the Court's assessment of the nature of the EU legal order and, in particular, its own position within it. On both matters, the Court is clear and uncompromising. The EU, it restates, is a 'new legal order', with its own constitutional framework, 'particularly sophisticated institutional structure' and 'full set of legal rules to ensure its operation'.[26] The Court of Justice's task is to preserve the specific characteristics and autonomy of Union law.[27] That task is not shared – and, moreover, cannot be shared – with any other internal or external institution. Accordingly, 'it should not be possible for the ECtHR to call into question the Court's finding in relation to the scope *rationale materiae* of EU law'.[28] This conclusion runs through Opinion 2/13 like a recurring literary motif.

The Court's robust defence of the specific characteristics and autonomy of EU law should not surprise seasoned observers. It is the backbone of judgments on constitutional matters. What is striking – and perhaps most disappointing for some – is the absence of a *positive* judicial voice as part of the process of ECHR accession. The Full Court's Opinion is noticeably silent on the virtues of the Union's commitment to accede to the Convention. The focus throughout its substantive assessment is squarely on *dismantling* the Draft Agreement in line with its interpretation of the EU legal system. The failure to adopt a more positive rights-focused approach is a standout feature of the Court's Opinion. Nowhere is this clearer than in its consideration of the Agreement's implications in the area of Common Foreign and Security Policy.[29] It will be recalled that, in that sphere of Union activity, the Court presently enjoys only restricted jurisdiction. On that basis, the Court might have been expected, at the very least, to acknowledge the fact that the introduction of a new (external) system of judicial review would actually *enhance* the protection of fundamental rights in that key policy field overall. Instead, the Court of Justice remained silent and did not waiver in its defence of the specific characteristics and autonomy of the EU legal order.

---

[25] 'The EU's Accession to the ECHR,' at note 12 above at p.1.
[26] Opinion 2/13 at para. 158.
[27] At para. 174.
[28] At para. 186.
[29] See here also 'The EU's Accession to the ECHR,' at note 12 at p. 13.

© 2015 The Author(s) JCMS: Journal of Common Market Studies © 2015 John Wiley & Sons Ltd

Opinion 2/13 leaves the prospect of EU accession to the ECHR in serious difficulties. As others argue, the only solution may be to amend the EU Treaties and mandate ECHR accession 'notwithstanding' the Full Court's Opinion.[30] However, in view of the Court's assessment of the nature of Union law and its own institutional role within the EU legal order, even such an explicit political move by the Member States may not be enough to deliver on the Union's Art 6 TEU commitment to accede to the ECHR.

II. Data Protection

Alongside Opinion 2/13, data protection should also feature prominently in discussion of legal developments in 2014. During the year, the Court delivered two key rulings on different aspects of that policy area. First, in *Digital Rights Ireland* and *Seitlinger and Others* (Joined Cases), the Court struck down as invalid Directive 2006/24 EC on the retention of personal data by public communication providers for the purposes of the prevention of serious crime and acts of terrorism.[31] Second, in *Google Spain*, the Court ruled that internet search engine providers are required to block links to third-party webpages that are accessible through their search engines where the pages concerned contain 'inadequate' or 'irrelevant' information about individuals.[32]

The Court's conclusions in both decisions make important, defining contributions to ongoing political efforts to reform data protection law at Union level. In summary, these efforts seek to recalibrate existing EU data protection instruments to meet the demands of the digital age whilst at the same time tackling threats from organized crime and terrorism through the introduction of potentially far-reaching derogations to data protection laws.

Data Retention, Crime Prevention, and the EU Charter of Fundamental Rights

In *Digital Rights Ireland* and *Seitlinger and Others* (*Digital Rights Ireland*), the Court of Justice was requested to assess the validity of Directive 2006/24 EC on the retention of personal data by public communication providers for the purposes of the prevention of serious crime and acts of terrorism.[33] The applications for judicial review arrived at the Court separately by way of preliminary references from the High Court in Ireland and the Austrian Constitutional Court, respectively, and were subsequently joined.[34] Before the Irish and Austrian courts, both sets of applicants had called into question the compatibility of Directive 2006/24 EC with the EU Charter of Fundamental Rights.

Directive 2006/24 EC was enacted in direct response to public security concerns in the wake of terrorist attacks in Madrid (2004) and London (2005).[35] In summary, it required

---

[30] See e.g., Besselink (2015) 'Acceding to the ECHR notwithstanding the Court of Justice Opinion 2/13.' *VerfassungsBlog*, 23 December 2014. Available at http://www.verfassungsblog.de/en/acceding-echr-notwithstanding-court-justice-opinion-213 (accessed 28 March 2015).

[31] *Digital Rights Ireland and Seitlinger and Others* (C-293/12 and C-594/12) EU:C:2014:238.

[32] *Google Spain* (C-131/12) at para. 93.

[33] Directive 2006/24/EC of the Parliament and Council on the retention of data generated or processed in connection with the provision of publicly available electronic communications services or of public communications networks [2006] OJ L105/54.

[34] Pursuant to Art 54, Consolidated Version of the Rules of Procedure of the Court of Justice [2012] OJ L265/1. Preliminary references are frequently joined under this provision.

[35] http://europa.eu/rapid/press-release_STATEMENT-14-113_en.htm (accessed 28 March 15). See also Directive 2006/24/EC, Preamble 10.

© 2015 The Author(s) JCMS: Journal of Common Market Studies © 2015 John Wiley & Sons Ltd

Member States to introduce legislation obliging telecommunications operators to retain specific items of data generated and processed by them and, further, to make that data accessible to competent national authorities.[36] These measures developed existing provisions that already provided for possible derogations to EU data protection laws. In particular, Art 15(1) of Directive 2002/58 EC empowered *Member States* to enact legislation providing for the retention of communications data for limited periods on the grounds of, inter alia, state security, defence and crime prevention.[37]

In *Digital Rights Ireland*, the applicants argued that the Union legislature's intervention to *harmonize* Member State provisions on data retention through Directive 2006/24 EC was incompatible with Articles 7, 8 and 11 EUCFR on respect for privacy, the protection of personal data and the freedom of expression respectively. Directive 2006/24 EC had already survived direct attack before the Court of Justice: in *Ireland v Parliament and Council*, the Irish Government had unsuccessfully argued that the Directive had been adopted using an incorrect legal base in the Treaty.[38]

Nevertheless, the Court of Justice upheld the applicants' complaints in *Digital Rights Ireland* and struck down the Directive as invalid. It concluded that the framework for data retention established by Directive 2006/24 EC, together with the rules providing for data access by national authorities, constituted a 'serious interference' with the fundamental rights of EU citizens protected in Arts 7 and 8 EUCFR.[39] Moreover, the Court held that the particular degree of interference with citizens' rights to privacy and the protection of personal data could not be justified.[40] With regard to the Directive's provisions on data retention, the Grand Chamber noted that, taken together, the obligations to store data across the five individual categories enabled national authorities to draw 'very precise conclusions' about the private lives of its citizens.[41] The stored data could be used, the Court observed, to track 'the habits of everyday life, permanent or temporary places of residence, daily or other movements, the activities carried out, the social relationship of those persons and the social environments frequented by them'.[42]

Pursuant to Art 52(1) EUCFR, the Court acknowledged that Union law permits restrictions to fundamental rights, including the right to privacy and the protection of personal data. However, such restrictions must be provided for by law; respect the essence of the rights at issue; genuinely serve objectives in the general interest; and comply with the proportionality principle.[43] Appraising Directive 2006/24 EC, the Grand Chamber accepted that the fight against international terrorism and serious crime constitute objectives in the general interest that could, as a matter of principle, serve to justify restrictions to the right to privacy and data protection in Arts 7 and 8 EUCFR.[44]

Nonetheless, on the facts, the Grand Chamber concluded that the restrictions placed on the exercise of Charter rights by the Directive were disproportionate to those objectives.

---

[36] See Directive 2006/24 EC, Arts 5 and 6.

[37] Directive 2002/58/EC of the Parliament and Council concerning the processing of personal data and the protection of privacy in the electronic communications sector [2002] L201/37.

[38] *Ireland v Parliament and Council* (C-301/06) EU:C:2009:68.

[39] *Digital Rights Ireland* (C-293/12 and C-594/12) at paras 37 and 65.

[40] At paras 38–69.

[41] At para. 27.

[42] *Ibid.*

[43] At para. 38.

[44] At para. 42.

In particular, it criticized the scope of the Directive's data retention obligations and the absence of substantive limits and procedural guarantees governing subsequent access to stored information by national authorities. According to the Court, the Directive 'entail [ed] a wide-ranging and particularly serious interference with [Arts 7 and 8 EUCFR], without such an interference being precisely circumscribed by provisions to ensure that it is actually limited to what is strictly necessary'.[45] Remarkably, there was no requirement in Directive 2006/24 EC to establish any link whatsoever between individual activity and the general interest objectives of serious crime and terrorism prevention. Moreover, the Directive placed no real limits on data access by national authorities. Indeed, the Court pointed expressly to the fact that access to data was not conditional on prior judicial authorization.[46]

Digital Rights Ireland is certain to become a touchstone decision in connection with future attempts to introduce key derogations to EU data protection instruments. The relevance of that decision extends far beyond immediate concerns to replace Directive 2006/24 EC – a matter that has, of course, gained renewed impetus in light of the most recent terrorist attacks in France in January 2015. *Digital Rights Ireland* will undoubtedly also have important implications for the adoption of other sector-specific data retention measures. First and foremost in that regard is the proposed Directive on the use of passenger name record data for the prevention, detection, investigation and prosecution of terrorist offences and serious crime (the so-called 'PNR Directive').[47] Prior to the Court's ruling on Directive 2006/24 EC, the Draft PNR Directive had already attracted critical attention, and is now subject to calls for review in light of the Court's data retention ruling.[48]

At a more abstract level, *Digital Rights Ireland* is also a rather neat illustration of the Court of Justice's function within the EU institutional framework as a 'specialist legislature chamber' (Stone Sweet, 2000, p. 61). On that interpretation, the Grand Chamber's decision is principally concerned with the fixing of parameters for *future* constitutionally legitimate policy-making by the EU legislature in the relevant policy area. Further illustrations of this same model of judicial adjudication can be found across other areas of EU law. For instance, in EU internal market law, the case law on Art 114 TFEU (the principal legal basis for internal market legislation) has also resulted in the establishment by the Court of a circumscribed framework for constitutionally legitimate EU policy-making.[49] Indeed, it has been argued that the jurisprudence on Art 114 TFEU has evolved into nothing less than a 'Drafting Guide' on the limits for Treaty-compliant policy-making (Weatherill, 2011, p. 827).

With regard to data protection, the Grand Chamber's prescription to the EU legislature on the parameters for future policy-making is clear. To comply with the demands of Charter rights on privacy and data protection, derogations to the general EU framework must satisfy a strict proportionality test. Following the terms of the Court's ruling, future EU

---

[45] At para. 65. See also para. 57.

[46] At para. 62.

[47] Proposal for a Directive of the Parliament and Council on the use of Passenger Name Record Data for the prevention, detection, investigation and prosecution of terrorist offences and serious crime COM (2011) 32 Final.

[48] See e.g. European Parliament resolution of 11 February 2015 on anti-terrorism measures (2015/2530(RSP)) at para. 13.

[49] See, in particular, the jurisprudence on the scope of Art 114 TFEU incl. *Germany v Parliament and Council* (*Tobacco Advertising*) (C-376/98) EU:C:2000:544.

© 2015 The Author(s) JCMS: Journal of Common Market Studies © 2015 John Wiley & Sons Ltd

acts must 'must lay down clear and precise rules governing the scope and application of the measure in question and imposing minimum safeguards so that the persons whose data have been retained have sufficient guarantees to effectively protect their personal data against the risk of abuse and against any unlawful access and use of that data.'[50]

Given the sensitive nature of the issues, and the readiness of EU citizens to challenge restrictions on their privacy, the Court of Justice will no doubt have an opportunity to assess the Union legislature's compliance with its prescription in the near future.

A Right to be Forgotten in EU Law?

In *Google Spain*, the Court was requested to determine whether internet search engine providers are required to block links to third-party webpages that are accessible through their search engines where the pages contain inadequate or irrelevant information about individuals. That request again arrived at the Court by way of preliminary reference – on this occasion from the National High Court in Spain. The reference has its origins in a dispute between Mr Costeja González, a Spanish national, and Google Spain and its parent, Google Inc., as providers of internet-related products and services. Mr González sought to compel Google to remove search engine links to two news items published in a Spanish newspaper that announced his name in connection with historic (and now settled) proceedings for the recovery of social security debts. His action was successful before the Spanish Data Protection Authority and was now subject to appeal before the referring National High Court.

The outcome of the dispute before the Spanish Court turned on the Court of Justice's interpretation of Directive 95/46 EC on the protection of individuals with regard to the processing of personal data and the free movement of such data.[51] Did the scope of that instrument – enacted prior to the internet revolution and, strikingly, not amended since its adoption in 1995[52] – extend to include the activities of search engine providers? To answer this question, it was necessary to determine three preliminary issues. First, does the execution of internet searches constitute 'data processing' for the purposes of the Directive? Second, are search engine providers such as Google Spain acting as 'controllers' of processed data? And, third, do Google's activities as an internet search engine fall within the territorial scope of the Data Protection Directive?

Advocate Niils General Jääskinen and the Grand Chamber of the Court had little difficulty in concluding that the provision of internet searches constituted 'data processing' within the terms of Directive 95/46 EC. Equally, the two parties were in full agreement that Google Spain's activities fell within the territorial scope of that instrument. However, there was marked disagreement between the Court and the Advocate General over the second issue of Google's status as a 'controller' of personal data. Advocate General

---

[50] *Digital Rights Ireland* (C-293/12 and C-594/12) at para. 54. Further detail on specifics may be gleaned from individual paragraphs of the judgment, especially paras 38–69.
[51] Directive 95/46/EC of the Parliament and Council on the protection of individuals with regard to the processing of personal data and on the free movement of such data [1995] OJ L281/31.
[52] The failure to date (April 2015) to revise Directive 95/46 EC to meet the challenges of the digital age is a standout feature of *Google Spain*. As Advocate General Jääskinen observed, 'Nowadays almost anyone with a smartphone… could be considered to be engaged in activities on the Internet to which the [1995] Directive could potentially apply'. See the Opinion of AG Jääskinen in *Google Spain SL and Google Inc. v Agencia Española de Protección de Datos (AEPD) and Costeja González* (C-131/12) EU:C:2013:424 at para. 10.

© 2015 The Author(s) JCMS: Journal of Common Market Studies © 2015 John Wiley & Sons Ltd

Jääskinen advised the Grand Chamber to conclude that internet search engine providers such as Google Spain are not 'controllers' of personal data held on third-party source webpages.[53] He argued, with close reference to the conclusions of the independent Working Party on data protection established by the Directive,[54] that classification as 'data controller' requires the exercise of 'factual influence' over personal data by the relevant party.[55] The act of simply supplying – through the provision of intermediary search facilities – the *location* of information published by third parties elsewhere does not, the Advocate General argued, meet this test.

The Grand Chamber chose not to follow the Advocate General on the matter of Google's status as a 'data controller' under the Directive. By adopting its own distinctive approach, the Court may also been seen to reject implicitly the independent Working Party's Opinions on the topic, which Advocate General Jääskinen had found particularly 'helpful'.[56] There is, of course, no constitutional obligation on the Court's part to follow (or indeed refer to) such materials in its decision. Nevertheless, it may seem surprising that the Court opted not to do so, especially given the Working Party's expertise, independent advisory status and prior detailed assessments of the topic. The Grand Chamber's decision is instead entirely self-referential and, as such, characterizes a continuation of its own, largely freestanding effort to recalibrate Directive 95/45 EC to meet the challenges of the internet age.[57] The protection of individual privacy and personal data – as now safeguarded in the EU Charter – are key drivers of its approach and directly colour the standard of protection guaranteed within the EU.

Accordingly, the Grand Chamber was clear that the activities of search engine providers such as Google encompass those of 'data control'. In particular, the Court noted that 'search engines [play] a decisive role in the overall dissemination of… data in that [they render] the latter accessible to any internet user making a search on the basis of the data subject's name, including to internet users who would otherwise not have found the web page on which those data are published'.[58] Further, it emphasized that the quality of internet search engines is such that users who search an individual's name may quickly and easily 'establish a more or less detailed and profile' of the relevant individual.[59]

The Court then ruled that, interpreted in light of Arts 7 and 8 EUCFR, Directive 95/46 EC guaranteed individuals the right to request internet search providers to delete certain links to webpages that appear in the list of results following a search under their name.[60] The links to be deleted cover webpages that contain information that is 'inadequate, irrelevant or no longer relevant, or excessive in relation to the purposes of the processing at issue'. The Grand Chamber's judgment is very clear that, as a general rule, an individual's rights to privacy and protection of personal data should trump the interests of other internet users in being able to access (and make independent judgements on) all information

---

[53] Opinion of AG Jääskinen in *Google Spain* at para. 89.
[54] Article 29 Working Party, Opinion 1/2010, available at http://ec.europa.eu/justice/data-protection/article-29/documentation/index_en.htm (accessed 28 March 2015)
[55] *Google Spain* (C-131/12) at para. 88.
[56] At para. 31.
[57] See e.g., Case C 101/01 *Lindqvist* EU:C:2003:596.
[58] *Google Spain* (C-131/12) at para. 36.
[59] At para. 37.
[60] At para. 97.

© 2015 The Author(s) JCMS: Journal of Common Market Studies © 2015 John Wiley & Sons Ltd

linked by name to the individual concerned and lawfully published online by third parties.[61] Nevertheless, the Court noted that, in specific cases, the primacy of the data subject's Charter rights may be qualified in particular instances – for instance, to take account of the data subject's role in public life and the consequential public interest in having access to the information in question.[62]

Media soundbites proclaiming that the Court of Justice established a new 'right to be forgotten' in *Google Spain* are somewhat misleading.[63] Art 12(b) of Directive 95/46 EC already guaranteed data subjects the right to obtain, from data controllers directly, the correction, deletion or blocking of data that was incomplete, inaccurate or otherwise incompatible with the Directive. The standout feature of *Google Spain* is the Grand Chamber's decision to categorize internet search engine operators as 'data controllers'. It was that move that effectively brought Google within the scope of the Directive and, as such, subject to full compliance with its data protection provisions as interpreted by the Court in light of EU Charter rights.

In any case, *Google Spain* has significant implications for the regulation of online privacy in EU law. The decision effectively imposes on Google (and, by extension, other market operators) a legal responsibility to balance, in individual instances, the data subject's rights to privacy and the protection of personal data with the public interest in the freedom of expression. This is an important responsibility that presents obvious challenges for search engine providers. As a Google spokesperson put it, 'the Court's ruling requires Google to make difficult judgments about an individual's right to be forgotten and the public's right to know'.[64] Critics argue that market operators should not be entrusted (or burdened) with such a responsibility. [65]

The issue of horizontal effect (the obligation imposed on market operators to balance competing fundamental rights) is an important one, especially in light of the scale and significance of the subject matter. However, as the Grand Chamber's judgment makes clear, the responsibility entrusted to market operators is imposed only at first instance. *Google Spain* does not leave the task of weighing competing fundamental rights entirely to market operators and individual citizens as a matter of private concern. Under the terms of Directive 95/46 EC, the decisions of search engine operators on the balance of competing fundamental rights in individual instances remain subject to full regulatory and/or judicial oversight.[66] The regulatory framework governing the implementation of *Google Spain* will, therefore, be constructed in part and over time through direct interactions with, first and foremost, Member State data protection authorities.

The Court's decision to place a central aspect of online EU data protection law principally in the hands of a stakeholder/supervisor partnership – ahead of efforts to revise Directive 95/46 EC through the ordinary EU legislative process[67] – is a bold move. It may

---

[61] At para. 94.

[62] At para. 97.

[63] See e.g. *Time Magazine*, 15 May 2014 and *The Economist*, 4 October 2014.

[64] *Reuters*, 30 May 2014.

[65] See here the Opinion of AG Jääskinen at para. 133.

[66] At para. 77.

[67] The Commission's Proposal for a Regulation on the protection of individuals with regard to the processing of personal data and on the free movement of such data (the 'General Data Protection Regulation') COM (2012) 11 Final is, at the time of writing (April 2015), still under negotiation.

© 2015 The Author(s) JCMS: Journal of Common Market Studies © 2015 John Wiley & Sons Ltd

also yet prove an effective regulatory strategy. At the same time, however, that strategy may be criticized for sacrificing too readily the virtues of legislative deliberation for the efficiency of an involuntary operator-led response. For its part, Google acted promptly to implement the Grand Chamber's decision. In May 2014, and within weeks of the judgment, the company launched an online form to enable citizens to request the removal of specific links that appear in results following searches that include their name.[68] On its first day of operation over 12,000 individual requests were made through the company's online application process.[69] By October 2014, that total had risen to 143,000.[70]

Of greater concern perhaps is the Court's substantive conclusion in *Google Spain* – in the form of its guidance to Google and Member State data protection agencies – on the balancing of fundamental rights. The judgment is certainly is open to criticism that the Court attached insufficient weight to the freedom of expression – also protected in the Charter (Art 11 EUCFR) – when it sought to establish the parameters for the assessment of competing fundamental rights. Indeed, it is a striking feature of the decision that Art 11 EUCFR is not cited at all in the operative paragraphs of the Grand Chamber's reasoning on the scope of the Directive.

III. The Scope of Application of the Charter – Further Insights

The data protection jurisprudence clearly illustrates the powerful impact of the EU Charter of Fundamental Rights on the interpretation of primary and secondary Union law. During 2013 and 2014, the Court of Justice also moved to clarify further key aspects of the Charter's application. In particular, the Court considered the scope of application of the Charter to the Member States (Art 51 EUCFR)[71] ; the interaction of Charter rights with other international and domestic fundamental rights provisions (Art 53 EUCFR)[72] ; and the direct effect of individual EU Charter provisions.[73] For reasons of space, this contribution will comment only on key aspects related to the first two issues – with a focus on headline developments in each field.

Art 51 EUCFR: The Charter and Member State Activity

In 2013, the Court of Justice outlined its approach to the interpretation of Art 51 EUCFR. That provision determines the extent to which the Charter extends to capture Member State activity. Art 51 provides that Member States are subject to the Charter 'when they are implementing Union law'. In *Fransson*, the Grand Chamber held that the concept of 'implementing Union law' in Art 51 EUCFR should be interpreted in line with its pre-existing case law governing the scope of application of EU fundamental rights – as unwritten 'general principles' of Union law – to Member State activity.[74] In both instances, the decisive factor is whether Member States are 'acting in the scope of European Union law.'

---

[68] https://support.google.com/legal/contact/lr_eudpa?product=websearch (accessed 28 March 15).
[69] *Reuters*, 30 May 2014.
[70] *EU Observer*, 10 October 2014.
[71] *Fransson* (C-617/10).
[72] *Melloni* (399/11).
[73] *Association de médiation sociale v Union locale des syndicats CGT and Others* (C-176/12) EU:C:2014:2.
[74] *Fransson* (C-617/10) at para. 21.

© 2015 The Author(s) JCMS: Journal of Common Market Studies © 2015 John Wiley & Sons Ltd

By aligning the 'implementing Union law' with reference to the jurisprudence on the general principles of Union law, the Court of Justice has, to a certain extent, invoked one riddle to resolve another. The case law on the 'scope of Union law' is no vision of clarity and itself warrants further judicial rationalization (and academic assessment).[75] With specific regard to the Charter, the Court has, however, subsequently formulated the following guidance to assist national courts in determining when Member State activity falls within the scope of Union law. According to the Court:

> [In] order to determine whether a national measure involves the implementation of EU law for the purposes of Article 51(1) of the Charter, it is necessary to determine, inter alia, *whether that national legislation is intended to implement a provision of EU law*; the *nature of the legislation at issue* and *whether it pursues objectives other than those covered by EU law*, even if it is capable of indirectly affecting EU law; and also *whether there are specific rules of EU law on the matter* or rules which are capable of affecting it.[76]

In *Fransson*, the Grand Chamber adopted a rather expansive view of the 'scope of Union law' on the facts. That decision requested the Court to consider in light of Art 50 EUCFR (*ne in bis idem*) the legality of Swedish measures that had led to the applicant being punished twice for the same infringements of national tax law. The Grand Chamber grounded its jurisdiction to apply the Charter by establishing a link between the subject matter giving rise to the national proceedings at issue (Mr Fransson's underpayment of VAT) and the existence of a combination of Union instruments and Treaty obligations in the same substantive area (Directive 2006/112 EC on the common system of VAT, Art 4(3) TEU and Art 325 TFEU).[77] The fact that the relevant national tax penalties and criminal proceedings had not been adopted formally to transpose, in particular, Directive 2006/112 EC was considered irrelevant.[78] The Court read into the *application* of the national measures in the specific instance an *intention* on the part of the Swedish authorities to penalize an infringement of the aforementioned EU Directive.

Subsequent decisions from ordinary Chambers of the Court appear to suggest a more cautious judicial approach to defining the scope of the Charter's application to the Member States. In both *Hernandez* and *Siragusa*, for instance, the Court stressed that the concept of 'implementation' in Art 51 EUCFR 'presupposes a degree of connection between the measure of EU law and the national measure at issue *which goes beyond the matters covered being closely related or one of those matters having an indirect impact on the other*'.[79] Thus, 'the mere fact that a national measure comes within an area in which the European Union has powers cannot bring it within the scope of EU law, and, therefore, cannot render the Charter applicable'.[80] Nevertheless, it is suggested that the door has not yet closed on judicial ambition in this particular dimension of EU constitutional law. The overriding impression emerging from the case law is of a Court that is continuing to refine its approach to the scope of the Charter – with a careful eye on its own sphere of influence in the field of fundamental rights.

---

[75] See here e.g. the forthcoming contribution by Dougan in the *CML Rev.* (forthcoming, 2015).

[76] *Hernández and Others* (C-198/13) EU:C:2014:2055 at para. 37 (emphasis added). See also e.g. *Siragusa v Regione Sicilia* (C-206/13) EU:C:2014:126 at para. 25.

[77] *Fransson* (C-617/10) at paras 24–27.

[78] At para. 28.

[79] *Hernández and Others* (C-198/13) at para. 34 and *Siragusa* (C-206/13) at para. 24 (emphasis added).

[80] *Hernández and Others* (C-198/13) at para. 36.

© 2015 The Author(s) JCMS: Journal of Common Market Studies © 2015 John Wiley & Sons Ltd

Should the Court settle for a more restrained reading of the criterion of 'implementing Union law' (and, in parallel, that of 'acting within the scope of Union law'), then this would sit comfortably with the demands of Art 6 TEU and Art 51(2) EUCFR. These two provisions make clear that the introduction of a legally binding Charter at Lisbon was not intended '[to] extend the field of application of Union law beyond the powers of the Union or establish any new power or task for the Union, or modify powers and tasks as defined in the Treaties'.[81] The Court's evolving jurisprudence on the scope of the Charter's application to the Member States should be read in the shadow of both provisions.

Member States Give Way: Interactions between Charter Rights and National Fundamental Rights Standards

In 2013, the Court of Justice was also invited to consider the scope of another of the EU Charter's key horizontal provisions: Art 53 EUCFR. That provision is one of several that cite the Charter within the broader legal framework governing the protection of fundamental rights within Europe. It reads:

> Nothing in this Charter shall be interpreted as restricting or adversely affecting human rights and fundamental freedoms as recognised, in their respective fields of application, by Union law and international law and by international agreements to which the Union or all the Member States are party, including the [ECHR] and by the Member States' constitutions.

In *Melloni*, the Court was requested to determine whether Art 53 EUCFR provided a basis for Member States to maintain *higher national* standards of fundamental rights protection when acting 'within the scope of Union law'.[82] The applicant, Mr Melloni, had been convicted *in absentia* in Italy for bankruptcy fraud and now faced extradition from Spain to Italy pursuant to a European Arrest Warrant issued by the Italian authorities. Before the referring Spanish Constitutional Court, Mr Melloni argued that the Spanish authorities should not execute the arrest warrant on the ground that his conviction was not open to review before the Italian courts. The possibility for review in the issuing Member State, he argued, was necessary to safeguard his fundamental rights to a fair trail and defence as enshrined, in particular, in Spanish constitutional law.

The Grand Chamber, supported by the Advocate General, had little difficulty in rejecting the applicant's argument. The Court concluded that Art 53 EUCFR did not permit the Spanish authorities, on the basis of national constitutional law, to make surrender of a person convicted *in absentia* conditional upon the relevant conviction being open to review in the issuing Member State. In the Court's view:

> That interpretation of Article 53 of the Charter would undermine the principle of the primacy of EU law inasmuch as it would allow a Member State to disapply EU legal rules which are fully in compliance with the Charter where they infringe the fundamental rights guaranteed by that State's constitution.[83]

The Court's direct appeal to the primacy of Union law in *Melloni* indicates that, in instances of conflict between EU Charter rights and national fundamental rights standards,

---

[81] Art 51(1) EUCFR.
[82] *Melloni* (C-399/11).
[83] At para. 58.

© 2015 The Author(s) JCMS: Journal of Common Market Studies © 2015 John Wiley & Sons Ltd

the former must prevail. Art 53 EUCFR does not, therefore, introduce a further, exceptional qualification to the Court's established case law on the relationship between supranational and domestic law.[84] At the same time, the decision in *Melloni* does not completely displace scope for Member State input in the area of fundamental rights. As the Grand Chamber noted, pursuant to Art 53 EUCFR, Member States remain free to apply national standards of fundamental rights protection when implementing Union law, provided that this does not compromise 'the level of protection provided for by the Charter' and/or the 'primacy, unity, and effectiveness of Union law'.[85]

The scope of residual Member State input in the sphere of fundamental rights protection is often ultimately determined by the extent of Union intervention in the relevant field. In *Melloni*, the rules governing the extradition of persons convicted *in absentia* in other Member States had been fully harmonized at Union level.[86] This left Spain no scope to impose additional conditions as executing Member State on the basis of national fundamental rights law. By way of contrast, subsequent decisions confirm that Member States retain scope to influence fundamental rights standards at Union level in instances where Union measures do not regulate matters exhaustively. In *Jeremy F*, for example, the Court was requested to determine whether the United Kingdom could provide for 'appeals with suspensive effect' against decisions related to a European Arrest Warrant.[87] Framework Decision 2002/584 JHA was silent on the possibility of such appeals.[88] The Court concluded that, subject to its oversight for compliance with Union law, Member States remained free to apply their own constitutional guarantees relating to, inter alia, the right to a fair trial.[89]

At first sight, it is tempting to take a highly critical view of the *Melloni* judgment. The Grand Chamber, it would appear, selfishly defended the primacy of Union law (and, thereby, its own sphere of influence) at the expense of efforts to *enhance* the protection of the applicant's fundamental rights. Yet, considered in its broader context, that reading of the decision does not stand up to rigorous scrutiny. The Court's reasoning – including in *Melloni* itself – on the right to a fair trial and rights of defence (Arts 47 and 48(2) EUCFR) confirms that EU standards of rights protection under the Charter are very much in keeping with the scope of rights recognized by the ECtHR in the same areas. Indeed, the Grand Chamber makes this point expressly in its assessment of the compatibility of Framework Decision 2002/584 JHA (European Arrest Warrant) with Arts 47 and 48(2) EUCFR.[90]

If *Melloni* carries any warning message, then that message targets the EU legislature. It is a reminder of the potential weaknesses inherent in decisions to harmonize Member State provisions *exhaustively* around *minimum* (ECtHR compliant) standards. By agreeing to adopt minimum baselines as the regulatory ceiling, the Member States (acting through the Council) effectively forfeit the right to invoke national law as a means subsequently to adjust – and *trade up* – the agreed common regulatory framework. That is the direct consequence of the primacy of EU law. Ordinarily, the consequences of that move

[84] Contrast e.g. *Asda Stores Ltd* (C-108/01) EU:C:2003:296.
[85] *Melloni* (C-399/11) at para. 60.
[86] At para. 62. See also the Opinion of Advocate General Bot at para. 86.
[87] *Jeremy F. v Premier minister* (C-168/13 PPU) EU:C:2013:358.
[88] Council Framework Decision on the European arrest warrant and the surrender procedures between Member States [2002] OJ L190/1.
[89] *Jeremy F. v Premier minister* (C-168/13 PPU) at para. 53.
[90] *Melloni* (C-399/11) at para. 50.

may simply frustrate certain Member States on specific occasions. In the sensitive areas of criminal justice and fundamental rights protection, the consequences of failing to raise the regulatory floor sufficiently at the legislative stage may be much more profound for both Member States and individual citizens.

IV. Union Citizenship: Economically Inactive Citizens

A survey of EU legal developments would not be complete without mention of the case law on EU citizenship. 2013–14 was another busy period for the Court in the field of Union citizenship, with a total of 29 judgments. The highlight from the preceding two-year period is undoubtedly the case law addressing the rights of *economically inactive* Union citizens.[91] In what will likely be read as a concession to certain Member State governments (notably the UK and German governments), the Court of Justice has made subtle, yet potentially significant adjustments to its case law. In summary, it has accepted that Member States may refuse to grant social assistance to economically inactive Union citizens who exercise their right to freedom of movement without sufficient resources of their own.

C-333/22 Dano v. Jobcenter Leipzig

The Court affected its key shift in approach with respect to economically inactive Union citizens in its *Dano* judgment. In that decision, the Grand Chamber concluded that Union law did *not* preclude Member State legislation under which economically inactive nationals of other Member States are excluded from accessing non-contributory benefits granted to nationals of that state who are in the same situation. The applicant, Ms Dano, was a Romanian national, who had resided in Germany together with her son, Florin (also a Romanian national) since July 2011. Ms Dano and Florin resided with the applicant's sister, who also provided for them materially. As the preliminary reference makes clear, Ms Dano was not working (and had not previously worked) in either Germany or Romania. Moreover, there was nothing to indicate that the applicant was searching (or had previously searched for) employment. To cover material needs, Ms Dano had applied unsuccessfully for a social assistance grant pursuant to provisions of Book II of the German Social Code ('Sozialgesetzbuch Zweites Buch'; SGB II).

The judgment in *Dano* is highly significant. At the level of political analysis, the decision may be viewed as offering a judicial olive branch to (certain) Member State governments. In recent years, Union citizenship – and, in particular, the rights of economically inactive EU citizens – has become a highly politicized legal status within key Member States. A rising tide of euroscepticism within, inter alia, the United Kingdom and Germany has given a powerful voice to criticism that the European Union, and the Court of Justice in particular, empowers Union citizens to engage in so-called 'benefit tourism.'[92] Notwithstanding the absence of objective data to support such arguments, the governments of certain Member States have taken unilateral steps to address perceived concerns regarding the domestic social and economic costs of Union

---

[91] In particular, *Dano and Florin Dano v Jobcenter Leipzig* (C-333/13) EU:C:2014:2358 and *Pensionsversicherungsanstalt v Brey* (C-140/12) EU:C:2013:565.

[92] See e.g. 'The Free Movement of Persons in the European Union: Salvaging the Dream while Explaining the Nightmare' (Editorial) (2014) 51 *CML Rev.* 726.

© 2015 The Author(s) JCMS: Journal of Common Market Studies © 2015 John Wiley & Sons Ltd

citizenship.[93] The United Kingdom, for instance, has repeatedly amended its implementing regulations on Union citizenship in recent years and introduced new restrictions on EU residence rights and social benefit entitlements.

In *Dano*, the Grand Chamber sets out a clear statement of principle with regard to the scope of EU citizenship rights. Union law does not guarantee economically inactive Union citizens a right to access the welfare systems of host Member States to fund their subsistence. To conclude otherwise, the Court ruled,

> [w]ould run counter to an objective of [The Citizens' Rights Directive, 2004/38 EC] set out in recital 10 in its preamble, namely preventing Union citizens who are nationals of other Member States from becoming an unreasonable burden on the social assistance system of the host Member State.[94]

To a greater extent, it was already apparent from both primary and secondary Union law that *economically inactive* Union citizens enjoy only conditional rights of residence and qualified equal treatment (see Thym, 2015). By contrast, *economically active* citizens and those of independent means are afforded far greater constitutional protection. *Dano* leaves this underlying dynamic unchanged. What the Grand Chamber judgment does adjust, however, is the constitutional framework governing the assessment of the right to equal treatment afforded to economically inactive Union citizens under Union law. This second layer of legal analysis is potentially of great importance, with clear potential to 'tighten up' the scope of EU citizenship rights overall – at least for the economically active.

The striking feature in *Dano* is the Court's decision to determine the scope of EU citizenship rights with express, and apparently exhaustive, reference to *secondary* Union law. In part, this characterizes a novel and noteworthy shift in approach. First, and less remarkably, the Court concluded that Ms Dano's right to equal treatment was derived from Art 24 of Directive 2004/38 and Art 4 Regulation 883/2004.[95] Both provisions were taken as 'specific expressions' of the general prohibition on discriminatory treatment set out in Art 18 TFEU. Far more significantly, however, the Court then ruled that the protection guaranteed by the aforementioned provisions could *only* be invoked if the applicant could establish a residence right *under Directive 2004/38 EC* (i.e. secondary EU law). According to the Court,

> So far as concerns access to social benefits… a Union citizen can claim equal treatment with nationals of the host Member State only if his residence in the territory of the host Member State complies with the conditions of Directive 2004/38.[96]

The decision to tie the establishment of a right of *residence* under Union law to compliance with the terms of Directive 2004/38 EC is a key structural innovation. Traditionally, the Court has accentuated *primary* Union law as the basis of Union citizens' residence rights. The provisions of Directive 2004/38 EC – while central to the enquiry – are thus classically interpreted as subject to compliance with the demands of the Treaty.

---

[93] For a comprehensive review, see the respective national reports prepared for the XXVI FIDE Congress (Copenhagen, 2014), published in Neergaard *et al.* (2014)

[94] *Dano* (C-333/13) at para. 74.

[95] Directive 2004/38/EC of the Parliament and Council on the right of citizens of the Union and their family members to move and reside freely within the territory of the Member States [2004] OJ L158/77 and Regulation 883/2004/EC of the Parliament and Council on the coordination of social security systems [2004] OJ L166/1.

[96] *Dano* (C-333/13) at para. 69.

© 2015 The Author(s) JCMS: Journal of Common Market Studies © 2015 John Wiley & Sons Ltd

Accordingly, the Court has frequently invoked Arts 20 and 21 TFEU in order to emancipate the substantive rights of residence and equal treatment guaranteed to Union citizens from the strict letter of Directive 2004/38 EC.[97] The provisions of that Directive are typically taken by the Court as *part of* the range of conditions and limits imposed on Union citizens' Treaty rights as opposed to the direct source of substantive rights *per se*. In result, this approach has generally supported the progressive judicial expansion of EU citizenship rights under primary Treaty law.

The Court's decision to sharpen the substantive rights of Union citizenship around Directive 2004/38 EC will be welcomed by those with concerns about the extent of Member State solidarity obligations towards economically inactive EU citizens. Indeed, certain Member State governments will find particular comfort in the Grand Chamber's structural adjustment. The United Kingdom government, for instance, had already expressly linked entitlement to equal treatment with respect to social assistance to the establishment of a 'right to reside' under Directive 2004/38 EC – a move upheld by the UK Court of Appeal but challenged by the EU Commission.[98] For Ms Dano, the Court's decision effectively makes her residence in Germany subject to immigration control under *national* law. Given the relatively low thresholds set for 'sufficient resources'[99] and, by analogy, the ease by which EU nationals may trigger Treaty protection as economic actors (e.g. workers),[100] the gap in rights protection that defines Ms Dano's situation is arguably relatively small. Nevertheless, for the applicant and her dependent child, it is unquestionably very real.

In time, the Court will likely offer further clarification on the nature of its apparent tightening of the legal framework governing the residence and equal treatment rights of economically inactive citizens. In particular, it is hoped that the Court will set out where its *Dano* judgment fits with the other 'layers'[101] of its case law on EU citizenship. For instance, does it remain open to non-economically active EU nationals to access the right to equal treatment in EU law on the basis of lawful residence under *national* law? Similarly, are the requirements for lawful residence under Directive 2004/38 EC still open to review (and potential 'loosening') by the Court of Justice against primary Union law? Finally, is the concept of a 'real' or 'genuine link' to the host state relevant to the assessment of the residence rights of inactive EU citizens post-*Dano*?

What is already clear, however, is that the assessment of Union citizens' own resources for the purposes of establishing residence under Art 7(1)(b) of Directive 2004/38 EC must take the form of an individualized review.[102] Member States must carefully examine the financial situation of every Union citizen specifically, and without taking into account the social benefits claimed, in order to determine whether or not that person satisfies the condition of having 'sufficient resources' under that provision of the Directive.[103] Recourse to generic thresholds to guide the application of EU citizenship rights is not permitted.[104]

---

[97] See e.g. *Baumbast and R* (C-413/99) EU:C:2002:493 and *Grzelczyk* (C 184/99) EU:C:2001:458.

[98] *Abdirahman v Secretary of State for Work and Pensions* [2007] EWCA Civ 657 and http://europa.eu/rapid/press-release_IP-13-475_en.htm respectively (accessed 28 March 15).

[99] Art 8(4), Directive 2004/38/EC.

[100] See e.g., *Trojani* (C-456/02) EU:C:2004:488 at para. 15.

[101] This label is borrowed from Thym, 2015.

[102] Art 8(4), Directive 2004/38/EC.

[103] *Dano* (C-333/13) at para. 80.

[104] Art 8(4), Directive 2004/38/EC and *Brey* (C-140/12) at para. 68.

© 2015 The Author(s) JCMS: Journal of Common Market Studies © 2015 John Wiley & Sons Ltd

Concluding Remarks: Continuity and its Power

2014 was a year of considerable political and institutional change within the European Union.[105] That year was marked, of course, by elections to the European Parliament; the appointment of new figures to the key positions of President of the European Council and High Representative for Foreign Affairs; and the (rather tumultuous) election of a new EU Commission President. In sharp contrast, developments in the legal sphere in the same year are remarkable only for their obvious continuity – not merely at an institutional level, but principally in terms of their guiding narrative. As before, EU law, and the Court of Justice in particular, can clearly be seen to be exercising definite influence over the nature, scope, and trajectory of European integration.

This contribution has surveyed a selection of judicial highlights from the previous year. To address a gap in last year's *Review*, it also considered two sets of key decisions delivered in 2013. In isolation, the case law illuminates particular points of advancement, refinement and fracture in the protection of EU fundamental rights across a broad spectrum of EU policy areas. In *Digital Rights Ireland* and *Google Spain*, for instance, Union citizens saw their EU fundamental rights to privacy and data protection further enhanced through judicial adjudication. On the other hand, in the area of EU citizenship, the Grand Chamber's decision in *Dano* may be seen to have adjusted (downward) the legal framework governing the extent of Member State solidarity obligations towards economically inactive EU citizens. *Fransson* and *Melloni* offer welcome – if yet incomplete – clarification on the scope application of the EU Charter of Fundamental Rights to Member State activity. Finally, in Opinion 2/13, the Full Court squarely rejected the terms of political agreement regarding the EU's accession to the ECHR, casting doubt over the viability of the entire accession project.

Through the lens of EU fundamental rights, the legal developments explored in this contribution also offer powerful insights into the nature and impact of the Court's role vis-à-vis the Union institutions, Union citizens and the Member States. The case law selected for analysis touches on each of these constellations and, in all three, exposes – once again – the position of the Court of Justice at the very epicenter of Union policy-making. Thus, in *Digital Rights Ireland*, the Court may be seen to circumscribe the parameters for *future* constitutionally legitimate policy-making by the EU legislature in the field of data protection. In *Google Spain*, its interpretation of the legal framework regulating data management affected significant legal reform ahead of, and very much detached from, contemporaneous political efforts at Union level to recalibrate EU data protection policy for the digital age. *Dano* represents an apparent refinement of the Court's *own* earlier creativity in the field of EU citizenship. Perhaps most strikingly, in Opinion 2/13 the Full Court may even be seen to act as the ultimate guardian of European integration – protecting the Union *from what it sees* as interference by the Member States themselves. These decisions are not isolated phenomena, but examples of the thickest and most colourful threads that form part of the rich tapestry that characterizes EU judicial adjudication.

The prominence of the Court's institutional role in EU integration is again attracting the attention of EU legal scholars. A growing body of legal writing is refocusing the analytical spotlight on judicial law-making and its legitimacy. This shift in emphasis signals

[105] See the accompanying contributions to this volume.

© 2015 The Author(s) JCMS: Journal of Common Market Studies © 2015 John Wiley & Sons Ltd

a renewed awareness among legal scholars of the continuing centrality of the Court's role in EU integration – a position reinforced by the conclusions of the present contribution. It also reflects scholarly concerns with, in particular, the quality of EU judicial decision-making and the nature of the institutional relationship between the Court and the Union legislature. Key contributions include those by Adams *et al.* (2013); Beck (2013); Conway (2012); Dawson, De Witte and Muir (2013); Horsley (2013); Micklitz and De Witte (2012); Nic Shuibhne (2013); and Rosas *et al.* (2013). Overall, recent studies by legal scholars of the Court and its role in EU integration demonstrate an increased openness to the adoption of more critical perspectives. Several recent contributions also integrate inter-disciplinary perspectives into legal analysis of judicial law-making and its legitimacy. Both developments represent welcome and enriching scholarly trends.

References

Adams, M., de Waele, H., Meeusen, J. and Straetmans, G. (eds) (2013) *Judging Europe's Judges*: *The Legitimacy of the Case Law of the European Court of Justice Examined* (Oxford: Hart Publishing).

Amtenbrink, F. (2013) 'Legal Developments'. *JCMS*, Vol. 51, No. s1, pp. 139–54.

Beck, G. (2013) *The Legal Reasoning of the Court of Justice of the EU* (Oxford: Hart Publishing).

Besselink, L.F.M. (2015) Acceding to the ECHR Notwithstanding the Court of Justice Opinion 2/13. *VerfassungsBlog*, 23 December 2014. Available at «http://www.verfassungsblog.de/en/acceding-echr-notwithstanding-court-justice-opinion-213»

Conway, G. (2012) *The Legal Limits of Legal Reasoning and the European Court of Justice* (Cambridge: Cambridge University Press).

Dawson, M., De Witte, B. and Muir, E. (eds) (2013) *Judicial Activism at the European Court of Justice* (Cheltenham: Edward Elgar Publishing).

Editorial (2014) 'The Free Movement of Persons in the European Union: Salvaging the Dream while Explaining the Nightmare'. *Common Market Law Review*, Vol. 51, No. 3, pp. 726–40.

Editorial (2015) 'The EU's Accession to the ECHR – a "NO" from the ECJ!' *Common Market Law Review*, Vol. 52, No. 1, pp. 1–15.

Horsley, T. (2013) 'Reflections on the Role of the Court of Justice as the "Motor" of European Integration: Legal Limits to Judicial Lawmaking'. *Common Market Law Review*, Vol. 50, No. 4, pp. 931–64.

Micklitz, H-W. and De Witte, B. (eds) (2012) *The European Court of Justice and the Autonomy of the Member States* (Cambridge/Antwerp/Portland, Intersentia Publishing).

Neergaard, U. and Jacqueson, C. and Holst-Christensen, N. (eds.) (2014) *Union Citizenship*: *Development, Impact and Challenges* (Copenhagen: DJØF Publishing).

Shuibhne, N. (2013) *The Coherence of EU Free Movement Law*: *Constitutional Responsibility and the Court of Justice* (Oxford: Oxford University Press).

Rosas, A., Levits, E. and Bot, Y. (eds.) (2013) *The Court of Justice and the Construction of Europe*: *Analyses and Perspectives on Sixty Years of Case-law* (The Hague: Springer Verlag).

Stone Sweet, A. (2000) *Governing with Judges* (Oxford: Oxford University Press).

Thym, D. (2015) 'The Elusive Limits of Solidarity: Residence Rights of and Social Benefit for Economically Inactive Union Citizens'. *Common Market Law Review*, Vol. 52, No. 1, pp. 17–50.

Weatherill, S. (2011) 'The Limits of Legislative Harmonization Ten Years after Tobacco Advertising: How the Court's Case Law has become a "Drafting Guide"'. *German Law Journal*, Vol. 12, No. 3, pp. 827–64.

© 2015 The Author(s) JCMS: Journal of Common Market Studies © 2015 John Wiley & Sons Ltd

JCMS 2015 Volume 53 Annual Review pp. 128–143　　　　　　　　　　　　DOI: 10.1111/jcms.12261

Justice and Home Affairs

JÖRG MONAR
College of Europe

I. Introduction

The last year of the 2009–14 Stockholm Programme for the development of the 'Area of Freedom, Security and Justice' (AFSJ) found the EU struggling not very successfully with increasing asylum and refugee flows across the Mediterranean, but making some legislative progress in the difficult field of legal immigration. Judicial co-operation in both civil and criminal matters also saw advances through the adoption of several legal instruments, the latter in particular through the introduction of the highly innovative European Investigation Order. In the internal security domain the terrorist threat posed by returning 'foreign fighters' became a major preoccupation for the Council whose traditionally strong reliance on data collection and processing instruments for countering internal security threats was challenged during the year by both the Court of Justice and the European Parliament on fundamental rights and data protection grounds. Two major joint operations – 'Triton', focused on maritime border management, and 'Archimedes', on the fight against cross-border crime – showed the growing operational dimension and capabilities of the AFSJ. Rather than adopting a successor to the 'Stockholm Programme' the European Council adopted more modest 'Strategic Guidelines' focused on consolidation and better implementation.

II. Developments in Individual Policy Areas

Asylum and Migration

The crises in the Union's wider neighbourhood not only posed major challenges to its foreign and security policy in 2014 but also contributed to a major increase of the pressures on its asylum system. Over the entire year asylum applications increased by 44 per cent in comparison with the year before, with a total number of 626,026: while applications by Syrians topped the list with 122,790, the number of Ukrainians seeking asylum increased by 13 times compared to the year before to a total of 14,040 (Eurostat, 2015). The increasing numbers repeatedly made the headlines in EU media because of a continuing series of incidents in the Mediterranean that cost the lives of refugees as victims of the unscrupulous people smugglers with their unseaworthy boats. The Union faced again severe criticism from various sides, including by German Federal President Joachim Gauck who, when referring to the Mediterranean incidents at a refugee policy conference in Berlin in June, accused both national and EU policy-makers of not doing enough in response to the plight of the refugees (Bundespräsident, 2014). With nearly one-third of total EU asylum applications lodged in Germany (202,645), at the time the country went through a new acrimonious asylum debate, although it was

© 2015 The Author(s) JCMS: Journal of Common Market Studies © 2015 John Wiley & Sons Ltd, 9600 Garsington Road, Oxford OX4 2DQ, UK and 350 Main Street, Malden, MA 02148, USA

actually Sweden that received the highest number of applications in relation to its population size with 8,415 per million inhabitants, three times more than Germany (Eurostat, 2015).

Reinforced by the completion of the recast legislative package of the Common European Asylum System (CEAS) the year before, the EU was less passive in the face of the mounting asylum challenges than some criticisms made it appear. The Commission stepped up emergency funding for national asylum structures under pressure – with Greece and Italy as primary beneficiaries – and used the newly operational Asylum, Migration and Integration (AMIF) Fund to support the promotion of best practice in asylum procedures for asylum seekers with special needs, including information campaigns in co-operation with the United Nations High Commissioner for Refugees (UNHCR) on the risks for refugees to use illegal immigration channels and resettlement and relocation projects (European Commission, 2014a). The Commission also reported in May that in response to a call by the UNHCR, 11 Member States had offered more than 13,100 places for the resettlement and humanitarian admission of persons from Syria, although this still fell well short of the 30,000 the UNHCR had asked for by the end of 2014 (European Commission, 2014b).

The European Asylum Support Office (EASO) expanded again its practical and technical support to EU Member States and institutions and adjusted its work programme with more emphasis on Member States' implementation of the recast asylum package through training, practical co-operation activities, country-of-origin information and quality reports as well as on the further development of EASO's early warning and preparedness system (European Asylum Support Office, 2014a). The Office reported in July that it had deployed 56 asylum support teams (ASTs) under the second operating plan for Greece. The deployment to this geographically exposed Member State provided continuous training for the staff and first-instance caseworkers of the new Greek Asylum Service, to help provide relevant country-of-origin information to first-instance caseworkers and the staff of appeal authorities. It also strengthened the quality management of the first-instance asylum decision-making procedure. The deployment also provided organizational advice for the clearing of the huge backlog of Greek asylum cases. Yet over 35,000 of such cases still remained unresolved in June, which led EASO to estimate that the backlog would not be cleared before mid-2017 (European Asylum Support Office, 2014b). Both the Greek case and the limited response of Member States to the UNHCR appeal in favour of the Syrian refugees demonstrated again the almost complete dependence of EU asylum policy effectiveness on national capabilities and responses.

One of the major recent institutional innovations in EU asylum policy has been the creation – in October 2013 after the Lampedusa refugee boat tragedy – of the 'Task Force Mediterranean' (TFM), composed of representatives of the Commission, the Member States, the EEAS and relevant EU agencies. Established to optimize the use of EU instruments in order to avoid a repetition of the Lampedusa tragedy, the Task Force had asylum policy measures within its remit right from the start. While the TFM has provided an impetus for the establishment of regional protection programmes for refugees from Syria and Northern Africa and made EASO action part of a integrated approach to asylum and migration, challenges in the Mediterranean listed in the Commission's first implementation report of 22 May clearly showed that the Task Force has been focusing on migration and sea border management issues, with overall little added value on the asylum policy side (European Commission, 2014c).

© 2015 The Author(s) JCMS: Journal of Common Market Studies © 2015 John Wiley & Sons Ltd

With some of the refugee movements across the Mediterranean being clearly motivated by economic migration motives, and migratory pressures remaining substantial also on the Greek and Bulgarian land borders to Turkey as well as in the Western Balkans, migration management continued to figure high on the EU agenda. At an informal meeting of JHA ministers in Milan on 8 July an effort was made to overcome the at times tense polarization between (mostly southern) Member States demanding more intra-EU solidarity and (mostly northern) Member States emphasizing more responsibility in terms of more effective migration and border management. The Italian Presidency of the second half of the year,[1] to which the deteriorating situation in the Mediterranean was of obvious concern, subsequently introduced a paper aimed at a sustainable approach beyond short-term emergency measures in the migration field. This was transformed into formal Council conclusions on 'Taking action to better manage migration flows' by the JHA Council of 8–9 October. These Council conclusions identified three 'pillars' for the new approach, consisting first of co-operation with third countries with a primary focus on the fight against smugglers and trafficking in human beings; second, the strengthening of the ability of Frontex (see next section) to respond in a flexible and timely manner to emerging risks and pressures; and finally, actions within the EU to uphold and implement the CEAS fully with a special emphasis on operational co-operation (Council of the European Union, 2014a).

The new strategy document dedicated much of its space – two-thirds of the total – to co-operation with third countries of transit and origin in order to reduce migratory pressures, but contains little in terms of assessment of the likely chances of success of co-operation objectives with the different countries in question. It is, for instance, foreseen that, together with the Tunisian, Egyptian and Libyan authorities, ways will be identified of curtailing the supply of vessels from Tunisia and Egypt for the illegal immigration trade, in parallel with supporting those countries in managing migratory flows. In the case of Tunisia, the basis for such co-operation was reinforced during 2014 not only by the continuing post-Arab Spring political and constitutional stabilization of the country, but also through the agreement on a 'Mobility Partnership' between Tunisia, the EU and ten Member States,[2] which was formally established on 3 March and includes co-operation on visa facilitation, integration of Tunisian migrants, easier mutual recognition of professional and university qualifications, readmission and the prevention of human trafficking and the smuggling of migrants (European Commission, 2014d). No comparable basis for co-operation on migration issues could so far be achieved with Egypt – and, because of major political instability, even less so with Libya – which shows the persisting obstacles to an effective overall external EU migration policy.

Some distinct progress was also made on the legal immigration side with the adoption of two directives aimed at facilitating access to work in the EU for two specific categories of third-country workers, but this progress was achieved at the expense of further differentiation as Denmark, Ireland and the United Kingdom opted out from both instruments.

On 17 February – after more than three years of negotiations – the Council adopted Directive 2014/36/EU on the conditions of entry and stay for third-country nationals for the purpose of employment as seasonal workers (European Parliament/Council of the

---

[1] See Carbone's contribution to this volume.
[2] Belgium, Denmark, France, Germany, Italy, Poland, Portugal, Spain, Sweden and the United Kingdom.

© 2015 The Author(s) JCMS: Journal of Common Market Studies © 2015 John Wiley & Sons Ltd

European Union, 2014a). It had to find a difficult balance between addressing the Member States' different needs in seasonal work – mostly in agriculture and tourism; their interest in keeping numbers under control and avoiding temporary stays turning into permanent ones; and the aim of providing sufficient rights for seasonal workers to avoid their exploitation. To qualify as a 'seasonal worker' under the terms of the directive, a third-country national must comply with a range of conditions. In particular, he has to retain his principal residence in his own country, stay legally and temporarily in the territory of a Member State to carry out an activity dependent on the 'passing of the seasons', come with a valid work contract or binding job offer of fixed duration, provide – if applicable – evidence that he can comply with the conditions of regulated professions in the EU and evidence of sickness insurance and accommodation arrangements (Articles 3, 5 and 6). It is left to the Member States to determine during transposition the sectors of employment which include activities that are dependent on the 'passing of the seasons' (Article 2(2)) and a maximum period of stay for seasonal workers of not less than five months and not more than nine months in any 12-month period (Article 14(1)). This already large margin of discretion left to the national level is further extended by the option for Member States to reject an application for seasonal work under the directive if the vacancy can be filled by its own nationals, other EU citizens or other already lawfully resident third-country nationals (Article 8(3)). If eligible, however, the third-country seasonal worker benefits not only from a single authorization procedure combining the issuing of a visa (or, if applicable, visa exemption) and work permit (Article 12) but also, depending on national conditions, from facilitated extensions of stay and re-entry (Articles 15 and 16) and – more importantly – a right to accommodation that ensures an adequate standard of living (Article 20) and equal treatment with EU nationals as regards the terms of employment, the right to strike, social security, education and vocational training, as well as tax benefits (Article 22). While the directive has its fair share of complexity – a distinction between stays based on short-term Schengen visas and longer non-Schengen visas runs through several provisions – and leaves Member States a large margin of discretion, it nevertheless marks a major step ahead both for EU-wide recognition that third-country workers have their role to play in European economies and – a point much insisted upon by the European Parliament during the lengthy negotiations with the Council – for ending widespread discriminatory practices regarding them.

The other instrument of migration relevance, which the Council adopted on 13 May, was the directive 2014/66/EU on the conditions of entry and residence of third-country nationals in the framework of an intra-corporate transfer (European Parliament/Council of the European Union, 2014b). The directive is aimed at making it easier and quicker for multinational companies to transfer highly skilled employees temporarily to subsidiaries within the EU – and thus to enhance EU competitiveness – while at the same time preventing their exploitation and risks of distorting competition. The directive is applicable to third-country managers, specialists or trainee employees who are temporarily seconded for occupational or training purposes by companies established in third countries to subsidiaries within the EU who have been employed for at least three months by their company and provide the necessary work contract and qualification evidence for taking up the transfer assignment, including an undertaking to be taken back by the company to employment outside of the EU after the termination of their assignment (Articles 3 and 5). To avoid potential abuse by multinational companies, the remuneration granted to the third-country national during the entire intra-corporate transfer is not less favourable than that granted to nationals of the Member State where the work is carried out occupying comparable positions (Article 5(4)). Member States can also refuse an intra-corporate transferee application if the host entity has only been set up for the purpose of receiving transferees or if it has not respected its legal obligations regarding social security, taxation, labour rights or working conditions (Article 7). Member States also remain free to reject applications on grounds of their right to determine volumes of admission of third-country nationals (Article 6), and the maximum duration of the intra-corporate transfer is three years for managers and specialists and one year for trainee employees (Article 12). The transferees themselves benefit not only from a simplified permit issuing procedure, but also from a right to equal treatment and family reunification largely aligned with that of EU nationals (Articles 18 and 19). An innovative feature is the entitlement of intra-corporate transferee permit holders – subject to a number of conditions – to stay in any second Member State and work in any other entity established in the latter and belonging to the same undertaking or group of undertakings within the maximum periods of their assignment, and this without being subject to the usual Schengen visa requirement (Article 21 and 22).

Although politically less sensitive than the seasonal workers instrument, because of the lower numbers of third-country nationals involved, the intra-corporate transferee directive also took more than three years of negotiations because of Member States' concerns about fraud, abuse and circumvention of national control possibilities. This has led to the inclusion of many more conditions than originally proposed by the Commission; nevertheless, the directive does cover some new ground as regards intra-EU mobility of third-country workers. The adoption of both the intra-corporate transferee and the seasonal workers directives may be regarded as no minor achievement, as the continuing negotiations on the recast directive on the conditions of entry and residence of third-country nationals for the purposes of research, studies, pupil exchange, training, voluntary service and au pairing showed that any EU progress on facilitating legal immigration remains difficult, especially at times of particular challenge to labour markets in some Member States. At the end of the year there were still major concerns on the part of national delegations regarding the scope of the directive, the intra-EU mobility of the categories of third-country nationals concerned and the rights granted to third-country nationals (Council of the European Union, 2014b).

Border Management

In its annual risk assessment for 2014, the Union's external border management agency, Frontex, highlighted the continuing heavy illegal immigration pressure on the Southern Mediterranean coast and the borders with Turkey. It underlined also the fluidity of the situation at the EU's external borders, as enhanced surveillance along the Greek land border with Turkey had resulted in a displacement to the Eastern Aegean Sea and the Bulgarian land border with Turkey. Frontex also placed a major emphasis on the increasing workload of European external border authorities in a time of steadily increasing air and land travel flows, increasingly sophisticated document fraud and rapid route changes of the gangs involved in illegal immigration facilitation and people smuggling. In this context, the coming into full operation of the EU's new Visa Information System

(VIS) – whose three-year transitional period ended in October – also had two sides to it. On the one hand, VIS brings enhanced visa issuing and control security; on the other hand, it also means that the border authorities of all Schengen countries are expected to be able to carry out VIS fingerprint verifications at all border crossing points and also be able to issue VIS visas with biometric components at the border when necessary (Frontex, 2014a).

In the context of its monitoring of the Schengen system's functioning, the European Commission identified a five-fold increase of illegal immigration over the Central Mediterranean route and a 35 per cent increase in detections of illegal stays inside of the Schengen zone compared to the same period the year before as major indicators of strain on the system. Yet in its 6th Schengen Report in November the Commission arrived at an overall positive assessment of the operation of the system with few truly justified temporary reintroductions of controls at internal borders, one completed investigation on an alleged incompatibility of national legislation with the Schengen rules on the absence of internal border controls (a German case) and the preparations for extending the European Border Surveillance System 'Eurosur' from the initial 19 to all 30 Schengen countries by 1 December 2014 being kept on track. The details of the improved Schengen evaluation mechanism – already decided upon in 2013, which aimed at improving both compliance with the Schengen acquis and allowed an earlier detection of compliance problems of Schengen members – were also finalized, with the first application of the mechanism scheduled for February 2015. The new second-generation Schengen Information System (SIS II) saw increased use of its new categories of objects and functionalities after the necessary adaptions of the national police systems, but the Commission also reported concerns regarding the security of the system after a previous hacker attack on the Danish national system and an investigation into the physical security of the system at Polish external borders (Commission, 2014e). The interaction between so many still organizationally and legally autonomous national border management systems will inevitably remain a challenge not only for the SIS II but also for the Schengen system in general.

The ultimate test of effective border management always lies in the operational sphere, and in this respect Frontex, with its now 317 staff members, continued to play a crucial role (Frontex, 2014b). It was not only tasked with helping to bring the remaining 11 Schengen countries (which had needed a longer preparatory time) with their National Coordination Centres into 'Eurosur' and to feed national border situational data into an operationally usable 'European Situational Picture', but also continued to play a key role in the planning and co-ordination of a series of joint external border operations. One of the largest of these operations in recent years – with a monthly budget of €2.9 million and the involvement of seven patrol ships, four patrol aircraft and one helicopter and personnel from 21 Member States – was launched under the name of 'Triton' on 1 November, covering the territorial waters of Italy and part of the search and rescue (SAR) zones of Italy and Malta. This operation replaced the major Italian migration control and SAR operation 'Mare Nostrum' which had put an increasing strain on Italian resources, but with a more limited operational range of only 30 miles off the Italian coast. As an important part of the EU's response to the major increase of refugee and migration pressure via the Central Mediterranean route, 'Triton' was focused on sea border control and the interception of people smugglers in combination with a search and rescue mandate. Although of a more limited reach than the Italian 'Mare Nostrum' Frontex was able to report on 'Triton' at the end of the year the rescue of 11,400 migrants, with around

© 2015 The Author(s) JCMS: Journal of Common Market Studies © 2015 John Wiley & Sons Ltd

10,000 having found themselves in a 'distressed' situation in a total of 77 SAR operations. With some of the intercepted freighters filled with up to 600 people and Syrian refugees having to pay the smugglers up to €6,000 each only to get to the embarkation point, the operation showed again the profitability of the situation for the criminal gangs and the extent of the challenge (Frontex, 2014c).

Judicial Co-operation

Judicial co-operation in civil matters has attracted few headlines since the establishment of the Union's AFSJ but it has made a steady contribution to improved access to justice, legal certainty and predictability in cross-border legal proceedings to the benefit of both citizens and companies. This contribution was further strengthened by the Council's adoption on 13 May of Regulation (EU) 655/2014, establishing a European Account Preservation Order procedure to facilitate cross-border debt recovery in civil and commercial matters (European Parliament/Council of the European Union, 2014c). The Regulation enables a creditor to obtain a protective measure in the form of a *European Account Preservation Order* (EAPO) preventing the transfer or withdrawal of funds held by his debtor in a bank account maintained in a Member State if there is a risk that, without such a measure, the subsequent enforcement of his claim against the debtor, who may wish to dissipate the funds to frustrate recovery efforts, will be impeded or made substantially more difficult. Such protective measures exist in all Member States, but their conditions and efficiency vary considerably, and the recourse to national protective measures can be rather cumbersome in cases with cross-border implications, in particular when the creditor seeks to preserve several accounts located in different Member States.

The EAPO will be available to a creditor as an alternative to national procedures either (a) before he initiates proceedings in a Member State against the debtor on the substance of the matter, or at any stage during such proceedings up until the issuing of the judgment or the approval or conclusion of a court settlement, or (b) after the creditor has obtained in a Member State a judgment, court settlement or authentic instrument which requires the debtor to pay the creditor's claim (Article 5). In order to ensure the surprise effect of the EAPO, the Order will be issued without a prior notification of the debtor ('ex parte procedure', Article 11). In order to counterbalance the absence of a prior hearing of the debtor, the Regulation foresees a range of remedies available to the debtor so that he can challenge the order as soon as he is informed of the freezing of his accounts (Article 33). As a further safeguard, Article 12 obliges the creditor to provide security for an amount sufficient to prevent abuse of the procedure and to ensure compensation for any damage suffered by the debtor as a result of the order. While the reach of the Regulation has been reduced by a rather narrow definition of 'account' – limiting it essentially to deposits in money – and its accessibility to creditors by the (heavy) condition to provide security, it can be still expected to make an important contribution to the reduction of the length, cost and legal uncertainty of cross-border debt recovery. The non-participation of Denmark and the United Kingdom – on the basis of their 'opt-outs' – appears all the more regrettable from the perspective of the Union as an 'area of justice'.

While the adoption by the Council on 6 May of Regulation (EU) 542/2014 amending the 'Brussels I Regulation' on jurisdiction and the recognition and enforcement of judgments in civil and commercial matters had a more technical objective – to render the latter's rules applicable to two courts common to several Member States, the Unified Patents Court and the Benelux Court of Justice (European Parliament/Council of the European Union, 2014d) – the Council's approval on 4 December of the 2005 Hague Convention on Choice of Court Agreements had a wider significance (Council of the European Union, 2014c). The Convention defines uniform rules for the conferral of jurisdiction on a court designated by parties to a cross-border dispute in civil and commercial matters, and determines the conditions upon which a judgment rendered by a court by a contracting state so designated shall be recognized and enforced in all other contracting states. The Council Decision approving the conclusion of the Convention on behalf of the Union was one important consequence of the 2006 Lugano Opinion of the Court of Justice (Opinion 1/03), asserting the exclusive external competence of the Union in matters on jurisdiction, and the recognition and enforcement of judgments in civil and commercial matters, underlining the international reach of the Union's internal competence in the civil justice field.

In the criminal justice field, substantial legislative progress was made with the finalization of three new legal instruments. The most innovative of the three is Directive 2014/41/EU establishing a European Investigation Order (EIO) in criminal matters which the Council adopted on 14 March (European Parliament/Council of the European Union, 2014e). The directive constitutes one of the most advanced applications of the principle of mutual recognition in EU criminal justice to date by enabling a judicial authority in one Member State (the 'issuing' state) to have, via the issuing of an EIO, one or several specific investigative measure(s) carried out in another Member State (the 'executing' state) to obtain evidence in criminal proceedings (Article 1), with the executing state having only a strictly limited range of grounds, such as a potential incompatibility of the order with the freedom of the press or expression rights, for non-recognition or non-execution of the EIO (Article 11). The investigative measures which can be ordered via the EIO include, *inter alia*, the obtaining of information or evidence already in the possession of the executing authority, the hearing of witnesses and (with additional safeguards) the temporary transfer to the issuing state of persons held in custody for the purpose of carrying out an investigative measure, covert investigations and information on and monitoring of bank accounts and the interception of telecommunications. The executing authority in the other Member State shall acknowledge the receipt of an EIO within 30 days and carry out the investigation measure within 90 days, and the decision on the recognition or execution must be taken and the investigative measure carried out with the same celerity and priority as for a similar domestic case (Article 12). As a safeguard against over-frequent use of the EIO it is provided that the order should only be issued if 'necessary and proportionate' for the purpose of the criminal proceedings and if the investigative measure(s) indicated in the EIO could have been ordered under the same conditions in a similar domestic case (Article 6). The rights of the suspected or accused person have to be taken into account in the issuing decision, and Member States have to ensure that legal remedies are equivalent to those available in a similar domestic case (Article 14).

In terms of scope and binding effects on the executing authorities, the introduction of the EIO marks a significant step beyond the 2008 European Evidence Warrant (EEW) directive, which had been a rather ineffective instrument. Once fully effective – Member States have been given the generous deadline of 22 May 2017 for full compliance – it will replace a complex patchwork of existing mutual legal assistance rules.

© 2015 The Author(s) JCMS: Journal of Common Market Studies © 2015 John Wiley & Sons Ltd

While the United Kingdom decided to 'opt in', Denmark and Ireland did not – a further element of differentiation which is not serving the objective of a single (and effective) EU area of justice. The Danish and Irish non-participation has also made a full replacement of the EEW impossible; as a result, it will co-exist with the much more effective EIO.

On the same day as the EIO directive the Council also adopted Directive 2014/42/EU on the freezing and confiscation of instrumentalities and proceeds of crime (European Parliament/Council of the European Union, 2014f). It provides for enhanced possibilities for confiscating proceeds of crime in cases of illness or the absconding of the person concerned (Article 4); as well as for extended powers of confiscation where a court, on the basis of the circumstances of the case, such as that the value of the property being disproportionate to the lawful income of the convicted person, is satisfied that the property in question is derived from criminal conduct (Article 5); and in cases in which property has been directly or indirectly transferred by a suspected or accused person to third parties. The directive addresses some of the weaknesses of existing EU instruments in enabling national authorities to confiscate and recover profits from cross-border crime and responds, in particular, to the increasing sophistication of transnational organized crime operations.

A rather different type of criminal activity was targeted by the adoption by the Council on 14 April of Directive 2014/57/EU on criminal sanctions for market abuse (European Parliament/Council of the European Union, 2014g). This directive complements, on the criminal justice side, the parallel adoption of the new EU Market Abuse Regulation (EU 596/2014) and reflects the political consensus reached at EU level after the experiences of the 2008–09 financial crisis that criminal sanctions for serious forms of market abuse are needed to set clear boundaries for types of financial trading behaviour that are considered to be particularly unacceptable, and to send a corresponding message to both the public and potential offenders. The directive establishes minimum rules for criminal sanctions for insider dealing, for unlawful disclosure of inside information and for market manipulation (Articles 1 and 3 to 5). It provides for both the necessary technical definitions of the different types of financial market abuse offences and a mandatory sanction level of a maximum term of imprisonment of at least four years (Article 7). Inciting, aiding and abetting the above types of abuse are also defined as offences, but with the lower sanction level of at least two years of imprisonment (Articles 6 and 7). Sanctions for legal persons – including potential permanent closure – are also foreseen (Article 9). Given that previously not all Member States had provided for effective sanctions for the financial market abuse forms covered by the directive, and that different national approaches affected negatively both the effectiveness of prosecution and the uniformity of conditions of operation within the internal market, the instrument should make a substantial contribution to ensuring the integrity of EU financial markets and strengthening investor protection and confidence.

Throughout the year, negotiations continued on the establishment of a European Public Prosecutor's Office (EPPO) for combating criminal offences affecting the financial interests of the Union, with a majority of Member States favouring a much more decentralized organization of the Office than originally aimed at by the Commission. At the end of the year there seemed to be strong support in the JHA Council for the EPPO being organized in such a way that the European Prosecutors Members of the EPPO

© 2015 The Author(s) JCMS: Journal of Common Market Studies © 2015 John Wiley & Sons Ltd

College and forming the backbone of the Office would, as a rule, supervise the work of European Delegated Prosecutors in their Member States of origin, rather than exercise investigation and prosecution powers themselves. Considering that this approach could raise questions as regards the effective independence of the Office, the Italian Presidency suggested, as a balancing measure, that the independence of the European Chief Prosecutor, chairing the EPPO College, and the European Prosecutors should be reinforced through more transparent and 'European' rather than purely national appointment procedures. A majority of ministers then agreed that the independence of the European Prosecutors should be strengthened in order to balance the proposed supervision mechanism, including through a more transparent and objective procedure of nomination and appointment of the Members of the College (Council of the European Union, 2014d). The negotiations revealed again the preference of most Member States for a horizontal co-ordination rather than vertical integration approach to criminal justice in the Union, although the intensity of the negotiations also showed at least a willingness to move beyond an institutional status quo which still provides ample opportunities for fraud against the EU budget to escape effective prosecution.

Internal Security Co-operation

The fight against terrorism ranked again high on the Union's internal security agenda. In its annual 'Terrorism Situation & Trend Report', Europol placed a particular emphasis on the threat posed by the substantial and increasing numbers of EU citizens travelling to Syria in particular, to fight alongside al-Qaeda-affiliated groups. Europol concluded on a likely 'exponential' rise of the threat to the EU in the wake of the civil war in Syria, as these European fighters may have sought to set up logistical, financial or recruitment cells, serve as role models to individuals within extremist communities and come back to the EU with their resolve strengthened by the combat experience and the skills and contacts necessary to carry out attacks (Europol, 2014). Later in the year, evidence about young European radical Islamists joining the ranks of the murderous advance in Iraq of the so-called 'Islamic State in Iraq and the Levant' added further urgency to the Europol threat assessment.

The challenge posed by European 'foreign fighters' was discussed thoroughly by the JHA Council in its meeting on 5–6 June, during which the ministers confirmed the importance of more action on prevention, information exchange, detection of travel, criminal justice responses and co-operation with third countries. On the same occasion the Council adopted a revised 'EU Strategy for Combating Radicalisation and Recruitment to Terrorism' providing, *inter alia*, for a range of objectives on improving communication work countering terrorism, measures against online radicalization and recruitment, civil society counter-terrorism, capacity-building, promoting initiatives aimed at encouraging disengagement of potential terrorists and the alignment of internal external counter-radicalization work (Council of the European Union, 2014e). Through its very comprehensive approach, the revised strategy, which was complemented by implementation guidelines adopted by the Council at its 4–5 December meeting (Council of the European Union, 2014f), appears better adapted to the complex social, psychological, cultural and political context of terrorist radicalization and recruitment. However, the Member States felt it necessary to emphasize again their primary responsibility for combating the

© 2015 The Author(s) JCMS: Journal of Common Market Studies © 2015 John Wiley & Sons Ltd

phenomenon as well as the nationally 'specific nature' of the threat, an insistence on national competences and priorities which may explain a regrettable absence of more precise and binding targets in both the strategy and the implementation guidelines.

On 30 August the 'foreign fighters' threat reached the top EU political level when the European Council called for an 'accelerated implementation' of counter-measures and asked the Council to review the effectiveness of the measures and to propose additional action until December (European Council, 2014a). In December, the Italian Presidency was in a position to report some progress, such as the establishment of a European Commission-organized forum with representatives from EU institutions, governments and industries on how to remove illegal content from the Internet, the creation of a 'Syria Strategic Communications Advisory Team' providing expertise to governments and EU institutions on counter-terrorist strategic communications and advanced preparations for the putting into place of an 'Radicalisation Awareness Network' (PREVENT-RAN) Centre assisting Member States in setting up practical counter-radicalization or disengagement projects (Council of the European Union, 2014g). However, the Presidency's report remained silent on the strong insistence of the EU's Counter-Terrorism Coordinator, Gilles de Kerchove, in a paper submitted to the Council on 2 December, that an update of the EU's criminal law legislation would be needed as part of the response to the foreign fighters and returnees phenomenon (Council of the European Union, 2014h). This was contested by several Member States which considered additional action at the national level more effective, so the December JHA Council could agree on no more than 'assessing' the need for a revision of the relevant Framework Decision on combating terrorism reached in 2002.

The Council's strong reliance on personal data collection and analysis as a core element of the EU counter-terrorism strategy and the fight against cross-border crime in general suffered a partial setback on 8 April when the Court of Justice of the EU declared the Directive 2006/24/EC on the retention of telecommunication data invalid. Given its aim to harmonize national rules on the retention of data generated or processed by providers of publicly available electronic communications services for the purpose of the prevention, investigation, detection and prosecution of serious crime, the directive had remained controversial ever since its adoption in 2006. The Court had been asked by the Irish High Court and the Austrian Constitutional Court (Joined Cases C-293/12 and C-594/12) under a preliminary rulings procedure to examine the validity of the directive, in particular in light of two fundamental rights under the Charter of Fundamental Rights of the EU, namely the fundamental right to respect for private life and the fundamental right to the protection of personal data. In its judgment the Court accepted, on the one hand, that the retention of data for the purpose of their possible transmission to the competent national authorities genuinely satisfied an objective of general interest, namely the fight against serious crime and, ultimately, public security. On the other hand, however, the Court ruled that the wide-ranging and particularly serious interference of the directive with the fundamental rights at issue is not sufficiently circumscribed to ensure that that interference was actually limited to what is strictly necessary and thus failed to comply with the principle of proportionality. The Court referred, in particular, to serious shortcomings of the directive in terms of differentiations, limitations and exceptions, as well as the definition of objective criteria in relation to the retention and use of the data by national authorities in the light of the objective of fighting against serious crime (Court

© 2015 The Author(s) JCMS: Journal of Common Market Studies © 2015 John Wiley & Sons Ltd

of Justice, 2014). As the Court also criticized a lack of objective criteria in the rules applicable to the data retention period, the absence of sufficient safeguards to ensure effective protection of the data against the risk of abuse and unlawful access and use of the data, as well as inadequate provisions for ensuring control of compliance with the requirements of protection and security in the case – for which the directive allows – that the data are not retained within the EU, it was clear that a completely new instrument would be needed. While support for a new instrument remained strong in the Council, the invalidation of the directive and the Court's reasoning was welcomed by the European Data Protection Supervisor (European Data Protection Supervisor, 2014) and many Members of the European Parliament. At the end of the year, the European Commission was still treading carefully, declaring it would consider different options rather than committing itself to making a new proposal soon (Commission, 2014f).

The invalidation of Directive 2006/24/EC also strengthened opposition within the European Parliament against parts of the proposed EU directive on the use of Passenger Name Record (PNR) data for the prevention, detection, investigation and prosecution of terrorist offences and serious crime, now under negotiation since 2011. Although the Council put strong pressure on the Parliament to endorse the measure, with the European Council calling even in August upon the Parliament to finalize it before the end of the year in the light of the terrorist foreign fighters threat (European Council, 2014a), a majority of the Parliament's Civil Liberties (LIBE) Committee stressed in a session on 11 November (focused on the PNR proposal), and following the Court's ruling of 8 April, the need to assess whether existing measures would be sufficient before adopting new ones and to put in place adequate data protection safeguards (European Parliament, 2014a). A further indication of Parliament's critical attitude towards the issue was its vote on 25 November – by a majority of 383 to 271 (with 47 abstentions) – to refer the new EU–Canada agreement on the transfer of PNR to the Court of Justice for an opinion on its compatibility with the EU Treaties and Charter of Fundamental Rights (European Parliament, 2014b).

With one of the pillars of its internal security approach – data collection and analysis – being partially put into question by both Court and Parliament, the Council could at least note with some satisfaction that progress continued to be made on the operational side. In October, Europol reported to the Council the overall very satisfactory results of the large-scale joint law-enforcement 'Operation Archimedes', running from 15 to 23 September, which had involved all 28 Member States and six third countries who committed thousands of police officers to co-ordinated actions in 260 locations to disrupt organized crime groups engaged in the trafficking and production of drugs, the trafficking of human beings, the facilitation of illegal immigration, organized property crime, the trade in firearms and counterfeit goods. According to the consolidated report submitted on 2 December, the operation resulted in 1150 arrests, more than 350 seizures and the freeing of nearly 200 victims of trafficking in human beings. While there were also a number of weaknesses identified – in particular insufficient planning time and problems with the transfer of frontline operational information to Europol – the contribution the operation had made was generally appreciated, with most Member States being keen on repeating the exercise, although perhaps on a smaller, more regionally focused scale. The fact that Europol noted in its report – with apparent satisfaction – that the operation had been reported in the media 3245

© 2015 The Author(s) JCMS: Journal of Common Market Studies © 2015 John Wiley & Sons Ltd

times suggested that public visibility is increasingly becoming a consideration for the agency (Council of the European Union, 2014i).

III. Development Perspectives

With the 2009–14 'Stockholm Programme' ending during the year, the Member States had to address the question of a potential successor in line with the five-year programming cycle for the AFSJ which had been applied since the 1999–2004 'Tampere Programme'. The overall balance sheet of the Stockholm Programme appeared to be rather mixed. On the one hand it had defined several strategic priorities and helped the EU to focus on, and make progress in, a number of areas: the adoption of the second-generation asylum legislation package in 2013; the creation of the European Asylum Support Office and the reinforcement of technical operational support through the passage to the second-generation Schengen Information System (SIS II); the establishment of the agency for the operational management of large-scale IT systems in the AFSJ (EU-LISA), EUROSUR and the Visa Information System (VIS); as well as substantial advances on mutual recognition in the civil law domain (including on the sensitive issue of divorce and legal separation) and with respect to the strengthening of procedural rights in the criminal justice domain. All these developments count heavily on the positive side of the balance.

On the other hand, however, progress in the fields of both legal immigration and the harmonization of substantive criminal law have been rather modest, and in spite of the new asylum package the Stockholm Programme has not been able to change the afore-mentioned almost complete dependence of EU asylum policy effectiveness on national capabilities and responses. The Stockholm Programme has also failed to enable the Union to react more effectively to crisis situations in the AFSJ (such as the Mediterranean refugee surges), to arrive at a sustainable system of solidarity in response to asymmetric pressures on Member States (such as Greece and Malta) and to address the mounting civil society and parliamentary concerns about the more extensive use of cross-border personal data collection and processing instruments for law-enforcement purposes.

Given the chequered outcome of the Stockholm Programme and after much reflection and inputs from several sides (including the European Commission), the answer to the question about a potential successor came in the form of the 'Strategic guidelines for legislative and operational planning within the area of freedom, security and justice' which were formally adopted by the European Council in its session of 26–27 June and inserted in its 'Conclusions' (European Council, 2014b). It was just as well that the term 'Programme' was not used, as these 'Guidelines' can clearly not match any of the previous five-year frameworks in terms of programmatic ambition.

The core rationale of the Guidelines – which operate on the same five-year horizon with a mid-term review in 2017 – is given in paragraph 3, which states that 'the overall priority now is to consistently transpose, effectively implement and consolidate the legal instruments and policy measures in place'. Most of the objectives listed are exceedingly general – such as 'addressing smuggling and trafficking of human beings more forcefully' or 'enhance mutual recognition of decisions and judgements in civil and criminal matters' – and none of them goes beyond the horizon of the preceding Stockholm Programme. Controversial issues are addressed in the most innocuous way. The EPPO, for instance, is addressed only in relation to the protection of the EU's financial interests with merely the objective of 'advancing negotiations' on it, which – given the 2020 time horizon – is surely to keep pressure for progress at a minimum.

While there is undeniably a lot of scope in the EU justice and home affairs domain for better implementation and the consolidation of existing instruments and mechanisms, the absence of any more substantial and clearly new strategic objectives and commitments in the 'Guidelines' can be taken as an indication that the period of rapid expansion of the AFSJ in the first decade after the Tampere European Council of 1999 has now definitely come to an end. There is simply no sufficient political consensus among the Member States about the ultimate aims of the AFSJ to warrant more substantial deadline-linked objectives – a lack of consensus highlighted not least by the coming into effect on 1 December 2014 of the UK's block opt-out from 130 pre-Lisbon 'third-pillar' measures in combination with a re-opt-in into 35 of those, as decided the year before. However, the absence of a strategic consensus with corresponding objectives does not necessarily mean stagnation for the coming years: not only can the European Commission play a dynamic role because of its right of initiative, but Member States are also very likely to continue to consider common action whenever common challenges generate enough pressure and additional action can bring evident benefits to all. This was shown once again on 4 December when the Council adopted conclusions on an 'Renewed European Internal Security Strategy' to be prepared for 2015 which placed an emphasis on better matching EU action with emerging security threats and identified some potential innovations such as the possible introduction of a European Police Record Index System (EPRIS) (Council of the European Union, 2014j). More short-term and instrumental responses to common challenges may be less 'programmatic' and 'strategic' in nature – but they can nonetheless generate some significant progress.

References

Bundespräsident (2014) 'Berliner Symposium zum Flüchtlingsschutz'. 30 June.
Council of the European Union (2014a) 'Council Conclusions on "Taking action to better manage migratory flows"'. 14141/14, 10 October.
Council of the European Union (2014b) 'Proposal for a Directive of the European Parliament and of the Council on the conditions of entry and residence of third-country nationals for the purposes of research, studies, pupil exchange, remunerated and unremunerated training, voluntary service and au pairing [Recast] [First reading] – Approval of negotiation mandate'. 16512/14, 9 December.
Council of the European Union (2014c) 'Council Decision of 4 December 2014 on the approval, on behalf of the European Union, of the Hague Convention of 30 June 2005 on Choice of Court Agreements'. OJ L 353, 10 December.
Council of the European Union (2014d) 'Proposal for a Council Regulation on the establishment of the European Public Prosecutor's Office – Report on the State of Play'. 16993/14, 18 December.
Council of the European Union (2014e) 'Revised EU Strategy for Combating Radicalisation and Recruitment to Terrorism'. 9956/14, 19 May.
Council of the European Union (2014f) 'Guidelines for the EU Strategy for Combating Radicalisation and Recruitment to Terrorism'. 13469/1/14 REV 1, 27 November.
Council of the European Union (2014g) 'Report on measures with regard to foreign fighters'. 16915, 16 December.

© 2015 The Author(s) JCMS: Journal of Common Market Studies © 2015 John Wiley & Sons Ltd

Council of the European Union (2014h) 'Foreign fighters and returnees: discussion paper'. 15715/2/14, REV2, 2 December.

Council of the European Union (2014i) 'Operation Archimedes – Evaluation Report'. 16442/14, 4 December.

Council of the European Union (2014j) 'Council conclusions on the development of a renewed European Union Internal Security Strategy'. 14186/6/14 REV 6, 13 November.

Court of Justice (2014) 'Judgment of the Court (Grand Chamber) of 8 April 2014 (requests for a preliminary ruling from the High Court of Ireland (Ireland) and the Verfassungsgerichtshof (Austria)) – Digital Rights Ireland Ltd (C-293/12) v Minister for Communications, Marine and Natural Resources, Minister for Justice, Equality and Law Reform, The Commissioner of the Garda Síochána, Ireland and the Attorney General, and Kärntner Landesregierung, Michael Seitlinger, Christof Tschohl and Others (C-594/12)'. Luxembourg, 8 April.

European Asylum Support Office (2014a) 'EASO work programme 2014'. Valetta, 1 August (adjusted version).

European Asylum Support Office (2014b) 'EASO Operating Plan for Greece. Interim Assessment of Implementation'. Valetta, 28 July.

European Commission (2014a) 'Annex to the Commission Implementing Decision concerning the adoption of the work programme for 2014 and the financing for Union actions and emergency assistance within the framework of the Asylum, Migration and Integration Fund'. C(2014) 5652, 8 August.

European Commission (2014b) '5th Annual Report on Immigration and Asylum'. COM(2014) 288, 22 May.

European Commission (2014c) 'Implementation of the Communication on the Work of the Task Force Mediterranean'. SWD(2014) 173, 22 May.

European Commission (2014d) 'Déclaration conjointe pour le Partenariat de Mobilité entre la Tunisie, l'Union Européenne et ses Etats membres participants'. Brussels, 3 March.

European Commission (2014e) 'Sixth bi-annual report on the functioning of the Schengen area 1 May – 31 October 2014'. COM(2014) 711, 27 November.

European Commission (2014f) 'Exchange of Views between Commissioner Dimitris Avramopoulos and MEPs at the LIBE Committee in the European Parliament'. Brussels, 3 December.

European Council (2014a) 'Special meeting of the European Council (30 August 2014) – Conclusions'. EUCO 163/14, 30 August.

European Council (2014b) 'European Council 26/27 June 2014 – Conclusions'. EUCO 79/14, 27 June.

European Data Protection Supervisor (2014) 'Press Statement: The CJEU rules that Data Retention Directive is invalid'. Brussels, 8 April.

European Parliament (2014a) 'MEPs debate plans to use EU Passenger Name Record (PNR) data to fight terrorism'. Press release 20141110IPR78121, 11 November.

European Parliament (2014b) 'MEPs refer EU-Canada air passenger data deal to the EU Court of Justice'. Press release 20141121IPR79818, 25 November.

European Parliament/Council of the European Union (2014a) 'Directive 2014/36/EU [...] of 26 February 2014 on the conditions of entry and stay of third-country nationals for the purpose of employment as seasonal workers'. OJ L 94, 28 March.

European Parliament/Council of the European Union (2014b) 'Directive 2014/66/EU [...] of 15 May 2014 on the conditions of entry and residence of third-country nationals in the framework of an intra-corporate transfer'. OJ L 157, 27 May.

European Parliament/Council of the European Union (2014c) 'Regulation (EU) No 655/2014 [...] of 15 May 2014 establishing a European Account Preservation Order procedure to facilitate cross-border debt recovery in civil and commercial matters'. OJ L 189, 27 June.

European Parliament/Council of the European Union (2014d) 'Regulation (EU) No 542/2014 [...] of 15 May 2014 amending Regulation (EU) No 1215/2012 as regards the rules to be applied with respect to the Unified Patent Court and the Benelux Court of Justice'. OJ L 163, 29 May.

European Parliament/Council of the European Union (2014e) 'Directive 2014/41/EU [...] of 3 April 2014 regarding the European Investigation Order in criminal matters'. OJ L 130, 1 May.

European Parliament/Council of the European Union (2014f) 'Directive 2014/42/EU [...] of 3 April 2014 on the freezing and confiscation of instrumentalities and proceeds of crime in the European Union'. OJ L 127, 29 April.

European Parliament/Council of the European Union (2014g) 'Directive 2014/57/EU [...] of 16 April 2014 on criminal sanctions for market abuse (market abuse directive)'. *OJ L 173, 12* June.

Europol (2014) 'EU Terrorism Situation & Trend Report'. The Hague: Europol.

Eurostat (2015) 'Asylum applicants and first instance decisions on asylum applications: 2014'. Data in focus, 3/2015.

Frontex (2014a) 'Annual Risk Analysis 2014'. Warsaw 2014.

Frontex (2104b) 'Frontex' Programme of Work 2014'. Warsaw 2014.

Frontex (2014c) 'Operation Triton – Winter developments'. Warsaw, 24 December.

© 2015 The Author(s) JCMS: Journal of Common Market Studies © 2015 John Wiley & Sons Ltd

JCMS 2015 Volume 53 Annual Review pp. 144–161   DOI: 10.1111/jcms.12263

Eurozone Governance: Deflation, Grexit 2.0 and the Second Coming of Jean-Claude Juncker

DERMOT HODSON
Birkbeck College, University of London

Introduction

The global financial crisis continues to cast a long shadow over the eurozone and, in spite of an occasional break in the clouds, blue skies remain a distant prospect. As discussed in last year's review (Hodson, 2014), the eurozone's exit in 2013 from its double dip recession provided some grounds for optimism, as did the emergence of Ireland and Spain from their loan agreements with the European Union (EU) and, in the case of the former, the International Monetary Fund (IMF). The eurozone economy continued to recover in 2014 but its recovery was beset by economic and political problems. The principal economic problem was a sharp deceleration in the rate of inflation, driven mainly by falling oil prices, which left the eurozone on the cusp of deflation. The ECB stopped short of fully fledged quantitative easing in its response to falling prices – giving credence to the view that it has been behind the curve in dealing with the euro crisis (De Grauwe, 2011) – but it stepped up its purchases of asset-backed securities and experimented with negative interest rates. If this deflationary scare served as a quiet reminder that the euro crisis was not over, the fall of the Greek government in December 2014 shouted this message from the rooftops. By the year's end, Greece's Coalition of the Radical Left, Syriza, were on the verge of winning power on an anti-austerity platform. Syriza won plaudits at home for promising to put an end to the painful reforms undertaken by Greece in exchange for financial support from the EU and IMF, but its policies cast doubt on Greece's commitment to its international creditors and its fate in the eurozone. This was a dramatic turn of events for Greece, which saw long-term interest rates fall in the first half of 2015 to their lowest levels since 2009, only to see them spike in the second half of the year as the risk of Grexit (Greece's departure from the eurozone) returned (Alcidi *et al.*, 2012; Panagiotarea, 2013).

It was against the backdrop of these turbulent events that Jean-Claude Juncker succeeded José Manuel Barroso as president of the European Commission in November 2014.[1] This was an inauspicious year to change the EU's policy-making guard, but Juncker arrived at the Berlaymont with a wealth of experience after nine years as Eurogroup president and twice as long as Luxembourg Prime Minister. Yet Juncker also had a reputation as a prickly customer, with a particular view of eurozone governance and strained relations with some players in EU policy-making. He also introduced radical reform to the internal governance of the European Commission, which raised questions over its ongoing role in managing the euro crisis.

---

[1] See Dinan's contribution to this volume.

© 2015 The Author(s) JCMS: Journal of Common Market Studies © 2015 John Wiley & Sons Ltd, 9600 Garsington Road, Oxford OX4 2DQ, UK and 350 Main Street, Malden, MA 02148, USA

Figure 1: Bond Yields for Selected Eurozone Members, 2007–2014.

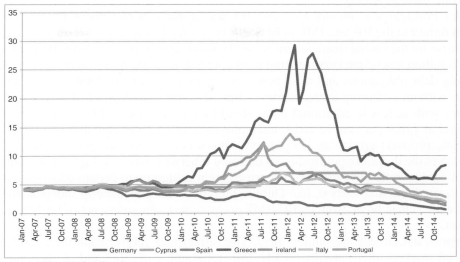

Source: ECB Statistical Warehouse
Note: 10 Year Government Benchmark Bond Yields

This contribution takes stock of these and other developments in eurozone governance in 2014. Section I gives an update on the euro crisis, focusing on the reemergence of concerns over Grexit. Section II looks at the economic outlook in 2014 and the factors driving deflation in the eurozone.[2] Section III explores key developments in eurozone monetary policy, including the ECB's experiment with negative interest rates. Section IV focuses on financial surveillance in the eurozone and the emerging relationship between the ECB Governing Council and the new Single Supervisory Mechanism. Section V turns to economic policy co-ordination and reviews the Six-Pack's third year in operation. Section VI offers tentative thoughts on what we might expect from Juncker's tenure as Commission president based on his past, and at times problematic, performance as Eurogroup president.

I. The Euro Crisis in 2014: Grexit 2.0

The year 2013 provided some breathing space for the eurozone after three years of fiscal turmoil. Mario Draghi's commitment 'to do whatever it takes' (Draghi, 2012) to save the euro remained untested but still credible, as evidenced by falling long-term interest rates for Member States at the epicentre of the crisis (see Figure 1). Long-term interest rates, as measured by the yield on ten-year government bonds, provide a proxy for the risk of sovereign default. Since the start of the euro crisis, financial market analysts have treated bond yields of 7 per cent as the dividing line between sustainable and unsustainable debt. Seen in these terms, the fact that yields fell below 3 per cent in Spain, Italy, Ireland and

---

[2] On developments in the European economy as a whole see Benczes and Szent-Ivanyi's contribution to this volume.

© 2015 The Author(s) JCMS: Journal of Common Market Studies © 2015 John Wiley & Sons Ltd

Portugal by the end of 2014 can be seen as a vote of confidence in these countries and the eurozone more generally.

That Portugal was included on this list was a major achievement for this country, which turned to the EU and IMF in May 2011 after its deficit reduction plans were blown off course by the global financial crisis (see Hodson, 2012). In May 2014, Portugal exited its €78 billion rescue package, leaving it reliant once again on financial markets to service existing debt obligations and raise new loans. Like Ireland in December 2013, Portugal did so without obtaining a precautionary line of credit, which would have provided the country with access to additional loans should the need arise. With government debt in Portugal at 128.9 per cent in 2014, unemployment at 14.2 per cent and real GDP (gross domestic product) growth at 1.0 per cent, this was an economic gamble (Wolff *et al.*, 2014). Yet the domestic political costs of doing otherwise were too high. A precautionary line of credit would have required the government to sign up to certain economic policies with its creditors and Lisbon, like Dublin, preferred the semblance of independence that came with a clean break from its EU–IMF programme to the safety net of further financial support.

Cyprus and Greece are outliers here. The former had yet to regain the confidence of financial markets after entering an EU–IMF programme in 2013 and so its bond yields remained higher in 2014 than for other peripheral eurozone members. Greece's problems were, in the short term at least, of its own political making. Greek bond yields fell below 7 per cent in March 2014 for the first time in four years but they returned to 8.4 per cent by the year's end. The turning point here occurred in May 2014 when Syriza, the Greek Co-alition of the Radical Left, won 26.5 per cent of Greek votes in the European Parliament elections, more than any other party. The European Parliament has not been a first-order player in the euro crisis, but this result was significant because it sent a clear signal that Syriza could, and probably would, form the next Greek government.

In September 2014, Syriza's leader Alexis Tsipras put forward a €13.5 billion pro-gramme of economic policies that included further haircuts on Greek debt, tax cuts, a minimum wage, subsidized electricity for individuals and improved social security bene-fits. These proposals proved understandably popular with an electorate that had seen the Greek economy contract by an astonishing 25 per cent between 2008 and 2013.[3] Finan-cial markets, however, were less sympathetic. The problem here was that Tsipras simply failed to convince that a Syriza government could pay for such economic measures, meet its obligations to its international creditors and keep Greece in the euro. Grexit, in other words, was back on the cards.

Questions over Greece's fate in the eurozone ceased to be hypothetical when, in De-cember 2014, Greek Prime Minister Antonis Samaras brought forward by two months a parliamentary vote for a new president of the Hellenic Republic. Why Samaras did not wait here is unclear, but the move triggered a general election when Stavros Dimas – a former European commissioner and the governing coalition's candidate for president – failed to win the required super-majority in the Greek Parliament. It seems doubtful that Samaras' government could have hung on for its full term, which was due to expire in 2016, but its mishandling of the presidential election was badly timed. Having begun 2014 with falling bond yields amid talk of exiting its EU–IMF programme or negotiating

---

[3] *Financial Times*, 4 March 2015.

© 2015 The Author(s) JCMS: Journal of Common Market Studies © 2015 John Wiley & Sons Ltd

a third but smaller financial support package, Greece found itself facing rising bond yields and a general election by the year's end. Syriza emerged as the largest party in the January 2015 election and by the time it had formed a governing coalition with the Independent Greeks, a populist right-wing party, Greek bond yields had reached double digits once again. In consequence, the euro crisis entered a new and deeply worrying phase in which the future of the single currency was once again in doubt.

II. The Economic Outlook: Recovering Slowly but Unsurely

The eurozone's economic recovery continued in 2014, albeit tentatively (see Figure 2). Real GDP in the eurozone increased by 0.8 per cent in 2014, which was an improvement on the −0.5 per cent growth rate recorded in 2013, but still disappointing. The United States, in contrast, saw real GDP rise by 2.4 per cent in 2014. A key difference between the two economies (see Figures 2 and 3) was domestic demand, which increased by just 0.8 per cent in the eurozone in 2014 compared to 2.5 per cent in the United States. Looking at some of the components of domestic demand, the eurozone lagged behind the United States in terms of private rather than public consumption, which is illustrative of weaker consumer confidence and higher unemployment in Europe. A puzzle for the eurozone is why external demand, which was so vital to its recovery from the great recession of 2009, is declining. In 2012, net exports of goods and services to eurozone growth contributed 1.4 percentage points to real GDP growth. In 2014, this figure had fallen to 0.1 percentage point. This reversal is linked to a cyclical slowdown in the world economy since 2010, although longer-term structural shifts might be at play. One such shift is that China is now importing fewer parts and components as part of its production of goods to be exported to the rest of the world, which suggests that the Chinese economy is no longer

Figure 2: Real GDP Growth and Selected Components, Eurozone 2007–2014.

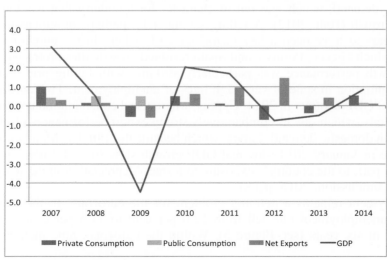

Source: European Commission AMECO database

© 2015 The Author(s) JCMS: Journal of Common Market Studies © 2015 John Wiley & Sons Ltd

Figure 3: Real GDP Growth and Selected Components, United States 2007–2014.

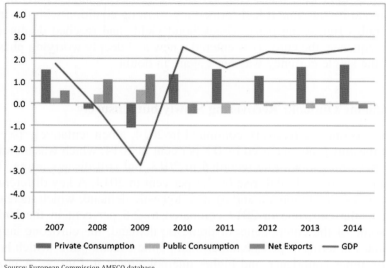

Source: European Commission AMECO database

the same turbo-charged engine of global trade that it once was (see European Commission, 2015; Mattoo and Ruta, 2015).

As always, the economic performance of eurozone members varied (see Figure 4). Real GDP in France and Germany increased by 0.4 per cent and 1.5 per cent respectively in 2014. For France, weak domestic demand and a negative contribution from net exports underlined president François Hollande's failure to boost growth in spite of his turn towards 'supply-side socialism' in 2014.[4] Germany's recovery in 2014 was primarily built on domestic demand, which was out of character for a country that has long relied on export-led growth (Hall, 2012). A falling savings rate, perhaps in anticipation of rising wages, appears to have been a key factor here. Elsewhere in the eurozone, 2014 was the year in which Greece, Portugal and Spain resumed growth after protracted recessions. Spain's growth performance was particularly striking, with falling prices encouraging greater consumption in spite of very high rates of unemployment. Two eurozone economies saw real GDP contract in 2014: Cyprus, where fiscal consolidation continues to take its toll, and Italy, which saw its comparatively strong export performance offset by a sharp contraction in domestic demand. Latvia, which became the 18th EU Member State to join the eurozone in January 2014, saw real GDP growth slow from 4.2 per cent to 2.6 per cent, due, in part, to the country's exposure to a sharp depreciation in the Russian rouble (European Commission, 2015, p. 88).

Unemployment remains a defining problem for the eurozone. In the eurozone as a whole, the unemployment rate fell from 12.0 per cent to 11.6 per cent, a modest fall but the first in six years (see Figure 5). Within the eurozone, nine members recorded

[4] *Financial Times*, 22 January 2014.

© 2015 The Author(s) JCMS: Journal of Common Market Studies © 2015 John Wiley & Sons Ltd

Figure 4: Real GDP Growth, Eurozone and its Members 2013 and 2014.

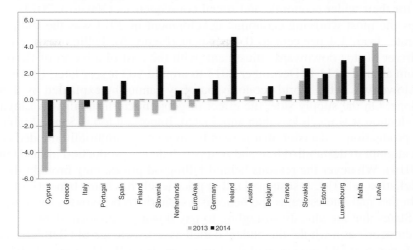

Figure 5: Unemployment Rate in the Eurozone and its Members 2013 and 2014

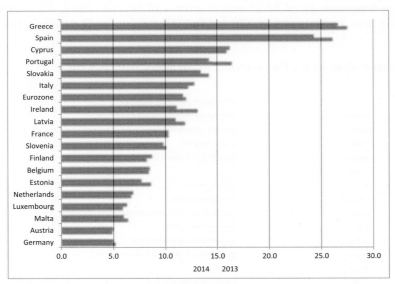

Note: Unemployment as a percentage of the civilian labour force.
Source: European Commission AMECO database

unemployment rates in excess of 10 per cent in 2014 and, of these, two saw rates in excess of 24 per cent. The Member States in question, Greece and Spain, saw their unemployment rates fall in 2014. The resumption of growth in 2014 in these countries undoubtedly helped. Spain's performance in dealing with this labour market crisis is the more impressive of the two. A set of labour market reforms adopted in 2012 which make it cheaper for firms to dismiss workers on permanent contracts while promoting a more decentralized approach to collective wage bargaining won high praise from the Organization for

© 2015 The Author(s) JCMS: Journal of Common Market Studies © 2015 John Wiley & Sons Ltd

Economic Cooperation Development (2014) for promoting greater flexibility, as well as criticism for their wider economic and social consequences (Navarro, 2014).

Perhaps the most worrying economic development in 2014 was the sharp fall in the inflation rate, from 1.4 per cent to 0.4 per cent (Figure 6). Falling energy prices were the key driver of this downward adjustment, with the cost of a barrel of Brent crude oil falling from around $111 in December 2013 to around $62 a year later. Falling prices reflect the slowdown in the world economy but they cannot be explained by demand-side factors alone. On the supply side, the effect of geopolitical instability in Libya and Iraq on oil production was much less than anticipated. Important too is Saudi Arabia's refusal to cut oil production, a decision that is seen by more conspiratorially minded commentators as an attempt to destabilize Iran and scupper shale gas production in the United States (Bazzi, 2014). Whatever the reasons behind falling oil prices, they brought the eurozone close to deflation in 2014. A sustained fall in price levels has some benefits, of course, but it means higher real interest rates and hence is a scenario to be avoided for those eurozone Member States that are already struggling to pay down government debt.

In the eurozone as a whole, the budget deficit as a percentage of GDP fell from 2.9 per cent to 2.6 per cent and government debt increased from 93.1 per cent to 94.3 per cent (see Table 1). Of 18 eurozone members, 11 found themselves with government borrowing below the excessive deficit procedure's 3 per cent of GDP threshold, although government debt as a percentage of GDP was in excess of 60 per cent in 13 countries. Fiscal consolidation was most severe in Greece, which saw its budget deficit fall from 12.2

Figure 6: Inflation Rate for the Eurozone and its Members 2013 and 2014.

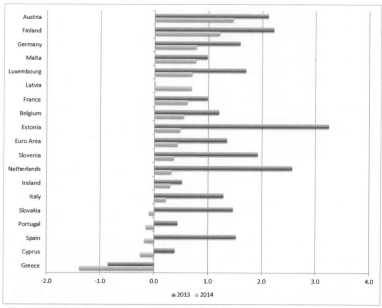

Source: European Commission AMECO database
Note: Annual change in Harmonized Index of Consumer Prices

© 2015 The Author(s) JCMS: Journal of Common Market Studies © 2015 John Wiley & Sons Ltd

Table 1: Governing Borrowing in the Eurozone and its Members as % of GDP, 2014

	Net lending	Government debt	Primary balance
Eurozone	−2.6	94.5	0.1
Belgium	−3.2	106.4	−0.1
Germany	0.4	74.2	2.2
Estonia	−0.4	9.8	−0.2
Ireland	−4.0	110.8	0.1
Greece	−2.5	176.3	1.7
Spain	−5.6	98.3	−2.3
France	−4.3	95.3	−2.1
Italy	−3.0	131.9	1.6
Cyprus	−3.0	107.5	0.1
Latvia	−1.5	40.4	−0.1
Luxembourg	0.5	22.7	0.9
Malta	−2.3	68.6	0.5
Netherlands	−2.8	69.5	−1.3
Austria	−2.9	86.8	−0.3
Portugal	−4.6	128.9	0.4
Slovenia	−5.4	82.2	−2.0
Slovakia	−3.0	53.6	−1.2
Finland	−2.7	58.9	−1.4

Source: European Commission AMECO database.

per cent in 2013 to 2.5 per cent in 2014. In spite of this fact, Greek government debt increased from 174.9 per cent to 176.3 per cent in this period. Posting a positive primary balance (i.e. a measure of government borrowing that excludes interest repayments) is a conventional indicator of a country's ability to reduce its government debt. In 2013, Greece, Ireland, Portugal and Cyprus all posted primary surpluses for the first time since the sovereign debt crisis hit. This fact is testament to the considerable fiscal consolidation undertaken by these countries, even if these efforts were not sufficient to convince markets that the euro crisis is over (see Section I).

III. Monetary Policy: All eyes on the ECB (Again)

Faced with sharp falls in price levels and forecasts of deflation, the ECB came under considerable pressure in 2014 to go further in its response to the euro crisis. Conventional monetary policy had little room for manoeuvre here, the ECB Governing Council having cut the interest rate on its main deposit facility nine times since the global financial crisis struck in 2007. As a result of these cuts, the interest rate on the main deposit facility reached zero in November 2013. In spite of historically low nominal interest rates, the European Commission's monetary conditions index for the euro area tightened in 2013 and the early months of 2014 (Figure 7). This index is a weighted average of real interest rates and the real effective exchange rate. The real interest rate is defined here as the nominal interest rate minus anticipated consumer price inflation and the real effective exchange rate measures changes in euro area unit labour costs relative to key trading partners. The monetary conditions index fell (i.e. tightened) between July 2012 and February 2014, chiefly because the euro-area real effective exchange rate experienced sustained appreciation over this period. If a rise in the euro exchange rate thus countered the effects of

© 2015 The Author(s) JCMS: Journal of Common Market Studies © 2015 John Wiley & Sons Ltd

Figure 7: Monetary Conditions Index, Eurozone, January 1999–December 2015.

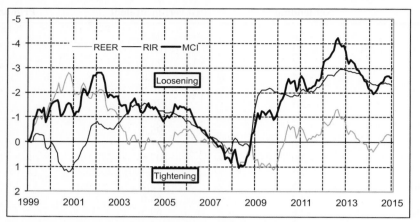

Note: Real interest rates (RIR), Real Effective Exchange Rate (RIR) and Monetary Conditions Index (MCI)
Source: European Commission

low nominal interest rates, the risk of deflation threatened to make matters worse by caus-ing real interest rates to rise too. It was against this backdrop that the ECB Governing Council decided in June 2014 to cut the interest rates on its main deposit facility to −0.1 per cent, followed by a further cut to −0.2 per cent three months later.[5]

The ECB is not alone in embracing negative interest rates in the wake of the global fi-nancial crisis – Denmark, Sweden, and Switzerland have taken similar steps – but this is an experimental move nonetheless (Ilgmann and Menner, 2011). Practically speaking, it means that commercial banks holding deposits at the European Central Bank will be charged for this service rather than receiving an interest payment. The rationale for this switch is to encourage commercial banks to lend to individuals and businesses rather than keeping their money in central banks and to incentivize consumption and investment by individuals and businesses. Negative interest rates can also serve as a spur for exchange rate depreciation as investors sell domestic for foreign currency in search of higher rates of return on their investment. The gains from negative interest rates are by no means guar-anteed and an additional concern here is that they could harm the profitability of banks, especially those that are heavily dependent on deposits to finance loans. It is too soon to judge the effects of negative interest rates in the euro area but it may have encouraged a depreciation of the euro real effective exchange rate in the second half of 2014 and, hence, a loosening of monetary conditions. Negative interest rates certainly proved to be unpopular with Germany's public banks, the Sparkassen, which criticized the ECB and put pressure on the German government to support savers (Ross and Jones, 2014).

Negative interest rates are an interesting experiment but they are most certainly not a panacea for the eurozone. For one thing, there are limits to how far into negative territory

[5] Between June and September 2014, the ECB also cut the interest rates on its main refinancing operations and marginal lending facility to 0.05 per cent and 0.30 per cent respectively.

© 2015 The Author(s) JCMS: Journal of Common Market Studies © 2015 John Wiley & Sons Ltd

interest rates can go, even though economists disagree on what the true lower bound on interest rates actually is. Furthermore, negative interest rates are just one of several unconventional monetary policies considered by the ECB in 2014. Others include a four-year targeted long-term operation (TLTRO) launched in June 2014 and designed to provide over €400 billion in additional liquidity support to euro-area banks. A policy response that was much debated in 2014, but not realized until early 2015, was quantitative easing: the large-scale purchase of public and private bonds by the central bank, financed through the expansion of its balance sheet. ECB president Mario Draghi dropped a strong hint that the bank was moving in this direction in his speech at the Annual Central Bank Symposium in Jackson Hole in August 2014. In this intervention, Draghi expressed concerns over rising real interest rates and announced that 'The Governing Council will acknowledge these developments and within its mandate will use all the available instruments needed to ensure price stability over the medium term' (Draghi, 2014).

In September 2014, the ECB Governing Council put forward new instruments in the form of its Asset Backed Securities Purchase Programme (ABSPP) and an Expanded Covered Bond Purchase Programme (CBPP3). Under these programmes, the ECB agreed to buy a wider range of private bonds over a two-year period in order to 'facilitate credit provision to the euro-area economy, generate positive spill-overs to other markets and, as a result, ease the ECB's monetary policy stance' with the overarching aim being 'a return of inflation rates to levels closer to 2 per cent'.[6] This statement is an interesting one for ECB watchers since it recalls discussions in the early days of Economic and Monetary Union (EMU) about the existence of a deflationary bias in euro-area monetary policy (Arestis and Sawyer, 2001). In October 1998, the fledgling ECB Governing Council agreed on a quantitative definition of price stability as 'a year-on-year increase in the Harmonised Index of Consumer Prices (HICP) for the euro area of below 2 per cent' (ECB Governing Council, 1998). The ECB Governing Council provided further guidance here in June 2003 when it announced that it would seek to maintain inflation rates 'below, but close to, 2 per cent over the medium term' (ECB, 2003). This clarification was, in one sense, a fudge that satisfied the hawks on the ECB Governing Council by keeping the original asymmetric definition of inflation while offering a more symmetric clarification to the doves. Providing greater clarity at this juncture might have cleared the way for quantitative easing by the ECB, which arrived only in January 2015 when the ECB Governing Council unveiled its Expanded Asset Purchase Programme. Under this scheme, the ECB finally agreed to the large-scale purchase of bonds issued by euro-area governments, agencies and institutions, some seven years after the US Federal Reserve had embarked on a similar course of action.

IV. Financial Supervision: The Strange Case of the Single Supervisory Mechanism

The year 2014 was another high-stakes one for eurozone financial supervisors. In October 2014, the ECB published the results of its so-called comprehensive assessment of the eurozone's biggest 130 banks (ECB, 2014). The first part of this assessment involved an asset quality review to determine whether these banks were sufficiently capitalized.

---

[6] Decision of the European Central Bank of 19 November 2014 on the implementation of the asset-backed securities purchase programme (ECB/2014/45).

© 2015 The Author(s) JCMS: Journal of Common Market Studies © 2015 John Wiley & Sons Ltd

Twenty-five banks failed this test. Twelve of these institutions had already taken sufficient steps to increase their capital, the ECB concluded, but 13 others from Italy, Greece, Belgium and Slovenia were required to take immediate remedial action. The second part of the assessment was a stress test that sought to establish whether the eurozone's banks could withstand unfavourable economic shocks. Here the ECB, working with national authorities and the European Banking Authority, concluded that such a scenario would deplete banks' so-called common equity tier 1 capital – a key proxy for the financial strength of an institution – by not more than minimum requirements. Euro-area banks, in other words, were adjudged to be in a position to withstand hard economic times. The comprehensive assessment was not the game-changer that the United States government's stress test in 2009 seems to have been (see Geithner, 2014, for an insider account). For some commentators, the ECB erred by failing to consider a large deflationary shock as part of its stress tests, but the exercise was otherwise deemed credible (Arnold et al., 2014). The ECB certainly did a better job here than the EU's Committee of European Banking Supervisors. In 2010, the latter, which was later transformed into the European Banking Authority, conducted a euro-wide stress test that provided a clean bill of health to Allied Irish Bank just months before Ireland's second largest financial institution required recapitalization by the government.

The Single Supervisory Mechanism (SSM) began operating in November 2014, 12 months after EU finance ministers and the European Parliament agreed on the legislation underpinning the bank's new role in EU financial supervision. As discussed in last year's review, the Single Supervisory Mechanism entails a significant transfer of powers to the ECB when it comes to the supervision of financial institutions. As of November 2014, the ECB assumed responsibility for 'contributing to the safety and soundness of credit institutions and the stability of the financial system within the EU and each Member State'.[7] This means, in practice, that the ECB will be responsible for licensing financial institutions, enforcing prudential standards and carrying out supervisory reviews. And yet, in spite of – or, more accurately, because of – the wide-ranging scope of these powers, the ECB's control over the Single Supervisory Mechanism has been heavily constrained by national governments.

For students of EU governance (see Wallace et al., 2014), the Single Supervisory Mechanism is a curious exhibit. Situated within the ECB's decision-making structures, the Single Supervisory Mechanism also operates at one remove from the bank. A Supervisory Board is responsible for the day-to-day functioning of the Single Supervisory Mechanism and for preparing decisions to be approved by the ECB Governing Council. The Supervisory Board's right of initiative here is powerful; the ECB Governing Council is able to object to, but not modify, draft decisions by the Supervisory Board and – under the so-called principle of non-objection – the ECB Governing Council has no more than ten days to register objections before draft decisions by the Supervisory Board take effect.

If this approach limits the ECB's authority over the Single Supervisory Mechanism, then so too do the procedures for appointing members to the Supervisory Board. The chair is not an internal appointment made by the ECB Governing Council. Instead it falls to the ECB Governing Council to propose a candidate on the basis of an open procedure

---

[7] Council Regulation (EU) No 1024/2013 of 15 October 2013 conferring specific tasks on the European Central Bank concerning policies relating to the prudential supervision of credit institutions, Official Journal, L 287/63, 29.10.2013.

© 2015 The Author(s) JCMS: Journal of Common Market Studies © 2015 John Wiley & Sons Ltd

who is then approved by the European Parliament and confirmed by the Council of the European Union. The Vice Chair of the Supervisory Board is chosen from the members of the ECB Executive Board but the chair cannot be a member of either the ECB Executive Board or the ECB Governing Council. The other members of the Supervisory Board include four representatives of the ECB and a representative from each national financial supervisor, this being the national central bank in some cases or a government agency in others. As such, national representatives exercise an even stronger grip on the ECB Supervisory Board than is the case with the ECB Governing Council.

The ECB's control over the Single Supervisory Mechanism is also limited by a strict division of labour between European and national authorities over the direct supervision of financial institutions. The Single Supervisory Mechanism has overall responsibility for the supervision of around 4700 financial institutions but it is directly responsible for the supervision of only around 1200 significant entities. Significance is determined by a set of criteria that covers: credit institutions with total assets exceeding €30 billion; those with assets below €5 billion but which account for 20 per cent of national GDP; the three most significant credit institutions in a Member State irrespective of these criteria; those institutions that are being directly supported by the European Stability Mechanism; and those with significant cross-border assets and liabilities. Those credit institutions that do not fall within this category are supervised directly by national supervisors, albeit under the gaze of the ECB.

A final way in which the ECB's powers over the Single Supervisory Mechanism are constrained concerns the conduct of supervisory missions. Day-to-day supervision is carried out by so-called Joint Supervisory Teams, which include officials from both the ECB and national supervisors. Each team will be led by an ECB official and their work will be supported by the bank's newly created Directorate General for Micro-Prudential Supervision IV. In spite of such support, it is clear that national supervisors will play a decisive role in the supervision of even significant financial institutions in their own countries.

V. Economic Policy Co-ordination: Softly Goes the Six-Pack

For Scharpf (2013, p. 12), who has been as a vocal critic of EU economic governance, it can be 'treated as given … that the Fiscal Pact and the Six-Pack and Two-Pack regulations have strengthened, rather than relaxed, the rules preventing the use of expansionary fiscal policies at the national level'. As discussed in recent reviews (Hodson, 2011a, 2012, 2013, 2014), the track record of EU economic surveillance following these reforms calls for a closer look at this issue. Member States have been subject to no shortage of peer pressure but none have faced financial penalties since the reforms took effect, and most countries have been given a margin of flexibility to get government borrowing under control. The interim conclusion, then is that the Six-Pack, Fiscal Compact and Two-Pack are softer than they look. It is important to note, however, that 'softer' does not mean 'weaker' here, since a system relying on peer pressure and flexible interpretations of compliance can be more credible than harder forms of co-ordination. A recurring problem for the latter is that pecuniary sanctions impose costs on the sender as well as the target, and they can also lead more easily to a breakdown in co-operation between the parties involved (Hodson and Maher, 2004).

© 2015 The Author(s) JCMS: Journal of Common Market Studies © 2015 John Wiley & Sons Ltd

Events in 2014 confirmed this 'soft' interpretation of EU economic governance in the light of the global financial crisis. Out of the 11 eurozone members that found themselves with excessive deficits at the beginning of the year, four – Belgium, the Netherlands, Austria and Slovakia – saw disciplinary proceedings brought to a close after the Commission and ECOFIN Council agreed that government borrowing in these countries had fallen below 3 per cent of GDP. Six of the remaining states – Cyprus, Spain, Greece, Ireland, Portugal and Malta – faced no additional sanctions, EU authorities being content that these Member States had taken sufficient action in response to earlier calls for corrective action. The only problematic case in 2014 was France, which the Commission adjudged to be at 'significant risk of non-compliance with the recommended fiscal effort [by EU finance ministers] both in 2013 and 2014' (European Commission, 2014, p. 3). The French government was duly invited to come forward with additional measures designed to get government borrowing under control in its stability programme, which it presented to the Commission in May 2014. Acting on the recommendation from the Commission, the ECOFIN Council concluded in June that France's 'stability programme broadly responded to the Commission recommendation'.[8] Given France's fiscal leeway at a time of moribund growth this was probably the right call here, and it confirms the flexibility of EU fiscal rules even after the reforms of recent years. Be that as it may, these rules provide limited incentives for Member States to engage in the kind of co-ordinated fiscal policies that might be needed to prevent prolonged economic stagnation in the eurozone.

VI. The Future of Euro-Area Governance: The Return of Jean-Claude Juncker

In November 2014, Jean-Claude Juncker took office as the 12th president of the European Commission, having served as Prime Minister of Luxembourg from 1995 to 2013. Juncker's appointment signified change and continuity in the selection procedure for Commission presidents. It was novel insofar as Juncker was first put forward by the European People's Party as a candidate for the Commission presidency as part of the *Spitzenkandidaten* process (Hobolt, 2014) rather than emerging as a compromise candidate after negotiations between EU heads of state or government.[9] Juncker's appointment was also a conservative move that resulted, yet again, in the Commission president being chosen from the (recent) ranks of the European Council. Between 1958 and 1994, only one out of eight Commission presidents had previously served as a head of state or government, although all had held senior positions in government. Since 1995, all four Commission presidents have served as Prime Minister of their country before coming to Brussels. This tendency may reflect the increased complexity of leading the Commission in the post-Maastricht period, but only partly so. It can also be seen as an attempt by the members of the European Council to appoint 'one of their own' to the Berlaymont rather than an unknown quantity. Martin Schulz, the Socialists and Democrats' candidate for the Commission president and someone who rose through the ranks of local politics before becoming a member of the European Parliament, would have been a much more controversial choice here – so much so, in fact, that the heads of state or government might not

[8] Council Recommendation of 8 July 2014 on the National Reform Programme 2014 of France and delivering a Council opinion on the Stability Programme of France, 2014. Official Journal of the European Union C 247/42, 29.7.2014.
[9] See Dinan's contribution to this volume.

© 2015 The Author(s) JCMS: Journal of Common Market Studies © 2015 John Wiley & Sons Ltd

have agreed to his appointment had the Socialists and Democrats come top in the European Parliament elections.

Juncker is not only an alumnus of the European Council; he also has a close personal connection to eurozone governance from his time as the Eurogroup's first 'permanent' president (2004–13). What, in the light of this turbulent time in this role (see Hodson, 2011b), can we expect from Juncker's presidency of the Commission in relation to EMU? First, and perhaps most fundamentally, Juncker has a track record of flexibility in relation to the enforcement of the EU's fiscal rules. One of his first major contributions as Eurogroup president was to chair talks between euro-area finance ministers over the re-form of the stability and growth pact following the ECOFIN Council's de-facto suspension of disciplinary measures against France and Germany in 2003. Juncker played a critical and pragmatic role in these negotiations by convincing France and Germany to re-commit to the effective and timely enforcement of the excessive deficit procedure by giv-ing Member States more time to get government borrowing under control and by ensuring that financial penalties would be used only in extremis. While this compromise has been judged harshly in the light of the euro crisis, such criticism forgets that most Member States had reduced government borrowing below 3 per cent of GDP by the time that the global financial crisis struck.

A second observation is that Juncker is likely to be a much less emollient figure than his predecessor as Commission president, José Manuel Barroso. Aside from a high-profile spat with French president Jacques Chirac over the European Constitution, Barroso devel-oped a reasonable working relationship with key players in EU politics during his ten years in the Berlaymont. As Eurogroup president, Juncker had run-ins with several key players. One was with ECB president Jean-Claude Trichet, who bristled at Juncker's will-ingness to speak out against interest rate increases in late 2005 and the Eurogroup presi-dent's attempts to foster a closer dialogue between euro-area finance ministers and the bank (Hodson, 2011b, chapter 3). Juncker also clashed with French president Nicolas Sarkozy over France's budget plans, and on the more fundamental question of who should speak for the eurozone; such tensions may explain Sarkozy's decision to block Juncker's appointment to the position of European Council president in 2009. Relations between Juncker and Angela Merkel, meanwhile, got off to a bad start when the former reportedly failed to brief the then German opposition leader about his plans in 2003 for an integrated defence policy between Belgium, France, Luxembourg and Germany. Cer-tainly, Merkel seems to have been a late convert to Juncker's candidacy for Commission president, with the German Chancellor refusing to endorse the former Luxembourg Prime Minister even in the immediate aftermath of the European Parliament elections in May 2014. It is tempting to put these spats down to personality – and Juncker's sarcastic style wins friends as well as foes – but they stem from the Luxembourger's attempt to show leadership on the European stage rather than, as Barroso so often did, to follow the lead of others.

Third, Juncker has a track record of seeking to enhance the euro area's role on the international stage. One of his more successful initiatives as Eurogroup president was his monetary diplomacy towards China (Hodson, 2011b, chapter 7). In November 2007, the Eurogroup dispatched Juncker to Beijing for talks with Chinese officials on the persistent depreciation of the renminbi against the euro after China ended its peg with the dollar to years earlier. The results of these talks were inconclusive, but they

© 2015 The Author(s) JCMS: Journal of Common Market Studies © 2015 John Wiley & Sons Ltd

provided an instance in which euro-area members showed themselves to be capable of speaking with one voice on international issues. Diplomatic initiatives of this sort are more difficult in multilateral settings, where EU Member States are over- rather than under-represented and supranational actors struggle to gain traction. Juncker learned this first-hand in 2010 when he was not invited to attend the landmark leaders' summit of the Group of Twenty (G-20) summit in London, the EU delegation being led by the president of the European Council. Juncker was an advocate of a more unified approach to the external representation of the euro area even before this snub. In July 2009, he tried but failed to convince euro-area finance ministers to support the idea of creating a single chair on the IMF Executive Board.

Seen in this historical context, the five priorities adopted by Juncker in April 2014 – in what was, in effect, a manifesto for his Commission presidency – read like a list of left-over business from his time as Eurogroup president. They include proposals to 're-balance the relationship between elected politicians and the European Central Bank', the creation of a 'full-time' presidency for the Eurogroup, a concern for social impact alongside fiscal sustainability and moves to strengthen the eurozone's voice in the IMF.[10] Commission presidents do not make the political weather of course and it remains to be seen whether Member States will support Juncker's plans to reform euro-area governance.

Juncker's presidency of the Commission – like those of his predecessors – hinge on whether his political aims for euro-area governance are aligned with those of the large Member States. Important too will be his management style within the European Commission. On the first of these points, the Juncker presidency began with a radical change to the internal structures of the European Commission. Like Barroso, Juncker has sought to exercise a high degree of control from the centre via the president's cabinet and strong secretariat, but the latter has also sought to use vice-presidents to constrain his other commissioners. The appointment of Pierre Moscovici as European Commissioner for Economic and Financial Affairs, Taxation and Customs was a controversial move given the French finance minister's mixed track record of compliance with the stability and growth pact. Significant, however, was the decision to appoint former Latvian Prime Minister Valdis Dombrovskis as Vice President for Economic and Monetary Affairs and the Euro. Moscovici finds himself tightly constrained by this arrangement; decisions for the College relating to EU economic co-ordination and surveillance – including any disciplinary measures against France – must now be jointly presented with Dombrovskis. A key question for the Juncker presidency is whether such constraints will slow decision-making in the Commission and whether the new vice-presidential veto players will allow Juncker to make his own mark on EMU and other policy issues.

A final issue to consider here when looking at Juncker's role in euro-area governance concerns his relations with Donald Tusk, who succeeded Herman Van Rompuy as president of both the European Council and the Euro Summit in December 2014. Van Rompuy played a key role in euro-area governance following the global financial crisis, helping to broker a deal over the involvement of the EU and IMF in providing emergency loans to Greece and leading on negotiations over the Six-Pack, the creation

---

[10] See: http://juncker.epp.eu/my-priorities.

© 2015 The Author(s) JCMS: Journal of Common Market Studies © 2015 John Wiley & Sons Ltd

of European banking union and wider reforms of euro-area governance. Institutional tensions between Van Rompuy and Barroso arose from time to time but they formed an effective working relationship. On paper, there is a potential imbalance between Tusk, a former Prime Minister of a non-euro area member, with Juncker, a self-styled founding father of the euro area and veteran of the European Council. That said, euro-area heads of state or government did not have to choose Tusk and the fact that they did may, as Puetter (2014) argues, be a calculated effort to build a bridge between euro and non-euro area members. Tusk also brings credibility by virtue of his successful stewardship of Poland's economy in recent years and his close working relationship with Angela Merkel and, as a politician from Central and Eastern Europe, brings more bite to the EU's dealings with Russia at a time of ongoing tension over the conflict in Ukraine. Key political decisions on the future of euro-area governance will, in any event, flow through the European Council and here Tusk will be at a distinct institutional advantage over Juncker.

Conclusion: One Step Forward, Two Steps Back

A student was late for class one icy day and, when asked by the teacher to explain himself, replied: 'It was so slippery that every time I took one step forward, I slid two steps back'. 'Then how did you get here?' asked the teacher. 'I tried to go home', said the student. As in this story, the eurozone took one step forward in its recovery in 2014 only to take two steps back towards crisis. On the positive side, the eurozone economy grew in spite of lacklustre external demand thanks to a tentative pick up in domestic demand. Welcome too was a sense of renewed financial market confidence in Portugal, which exited its EU–IMF programme, and Ireland and Spain, which continued to recuperate from their sovereign debt difficulties. On the down side, falling oil prices pushed the eurozone closer to deflation. Deeply worrying for the single currency too was the fall of the Samaras government in Greece in December 2014. This paved the way for Syriza's general election victory in January 2015 on an anti-austerity platform, a result that brought hope to some and fear to others, and fuelled concerns over Grexit for all.

Eurozone authorities responded to these challenges with a combination of ingenuity and conservatism. The ECB rarely sits still during crises, but nor does it move quickly. True to form, then, was the ECB Governing Council's decision in 2014 to embrace negative interest rates alongside more ambitious private bond buying schemes while stopping short of government bond purchases. Fully fledged quantitative easing – of the kind witnessed in the United States in 2008 – would come to the eurozone only in January 2015. The ECB, meanwhile, carried out its new responsibilities for eurozone financial supervision through its stress tests of eurozone banks, which were credible without being conclusive, and with the launch of the Single Supervisory Mechanism. On the fiscal side, events in 2014 lend weight to the hypothesis that the EU's fiscal rules are softer than they look, as evidenced by the leeway given to France in getting government borrowing under control.

The year 2014, finally, saw José Manuel Barroso make way for Jean-Claude Juncker as president of the European Commission. Barroso was a consensus candidate and a consensus-seeker who worked with the heads of state or government rather than seeking to forge a particular path for the eurozone following the global financial crisis. Juncker is an altogether more divisive figure. His presidency owes more to the *Spitzenkandidaten* process rather than the usual smoke and mirrors of EU summits and, as such, his relationship with the heads of state or government is more than usually complicated. How Juncker will adjust to this new role remains to be seen. He brings to the Berlaymont significant experience of eurozone governance from his time as Eurogroup president but also political baggage from his sometimes difficult dealings with other leaders. The former Luxembourg Prime Minister has already made his mark on the Commission through controversial reforms to the College that are likely to affect the EU executive's role in euro-area governance.

References

Alcidi, C., Giovannini, A. and Gros, D. (2012) '"Grexit": Who Would Pay for it?' Centre for European Policy Studies Brief No. 272 (Brussels: Centre for European Policy Studies).

Arestis, P. and Sawyer, M.C. (2001) 'Will the Euro Bring Economic Crisis to Europe?' Jerome Levy Economics Institute Working Paper No. 322 (Annadale-on-Hudson, NY Levy Economics Institute of Bard College).

Arnold, M., Fleming, J.C. and Ross, A. (2014) 'Bank Stress Tests Fail to Tackle Deflation Spectre'. *Financial Times,* 27 October.

Bazzi, M. (2014) 'Saudi Arabia is Playing Chicken with Its Oil'. The Great Debate Blog, Reuters, 15 December. Available at «http://blogs.reuters.com/great-debate/2014/12/15/saudi-arabia-is-playing-chicken-with-its-oil/»

De Grauwe, P. (2011) 'Only a More Active ECB can Solve the Euro Crisis'. *Centre for European Policy Studies Policy Briefs*, 250 (Brussels: Centre for European Policy Studies).

Draghi, M. (2012) 'Speech by Mario Draghi, President of the European Central Bank at the Global Investment Conference in London', 26 July 2012.

Draghi, M. (2014) 'Unemployment in the Euro Area'. Annual central bank symposium in Jackson Hole, 22 August. (Frankfurt am Main: ECB).

European Central Bank (1998) 'A Stability-Oriented Monetary Policy Strategy for the ESCB'. Press release, 13 October (Frankfurt am Main: ECB).

European Central Bank (2003) 'The ECB's Monetary Policy Strategy'. Press release, 8 May (Frankfurt am Main: ECB).

European Central Bank (2014) Aggregate Report on the Comprehensive Assessment (Frankfurt am Main: ECB).

European Commission (2014) 'Recommendation for a Council Recommendation on France's 2014 national reform programme and delivering a Council opinion on France's 2014 stability programme', COM(2014) 411 final, Brussels, 2 June.

European Commission (2015) 'European Economic Forecast - Winter 2015' European Economy No. 1 (Brussels: Commission of the European Communities).

Geithner, T. (2014) Stress Test: Reflections on Financial Crises (New York: Random House).

Hall, P.A. (2012) 'The Economics and Politics of the Euro Crisis'. *German Politics*, Vol. 21, No. 5, pp. 355–71.

Hobolt, S.B. (2014) 'A Vote for the President? The Role of Spitzenkandidaten in the 2014 European Parliament Elections'. *Journal of European Public Policy*, Vol. 21, No. 10, pp. 1528–40.

Hodson, D. (2011a) 'The Eurozone in 2011'. *JCMS*, Vol. 49, No. s1, pp. 178–94.

© 2015 The Author(s) JCMS: Journal of Common Market Studies © 2015 John Wiley & Sons Ltd

Hodson, D. (2011b) *Governing the Euro Area in Good Times and Bad* (Oxford: Oxford University Press).

Hodson, D. (2012) 'The Eurozone in 2012'. *JCMS*, Vol. 49, s2, pp. 178–194.

Hodson, D. (2013) 'The Eurozone in 2012:'Whatever It Takes to Preserve the Euro'?' *JCMS*, Vol. 51, No. s1, pp. 183–200.

Hodson, D. (2014) 'Eurozone Governance: Recovery, Reticence and Reform'. *JCMS*, Vol. 52, No. s1, pp. 186–201.

Hodson, D. and Maher, I. (2004) 'Soft Law and Sanctions: Economic Policy Co-ordination and Reform of the Stability and Growth Pact'. *Journal of European Public Policy*, Vol. 11, No. 5, pp. 798–813.

Ilgmann, C. and Menner, M. (2011) 'Negative Nominal Interest Rates: History and Current Proposals'. CAWM discussion paper/Centrum für Angewandte Wirtschaftsforschung Münster, No. 43.

Mattoo, A. and Ruta, M. (2015) The Global Trade Slowdown: Cyclical or Structure. IMF Working Paper, WP/15/6 (Washington DC: International Monetary Fund).

Navarro, V. (2014) 'Spain's Labour Market and Social Reforms have Exacerbated the Country's Unemployment Problem'. London School of Economics European Politics and Policy Blog. Available at «http://blogs.lse.ac.uk/europpblog/2014/04/09/spains-labour-market-and-social-reforms-have-exacerbated-the-countrys-unemployment-problem/» [Accessed 31 March 2015]

Panagiotarea, E. (2013) *Greece in the Euro: Economic Delinquency Or System Failure?* (Colchester: ECPR Press).

Puetter, U. (2014) 'Despite Attention Focusing on Juncker's New Commission, the European Council will Remain the Real Centre of EU Decision-making'. Availabe at «http://blogs.lse.ac.uk/europpblog/2014/10/20/despite-attention-focusing-on-junckers-new-commission-the-european-council-will-remain-the-real-centre-of-eu-decision-making/»

Ross, A. and Jones, C. (2014) 'Germany's Savings Banks Lash Out at ECB'. *Financial Times*, 4 June.

Scharpf, F.W. (2013) 'Political Legitimacy in a Non-optimal Currency Area'. MPIfG Discussion Paper 13/15.

Wallace, H., Pollack, H. and Young, A. (eds) (2014) *Policy-Making in the European Union* (7th edition) (Oxford: Oxford University Press).

Wolff, G.B., Darvas, Z. and Sapir, A. (2014) 'The Long Haul: Managing Exit from Financial Assistance'. Bruegel Policy Contribution Issue 2014/03, 20 February.

JCMS 2015 Volume 53 Annual Review pp. 162–180   DOI: 10.1111/jcms.12266

The European Economy in 2014: Fragile Recovery and Convergence*

ISTVAN BENCZES[1] and BALAZS SZENT-IVANYI[2]
[1]Corvinus University of Budapest. [2]Aston University

Introduction

In early 2014, six years after the outburst of the global financial-cum-economic crisis, most commentators on the European economy expected the year to bring a much-awaited breakthrough of slow but steady economic growth (European Commission, 2014c). Unfortunately, the numbers did not support these optimistic scenarios; economic recovery in the EU, while picking up to some extent after recession in 2012 and stagnation in 2013, remained fragile. As a result, by the second half of 2014, international institutions such as the European Commission (2014a), the IMF (2014a) and the OECD (2014) substantially downgraded their GDP growth forecasts for the EU and the eurozone in particular, and neither of them expected European real GDP growth to exceed 1.3 per cent in 2014.

Yet, as this contribution demonstrates, having an eye only on EU averages can be rather counterproductive. A more detailed analysis reveals that the economic performance of the 28 Member States was dramatically different in 2014. The principal aim of this contribution is, therefore, to decompose and explain Europe's economic performance in the past year. In doing so, it assesses Europe's performance in several key areas such as economic growth, employment, inflation, public finances and competitiveness, and systematically identifies countries that performed well above or well below the EU averages. Broad generalizations on the European level are often misleading due to the heterogeneity of Member States' economies. Moreover, the frequently used dichotomies, such as 'eurozone vs. non-eurozone' countries or 'old vs. new' members, are too often at odds with reality.

The second half of the contribution seeks to explore questions related to Europe's longer-term economic performance by investigating the convergence and divergence of income levels of Member States on the tenth anniversary of the 2004 enlargement. There are good reasons for expecting solid convergence in the period under investigation. Beyond standard economic theory, the facilitating forces of the single market (and, for some members, the single currency), along with the pro-growth policies of the EU's structural and cohesion funds, make it reasonable to assume the growth experiences of the new Member States would support the convergence hypothesis. The brief analysis of the data reveals, generally speaking, that the past ten years have substantially strengthened convergence, as many less developed Member States, especially the ones in Central and Eastern Europe, grew faster than the more advanced EU economies, thus making progress in closing income gaps. Unfortunately, there are also a number of countries which seem to have lost momentum in catching up with the core, especially Greece and, to a lesser extent, Italy, Portugal and Hungary.

*We are grateful to the editors of the *Annual Review*, Nathaniel Copsey and Tim Haughton, for insightful and constructive comments.

© 2015 The Author(s) JCMS: Journal of Common Market Studies © 2015 John Wiley & Sons Ltd, 9600 Garsington Road, Oxford OX4 2DQ, UK and 350 Main Street, Malden, MA 02148, USA

The contribution is structured as follows: Section I discusses Europe's performance in 2014 within the global economic context. This is followed by a presentation and discussion of the main economic indicators and individual Member State performance in Section II. Section III presents a brief analysis of income convergence within the EU. The final section offers some brief conclusions.

I. European Performance and the Global Economic Context

Europe's growth performance was much weaker than expected in 2014, with real GDP growth being around 1.3 per cent. This weak performance is especially striking when seen in the light of the sustained robust growth in other parts of the world. The global economy grew by 3.3 per cent in 2014, which, although far from spectacular, nonetheless provided opportunities that Europe failed to make use of (IMF, 2014a, p. xiii). Economic activity grew by more than 2 per cent in the US, whereas China achieved 7.4 per cent growth. World trade saw an even larger expansion, and financial market actors became exceedingly optimistic as well. Stock markets and long-term yields continued to rise and investors became less risk-averse. The spread and volatility of major assets declined to the low levels that were typical before 2007. These can be seen as highly encouraging developments, despite the fact that China's growth continued to decelerate, Japan performed below expectations and Brazil's economy stagnated, as did that of Russia, which was hit heavily by western sanctions due to its war with Ukraine and falling oil prices (see Table 1).

These overwhelmingly positive developments in the global economy, however, did not manage to push the European locomotive back on a solid and sustained growth path. Domestic demand did not increase and investment activity remained repressed. Weak domestic demand, coupled with decreasing global energy and commodity prices, significantly lowered inflation across the continent, and even led to deflation in the eurozone. Exports, which have traditionally been the main driving force of economies like Germany or many smaller open Member States, performed especially weakly. Additionally, although monetary policy was highly accommodating throughout the European Union, fiscal policies remained mostly neutral due to fears of increasing public debts – a legacy of the crisis and its resolution. Geopolitics did not help the EU recover either. The

Table 1: The global economic context – GDP growth rates

	2010	2011	2012	2013	2014*
World	5.4	4.1	3.4	3.3	3.3
Advanced economies	3.1	1.7	1.2	1.4	1.8
EU	2.1	1.7	-0.4	0.0	1.3
USA	2.5	1.6	2.3	2.2	2.2
Japan	4.7	-0.5	1.5	1.5	0.9
Emerging and developing economies	7.5	6.2	5.1	4.7	4.4
Brazil	7.5	2.7	1.0	2.5	0.3
China	10.4	9.3	7.7	7.7	7.4
India	10.3	6.6	4.7	5.0	5.6
Russia	4.5	4.3	3.4	1.3	0.2

Source: IMF (2014b), European Commission (2014a).
Note: *indicates forecast data.

© 2015 The Author(s) JCMS: Journal of Common Market Studies © 2015 John Wiley & Sons Ltd, 9600 Garsington Road, Oxford OX4 2DQ, UK and 350 Main Street, Malden, MA 02148, USA

turmoil in the Middle East and, especially, the sanctions against Russia, as well as Russia's retaliatory sanctions, have also caused serious concerns for many of the Member States.[1]

While the EU is still struggling to find the proper remedy for leaving behind the crisis, it also needs to face the medium- and long-term challenges of structural problems, such as the relatively weak growth in total factor productivity, the slow pace of sectoral and labour market reforms, an ageing population and structural unemployment, especially youth unemployment. These factors keep potential growth rates low, which in turn make investors reluctant to embark on large-scale investments. Sadly enough, none of these weaknesses has been really new for Europeans. By critically reflecting upon the so-called Sapir Report of 2003, put together by highly acclaimed experts on European economic integration just before the big bang enlargement of the EU, André Sapir (2014) acknowledged in last year's *Annual Review* that the EU needs a new and well-elaborated growth strategy much more than ever before. He called for the adoption of bold measures on both the demand and the supply sides. While the single market along with the single currency have laid down the foundations of a pro-growth economic environment, the EU should target its policies and financial resources much better in order to foster economic growth and development. The European Commission (2014a, p. ix) seems to share these ideas: in its economic forecast report, it claims that '[t]he dual challenge for economic policy consists in strengthening short-term economic dynamics and raising the economy's growth potential for the medium term'. Addressing such a multifaceted challenge requires concerted efforts from Member States, inviting both monetary authorities and governments to act.

Despite this generally gloomy picture, 2014 also showed some positive developments. The European Central Bank (ECB), as well as most non-euro area central banks, followed highly accommodating monetary policies with historically low interest rates and other liquidity boosting measures to increase aggregate demand.[2] Room for further manoeuvring, however, has been rather constrained in terms of lowering interest rates. Yet, central banks can do a lot by reducing financial fragmentation, strengthening banks' balance sheets and easing liquidity constraints in the private sector. Budget deficits have also generally decreased, which may indicate that there is space for fiscal policy to support growth-friendly restructuring, although throughout 2014 there was much political opposition to fiscal laxity, especially from Germany.

II. Main Economic Indicators and Member State Performance

Economic Growth

The lack of growth dynamics in general suggests that the EU has not been able to benefit from the most recent revival of the global economy. Nevertheless, the disappointing growth performance was no longer due to low levels of private consumption – as was clearly the case immediately after the crisis – but mostly resulted from record low investment ratios, both in the public and the private sectors. The level of investment dropped by

[1] *Reuters*, 7 August 2014.
[2] See Hodson's contribution to this volume.

© 2015 The Author(s) JCMS: Journal of Common Market Studies © 2015 John Wiley & Sons Ltd, 9600 Garsington Road, Oxford OX4 2DQ, UK and 350 Main Street, Malden, MA 02148, USA

15 per cent (around €430 billion) from its peak in 2007. As investment is the main driver of long-term growth, the tendencies in 2014 endangered the economic potential and well-being of the entire EU.[3]

However, the fact that the EU was unable to grow along with the major economic centres of the world was only one part of the problem; the EU was experiencing a multispeed recovery (see Table 2, which shows average EU growth rates between 2010 and 2014, and the major outliers on both ends). Convergence in terms of economic development was a strong indicator of success in the EU before the crisis. The steady convergence process was, however, severely halted by the crisis, and Member States exhibited rather diverging growth patterns (see more on economic convergence in Section III). In 2014, a handful of countries managed to reach at least 3 per cent growth rates: Ireland (4.6 per cent), the UK (3.1 per cent), Hungary (3.2 per cent), Luxembourg (3.0 per cent) Malta (3.0 per cent) and Poland (3.0 per cent). The three Baltic States were not in the group of best performers last year, but they did maintain above EU-average economic growth rates, thereby prolonging their spectacular post-2011 performance (following, of course, their similarly spectacular drop between 2007 and 2009). At the other end of the spectrum, Finland (−0.4 per cent), Italy (−0.4 per cent), Cyprus (−2.8 per cent) and the newest Member State, Croatia (−0.7 per cent), were struggling to find their way back to positive growth. The good news is that following a five-year contraction, Greece experienced a slight increase (0.6 per cent); so after several years, the country was able to escape from the group of worst performers. The major economies also showed an uneven performance. While Germany had a bad year in 2013 (0.1 per cent), it managed to bounce back to 1.3 per cent in 2014. Nevertheless, its turn was mainly due to its spectacular first-quarter performance, after which its economy started to slow down again. France was still stagnating and did not seem to have found a way to end its growth paralysis. The success story in the group of large economies, beyond the UK, has been Spain, which achieved a 1.2 per cent increase last year.

Employment

The generally slow and fragile European recovery has nonetheless generated jobs, with rates of unemployment decreasing in most countries, breaking the increasing trend of the past few years (see Table 3). However, differences between Member States are significant. Germany continued its trend of decreasing unemployment, and by the time of writing had the lowest level in the EU (5.3 per cent). Countries which have been struggling with very high levels of unemployment for years also made progress in 2014. Following the record high levels in 2013, Greece (26.8 per cent), Spain (24.8 per cent) and Portugal (14.5 per cent) managed to put a halt to further acceleration. Latvia (11.0 per cent) and Ireland (11.1 per cent) also experienced some moderation in their unemployment ratios. The trends in labour market data indicate a strong correlation with recoveries in economic growth. Only a handful of countries, including Austria, Luxembourg, the Netherlands (although these three had very low rates to begin with), Belgium, Croatia, Cyprus, Finland,

---

[3] The Commission launched an Investment Plan for Europe in November 2014, aimed at substantially raising investment activities across Europe (European Commission, 2014b).

© 2015 The Author(s) JCMS: Journal of Common Market Studies © 2015 John Wiley & Sons Ltd, 9600 Garsington Road, Oxford OX4 2DQ, UK and 350 Main Street, Malden, MA 02148, USA

Table 2: Average EU growth rates (in percentages) and the best and worst-performing Member States

	2010	2011	2012	2013	2014*
EU average	2.1	1.7	-0.4	0.0	1.3
Standard deviation	2.4	2.9	2.4	2.1	1.5
Best performers	Sweden (6.0)	Estonia (8.3)	Latvia (4.8)	Latvia (4.2)	Ireland (4.6)
	Luxembourg (5.1)	Lithuania (6.1)	Estonia (4.7)	Romania (3.5)	Hungary (3.2)
	Slovakia (4.8)	Latvia (5)	Lithuania (3.8)	Lithuania (3.3)	UK (3.1)
		Poland (4.8)		Malta (2.5)	Luxembourg (3)
					Malta (3)
					Poland (3)
Worst performers	Ireland (−0.3)	Portugal (−1.8)	Portugal (−3.3)	Greece (−3.3)	Finland (−0.4)
	Romania (−0.8)	Greece (−8.9)	Greece (−6.6)	Cyprus (−5.4)	Italy (−0.4)
	Croatia (−1.7)				Croatia (−0.7)
	Latvia (−2.9)				Cyprus (−2.8)
	Greece (−5.4)				

Source: authors, based on European Commission (2014a).
Notes: the 'best performers' are the countries which showed rates at least one standard deviation higher than the EU average. 'Worst performers' are at least one standard deviation lower.
*indicates forecast data.

Table 3: Average EU unemployment rates (in per cent of total labour force) and the best and worst-performing Member States

	2010	2011	2012	2013	2014*
EU average	9.6	9.6	10.4	10.8	10.3
Standard deviation	4.4	4.3	5.2	5.6	5.4
Best performers	Luxembourg (4.6)	Luxembourg (4.8)	Luxembourg (5.1)	Austria (4.9)	Germany (5.1)
	Netherlands (4.5)	Netherlands (4.4)	Austria (4.3)		
	Austria (4.4)	Austria (4.2)			
Worst performers	Slovakia(14.5)	Croatia (13.9)	Portugal (15.8)	Portugal (16.4)	Cyprus (16.2)
	Estonia (16.7)	Ireland (14.7)	Croatia (16.1)	Croatia (17.3)	Croatia (17.7)
	Lithuania (17.8)	Lithuania (15.4)	Greece (24.5)	Spain (26.1)	Spain (24.8)
	Latvia (19.5)	Latvia (16.2)	Spain (24.8)	Greece (27.5)	Greece (26.8)
	Spain (19.9)	Greece (17.9)			
		Spain (21.4)			

Source: authors, based on European Commission (2014a).
Notes: the 'best performers' are the countries which showed unemployment rates at least one standard deviation below the EU average. 'Worst performers' are at least one standard deviation higher.
*indicates forecast data.

France and Italy, experienced rising unemployment ratios. The case of France is especially worrying, where unemployment increased despite a slow but growing economy.

One of the most worrying social and economic phenomena in the European labour market is the persistently high level of youth unemployment, i.e. people without jobs between the ages of 15 and 24. The youth unemployment ratio was 15 per cent just before the crisis, and subsequently increased to a record high level of 23.6 per cent by early 2013 (Eurostat, 2014a). Due to somewhat accelerating economic growth rates in 2014, youth

© 2015 The Author(s) JCMS: Journal of Common Market Studies © 2015 John Wiley & Sons Ltd, 9600 Garsington Road, Oxford OX4 2DQ, UK and 350 Main Street, Malden, MA 02148, USA

unemployment decreased, but it was still close to 5 million people (or 21.6 per cent) by the end of 2014. The highest ratios, close to or even half of the young population, were measured in Spain (53.8 per cent), Greece (49.3 per cent), Italy (43.3 per cent) and Croatia (41.5 per cent) (Eurostat, 2014b).

Inflation

The past couple of years had seen a moderation of inflation across the EU, a trend that continued in 2014 as well, leading to deflation in several countries. By 2014, consumer price inflation averaged at an unusually low rate of 0.6 per cent, although the standard deviation was relatively high, leaving the EU rather divided (Table 4). The major reasons for decelerating inflation were the lack of growth dynamism, low energy prices, falling import prices (mostly due to the appreciation of the single currency) and a substantial drop in food prices, closely related to Russian sanctions on EU food exports. The 0.6 per cent average rate of inflation implies that the EU as a whole has entered a danger zone. While both the US and emerging markets have managed to thwart deflation in the last few years, a negative or close to zero consumer price index at the end of 2014 posed a serious challenge for some of the Member States, especially for crisis-hit economies such as Greece, which faced deflation for the past two years (−0.9 per cent in 2013 and −1.0 per cent in 2014), Spain (−0.1 per cent), Cyprus (−0.2 per cent) and more recently Bulgaria (−1.4 per cent) and Slovakia (−0.1 per cent). Only Austria, the UK and Romania (1.5 per cent in each case) managed to come close to the ECB's 2 per cent benchmark value for consumer price inflation. Importantly, the low inflation rate does not support the EU economies in their effort to dismantle public and private debts or to increase investment, as the real interest rate may remain stuck at a relatively high level. On the positive side, the extremely low (or even negative) inflation may help crisis-hit countries to partly capitalize on falling wage demands, which increase their competitiveness on international markets.

Faced with protracted low inflation, monetary policy has been rather accommodative in the EU in 2014, similar to other advanced economies. Nevertheless, if expectations continue to push price changes further down or even into the negative, both the ECB and the national central banks will need to adopt more unconventional policies.

Budget Deficit and Public Debt

While central banks did not have much room to stimulate growth in 2014, fiscal policy, remaining by and large neutral throughout the year, was not too active either in remedying the sluggish economic performance. After six years of persistently violating the 3 per cent general government deficit reference value enshrined in Article 126 of the Treaty, both the eurozone deficit average and the EU average decreased below 3 per cent in 2014 (see Table 5). According to the Commission forecast (2014a, p. 36), headline deficits will decrease further down to 2.7 per cent in 2015 and to 2.3 per cent in 2016.

The consolidation efforts of the past couple of years have seemingly delivered their much-awaited results. It is important to recall that almost every Member State engaged in sizeable fiscal stimuli during 2008 and 2009. The few exceptions were Greece, Portugal and Hungary, countries which pursued lax fiscal policies before the crisis and

© 2015 The Author(s) JCMS: Journal of Common Market Studies © 2015 John Wiley & Sons Ltd, 9600 Garsington Road, Oxford OX4 2DQ, UK and 350 Main Street, Malden, MA 02148, USA

Table 4: Average EU inflation rates (harmonized indices of consumer prices, in percentages) and countries with the lowest and highest values

	2010	2011	2012	2013	2014*
EU average	2.1	3.1	2.6	1.5	0.6
Standard deviation	1.6	1.1	0.9	1.0	0.7
High inflation	Romania (6.1) Greece (4.7) Hungary (4.7)	Romania (5.8) Estonia (5.1) UK (4.5) Latvia (4.2) Lithuania 4.1 Slovakia (4.1)	Hungary (5.7) Estonia (4.2) Poland (3.7) Slovakia (3.7) Czech Republic (3.5)	Estonia (3.2) Romania (3.2) Netherlands (2.6) UK (2.6)	Austria (1.5) Romania (1.5) UK (1.5)
Low inflation or deflation	Latvia (−1.2) Ireland (−1.6)	Czech Republic (2.1) Slovenia (2.1) Sweden (1.4) Ireland (1.2)	Greece (1.0) Sweden (0.9)	Bulgaria (0.4) Cyprus (0.4) Portugal (0.4) Sweden (0.4) Latvia (0.0) Greece (−0.9)	Bulgaria (1.4) Slovakia (−0.1) Spain (−0.1) Cyprus (−0.2) Greece (−1.0)

Source: authors, based on European Commission (2014a).
Notes: countries with 'low inflation or deflation' are the ones which showed inflation rates at least one standard deviation below the EU average. 'High inflation' countries are at least one standard deviation higher.
*indicates forecast data.

© 2015 The Author(s) JCMS: Journal of Common Market Studies © 2015 John Wiley & Sons Ltd, 9600 Garsington Road, Oxford OX4 2DQ, UK and 350 Main Street, Malden, MA 02148, USA

Table 5: Average general government budget balances (in percentages of GDP) in the EU, and the best and worst-performing Member States

	2010	2011	2012	2013	2014*
Mean	−6.3	−4.6	−3.8	−3.5	−2.8
Standard deviation	5.8	3.3	2.6	3.3	1.6
Best performers	Estonia (0.2)	Estonia (1.0)	Germany (0.1)	Luxembourg (0.6)	Germany (0.2)
	Sweden (0.0)	Luxembourg (0.3)	Luxembourg (0.1)	Germany (0.1)	Luxembourg (0.2)
		Sweden (−0.1)	Estonia (−0.3)*	Sweden (−0.9)	Estonia (−0.4)
		Germany (−0.9)	Bulgaria (−0.5)		Sweden (−0.9)
		Finland (−1.0)	Sweden (−0.9)		Denmark (−1.0)
					Latvia (−1.1)
					Lithuania (−1.1)
Worst performers	Ireland (−32.4)	Lithuania (−9.0)	Ireland (−8.0)	Spain (−6.8)	France (−4.4)
		Spain (−9.4)	UK (−8.3)	Greece (−12.2)	Slovenia (−4.4)
		Greece (−10.0)	Greece (−8.6)	Slovenia (−14.6)	Portugal (−4.9)
		Ireland (−12.6)	Spain (−10.3)		UK (−5.4)
					Croatia (−5.6)
					Spain (−5.6)

Source: authors, based on European Commission (2014a).
Notes: the 'best performers' are the countries which showed a budget position at least one standard deviation above the EU average. 'Worst performers' are at least one standard deviation below.
*indicates forecast data.

© 2015 The Author(s) JCMS: Journal of Common Market Studies © 2015 John Wiley & Sons Ltd, 9600 Garsington Road, Oxford OX4 2DQ, UK and 350 Main Street, Malden, MA 02148, USA

did not have any extra fiscal space by the time the global crisis hit Europe in 2008. As benchmark interest rates were close to zero right from the very start of the crisis, fiscal policy was expected to serve as the major tool for feeding aggregate demand in EU economies. As a corollary, the headline deficit number of the general government deteriorated by 6.1 percentage points, on average, between 2007 and 2009. Debt ratios have increased substantially and are still on the ascent. In 2007, the average debt ratio of EU economies was at 44.4 per cent, but by 2014 it got close to 90 per cent (European Commission, 2014a, p. 164).

From 2010 onwards, EU countries have been heavily engaged in robust consolidation efforts. By 2014, the Baltic States were among the best performers in terms of net lending and primary deficit. Greece managed to curb the general government deficit by more than 10 percentage points in a single year, from a strikingly high level of 12.2 per cent in 2013 to only 1.6 per cent in 2014. Denmark, Sweden and Germany were also among the best performers in terms of general government balance. In fact, Germany achieved a slight surplus by substantially repressing its aggregate demand as a result of a strong dedication to consolidating its public finances. The country had the highest primary balance in the EU in the past three consecutive years, which was also clearly reflected in its current account position. At the other end of the spectrum, crisis-hit economies such as Spain and Portugal, Slovenia, plus France and the UK had a deficit of at least 4.4 per cent in 2014. With the exception of the UK, this reflects disappointing growth dynamism. Public finances data demonstrate that eurozone membership itself, the core–periphery divide or the distinction between old and new Member States does not make a difference at all in terms of 'fiscal discipline'.

External Balance

Right from the beginning of the crisis, EU countries put great efforts into stabilizing external positions. The large creditors such as Germany maintained huge surpluses, while crisis-hit countries engaged in substantial cuts in their current account deficits. By 2014, the un-weighted average of current account balances showed a significant surplus of 1.3 per cent of GDP, though the spread around the mean was quite substantial. Only 12 countries out of the 28 members had a current account deficit in 2014 – but even those countries with deficits experienced solid improvements throughout the last couple of years (e.g. Greece, Portugal, Cyprus, Latvia. See Table 6 for more details).

Sadly, the considerable improvements have not been due to a general recovery in export performance. Instead, economies with high pre-crisis external imbalances implemented adjustments on the import side by substantially reducing their external demand. Improvements in current account balances have also been a clear sign of decreasing investment activity. The only exception to this trend was the UK, which had the largest external deficit last year, being an indication of strong import demand due to the country's good economic conditions. The countries showing large surpluses have been the same for considerable time, including Sweden, Denmark, Germany, the Netherlands and Luxembourg.[4] Without increased external demand of these creditor economies, however,

---

[4] Some other countries like Ireland, Slovenia and Hungary have also shown large surpluses in recent years, which can be seen as an indication of repressed domestic demand.

© 2015 The Author(s) JCMS: Journal of Common Market Studies © 2015 John Wiley & Sons Ltd, 9600 Garsington Road, Oxford OX4 2DQ, UK and 350 Main Street, Malden, MA 02148, USA

Table 6: Average EU current account deficit (as percentages of GDP) and Member States with highest deficits and surpluses

	2010	2011	2012	2013	2014*
EU average**	-1.0	-0.8	0.2	1.3	1.3
Standard deviation	5.2	4.2	3.9	3.4	3.4
Highest current account surpluses	Luxembourg (7.7)	Netherlands (7.1)	Netherlands (8.8)	Netherlands (8.5)	Netherlands (7.8)
	Netherlands (7.5)	Luxembourg (6.5)	Germany (7.2)	Denmark (6.9)	Germany (7.1)
	Sweden (6.5)	Germany (6.2)	Sweden (6.3)	Germany (6.9)	Denmark (6.2)
	Germany (5.9)	Sweden (5.9)	Denmark (5.8)	Sweden (6.5)	Slovenia (6.2)
	Denmark (5.7)	Denmark (5.7)	Luxembourg (5.7)	Luxembourg (5.2)	Sweden (5.7)
				Slovenia (4.8)	Ireland (5.5)
					Luxembourg (5.2)
Highest current account deficits	Malta (−6.4)	Poland (−5)	Poland (−3.8)	Czech Republic (−2.2)	Latvia (−2.2)
	Cyprus (−9.1)	Portugal (−5.6)	Greece (−4.3)	Latvia (−2.2)	Estonia (−2.8)
	Portugal (−10.4)	Greece (−10.5)	Romania (−4.7)	Greece (−2.7)	Greece (−2.8)
	Greece (−12)		Cyprus (−5.5)	UK (−4.2)	UK (−4)

Source: authors, based on European Commission (2014a).
Notes: countries with high current account deficits are ones which showed deficits at least one standard deviation below the EU average. Those with high surpluses are at least one standard deviation above.
*indicates forecast data.
**: un-weighted average of Member State current account balances.

© 2015 The Author(s) JCMS: Journal of Common Market Studies © 2015 John Wiley & Sons Ltd, 9600 Garsington Road, Oxford OX4 2DQ, UK and 350 Main Street, Malden, MA 02148, USA

no recoveries in the periphery can be expected to remain solid. That said, the robust re-covery in the current account positions of most EU countries cannot be interpreted as a success, since it has not been fed by accelerating net exports. Instead, the decreased aggregate demand due to fiscal adjustment (see above) and private sector deleveraging contributed to the further 'recovery' in external positions. The worst adjustment was experienced by Greece, where almost the entire recovery was delivered by constrained private and public demand.

Competitiveness

Changes in the real effective exchange rate (REER, defined as unit labour costs adjusted for nominal exchange rate movements) are often used to illustrate changes in the international competitive positions of the EU and of its Member States. Although this measure is only able to capture changes in the cost competitiveness of the export sector, it is perhaps a more straightforward indicator than the various composite competitiveness indicators and rankings. After a substantial appreciation in 2013, the REER appreciated again in the EU as a whole in 2014, making prospects for a stronger export-led recovery gloomy. The EU average, however, is slightly misleading, as it measures EU export competitiveness in relation to the EU's main *external* trading partners. Much of the trade of Member States is with other members; thus, Member State REERs can be more meaningful. Most Member States did not see any significant change in their competitive position, as the un-weighted average of Member State REER changes was zero in 2014. There were some exceptions though. The UK saw a substantial appreciation (6.1 per cent), and so did Latvia (2.9 per cent) and Estonia (2.5 per cent). Germany and Romania also experienced an appreciation of 2 per cent. On the other hand, export cost competitiveness improved mostly in smaller Member States, such as the Czech Republic (−5.9 per cent), Ireland (−4.8 per cent) and Cyprus (−4 per cent); Sweden (−3.2 per cent) also managed to improve on its cost competitiveness – see Table 7.

Going beyond cost aspects, the World Economic Forum's Global Competitiveness Index provides a measure of locational attractiveness (World Economic Forum, 2014). According to this index, some EU members, notably Finland, Germany, Sweden and the Netherlands, have been among the world's most competitive economies for some time. With the exception of Sweden, the other three managed to hold on to these positions in 2014. On the other hand, the least competitive EU countries are all from southern and eastern Europe. Greece had the worst position in 2014, though it substantially improved its rank from the previous year. Bulgaria, Latvia, Portugal and Romania, all belonging to the less competitive group of European countries, made impressive progress as well. On the other hand, Slovakia and Slovenia both experienced huge slumps in their rankings in recent years, and these continued in 2014.

III. Ten Years in Perspective: the Income Convergence Hypothesis

The ten-year anniversary of the EU's 'big bang' eastern enlargement in 2004, along with the rather diverse impacts of the global economic crisis and the ensuing slow recovery,

© 2015 The Author(s) JCMS: Journal of Common Market Studies © 2015 John Wiley & Sons Ltd, 9600 Garsington Road, Oxford OX4 2DQ, UK and 350 Main Street, Malden, MA 02148, USA

Table 7: Average real effective exchange rates, and highest appreciations and depreciations (unit labour costs relative to a group of industrialised countries, percentage change on preceding year)

	2010	2011	2012	2013	2014*
EU	−7.8	0.5	−5.1	8.9	3.3
Un-weighted average of Member States	−2.2	0.1	−2.1	2.0	0.0
Standard deviation	4.2	2.7	2.9	3.3	2.5
Highest REER depreciation	Ireland (−10.5)	Romania(−5.9)	Greece (−7)	Greece (−7.2)	Czech Republic (−5.9)
	Latvia (−10.5)	Ireland (−3.5)	Spain (−6.6)	Cyprus (−3.1)	Ireland (−4.8)
	Lithuania (−8.3)	Poland (−2.6)	Romania (−6)	Czech Republic (−3.1)	Cyprus (−4)
	Estonia (−6.4)	Estonia (−2.5)	Cyprus (−5.6)	Hungary　(−1.9)	Sweden (−3.2)
		Croatia (−2.5)	Portugal (−5.5)	UK (−1.6)	
			Ireland (−5.1)		
			Croatia (−5)		
Highest REER appreciation	Bulgaria (2.6)	Czech Republic (2.9)	Bulgaria (1.2)	Estonia (6.1)	Estonia (2.5)
	UK (2.8)	Malta (3.7)	Sweden (2.8)	Ireland (6.3)	Latvia (2.9)
	Czech Republic (3.0)	Bulgaria (3.9)	UK (4.9)	Latvia (6.3)	UK (6.1)
	Sweden (4.8)	Sweden (7.5)		Bulgaria (7.8)	
	Poland (8.4)				

Source: authors, based on European Commission (2014a).
Notes: countries with high REER depreciations are the ones which showed depreciations at least one standard deviation below the EU average. Those with high appreciations are at least one standard deviation above the average.
*indicates forecast data.

© 2015 The Author(s) JCMS: Journal of Common Market Studies © 2015 John Wiley & Sons Ltd, 9600 Garsington Road, Oxford OX4 2DQ, UK and 350 Main Street, Malden, MA 02148, USA

make the question of convergence among the economic performance of Member States especially compelling. Has EU membership managed to reduce differences in terms of national income and development over the course of the decade? Neoclassical growth theory, going back to the works of Solow (1956), predicts that countries with lower levels of income will tend to grow faster than richer countries due to differences in the capital/labour ratio and, in turn, with regard to the marginal product of capital. Assuming constant returns to scale and structural similarities, including applied technology, the neoclassical growth model predicts (an absolute) convergence in income (and economic development), making it only a matter of time for a less developed country to catch up with the more developed ones. Based on the neoclassical growth model, Martin *et al.* (2001) argued that economic integration can hugely bolster this convergence process among countries through the elimination of transaction costs, the increased efficiency of capital and the free flow of goods and services. In contrast, however, Krugman (1991) argued that due to scale economies and agglomeration effects, economic integration can instead foster divergence.

Reviewing the literature on empirical attempts to verify the neoclassical convergence hypothesis is beyond the scope of this contribution, but it is worth highlighting key findings on Europe. EU-wide studies focus on the performance of either countries or sub-national regions. At the country level, the empirical evidence overwhelmingly points to the relevance of the convergence hypothesis, at least for the EU-15. Cuaresma *et al.* (2008), for example, found that in case of the pre-2004 Member States, EU membership had a convergence-stimulating impact on long-term growth: relatively poor countries benefited more from membership than rich ones. Petrakos *et al.* (2011), however, showed that while convergence is clearly present on the country level, the picture is less evident on the level of regions. Analysing 70 regions from six EU members, Fagerberg and Verspagen (1996) concluded that convergence was present during the post-war decades, but there have been signs of reversal after the 1980s. They also argued that after the 1980s 'club convergence' became dominant, i.e. one could identify convergence within certain groups ('clubs') of regions, but no convergence between these groups. These conclusions were echoed by Fischer and Stirböck (2006), who identified two growth clubs: much of western Europe, including most of Spain, Northern Italy and Slovenia, versus the eastern Member States, parts of East Germany and Austria, plus the southern regions, including Portugal, Greece and some regions of Italy and Spain. The conflicting results between the national and the regional level can be traced back to the fact that growth in Member States is often driven by dynamic metropolitan centres, leaving the rest of the country untouched (Petrakos *et al.*, 2011).

So, have the less developed eastern and southern members grown faster in the past decade than the western and northern countries, thereby narrowing the gap between the two groups? The cross-country scatterplot diagram of Figure 1 seems to reinforce the income convergence hypothesis, showing a moderate negative relationship between the level of development (measured as a percentage of the EU15's average income) in the year of the big bang enlargement on the one hand, and the mean annual economic growth rate between 2004 and 2014 on the other.[5] By and large, EU countries can be split into two main

---

[5] Croatia and Luxembourg have been omitted from the analysis. Luxembourg was an outlier with 216 per cent of EU15 income in 2004. No data was available for Croatia.

© 2015 The Author(s) JCMS: Journal of Common Market Studies © 2015 John Wiley & Sons Ltd, 9600 Garsington Road, Oxford OX4 2DQ, UK and 350 Main Street, Malden, MA 02148, USA

Figure 1: Incomes in 2004 and subsequent economic performance

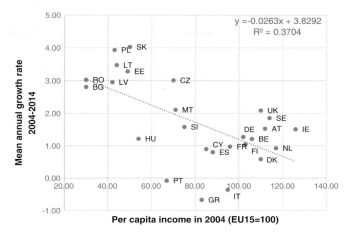

Source: authors, based on data from AMECO.
Note: per capita GDP in purchasing power parity.

clusters: the group of new Member States and the old Member States. Nevertheless, a handful of countries are somewhere midway in-between the two major clusters, often rather far from the trend line.

The Czech Republic, Estonia, Hungary, Latvia, Lithuania, Poland, Slovakia and Slovenia (CEE8) were at 53 per cent of the EU15 average in 2004. Ten years later the average score of the CEE8 was 68 per cent, demonstrating a massive wealth accumulation. Most of the eastern accession countries, such as Poland, Slovakia, the Czech Republic and the Baltic States, showed spectacular growth performances during the past ten years. For example, Poland's per capita income, measured in purchasing power parity, was only 43 per cent of that of the EU15's in 2004, but the ratio had increased by 20 percentage points to 63 per cent by 2014. The Baltic countries, on the other hand, were among the biggest losers of the crisis, suffering from an incredibly deep recession and losing about one-fifth of their national income. Yet, as Figure 1 demonstrates, they still managed to perform well above the trend line. With quick and unusually severe policy responses, each of them managed to bounce back and continued their convergence toward the core by 2011 (see Staehr, 2013).

The most surprising success story was achieved by Slovakia. After years of semi-isolation and a slow start to the EU accession process caused by the illiberal Mečiar regime in the second half of the 1990s, the pro-market reforms of the Dzurinda cabinet after 2001 unequivocally made Slovakia the most successful converger among the new EU Member States (Fisher et al., 2007; Győrffy, 2009).

Romania and Bulgaria, countries which joined the EU in 2007, also showed good convergence performance: both of them had incomes around a third of the EU15's average GDP per capita in 2004, but by 2014 they managed to reach 49 and 43 per cent, respectively. In fact, these two countries lie almost perfectly on the fitted line of Figure 1, just like Malta, which started the convergence process at 71 per cent in 2004 and reached 82 per cent 10 year later. Malta managed to outperform Slovenia, which was the most developed country of the 10 states acceding in 2004. Slovenia, in relative terms, did not

© 2015 The Author(s) JCMS: Journal of Common Market Studies © 2015 John Wiley & Sons Ltd, 9600 Garsington Road, Oxford OX4 2DQ, UK and 350 Main Street, Malden, MA 02148, USA

manage to approximate the EU15 average; it stayed where it was at the time of accession, at 75 per cent. Commentators on the Slovenian failure identify the lack of structural and institutional reforms, oversized state-controlled enterprises, the overregulated and unfavourable business environment and especially the deterioration of the country's export competitiveness as the main factors detrimental to growth (see especially European Commission, 2014b). The other CEE country which did not manage to capitalize on EU accession was Hungary. At the time of accession it had the third highest per capita income among the CEE8 countries, right behind Slovenia and the Czech Republic. Although Hungary, in sharp contrast to Slovenia, experienced some advances in its relative income position (it rose from 54 per cent to 62 per cent), it had been seriously outperformed by all the others by 2014. This conclusion is hardly moderated by the country's good economic performance in 2014, the long-run sustainability of which is seen as highly questionable. It is important to note, however, that both Slovenia and Hungary faced these deteriorating tendencies well *before* EU accession. As pointed out by Murn et al. (2002), Slovenia experienced worsening conditions, including low levels of foreign direct investment inflows, high unit labour costs and an excessive emphasis on labour-intensive production already at the turn of the millennium. The major blow to Hungary's economic development came around 2001 and 2002, when the public sector turned into the playground of short-sighted politicians (Benczes and Takács, 2014; Csaba, 2011).

At the other end of the trend line, old Member States displayed high starting per capita incomes and relatively low annual growth rates, as the income convergence hypothesis would predict. By and large, all the 'core' countries managed to slightly increase their relative income positions between 2004 and 2014, but there is ample evidence for spread around the trend here too. The United Kingdom and Sweden excelled, with an annual average growth rate of 2 per cent. Although neither of them avoided the impact of the financial crisis, a swift and robust recovery helped the two economies attain a far better performance than other old Member States. The UK experienced strong employment growth, along with a massive inflow of workers in the past ten years, hugely benefiting from the eastern enlargement of the EU. Additionally, from 2010 onwards, the country has been undertaking a series of austerity measures, mostly in the form of expenditure cuts – although the public deficit is still above the 3 per cent limit. The European Commission (2015a), however, points to sluggish productivity which undermines the sustainability of British performance. Sweden, on the other hand, avoided austerity. It managed to hold public debt at low levels and ran a balanced budget before, during and after the financial crisis. In fact, Sweden was even able to reduce taxes and increase spending on research, education and public investment, thereby boosting economic activity (European Commission, 2015b).

According to Figure 1, the third outlier on the positive side was, somewhat surprisingly, one of the 'programme countries': Ireland. Aside from Luxembourg, Ireland was the EU's richest country in 2004, yet it attained an impressive 1.5 per cent growth rate, ranking it in the top four among the old Member States. Compared to Ireland's staggering performance of the nineties (with often two-digit growth rates), the 1.5 per cent rate might seem rather modest. Yet if the more recent events, such as the bursting of the mortgage bubble and the consequent banking and fiscal crises, are taken into account, even such a 'moderate' rate is worth acknowledging (see Donovan and Murphy, 2013).

© 2015 The Author(s) JCMS: Journal of Common Market Studies © 2015 John Wiley & Sons Ltd, 9600 Garsington Road, Oxford OX4 2DQ, UK and 350 Main Street, Malden, MA 02148, USA

On the other hand, in line with the empirical literature cited above, southern countries suffered from further fall-backs. Clearly, Greece saw the most dramatic fall in its relative income (from 83 per cent of the EU15's average in 2004 to 66 per cent in 2014). But others, such as Italy and Portugal and, to a lesser extent, Cyprus and Spain, also fell behind. The global financial and economic crisis and the ensuing European sovereign debt crisis have seriously halted the convergence process of these economies. In contrast with Slovenia's and Hungary's performance, where problems began well before the crisis, some of the southern members did not do badly before 2007. In fact, Greece and Spain highly outperformed most of the old Member States between 2004 and 2007 (with annual average growth rates around 4.3 and 3.6 per cent, respectively; see Table 8). The two countries' performance was, in fact, in full harmony with the prediction of the income convergence hypothesis: they did not fare as outstandingly as the new Member States, but showed much better performance than, say, Germany, which achieved only 2.1 per cent. With the benefit of hindsight, Greece managed to maintain its relative position by

Table 8: Economic growth in EU Member States in 2004–7 and 2008–14

	2004–7	2008–14
EU average	4.4	0.2
Standard deviation	2.3	1.3
Countries above the EU average	Latvia (10.3)	Poland (3.1)
	Estonia (9.0)	Czech Rep (2.0)
	Lithuania (8.1)	Malta (2.0)
	Slovakia (7.6)	Slovakia (2.0)
	Romania (6.7)	UK (1.7)
	Bulgaria (6.0)	Bulgaria (1.0)
	Poland (5.4)	Romania (0.9)
	Slovenia (5.3)	Sweden (0.9)
	Ireland (5.2)	Germany (0.8)
	Czech Rep (4.8)	Lithuania (0.8)
		Austria (0.7)
		Belgium (0.5)
		France (0.4)
Countries below the EU average	Greece (4.3)	Ireland (−0.6)
	Cyprus (4.2)	Estonia (0.0)
	Finland (4.0)	Hungary (0.0)
	Spain (3.6)	Netherlands (−0.1)
	Sweden (3.5)	Denmark (−0.5)
	Hungary (3.4)	Slovenia (−0.5)
	Austria (2.9)	Finland (−0.7)
	UK (2.9)	Spain (−0.8)
	Netherlands (2.7)	Portugal (−0.9)
	Denmark (2.5)	Cyprus (−1.0)
	Belgium (2.4)	Italy (−1.2)
	Malta (2.4)	Latvia (−1.2)
	Germany (2.1)	Lithuania (−3.4)
	France (2.0)	Greece (−3.5)
	Portugal (1.4)	
	Italy (1.2)	

Source: authors, based on European Commission (2014a) and AMECO.

© 2015 The Author(s) JCMS: Journal of Common Market Studies © 2015 John Wiley & Sons Ltd, 9600 Garsington Road, Oxford OX4 2DQ, UK and 350 Main Street, Malden, MA 02148, USA

protracted fiscal profligacy and accumulation of public debt (Visvizi, 2012), whereas Spain's GDP growth was fuelled by a large mortgage bubble.

Portugal and Italy, on the other hand, were the laggards of the entire EU, with 1.4 and 1.2 per cent growth rates already between 2004 and 2007. Therefore, the deterioration of their economic performance could hardly be accounted for by the crisis itself. For Portugal, the divergence and the consequent decade-long stagnation coincided with the adoption of the single currency (Alves, 2014). In the case of Italy, the situation was even worse; the country was one of the worst performers already in the nineties (Commission, 2014a), and the adoption of the euro did not make things any better.

It is also reasonable to ask whether the EU as a whole was able to keep pace with the world's largest economy, the US, in the past ten years. US growth rates turned negative in 2007, but the country managed to slowly leave behind the crisis from 2009 onwards, and it was able to maintain steady growth in the years afterwards. Surprisingly, the development gap between the EU average and the US did not change at all between 2004 and 2014. In terms of current price per capita GDP, the EU-25 stood at two-thirds of US income in 2004 (€22,444 versus €33,649), exactly where the EU-28 stood in 2014 (€27,470 versus €40,946). This performance is partly due to the stunning convergence experience of most of the eastern member countries, but some old members were able to outperform the US in the ten-year period as well, most notably Austria, Germany, Luxembourg and Sweden.

Conclusions

The long-awaited recovery of the European economy did not arrive in 2014. Despite a generally accommodative global context, economic growth, while modestly accelerating after 2013, remained sluggish. Unresolved structural problems may be seen as the main reason for this continued eurosclerosis. While there were some initiatives to resolve some of these problems (such as the labour market reforms by Matteo Renzi's government in Italy or Manuel Walls' pro-business and pro-employment initiatives in France, along with Jean-Claude Juncker's Investment Plan for Europe), political will was just as evidently missing in 2014 as it had been the case in previous years (Copsey and Haughton, 2012). The consequences of persistently slow growth are several. Government debt is already at record high levels, making any further fiscal stimulus rather difficult. It is clear that any attempt to bolster fiscal consolidation would surely evoke serious opposition and even social unrest in many of the Member States (it is enough to mention the election victory of Syriza in Greece in January 2015). Unemployment did decrease in 2014, but this is not much consolation for the 26 million people without jobs Europe-wide. Youth unemployment is especially worrisome; it could easily result in the creation of a 'lost generation'. The opposing positions between Germany and France on the need for further austerity and especially on the rightness of the EU's fiscal rulebook do not help the community to hammer out the proper future methods of governance, including the sequencing and the depth of structural reforms. The lack of demand and decreasing global oil prices have practically annihilated inflation in Europe and have led to a very real threat of deflation which, if sustained, could paralyze Europe's growth for the foreseeable future, as it has paralyzed Japan since the 1990s. As we entered 2015, the basic question was whether the European Central Bank would be willing to take a more relaxed position on growth-supporting measures.[6]

---

[6] It seems that the ECB indeed wants to play a more active role: it announced an expanded asset purchase programme in January 2015.

© 2015 The Author(s) JCMS: Journal of Common Market Studies © 2015 John Wiley & Sons Ltd, 9600 Garsington Road, Oxford OX4 2DQ, UK and 350 Main Street, Malden, MA 02148, USA

This contribution has also examined the issue of convergence among EU Member States. By and large the income convergence hypothesis has been verified, as most of the new Member States, which were all well below the EU average in terms of GDP per capita at the time of their accession, have been able to grow faster than the core economies of the EU. Nevertheless, this bird's-eye view is rather biased, as there have been some outliers to this general trend. The very fact that some countries did not manage to capitalize on EU accession suggests that convergence is hardly an automatic, i.e. endogenous, outcome of EU membership. As the overview of country experiences in this contribution underlined, it would be extremely challenging to pinpoint any single reason for the co-existence of EU-level convergence and divergence of some national economies in the past ten years. Nevertheless, it would not be far off to claim that divergence can be explained by individual country factors in most of the cases, including policy mistakes and economic mismanagement on the one hand, and structural deficiencies and eroding competitiveness on the other. It is likely, however, that these countries would have fared even worse without EU membership (Jacoby, 2014, p. 67). The European financial-cum-economic crisis in fact made the convergence process a hard run for many; nevertheless, putting the blame solely on the crisis for laggard positions would be a huge mistake.

If someone, though, is looking for a European pattern, the current division of labour, along with the unique variety of capitalism(s) in Central and Eastern Europe and the Mediterranean region, may not help further convergence in the future (Epstein, 2014). Relying on foreign direct investment as a driver of growth and a source of knowledge needs to be supplanted by greater domestic innovation and knowledge creation in these countries, if the convergence momentum of the past decade is to be sustained.

References

Alves, A.A. (2014) 'In the Eye of the Storm: Portugal and the European Crisis'. In Ferreira-Pereira, L.C. (ed.) *Portugal in the European Union: Assessing Twenty-Five Years of Integration Experience* (New York: Routledge).

Benczes, I. and Takács, V. (2014) 'The Strategic Use of Public Debt in Central and Eastern Europe' In Benczes, I. (ed.) *Deficit and Debt in Transition: The Political Economy of Public Finances in Central and Eastern Europe* (Budapest and New York: CEU Press).

Copsey, N. and Haughton, T. (2012) 'Editorial: Desperate But Not Serious – The EU in 2011'. *JCMS*, Vol. 50, No. s2, pp. 1–5.

Csaba, L. (2011) 'And the First Shall be the Last'. *Hungarian Studies*, Vol. 25, No. 2, pp. 235–48.

Cuaresma, J.C., Ritzberger-Grünwald, D. and Silgoner, M.A. (2008) 'Growth, Convergence and EU Membership'. *Applied Economics*, Vol. 40, No. 5, pp. 643–56.

Donovan, D. and Murphy, A.E. (2013) *The Fall of the Celtic Tiger: Ireland and the Euro Debt Crisis* (Oxford: Oxford University Press).

Epstein, R.A. (2014) 'Overcoming 'Economic Backwardness' in the European Union'. *JCMS*, Vol. 52, No. 1, pp. 17–34.

European Commission (2014a) *European Economic Forecast Autumn 2014* (Brussels: European Commission).

European Commission (2014b) *An Investment Plan for Europe. COM*(2014) 903 final (Brussels: European Commission).

European Commission (2014c) *European Economic Forecast Spring 2014* (Brussels: European Commission).

© 2015 The Author(s) JCMS: Journal of Common Market Studies © 2015 John Wiley & Sons Ltd, 9600 Garsington Road, Oxford OX4 2DQ, UK and 350 Main Street, Malden, MA 02148, USA

European Commission (2015a) *Country Report United Kingdom 2015*. Commission Staff Working Document SWD (2015) 47 final. (Brussels: European Commission).

European Commission (2015b) *Country Report Sweden 2015*. Commission Staff Working Document SWD (2015) 46 final (Brussels: European Commission).

Eurostat (2014a) Unemployment Statistics, October 2014. Available at «http://ec.europa.eu/eurostat/statistics-explained/index.php/Unemployment_statistics».

Eurostat (2014b) 'Euro Area Unemployment Rate at 11.5 per cent'. *Eurostat Newsrelease, Euroindicators*, October.

Fagerberg, J. and Verspagen, B. (1996) 'Heading for Divergence? Regional Growth in Europe Reconsidered'. *JCMS*, Vol. 34, No. 3, pp. 431–48.

Fischer, M. and Stirböck, C. (2006) 'Pan-European Regional Income Growth and Club-Convergence'. *The Annals of Regional Science*, Vol. 40, No. 4, pp. 693–721.

Fisher, S., Gould J. and Haughton, T. (2007) 'Slovakia's Neoliberal Turn'. *Europe-Asia Studies*, Vol. 59, No. 6, pp. 977–98.

Győrffy, D. (2009) 'Structural Change Without Trust. Reform Cycles in Hungary and Slovakia'. *Acta Oeconomica*, Vol. 59, No. 2, pp. 147–77.

IMF (2014a) *World Economic Outlook. Legacies, Clouds and Uncertainties. October 2014* (Washington DC: IMF).

IMF (2014b) *World Economic Outlook Database*. Available at «http://www.imf.org/external/pubs/ft/weo/2014/02/weodata/index.aspx»

Jacoby, W. (2014) 'The EU Factor in Fat Times and in Lean: Did the EU Amplify the Boom and Soften the Bust?' *JCMS*, Vol. 52, No. 1, pp. 52–70.

Krugman, P.R. (1991) *Geography and Trade*. (Cambridge, MA: MIT Press).

Martin, C., Velázquez, F.J. and Funck, B. (2001) *European Integration and Income Convergence: Lessons for Central and Eastern European Countries*. World Bank Technical Papers (Washington, DC: World Bank).

Murn, A., Zupancic, R.K., Smrke, F., Barlic, N., and Horvat, E. (2002) *Development Report* (Ljubljana: UMAR, Institute of Macroeconomic Analysis and Development).

OECD (2014) *OECD Economic Outlook*, Vol. 2013, No. 2 (Paris: OECD).

Petrakos, G., Kallioras, D. and Anagnostou, A. (2011) 'Regional Convergence and Growth in Europe: Understanding Patterns and Determinants'. *European Urban and Regional Studies*, Vol. 18, No. 4, pp. 375–91.

Sapir, A. (2014) 'Still the Right Agenda for Europe? The Sapir Report Ten Years On'. *JCMS*, Vol. 52, No. s1, pp. 57–73.

Solow, R. (1956) 'A Contribution to the Theory of Economic Growth'. *Quarterly Journal of Economics*, Vol. 70, pp. 65–94.

Staehr, K. (2013) 'Austerity in the Baltic States during the Global Financial Crisis'. *Intereconomics*, Vol. 48, No. 5, pp. 293–302.

Visvizi, A. (2012) 'The Crisis in Greece and the EU-IMF Rescue Package'. *Acta Oeconomica* Vol. 62, No. 1, pp. 15–39.

World Economic Forum (2014) *The Global Competitiveness Report 2014–2015* (Geneva: World Economic Forum).

© 2015 The Author(s) JCMS: Journal of Common Market Studies © 2015 John Wiley & Sons Ltd, 9600 Garsington Road, Oxford OX4 2DQ, UK and 350 Main Street, Malden, MA 02148, USA

JCMS 2015 Volume 53 Annual Review pp. 181–199   DOI: 10.1111/jcms.12271

Supranational Banking Supervision in Europe: The Construction of a Credible Watchdog*

JAKUB GREN,[1] DAVID HOWARTH[1] and LUCIA QUAGLIA[2]
[1]University of Luxembourg. [2]University of York

Introduction

In 2014, a major development in the history of European integration took place with the start of supranational banking supervision through the Single Supervisory Mechanism (SSM). The creation of the SSM was the first step in the construction of banking union, which was initially proposed in June 2012 by the European Council president (Van Rompuy, 2012) and shortly thereafter endorsed by the euro area heads of government and state. The SSM was to be subsequently complemented by a common backstop for temporary financial support for struggling banks and a single framework for the managed resolution of banks. The creation of banking union amounted to a radical initiative to stabilize euro-periphery national banking systems exposed directly to rising sovereign debt loads and the growing risk of default – the 'sovereign debt-bank doom loop' – and to reverse the fragmentation of European financial markets (see Howarth and Quaglia, 2013, 2014). The European Council president presented banking union in terms of 'completing' economic and monetary union (EMU) and thus addressing a fundamental flaw in the design of EMU (Van Rompuy, 2012). Indeed, the architects of EMU – the central bank governors and expert members of the Committee for the study of economic and monetary union under the chairmanship of Commission President Jacques Delors – advocated the transfer of prudential supervision to the supranational level to complement monetary union. The Delors Committee's 'Report on economic and monetary union in the European Community' stated that the European System of Central Banks (ESCB) 'would participate in the coordination of banking supervision policies of supervisory authorities' (1989, para. 32). However, the transfer of supervisory powers was postponed given the opposition of a number of national governments (James, 2012).

By 2012, in the context of a devastating sovereign debt crisis and the very real menace of the imminent collapse of the Spanish banking system, Spanish government default and euro area collapse, most euro area governments had changed their policies on supranational banking supervision. Most had come to accept that a greater European Central Bank (ECB) role in prudential supervision and greater harmonization of national supervisory practices would improve the supervision of euro area headquartered banks, reducing the likelihood of supervisory forbearance – that is, the problem of

*David Howarth and Lucia Quaglia would like to thank the Luxembourg Fonds National de la Recherche, which funded Quaglia's stay in Luxembourg during the 2014–15 academic year and work on this contribution.

© 2015 The Author(s) JCMS: Journal of Common Market Studies © 2015 John Wiley & Sons Ltd, 9600 Garsington Road, Oxford OX4 2DQ, UK and 350 Main Street, Malden, MA 02148, USA

supervisors turning a blind eye to mounting problems within banks – which had such a devastating impact upon the large majority of Spanish savings banks, or *cajas* (Garicano, 2012). The creation of a credible SSM was also seen by many – notably in Germany – as a necessary first step to diminish the potential problem of moral hazard that could arise in the euro area periphery with the creation of European-level funding mechanisms to help national authorities to bail out or resolve banks, without adding to national sovereign debt (Boone and Johnson, 2011).[1]

The SSM agreed by the European Council in December 2012 should be seen as a compromise on the distribution of power between the ECB and national competent authorities (NCAs)[2] regarding bank supervision. On the one hand, the Member States agreed to assign the ECB responsibility 'for the overall effective functioning of the SSM' and 'direct oversight of the euro area banks' (European Council, 2012, p. 2). On the other, this supervision was to be 'differentiated' and the ECB would carry it out in 'close cooperation' with the NCAs. Direct ECB supervision – through joint supervisory teams (JSTs) – was to cover only those banks with assets exceeding €30 billion or those whose assets represent at least 20 per cent of their home country's annual GDP. On 4 February 2014, the European Central Bank (2014a) published a list of 128 such banks. The thousands of smaller, so-called 'less significant' banks headquartered in the euro area would continue to be under the direct supervision of NCAs, but according to increasingly harmonized rules and practices. This compromise of two-level supervision reflected above all the demands of the German government, which opposed transferring supervisory responsibilities for the country's regional public savings banks (*Sparkassen*) and co-operatives to the ECB. The compromise, however, raises doubts as to the construction of a credible mechanism that ensures the application of common supervisory standards to all euro area banks.

In 2014, five important SSM milestones were reached. First, on 11 March, the ECB published the manual for its asset quality review (AQR; European Central Bank, 2014b). Second, on 16 April, the ECB published its framework regulation for the operation of the SSM (European Central Bank, 2014d), putting meat on the bones of the SSM regulation adopted by Member States in the Council in 2013. Third, in September, the ECB endorsed the SSM Supervisory Manual and published a Guide to Banking Supervision which had been drawn up by the Work Stream of the ECB Task Force, consisting of ECB staff and experts from NCAs of the SSM (European Central Bank, 2015). Fourth, on 26 October the ECB published its comprehensive assessment of the 128 banks subject to its direct supervision (European Central Bank, 2014f). This comprehensive assessment consisted of the ECB's AQR and the European Banking Authority's (EBA's) stress tests. Fifth, the SSM officially began operation on 4 November – the date on which the ECB assumed full control of the prudential supervision of 128 euro area banks (European Central Bank, 2014g) and monitoring responsibility for the supervision of thousands of less significant banks.

---

[1] See, for example, the comments of the German Finance Minister, Wolfgang Schauble, in *New York Times*, 18 November 2011 and *European Voice*, 16 February 2012.
[2] 'National Competent Authorities' (NCAs) is a term used in the supervisory *acquis* to refer to national authorities responsible for banking. In some countries, the central bank controls supervision. In others, a separate body is responsible.

© 2015 The Author(s) JCMS: Journal of Common Market Studies © 2015 John Wiley & Sons Ltd

This contribution focuses on the important matter of the SSM's credibility, in terms of its institutional and operational design and its first assessment of the stability of systemically important (significant) European banks. What added value does the SSM provide over national supervision? Officially, the SSM is supposed to ensure the more effective supervision of all euro area-headquartered banks, and notably those institutions subject to direct ECB supervision because they meet the criteria set by the ECB to be classified as systemically important. The creation of the SSM was also part of a banking union package designed to help tackle the sovereign debt crisis by addressing the 'sovereign debt-bank doom loop' that affected the euro-periphery Member States. Thus, the broader effectiveness of the SSM – both in terms of good supervision and systemic stability – can only be judged in the future and hinges on a number of factors, some of which have little to do with the design and operation of the SSM itself.

This contribution seeks to answer a more modest but nonetheless important question: does the institutional design of the SSM and its first assessment of systemically important bank stability bolster the credibility of supranational banking supervision in Europe? One crucial measure of credibility with regard to the SSM and NCA supervision of less significant banks – the large majority of euro area headquartered banks not subject to direct ECB supervision – is the assurance of consistent supervision in the euro area. This involves some degree of convergence of NCA supervision in order to prevent national supervisory forbearance of struggling banks. It therefore becomes necessary to examine whether or not the design of the SSM provides the foundation to build convergence in euro area supervision of less significant banks, despite very different national supervisory practices and institutional frameworks. Section I assesses the credibility of the SSM design in terms of providing the foundation for consistent supervision with the help of the principal–agent analytical framework.

Section II of this contribution examines the credibility of the ECB's direct supervision of significant banks. The management of the ECB's comprehensive assessment of significant banks can be seen as the first step in demonstrating the capacity of the ECB to make difficult decisions with regard to the stability of euro area banks. Other measures by which to judge the credibility of the SSM are difficult to evaluate. The quality of the supervisory process agreed in the SSM's supervisory manual remains largely unknown. Ultimately, avoiding bank failure may be the best gauge of SSM credibility (as in Barth *et al.*, 2006). However, bank resolution through the SRM rather than bank bail-out with either national or European funds might lend more credibility to the SSM.

This contribution seeks to determine if the SSM has begun the unprecedented adventure of supranational banking supervision on the right foot. It argues that on both institutional design and on the first comprehensive assessment, credibility has been bolstered. Yet some features of the SSM's institutional design severely undermine the potential to ensure the effective supervision of less significant banks – notably the ECB's limited legal powers to require a change in NCA supervision short of assuming direct prudential control of a less significant bank – while the ECB's first comprehensive assessment attracted criticism from a range of credible and objective sources.

© 2015 The Author(s) JCMS: Journal of Common Market Studies © 2015 John Wiley & Sons Ltd

I. Credibility of Institutional Design: Ensuring the Consistent Supervision of Less Significant Banks

A significant part of the credibility of the SSM's institutional design has been about designing 'ex ante' and 'ex post' controls by the single supervisory board (SSB) of the ECB over the NCAs in order to ensure a degree of consistency in supervisory practice. These controls can be understood through an application of the principal–agent analytical framework (Weingast and Moran, 1983; Kiewiet and McCubbins, 1991). The ECB can be seen as a principal that adopts a range of controls to ensure that its policy preferences are enforced by the NCAs within the SSM. It then becomes important to assess whether these controls cover all 'zones of discretion'[3] the NCAs have with regard to supervisory tasks[4] which they carry out on the ECB's behalf. The credibility of the SSM design thus depends upon limiting the NCAs' 'zone of discretion' (what we refer to as 'black holes'). Clearly, in relation to the existing application of the principal–agent framework in national or European Union contexts, it is unusual to treat the non-majoritarian, but independent, ECB as a principal and the non-majoritarian national supervisors (NCAs), selected by national governments, as agents of the ECB. In the vast majority of political science studies, a government or governments are treated as the principal/collective principal.

With regard to EU policy-making, principal–agent analysis has been applied to improve our understanding of the relations between EU Member States and the Commission and the ability of the former to control the latter (Pollack, 1997); to examine the relations between the Member States and the European Central Bank, with the focus on the limited 'ex ante' and 'ex post' controls of the principals over the ECB agent (Elgie, 2002); and to explain the relations between EU Member States and the Council of Ministers (Ecofin) (Schuknecht, 2004; Hodson, 2009). However, to date, the application of principal–agent analysis to the relations between EU institutions and other agencies/authorities has been limited (see, for example, Thatcher, 2011; Egeberg and Trondal, 2011).[5] Principal–agent analysis has also been applied with regard to banking supervision at the national level (see, for example, Schuler, 2003; Masciandaro, 2004; Masciandaro and Pellegrina, 2008).

In the context of the SSM, three potential principal–agent relationships arise: between Member State governments (collectively) and the ECB (and its SSB); between Member State governments (individually) and NCAs;[6] and between the ECB and NCAs. It is the third relationship on which we focus here, given that the independence of both the ECB/SSB and NCAs is a starting point of the SSM — although it is very likely that NCA autonomy from Member State governments in the years to come will be tested, especially when politically difficult decisions over bank mergers and resolution arise. While EU Member States assigned powers to the ECB over supervision in the context of the

---

[3] The zone of discretion is 'the sum of delegated powers (policy discretion) granted by the principal to the agent, minus (b) the sum of control instruments, available for use by the principals to shape (constrain) or annul (reverse) policy outcomes that emerge as a result of the agent's performance of set tasks' (Thatcher and Stone Sweet, 2002, p. 5).

[4] 'Supervisory tasks' are understood in this contribution as specific tasks concerning policies relating to the prudential supervision of credit institutions in accordance with the SSM Regulation (Council, 2013).

[5] On the application of the principal–agent framework to the relations between two non-majoritarian institutions see Waterman and Meier (1998) and Terman (2015).

[6] The SSM Regulation provides no legal underpinning for the delegation of powers to the NCAs. Therefore, in the context of the operation of the SSM, the relationship between Member State governments and the NCAs has no direct legal basis per se. Nonetheless, NCAs remain agents of Member State governments.

© 2015 The Author(s) JCMS: Journal of Common Market Studies © 2015 John Wiley & Sons Ltd

SSM regulation, they imposed no specific institutional framework to govern the relationship of the ECB and NCAs. Therefore, the ECB had a very large margin of manoeuvre in designing this framework. The focus of this section is on the likelihood of the SSM design resulting in consistency in supervision, and thus most relevant is the principal–agent relationship between the ECB and the NCAs which carry out certain supervisory tasks on behalf of the ECB. As the ECB is solely responsible for the efficient functioning of the SSM, its relations with the NCAs are pivotal, in particular with regard to ensuring the ECB's supervisory policy preferences within the system.

The basic design of the SSM is outlined in its founding act: the SSM regulation (Council, 2013).[7] In light of this regulation, the SSM is a primarily[8] euro area banking supervisory system (regime) consisting of the ECB and NCAs (of euro area Member States) as bank supervisors (Council, 2013, article 6.1). The overarching objective of the SSM, for which the ECB is solely responsible, is to ensure that all banks of the Member States participating in the system are subjected to supervision of the highest quality implemented in a coherent and effective manner (Council, 2013). The direct NCAs' supervision of the less significant banks (Council, 2013, articles 6.4 and 6.5) is under the ECB's oversight (i.e. indirect ECB supervision).[9]

From a rationalist perspective, the ECB's core underlying interest is to ensure its control over supervision. From this stems a second interest: to ensure effective supervision – although the measurement of 'effectiveness' is potentially difficult, as noted above. From these interests stem the preference of consistent, and thus largely convergent, supervision. Many EU Member State governments accepted the legitimacy of these interests and preference because they accepted, at least in part, the argument that the financial crisis in the EU was exacerbated by the fragmentation in the supervision of large cross-border banks – in addition to ineffective 'light touch' regulation and supervision in some Member States – and national supervisory bias: and, notably, the tendency to demonstrate forbearance towards national champions.[10] If we are to interpret the foundation of the SSM as a decisive EU post-crisis measure, this suggests that the ECB's interest in the SSM framework should be to mitigate the factors which contributed to the impact of the recent financial crisis in the EU and to ensure the highest quality supervision. This interest – like that of ensuring ECB control – results in the preference to reduce the scope of national supervisory divergence and eradicate the remaining national bias among NCAs. However, there are good reasons to argue that in meeting this ECB preference the SSM design is far from optimal because the potential for agency 'shirking' is too great, which, in turn, undermines the credibility of SSM supervision of less significant banks.

The ECB's Mechanisms of Control over the NCAs

Even when the principal's policy preferences are clearly articulated, an agent should be seen as rational, opportunistic and capable of developing its own preferences (Ross,

---

[7] For legal analyses of the SSM see Ferran and Babis (2013) and Alexander (2015).

[8] The SSM Regulation provides the possibility for non-euro area Member States to opt in to a framework of 'close cooperation' (ECB, 2014d).

[9] The case of the SSM is a rare one where a political delegation is not formally followed by a legal delegation of tasks (Ferrarini and Chiarella, 2013; Wymeersch, 2014).

[10] For example, the Bundesbank (2014, p. 44) argued that the SSM 'will minimise the hazards of potentially inappropriate supervisory forbearance guided by national interests (known as "home bias")'.

© 2015 The Author(s) JCMS: Journal of Common Market Studies © 2015 John Wiley & Sons Ltd

1973; Kiewiet and McCubbins, 1991). The inherently asymmetrical distribution of information in a principal–agent relationship favours the agent and creates perverse incentives for the agent to pursue its own preferences (Holmstrom, 1979). In cases where agent preferences diverge from those of the principal, 'agency loss' occurs and an agent 'shirks'. The potential for agent 'slippage' – deliberate 'shirking' – can be created by the very structure of political delegation (Pollack, 1997). Therefore, the principal must find ways to limit potential 'shirking' by developing controls that encourage agent compliance with the principal's policy choices and discourage the creation of incentives for the agent to 'slip'.

The principal–agent relationship between the ECB and the NCAs in the SSM relating to supervision of less significant banks is likely to contribute to NCA slippage, because the SSM regulation confers on the ECB merely the responsibility for its efficient and consistent functioning. ECB–NCA relations are designed as '*relations of information*' (European Central Bank, 2014c).[11] The supervisory activities of the ECB are focused above all on significant banks (Lautenschläger, 2014). The interpretation of necessary consistency and degrees of convergence in the supervision of less significant banks remains subject to different views among supervisors themselves. The former head of BAFIN, the German federal banking supervisor Elke König (2014) (who was subsequently appointed to chair the Single Resolution Board based in Brussels), has repeatedly made clear her view that divergence in the supervision of less significant banks at the national level will continue in the immediate future, given very different national institutional and regulatory frameworks – although she noted that harmonization would take place gradually and in the long term.

Principal–agent analysis outlines two groups of mechanisms adopted to mitigate the agent 'shirking' and ensure agent alignment with the principal's policy preferences. These are the 'ex ante' and 'ex post' controls. As these controls are not costless measures, their usage is ultimately a trade-off between higher agency costs and limiting 'agency loss'. Here we examine the 'ex ante' and 'ex post' controls assigned to the ECB in relation to NCA supervision of less significant banks within the SSM framework and their likely effectiveness.

The principal's 'ex ante' controls, also known as administrative procedures, define the scope of agency, legal instruments available for the agent and the set of procedures the agent must follow (Pollack, 1997). These instruments and procedures delineate the agent's room for manoeuvre as to the execution of discretionary powers. The institutional design of the SSM provides a number of the ECB's 'ex ante' controls over the NCAs which are outlined in the SSM framework regulation, the supervisory manual,[12] the SSM common supervisory procedures and the NCAs' 'ex ante' reporting on 'material' decisions and procedures – that is, decisions and procedures that are of supervisory interest to the ECB. The ECB's power to issue regulations, guidelines and general instructions to the NCAs can be regarded as a mechanism situated in between the 'ex ante' and the 'ex post' controls (and is thus discussed below).

---

[11] Eduard Fernandez-Bollo (Chairman of the ECB's work stream (WS2) on the SSM legal framework and Ignazio Angeloni (Chair of DG Macro-Prudential Policy and Financial Stability at the ECB) at the ECB's Public Hearing on the SSM Framework Regulation, 19 February 2014, Frankfurt.

[12] The ECB supervisory manual is an internal and partially confidential ECB/SSM document addressed to the NCAs, covering all the tasks and supervisory processes of the SSM. As such, it complements both the SSM Regulation and the SSM Framework Regulation and constitutes an important part of common supervisory *acquis*.

© 2015 The Author(s) JCMS: Journal of Common Market Studies © 2015 John Wiley & Sons Ltd

In the SSM regulation (Council, 2013, article 6(7)), EU Member States assigned the ECB the obligation to establish the modalities of ECB–NCA relations – which, as noted above, allows us to treat the ECB as a principal. The single supervisory approach, which is both to precede and shape national supervisory practice, is outlined in the ECB's framework regulation and in the supervisory manual. The framework regulation divides supervisory tasks within the SSM. The supervisory manual provides more specific details as to the ECB–NCAs' non-public and confidential relationship in managing the supervision of less significant banks. These two documents set limits on the NCAs' discretion and may be considered as the ECB's 'ex ante' controls (procedures) on the NCAs' supervisory policies, aimed at ensuring the ECB's policy preference of reducing national divergence in supervisory approaches and eradicating the remaining national bias in supervisory practices.

Even though the SSM regulation assigns to the ECB direct supervisory powers only over more significant banks, the ECB's framework regulation (European Central Bank, 2014d) stipulates a number of specific supervisory powers which are a *direct* and *exclusive* competence of the ECB with regard to *all* banks, both significant and less significant. These powers are listed in Part V of the SSM framework regulation and described as 'common procedures'. The SSM common supervisory procedures encompass: bank authorization (European Central Bank, 2014d, articles 73–9); withdrawal of bank authorizations (European Central Bank, 2014d, articles 80–4); and assessment of the acquisition of a qualifying holding (European Central Bank, 2014d, articles 85–7). The role of the NCAs in these procedures is limited to serving as an 'entry point', as in the case of bank authorizations, or to initiating the procedure and non-binding consultations regarding withdrawals of bank authorizations and assessments of the acquisitions of qualifying holdings. The SSM common supervisory procedures are an example of the principal's involvement in important decision-making on the less significant banks and as such constitute 'ex ante' controls on the agents' discretion in key supervisory policies.

The SSM framework regulation obliges the NCAs to report ex ante – or, exceptionally, simultaneously – on 'material' supervisory procedures concerning the less significant banks (European Central Bank, 2014d, article 97). The ECB is empowered to provide opinions on the draft 'material' decisions and procedures, such as: the removal of bank management board members; the appointment of a receiver (European Central Bank, 2014d, article 97 (2a)); and procedures which have a 'significant impact' on a less significant bank (European Central Bank, 2014d, article 97 (2b)). The ECB shall define the general criteria for 'significant impact', based on the risk situation of the bank and the potential impact on the domestic financial system. As these NCA 'ex ante' reporting requirements on 'materiality' impose a burden on the execution of their discretionary powers, these requirements may be perceived in terms of the principal's 'ex ante' controls, which enable the ECB to oversee NCA actions.

In addition to these procedures, in which 'materiality' is defined either by law or at the ECB's discretion, the SSM framework regulation envisages another NCA 'ex ante' reporting procedure, the initialization of which is however at the NCAs' discretion. In cases where a NCA finds a procedure either to be 'material' and thus of supervisory interest for the ECB (European Central Bank, 2014d, article 97) or potentially to affect negatively the reputation of the SSM (European Central Bank, 2014d, article 97(4b)), the NCA can notify the ECB of such. According to the drafters' own interpretation, this procedure should be treated as a 'catch-up' clause for those NCA decisions which 'do not fulfill the

© 2015 The Author(s) JCMS: Journal of Common Market Studies © 2015 John Wiley & Sons Ltd

"materiality" premises, but should be assessed by the NCAs with regard to the quantitative criteria' (European Central Bank, 2014c). In the context of a principal–agent analysis, this NCA power of initiative may be problematic in that it potentially generates 'leaks' in the principal's control of its agents' 'zone of discretion'. The NCAs have the power to delineate the border between 'material' and 'non-material' procedures; that is, they can decide which supervisory procedures shall be of interest to the ECB and carry the burden of the 'ex ante' oversight and which shall not. This issue is examined further below.

According to the SSM regulation (Council, 2013), the ECB has the power to issue regulations, general instructions, guidelines and requests to the NCAs with regard to all supervisory tasks carried out by them within the SSM. From the perspective of principal–agent analysis, these instruments can be regarded as both 'ex ante' and 'ex post' ('hybrid') controls depending on the given circumstances. The role of ECB guidelines is to inform the NCAs how certain provisions of the supervisory *acquis* should be interpreted and applied and how the NCAs should use their discretionary powers. For example, the supervisory manual, which is – in substance – a guideline on the supervisory policies within the SSM, could be described as an 'ex ante' control. The ECB's regulations and general instructions are to steer the NCAs' supervisory actions. For example, an instruction directed by the ECB to an NCA 'to make use of their powers and to take action' would be an 'ex post' control (European Central Bank, 2014d, article 22). Given the sensitivity of banking supervision and its potential impact on financial markets, many of the ECB's regulations, general instructions, guidelines and requests directed to NCAs will be of a confidential nature and are likely to be (only partially) disclosed after a certain period of time.[13]

However, the legal status of some the ECB's supervisory acts regarding the NCAs, such as guidelines, (general) instructions and requests, remains ambiguous. In light of article 288 TFEU and article 34 of the ECB Statute, in order to exercise conferred tasks, the ECB can adopt legally binding regulations and decisions and non-binding recommendations and opinions. All of the abovementioned acts are known as EU 'typical acts'. Other legal instruments of the EU institutions not expressly listed in article 288 TFEU, are generally referred to as EU 'atypical acts' (see, for example, Snyder, 1993; Cosma and Whish, 2003; Grosse Ruse-Khan *et al.*, 2011). As the ECB's supervisory oversight acts (guidelines, general instructions and requests directed to the NCAs) are not provided by article 288 TFEU, they may be seen as EU atypical acts. The use of specific ECB supervisory oversight acts and the problem of their enforceability is explored further below.

The ECB's 'Ex Post' Controls over the NCAs

The principal's 'ex post' controls, known also as oversight procedures, allow the principal to monitor its agent's behaviour and impose sanctions in the event of 'agency shirking'. These 'ex post' controls are conventionally divided into 'police patrols' and 'fire alarms' (Kiewiet and McCubbins, 1991). 'Police patrols' consist of active surveillance of a sample of the agent's behaviour by the principal with the aim of detecting any non-

[13] Interviews, Commission de Surveillance du Secteur Financier (CSSF), Luxembourg, February/March 2014. The CSSF is Luxembourg's NCA for banking supervision within the SSM.

© 2015 The Author(s) JCMS: Journal of Common Market Studies © 2015 John Wiley & Sons Ltd

compliance with the principal's policy preferences. In classic form they include public hearings, studies, field observations and examinations of regular agent reports (Pollack, 1997). 'Fire alarms' are the principal's indirect 'ex post' controls because, while monitoring agents' activities, the principal relies on the support of third parties. 'Fire alarms' are less costly but at the same time are also less centralized and tend to be more superficial than 'police patrols'.

Among the 'police patrols' that the ECB has at its disposal to oversee NCA compliance with its policy preferences, three are particularly important: the NCAs' 'ex post' reporting requirements; the ECB's power to request supervisory information from any less significant banks and to conduct general investigations and send on-site inspections to any less significant bank; and, ultimately, the ECB's power to take over supervision of the less significant bank from the NCA. 'Police patrols' can be 'intrusive' or 'non-intrusive'. The latter may, in turn, be tentatively divided into 'yellow card' police patrols and 'red card' police patrols.

The NCAs' 'ex post' reporting requirements can be seen as instruments of the ECB's 'non-intrusive police patrols'. Articles 99 and 100 of the SSM framework regulation (European Central Bank, 2014d) obliges the NCAs to submit regular reports on their supervisory activities regarding the less significant banks, on the basis of which the ECB will assess the degree of the NCAs' compliance with its policy preferences. Furthermore, the NCAs may be requested to provide information on their supervisory activities, on either an *ad hoc* or continual basis (Council, 2013, article 6 (5e)).

The ECB's 'intrusive police patrols' include presenting a 'yellow card' to a NCA following its problematic supervision of a less significant bank. The section 'Investigatory Powers' of Chapter Three of the SSM regulation (Council, 2013) stipulates three procedures which can be classified as field observations (both on- and offsite) and can be treated as examples of 'yellow card' police patrols. These are: the ECB's power to request supervisory information directly from less significant banks (Council, 2013, article 10); and the ECB's powers to carry out general investigations (Council, 2013, article 11) and on-site inspections (Council, 2013, article 12). These procedures are completely separate from the NCA's 'ex ante' reporting on less significant banks. An ECB on-site inspection must be notified to the concerned NCA at least one week prior to the notification of the less significant bank concerned (European Central Bank, 2014d, article 145). Yet the ECB may decide that a less significant bank should not be informed about a planned on-site inspection if it could jeopardize the efficiency and proper conduct of an on-site inspection (European Central Bank, 2014d, article 145). The detailed procedures relating to the ECB's on-site inspections have been further outlined in the supervisory manual but remain closed to the public.

The second level of ECB 'intrusive police patrols' involves assigning a 'red card' to NCAs on the grounds of unacceptable performance relating to the supervision of less significant banks. The 'red card' results in direct ECB intervention in the NCAs' zone of discretion, with a view to reversing and improving the outcomes of their supervisory policies. The SSM regulation (Council, 2013, article 6 (5b)) provides the ECB the power, on its own initiative,[14] to take over direct supervision of a particular less significant bank

---

[14] But also upon request by a NCA (see Council, 2013).

© 2015 The Author(s) JCMS: Journal of Common Market Studies © 2015 John Wiley & Sons Ltd

from an NCA to ensure the consistent application of high supervisory standards (the 'take-over' clause). This is the most significant and potentially effective control mechanism in the ECB arsenal. However, it is also the most controversial and politically difficult to implement because, effectively, its use would amount to a public sanction of a NCA and would likely take place in the context of potential bank failure.

The SSM regulation (Council, 2013) also assigns the ECB both 'internal' and 'external' 'fire alarms' to prevent agent shirking. The ECB's power to relocate national supervisory personnel among the different NCAs participating in the SSM can be seen as an 'internal fire alarm' in that the procedure is foreseen with the framework of the SSM and no external institutions are engaged. This power can also be in part characterized as a 'police patrol' control. The ECB may find it 'appropriate' to involve staff from one NCA in supervisory teams of another NCA in order to interfere with the direct supervision of less significant banks (Council, 2013, article 31(2)). The vague wording of the SSM regulation's enabling clause for this 'ex post' control gives the ECB a considerable margin of manoeuvre in its interpretation and application. The ECB can make use of this control in order to ensure that its policy preference is followed by the agent, allowing the ECB to avoid having to make use of more centralized 'police patrol' controls. In this case, the personnel of one SSM NCA monitor another NCA as it carries out its supervisory tasks. The ECB thus acquires a decentralized source of information on possible agency shirking/slippage on the part of the NCAs. A caveat to treating this mechanism as a 'fire alarm' stems from the fact that personnel from another agent (or other agents) (and not a 'third party' per se) engage in the monitoring. The SSM consists of a single principal (the ECB) but multiple agents (NCAs) and, in this context, it may be justified to treat national supervisory staff of one NCA involved in the work of another NCA as the equivalent to a 'third party'. As the NCAs may compete among themselves for reputational reasons and for favours from their principal, it should not be assumed that NCA personnel will succumb to supervisory forbearance (and thus contribute to agency 'slippage') when engaged in supervisory work of their fellow NCAs.

'External fire alarms' are forms of decentralized oversight exercised by bodies that are external to the SSM framework (see, for example, Kiewiet and McCubbins, 1991). Two 'external fire alarms' regarding the operation of NCAs can be identified. First, the EBA has the power to identify breaches of EU law by NCAs – see article 17 of the EBA Regulation (Council and European Parliament, 2010). Second, national parliaments can request public hearings on SSM supervisory policies involving personnel from both the ECB's supervisory arm and the NCA concerned. On the supervision of less significant banks in the SSM, NCAs may be called to account by national parliaments in two ways. First, a NCA representative may be invited together with the chair or another member of the SSM's supervisory board to participate in an 'exchange of views' on supervisory policies and supervision (Council, 2013, article 21 (3)). Therefore, such an 'exchange of views' may also address the supervision of less significant banks in various contexts. This mechanism may be useful for the ECB to assess in an *ad hoc* manner the supervisory approach of a particular NCA and its conformity with its policy preferences. Second, the SSM regulation maintains national parliamentary oversight over NCAs, *even with regard* to their tasks carried out within the SSM (Council, 2013, article 21 (4)). This national-level 'external fire alarm', as with EBA judicial oversight, can bring agency discretion to the attention of the ECB principal.

The ECB's Struggle Ahead to Ensure its Policy Preferences

The ECB's mechanisms of control outlined above do not cover all the 'zones of discretion' that the NCAs enjoy when carrying out direct supervision of less significant banks on behalf of the ECB. There are three major challenges to the maintenance of the ECB's preferences that stem from the SSM's current institutional design: the NCAs discretion on 'materiality' reporting (in particular the usage of the 'catch-up clause'); the legal status of the ECB's regulations, guidelines and instructions directed to the NCAs; and the 'proportional' application of the SSM regulation and the ECB's framework regulation to the supervision of less significant banks. As noted above, the NCAs are required to notify 'ex ante' the ECB on a supervisory procedure which they consider to be 'material' and thus of potential supervisory interest to the ECB, or which may negatively affect the reputation of the SSM (Council, 2013, article 97; European Central Bank, 2014d, article 97 (4a and 4b)). The ECB added this provision into the framework regulation in order to enable the ECB to be informed on the major developments affecting less significant banks – which is clearly important in terms of ensuring the ECB's policy preferences. However, NCAs retain the power to determine whether or not a procedure is 'material' and thus of potential supervisory interest to the ECB.

As noted above, the ECB's supervisory oversight acts such guidelines, general instructions and requests that the ECB are empowered to adopt in relation to the NCAs should be seen as 'atypical acts'. It remains unclear which of these 'atypical acts' will be binding on the NCAs, and to what extent. Several core elements of the operation of the SSM are not legally binding: first, the ECB's *Guide to Banking Supervision*, which sets out the SSM's supervisory principles and clarifies its supervisory procedures (European Central Bank, 2014h, p. 2); second, the ECB instructions to NCAs with regard to the particular aspects of supervision of individual less significant banks (Lackhoff, 2013; König, 2014); third, neither the SSM regulation nor the framework regulation provides the ECB with direct instruments to enforce disciplinary actions addressed to the NCAs (Wymeersch, 2014, p. 39) – with the important exception of the 'take-over clause', which can be seen as the ultimate backstop of the SSM to ensure ECB control in the event of NCA non-compliance. Therefore, it follows that many ECB supervisory acts concerning the performance of tasks by the NCAs will not be enforceable, and these acts should be seen as 'soft law'.

The principle of proportionality (article 5 of TEU) applies to the operation of the SSM. The drafters of the SSM framework regulation claimed that the less significant banks would have simplified reporting requirements in comparison with significant banks. Also, the risk management standards enshrined in the supervisory *acquis* will be proportionally applied to the less significant banks (European Central Bank, 2014c).[15] Although proportionality may be necessary to simplify the supervision in the SSM,[16] the application of the principle gives the NCAs 'margin of discretion' and effectively undermines the ECB's policy preference of consistency in supervisory approach. Therefore, it will be crucial for the ECB to define necessary 'ex ante' procedures for the NCAs on how to apply the SSM supervisory *acquis*.

---

[15] Jukka Vessala (Director of DG Micro III) at the ECB's Public Hearing on the SSM Framework Regulation, 19 February 2014, Frankfurt. See European Central Bank (2014c).

[16] Ignazio Angeloni (Director of DG Macro-Prudential Policy and Financial Stability of the ECB) at the ECB's Public Hearing on the SSM Framework Regulation, 19 February 2014, Frankfurt. See European Central Bank (2014c).

© 2015 The Author(s) JCMS: Journal of Common Market Studies © 2015 John Wiley & Sons Ltd

II. The Credibility of ECB Supervision of Significant Banks: The Comprehensive Assessment

The credibility of the SSM's supervision of the 128 significant banks in the euro area depends upon the institutional design of supervision and the supervisory rules and procedures. Clearly, there are a number of persistent concerns as to the potential effectiveness of the design of the JSTs; the ability of a limited number of ECB supervisory staff to ensure adequate centralized control within the JSTs; and the precise supervisory model adopted (only part of which has been disclosed to the public in the supervisory manual). However, without the precedent of supranational supervision and without the hindsight of several years of operation, there are no objective gauges to evaluate effectively the credibility of the SSM supervision of significant banks. Nonetheless, as the first important undertaking by the SSM, the ECB's comprehensive assessment of 128 systemically important euro area banks – holding 81.6 per cent of all euro area assets – can be examined in terms of its contribution to the credibility of supranational bank supervision. The comprehensive assessment, undertaken in the summer and autumn of 2014, assumed a symbolic importance as to the future effectiveness of the SSM.[17] In this section we consider the importance of the comprehensive assessment and the reactions of the financial press, financial market operators (notably credit rating agencies) and leading financial economists.

The comprehensive assessment consisted of the AQR – undertaken by the ECB with regard to a total of 128 euro area headquartered banks based on data from the end of December 2013 – and stress tests of 123 EEA-headquartered banks conducted by the EBA. Information gained in the former was intended to feed into the latter (De Groen and Lannoo, 2014). Both the AQR and stress tests required banks to hold at least 8 per cent of regulatory capital – consisting mainly of equity and retained earnings – in relation to their risk-weighted assets under transitional Basel III/EU Capital Requirements Directive (CRD) IV rules. The publication of the AQR and the stress tests on the same day – 26 October – by two different bodies, on a different but largely overlapping sample of banks, created the potential for confusion (de Groen and Lannoo, 2014).[18] For the ECB, the AQR and broader comprehensive assessment were important to establish the central bank's credibility as a supranational bank supervisor. For the EBA, the 2014 stress tests were a matter of restoring the confidence the authority lost in the 2011 tests – widely criticized on the grounds that they offered a seriously inadequate assessment of the ability of European banks to withstand a major financial crisis (Buckley et al., 2012).[19] Infamously, the Franco–Belgian bank Dexia had to be bailed out in November 2012 for a third time in four years, and less than a year after having passed the EBA's 2011 stress tests. The ability of the ECB and EBA to work together in the future in a manner that reinforced the credibility of supranational banking supervision remained to be seen (Wymeersch, 2014).

The AQR became necessary because of German government insistence that banks with 'legacy problems' must not be assisted with European stability mechanism (ESM)

[17] *Financial Times*, 22 October 2014.
[18] De Groen and Lannoo (2014) show that only 103 banks were subject to both the AQR and the stress tests, while 27 banks were subject to the AQR and not the stress tests.
[19] *Financial Times*, 27 October 2014.

© 2015 The Author(s) JCMS: Journal of Common Market Studies © 2015 John Wiley & Sons Ltd

bail-out funds.[20] However, even without German insistence, a review of the assets of the euro area's largest banks could help – if undertaken with sufficient objective rigour – to bolster the credibility of the SSM and the role of the ECB as a new micro-prudential authority. To defenders, the AQR provided unprecedented scrutiny of bank loan books and collateral portfolios. The AQR involved over 6,000 ECB and NCA officials reviewing 800 portfolios, amounting to more than 57 per cent of the risk-weighted assets of the 128 banks examined. The ECB also stated that officials examined 119,000 borrowers, valued 170,000 items of collateral and built 765 models to challenge banks' own estimates of risk-weighted assets (European Central Bank, 2014e, p. 19).[21] Crucially, the AQR significantly improved the transparency and comparability of bank data across the then 18 euro area Member States plus Lithuania (which joined at the start of 2015). The AQR manual (European Central Bank, 2014b), published on 11 March, included the first set of bank supervision guidelines ever produced specifically for euro area NCAs – which were considerably more detailed and directing than existing EBA guidelines. The manual contains methodology for the AQR's 'phase 2' (the on-site inspection of banks), with detailed guidance on a range of matters including: procedures for validating data and checking model inputs; the valuation of material exposures and collateral and determine provisioning needs; the processes for quality assurance and progress tracking to ensure timely completion; when to use independent, external valuations for assets; and the use of industry benchmarks to assess market values. The AQR harmonized the definition of non-performing loans and uncovered hidden losses. In doing so, the ECB found massive shortfalls – €136 billion – in the loans that banks and national regulators classified as non-performing (i.e. bad). This figure amounted to 15 per cent more than the total previously announced by NCAs. The ECB found that banks had over-valued their assets by a total of €48 billion, pointing especially to an over-valuation of commercial loans.[22]

The success of the EBA's 2014 stress tests can be evaluated by three measures.[23] The first was sufficient transparency and comparability in the results. In 2014, there were to be 12,000 data points on the different scenarios (benchmark and adverse) and the EBA made use of AQR definitions. Earlier in the year, the EBA announced that for the first time it would publish fully loaded common equity Tier 1 ratios for each bank, whereas some market participants had previously refused to disclose these figures themselves. Second, rigorous tests could boost confidence in the capital position of European banks. The 2014 stress tests lowered Tier 1 capital by, on average, four points – even more than US Federal Reserve tests (a 2.9 per cent drop for participating banks in 2014). Both the ECB president, Mario Draghi, and the head of the SSM, Danièle Nouy, argued publicly that some banks would have to fail the stress tests in order to ensure the credibility of the new system.[24] Indeed, the number of banks failing in the adverse scenario of the 2014 stress tests far exceeded the results of previous tests: 24 banks failed with a capital shortfall under the adverse scenario of €24.6 billion; another 16 institutions, including seven in Germany, were left with capital ratios between 5.5 per cent to 7 per cent. After capital-raising in 2014, 14 banks still failed the tests, with a shortfall of €9.5 billion under

---

[20] *EUObserver*, 3 December 2012.
[21] *Financial Times*, 26 October 2014.
[22] *Financial Times*, 26 October 2014.
[23] *Financial Times*, 22 October 2014.

© 2015 The Author(s) JCMS: Journal of Common Market Studies © 2015 John Wiley & Sons Ltd

the adverse scenario, representing four per cent of total bank assets. While more rigorous than all previous EBA stress tests, the 2014 shortfall was lower than most expectations.[25]

Third, and most importantly, the tests were expected to encourage capital-raising and facilitate bank restructuring. Banks were given just two weeks to present plans to the ECB following the 26 October publication date, and up to a further 6–9 months to raise capital to cover shortfalls on the baseline and adverse scenarios respectively.[26] In part, the credibility of the comprehensive assessment on this measure was felt prior to the announcement of the November results. A range of larger euro area banks actively engaged in raising capital levels to avoid having to take corrective action later in the year. In the main, banks issued equity.[27] However, they also publicly listed subsidiaries, deleveraged by selling portfolios of assets, and sold businesses. Described as the 'announcement effect', when some banks raised capital this increased market pressure on other banks to improve their capital positions, regardless of the schedule set out in Basel III and the EU's CRDIV.[28] These pressures paralleled a fortuitous improvement in investor demand for bank equity in 2014 – which made failing the stress tests even less acceptable to management and investors.[29] For its part, the ECB actively encouraged banks to take advantage of favourable market conditions to issue equity.[30] In late October, the ECB estimated that banks had raised €57.1 billion from the start of the year (European Central Bank, 2014e).[31] However, a full assessment of this measure of credibility could be detected only following a period of significant writedowns – effectively a further clean-up – in the months following the November results.

The 25 (14 after earlier capital-raising in 2014) named banks that failed the comprehensive assessment were largely expected.[32] Nonetheless, after a brief rise, bank shares indexes dropped significantly.[33] Most bank analysts expected slow growth in bank lending as a large number of institutions would continue to boost their capital positions;[34] thus, the principal overarching objective of the comprehensive assessment – to build stable banking sectors that contribute to economic growth – was, at best, to be attained in the medium term.[35] Italian and Greek banks were the most exposed, with, respectively, nine and four failing, followed by three Austrian banks and two from each of Cyprus, Slovenia and Spain. Italian banks were responsible for a quarter of the total over-valued assets, just less than 1 per cent of their risk-weighted assets. Greek banks were responsible for €7.6 billion of the total over-valued assets, or almost 4 per cent of their risk-weighted assets. Once capital injections in early 2014 were taken into account, four Italian banks still faced shortfalls, including the country's third and fourth largest institutions: the Monte dei Paschi di Siena (MPS) and Banco Popolare. MPS, which needed to cover a shortfall of

---

[24] *Bloomberg Business*, 12 December 2014; *Financial Times*, 9 February 2014.
[25] *Financial Times*, 26 October 2014; *Financial Times*, 27 October, 2014.
[26] *Financial Times*, 17 July 2014.
[27] *Financial Times*, 6 May 2014.
[28] *Financial Times*, 3 July 2014.
[29] *Financial Times*, 3 July 2014.
[30] *Financial Times*, 24 April 2014.
[31] *Financial Times*, 26 October 2014.
[32] For a detailed analysis of the results of the Comprehensive Assessment see *Financial Times*, 27 October 2014.
[33] *Financial Times*, 27 October 2014.
[34] *Financial Times*, 27 October 2014.
[35] *Financial Times*, 27 October 2014.

© 2015 The Author(s) JCMS: Journal of Common Market Studies © 2015 John Wiley & Sons Ltd

€2.1 billion,[36] was the largest failure of the comprehensive assessment. Only one German bank failed – Münchener Hypothekenbank – but it had raised sufficient capital in 2014 to avoid additional capital action. German banks would have to lower the value of their assets by €6.7 billion, while French banks would only have to do so by €5.6 billion.

Italian banks were hit particularly hard by the harmonized definition of non-performing loans. In 2014, bad loans reached a total of €160 billion – more than double their level in 2010 – and they were expected to rise to nearly €200 billion in 2015.[37] About 17 per cent of Italian bank loans – €333 billion – were non-performing, according to the International Monetary Fund (Jassaud and Kang, 2015).[38] The Italian government responded to the comprehensive assessment by considering the possibility of setting up a 'bad bank' – that is, a vehicle designed to absorb some of the non-performing loans of the banking sector – as established previously in Spain (the SAREB).[39] Banks hoped that the establishment of a 'bad bank' would allow them to sell their bad loans at higher prices.[40]

Despite the widespread vote of confidence for the comprehensive assessment from a range of credible sources,[41] there were also voices critical of both the AQR and stress tests and the methodologies used, and there were calls for more work to be done to make them more rigorous (e.g. de Groen, 2014).[42] The ECB calculations on the basis of risk-weighted assets – which rely on the banks' own assessments of risk-weights assigned to assets and the assessments of credit rating agencies – were criticized. Despite improvement over previous stress tests, transparency was deemed to be inadequate, with only limited disclosure of banks' own funds and liability structures (de Groen, 2014). The tests ignored massive litigation costs facing banks[43] and ignored the tighter definition of capital to be imposed from 2019 which would deduct items such as goodwill and certain tax assets. Including this definition would, according to a Goldman Sachs study and the EBA's own figures, have quadrupled the actual capital shortfall of European banks and doubled the number of banks failing — including four large German banks.[44] Market expectations had already taken on board this reinforced definition.

With the Bank of England announcing a new leverage ratio standard at the end of October,[45] many bank analysts called for the EBA stress tests also to include the overall level of bank borrowing. A team at the Stern School of Business at New York University led by the economist Viral Acharya had developed an alternative methodology – SRISK, which takes into account the banks' total balance sheet without regard for risk (Acharya

---

[36] *The Economist*, 26 October 2014; *Financial Times*, 26 October 2014.

[37] *Bloomberg Business*, 16 April 2015.

[38] *New York Times*, 13 February 2015.

[39] *New York Times*, 13 February 2015.

[40] *New York Times*, 13 February 2015.

[41] *Financial Times*, 27 October 2014.

[42] See, for example, Finance Watch (2014). The strong position of German banks — including publicly owned *Landesbanks* — also attracted considerable scepticism. See *Financial Times*, 26 October 2014.

[43] *Financial Times*, 27 October 2014.

[44] *Financial Times*, 26 October 2014.

[45] *Financial Times*, 27 October 2014.

© 2015 The Author(s) JCMS: Journal of Common Market Studies © 2015 John Wiley & Sons Ltd

and Steffen, 2014).[46] The application of SRISK found a range of European banks suffered from worse shortfalls in an adverse scenario. French banks – which the EBA found had no shortfalls in an adverse situation[47] – were found to have shortfalls of €189 billion in the Stern School tests, far worse than the larger German and UK banking systems.

Conclusion

This contribution has discussed the main milestones in the establishment of the SSM in 2014, leading up to 4 November when the mechanism became operational. It has examined SSM credibility in terms of the mechanism's design, and specifically the relationship between the ECB and NCAs within the SSM, with the objective of consistent and high-quality euro area supervision. It has been argued that the principal–agent relationship between the ECB and the NCAs is likely to contribute to NCA slippage in the supervision of less significant banks, because of the 'soft law' character of most of the 'ex ante' and 'ex post' controls at the ECB's disposal. The use of the 'take-over' provision is an 'ex post' control which will likely be of great difficulty for the ECB to wield, given national political sensitivities surrounding inadequate NCA supervision and potential domestic bank failure. This contribution has also examined SSM credibility in terms of the effectiveness of the ECB's direct supervision of significant banks. In its comprehensive assessment, the ECB demonstrated its capacity to make difficult supervisory decisions, as evidenced by the AQR that revealed the poor state of several banks in the euro area, with Italy having the most troubled banks. However, there remain significant question marks over the ECB's methodology used in the AQR.

There is an interesting parallel between the quest for credibility in the establishment of the ECB/Eurosystem and that concerning the setting up of the SSM. In the first case, the quest for institutional credibility was triggered by the transfer of monetary policy from the national level to the supranational (euro area) level. In the second, this search for credibility was motivated by the transfer of banking supervision from the national to the supranational level (the euro area/banking union level). The main institutional difference between these two processes of delegation is that whereas in the case of monetary integration the transfer was complete (that is, there was no monetary sovereignty left at the national level), in the SSM the transfer was partly incomplete because the supervision of less significant banks remained primarily at the national level, leaving room for agent shirking.

This contribution has focused on the credibility of the institutional design of the SSM and its first major assessment of the solidity of the euro area's significant banks, which are the only gauges of credibility available at the birth of euro area supranational banking supervision. The credibility of the SSM will be determined by its empirical track record in the years to come, and specifically the ECB's ability to impose decisions (etc.) upon NCAs despite the ECB's lack of enforcement mechanisms; to assume control over the supervision of less significant banks from the NCAs; and to impose the resolution of a bank upon a reluctant NCA and national government. The credibility of the SSM will rely upon

[46] *Financial Times*, 27 October 2014.
[47] *Financial Times*, 26 October 2014.

© 2015 The Author(s) JCMS: Journal of Common Market Studies © 2015 John Wiley & Sons Ltd

developments beyond the immediate control of both the ECB and the NCAs – notably, the development of the 'sovereign debt-bank doom loop' in euro-periphery countries due to economic growth rates and the success or failure of government structural reforms. However, based on the assessment of this contribution, the SSM's institutional design and its first comprehensive assessment of significant euro area banks give reason to be wary of problems ahead which will undermine the credibility of the SSM and the role of the ECB as the world's first supranational bank supervisor.

References

Acharya, V. and Steffen, S. (2014) 'Making Sense of the Comprehensive Assessment'. SAFE Policy Letter, No. 32. Available at «http://nbn-resolving.de/urn:nbn:de:hebis:30:3-350190»

Boone, P. and Johnson, S. (2011) 'Europe on the Brink'. Policy Brief PB 11–13 (Washington DC: Peterson Institute for International Economics).

Alexander, K. (2015) 'European Banking Union: A Legal and Institutional Analysis of the Single Supervisory Mechanism and the Single Resolution Mechanism'. *European Law Review*, Vol. 40, No. 2, pp. 154–87.

Barth, J., Caprio, G. and Levine, R. (2006) *Rethinking Bank Regulation: 'Til Angels Govern* (Cambridge: Cambridge University Press).

Buckley, J., Howarth, D. and Quaglia, L. (2012) 'The Ongoing Struggle to "Protect" Europe from Its Money Men'. *JCMS*, Vol. 50, No. s1, pp. 99–115.

Bundesbank (2014) 'Launch of the Banking Union: the Single Supervisory Mechanism in Europe', Deutsche Bundesbank Monthly Report, October, pp. 43–64. Available at «https://www.bundesbank.de/Redaktion/EN/Downloads/Publications/Monthly_Report_Articles/2014/2014_10_banking_union.pdf?__blob=publicationFile».

Cosma, H., and Whish, R. (2003) 'Soft Law in the Field of Competition Policy'. *European Business Law Review*, Vol. 14, No. 1, pp. 25–56.

Council (2013) Regulation (EU) No 1024/2013 of 15 October 2013 conferring specific tasks on the European Central Bank concerning policies relating to the prudential supervision of credit institutions. L 287/63, Brussels. Available at «http://bit.ly/1dJpPy9».

Council and European Parliament (2010) Regulation (EU) No. 1093/2010 of the European Parliament and of the Council of 24 November 2010 establishing a European Supervisory Authority (European Banking Authority). L 331/12, Brussels. Available at «http://bit.ly/1pFzW7h».

De Groen, W.P. and Lannoo, K. (2014) 'The ECB AQR and the EBA Stress Test: What Will the Numbers Tell?'. CEPS Commentary, 23 October. Available at «http://www.ceps.eu/publications/ecb-aqr-and-eba-stress-test-what-will-numbers-tell».

de Groen, W.P. (2014) 'Was the ECB's Comprehensive Assessment up to standard?'. CEPS Policy Brief 325, 10 November (Brussels: Centre for European Policy Studies). Available at «http://www.ceps.eu/system/files/PB%20No%20325%20WPdG%20ECB%20Comprehensive%20Assessment.pdf».

Egeberg, M. and Trondal, J. (2011) 'EU-level Agencies: New Executive Centre Formation or Vehicles for National Control?'. *Journal of European Public Policy*, Vol. 18, No. 6, pp. 868–87.

Elgie, R. (2002) 'The Politics of the European Central Bank: Principal–Agent Theory and the Democratic Deficit'. *Journal of European Public Policy*, Vol. 9, No. 2, pp. 186–200.

European Central Bank (2014a) Decision of the European Central Bank of 4 February 2014 identifying the credit institutions that are subject to the Comprehensive Assessment. ECB/2014/3 (Frankfurt: ECB). Available at «http://www.ecb.europa.eu/pub/pdf/other/en_dec_2014_03_fen.pdf».

© 2015 The Author(s) JCMS: Journal of Common Market Studies © 2015 John Wiley & Sons Ltd

European Central Bank (2014b) Asset Quality Review: Phase 2 Manual. March (Frankfurt: ECB). Available at «https://www.ecb.europa.eu/pub/pdf/other/assetqualityreviewphase2manual201403en.pdf?e8cc41ce0e4ee40222cbe148574e4af7».

European Central Bank (2014c) Webcast of Public Hearing on Draft ECB SSM Framework Regulation [video]. February (Frankfurt: ECB). Available at «http://www.ecb.europa.eu/press/tvservices/other/html/webcast_140219.en.html».

European Central Bank (2014d) Regulation (EU) No 468/2014 of the European Central Bank of 16 April 2014 establishing the framework for cooperation within the Single Supervisory Mechanism between the European Central Bank and national competent authorities and with national designated authorities (SSM Framework Regulation). ECB/2014/17 (Frankfurt: ECB). Available at «http://bit.ly/19bRZRT».

European Central Bank (2014e) Aggregate Report on the Comprehensive Assessment. October (Frankfurt: ECB). Available at «https://www.ecb.europa.eu/pub/pdf/other/aggregatereportonthecomprehensiveassessment201410.en.pdf».

European Central Bank (2014f) Transcript of the Comprehensive Assessment Press Conference (with Q&A). October (Frankfurt: ECB). Available at «https://www.ecb.europa.eu/press/pressconf/2014/html/is141026.en.html».

European Central Bank (2014g) ECB Assumes Responsibility for Euro Area Banking Supervision. November (Frankfurt: ECB). Available at «https://www.ecb.europa.eu/press/pr/date/2014/html/pr141104.en.html».

European Central Bank (2014h) Guide to Banking Supervision. November (Frankfurt: ECB). Available at «https://www.bankingsupervision.europa.eu/ecb/pub/pdf/ssmguidebankingsupervision201411.en.pdf».

European Central Bank (2015) ECB Annual Report on Supervisory Activities 2014. March (Frankfurt: ECB). Available at «https://www.bankingsupervision.europa.eu/ecb/pub/pdf/ssmar2014.en.pdf?a88c90797b71eea2e8c133ef20a370d1».

European Council (2012) Council Agrees Position on Single Supervisory Mechanism. 17739/12, PRESSE 528, 13 December, Brussels. Available at «http://www.consilium.europa.eu/uedocs/cms_data/docs/pressdata/en/ecofin/134265.pdf».

Ferran, E. and Babis, V. (2013) 'The European Single Supervisory Mechanism'. *Journal of Corporate Law Studies*, Vol. 13, pp. 255–85.

Ferrarini, G. and Chiarella, L. (2013) 'Common Banking Supervision in the Eurozone: Strengths and Weaknesses'. *ECGI – Law Working Paper*, No. 223/2013, August 2013.

Finance Watch (2014) EU Bank Stress Tests and AQR Show the Need for a Binding Leverage Ratio, says Finance Watch'. 29 October. Available at «http://www.finance-watch.org/press/press-releases/965».

Garicano, L. (2012) 'Five Lessons from the Spanish Cajas Debacle for a New Euro-wide Supervisor'. In Beck, T. (ed.) *Banking Union for Europe – Risks and Challenges*. (London: Centre for Economic Policy Research).

Grosse Ruse-Khan, H., Jaeger, T. and Kordic, R. (2011) 'The Role of Atypical Acts in EU External Trade and Intellectual Property Policy'. *The European Journal of International Law*, Vol. 21, No. 4, pp. 901–39.

Hodson, D. (2009) 'Reforming EU Economic Governance: A View From (and On) the Principal–Agent Approach'. *Comparative European Politics*, Vol. 7, pp. 455–75.

Holmstrom, B. (1979) 'Moral Hazard and Observability'. *Bell Journal of Economics*, Vol. 10, No. 1, pp. 74–91.

Howarth, D. and Quaglia, L. (2013) 'Banking Union as Holy Grail'. *JCMS*, Vol. 51, No. s1, pp. 103–23.

Howarth, D. and Quaglia, L. (2014) 'The Steep Road to European Banking Union: Constructing the Single Resolution Mechanism'. *JCMS*, Vol. 52, No. s1, pp. 125–40.

© 2015 The Author(s) JCMS: Journal of Common Market Studies © 2015 John Wiley & Sons Ltd

James, H. (2012) Making the European Monetary Union (Cambridge: Harvard University Press).

Jassaud, N. and Kang, K. (2015) 'A Strategy for Developing a Market for Nonperforming Loans in Italy'. IMF Working Paper, WP/15/24 (Washington: International Monetary Fund). Available at «http://www.imf.org/external/pubs/ft/wp/2015/wp1524.pdf».

Kiewiet, D.R. and McCubbins, M.D. (1991) The Logic of Delegation: Congressional Parties and the Appropriations Process (Chicago: University of Chicago Press).

König, E. (2014) *The Role of National Supervisors in Banking Union [video]*. Available at «https://www.youtube.com/watch?v=rLHtYOtrqlA».

Lackhoff, K. (2013) 'How will the Single Supervisory Mechanism (SSM) Function? A Quick Overview'. *Journal of International Banking Law and Regulation*, Vol. 29, No. 1, pp. 13–28.

Lautenschläger, S. (2014) 'National Supervision in a European System: What is the New Balance?'. Member of the Executive Board of the ECB, Fifth FMA supervisory conference, Vienna, 30 September 2014. Available at «http://www.ecb.europa.eu/press/key/date/2014/html/sp140930_1.en.html».

Masciandaro, D. (2004) 'Central Banks or Single Financial Authorities? A Political Economy Approach'. *University of Lecce Economics Working Paper* No. 47/25.

Masciandaro, D. and Pellegrina, L. (2008) 'Politicians, Central Banks, and the Shape of Financial Supervision Architectures'. *Journal of Financial Regulation and Compliance*, Vol. 16. No. 4, pp. 290–317.

Pollack, M.A. (1997) 'Delegation, Agency and Agenda Setting in the European Community'. *International Organization*, Vol. 51, No. 1, pp. 99–134.

Ross, S. (1973) 'The Economic Theory of Agency: The Principal's Problem'. *American Economic Review, No.* 12, pp. 134–9.

Schuknecht, L. (2004) 'EU Fiscal Rules: Issues and Lessons from Political Economy'. European Central Bank Working Paper, No. 421 (Frankfurt: ECB).

Schuler, M. (2003) 'Incentive Problem in Banking Supervision: the European Case'. ZEW Discussion Papers, No. 03–62 (Mannheim: ZEW).

Snyder, F. (1993) 'Soft Law and Institutional Practice in the European Community'. EUI Working Paper Law No. 93/5 (Florence: European University Institute).

Terman, J. (2015) 'Reexamining the Assumptions of Bureaucratic Behavior'. *Journal of Public Administration Research and Theory* (online early DOI: 10.1093/jopart/muu087)

Thatcher, M. and Stone Sweet, A. (2002) 'Theory and practices of delegation to non-majoritarian institutions'. *West European Politics*, Vol. 25, No. 1, pp. 1–22.

Thatcher, M. (2011) 'The Creation of European Regulatory Agencies and its Limits: A Comparative Analysis of European Delegation'. *Journal of European Public Policy*, Vol. 18, No. 6, pp. 790–809.

Van Rompuy, H. (2012) 'Towards a Genuine Economic and Monetary Union: Report by President of the European Council Herman Van Rompuy'. EUCO 120/12, PRESSE 296, PR PCE 102; Brussels, 26 June. Available at «http://s3.documentcloud.org/documents/373846/towards-a-genuine-economic-and-monetary-union.pdf».

Waterman, R.W. and Meier, K.J. (1998) 'Principal–Agent Models: An Expansion?'. *Journal of Public Administration Research and Theory*, Vol. 8, No. 2, pp. 173–202.

Weingast, B.R. and Moran, M.J. (1983) 'Bureaucratic Discretion or Congressional Control?'. *Journal of Political Economy*, Vol. 91, pp. 765–800.

Wymeersch, E. (2014) 'The Single Supervisory Mechanism or "SSM", Part One of the Banking Union'. *ECGI – Law Working Paper* No. 240/014, February 2014.

© 2015 The Author(s) JCMS: Journal of Common Market Studies © 2015 John Wiley & Sons Ltd

JCMS 2015 Volume 53 Annual Review pp. 200–215   DOI: 10.1111/jcms.12281

Europe as a Regional Actor: Neighbourhood Lost?

ANA E. JUNCOS[1] and RICHARD G. WHITMAN[2]
[1] University of Bristol. [2] Global Europe Centre, University of Kent

Introduction

The irrelevance of the EU to shape or influence its European neighbourhood was fully apparent throughout 2014, marking a continuation of the downward trajectory of the EU's influence which has become the characteristic of the past half-decade in the region (Whitman and Juncos, 2011, 2012, 2013, 2014).

The EU now confronts an arc of crisis running from its neighbourhood to the east through and across its southern borders in which it is being confronted by multiple security challenges. To its east it faces a direct challenge from Russia, which is willing to use state power to alter borders and impose its will on its neighbours. In the Mashreq,[1] the emergence of the self-declared Islamic State has changed the dynamics of Syria's civil war and impacted on the wider Middle East. An Israel–Palestinian peace process remains absent while the blockade of Gaza by Israel, entering into its seventh year, escalated into a seven-week direct military intervention by bombardment and the deployment of ground forces by the Israeli Defence Forces from July 2014. Libya descended into civil war and state collapse, while in neighbouring Egypt military rule, established in July 2013, was consolidated amid rising political violence. The EU appears hapless and ill equipped to confront these challenges. Only the eastern Maghreb offered the EU some consolation, with Tunisia the only state to have come through the Arab Spring with a democratic government replacing authoritarianism.

If there is an area where the EU is expected to play a role as a regional actor and as a regional leader, it is in the case of enlargement. Enlargement has been hailed by policy-makers and academics alike as one of the most powerful tools of EU foreign policy (Rehn, 2006; Vachudova, 2014). Enlargement is said to have extended peace and security to other areas of the continent through the democratization processes fostered by the adoption of the *acquis communautaire*. In this way, the EU has been able to shape the perceptions and expectations, but also the behaviour, of candidate and potential candidate countries. However, over the past few years, EU policy in the Western Balkans and Turkey has remained atrophied and a state of economic and political malaise holds back the enlargement of the EU, with the exception of Croatia, which was already quite well advanced on the path to membership.

I. The EU's Regional Diplomacy

The EU's response to the challenges in the neighbourhood in 2014 has demonstrated three characteristics. First, the EU's structural diplomacy – its milieu, or region-shaping,

---

[1] This comprises the countries to the east of Egypt (i.e. Egypt, Jordan, Lebanon, Palestine and Syria).

© 2015 The Author(s) JCMS: Journal of Common Market Studies © 2015 John Wiley & Sons Ltd, 9600 Garsington Road, Oxford OX4 2DQ, UK and 350 Main Street, Malden, MA 02148, USA

role – has proven to have considerable weaknesses. Second, the EU's capacity for crisis management diplomacy has been enhanced since the Lisbon Treaty reforms, but it remains a work of considerable imperfection. Third, distinctions need to be drawn between the roles that different Member States and the different EU institutional actors such as the European External Action Service (EEAS) and the European Commission are able to play, with the Member States still dominating issues of high politics.

II. The EU as a Regional Actor in the Southern Neighbourhood

2014 was another sobering year as far as relations with the Southern neighbourhood are concerned. The high expectations that followed the Arab Spring revolutions failed to materialize for another year, with a new war in Gaza in the summer, the crises in Syria and Libya worsening and Islamic terrorism on the rise. Libya exemplified many of the problems in the region. International intervention failed to bring any peaceful and sustainable change in the medium term, with the country even more divided between two rival coalitions: 'Libyan Dignity' and the 'Libyan Dawn'. Although the Muslim Brotherhood and other Islamist parties lost in the general elections in June, they refused to accept the election results and forced the newly elected House of Representatives to flee Tripoli. Libyan Army General Khalifa Haftar then sought to oust the Islamists from power by launching 'Operation Dignity', which then led to the rise of the opposition in the so-called operation 'Libyan Dawn'.

The EU's ability to influence events on the ground has been very limited. Its strategy in Libya has focused on medium and long-term reconstruction and democratization, and as a result the EU does not have the capabilities necessary to deal with the deterioration of the security situation in Libya (Kostanyan and Blockmans, 2014). Its only CSDP instrument in the country, an integrated border management assistance mission (EUBAM Libya) launched in May 2013, is not a crisis management instrument and was forced to relocate to Tunisia in the summer of 2014. Its EU Delegation, one of the newest delegations opened after the entry into force of the Lisbon Treaty, was forced to repatriate its staff due to the security situation in the country. What is more, according to Kostanyan and Blockmans, Member States have put commercial interests before an effective collective response to the Libyan crisis. In their words,

> Rome, Paris and London competed with each other to secure contracts with Libya for their own defence industries. Other European countries simply stood by and watched how, instead of disarmament, demobilisation and reintegration, Libyan armed forces received training from Egypt and its partners to counter successful attacks by fundamentalist militias (Kostanyan and Blockmans, 2014, p. 2).

In relation to the Middle East peace process, the EU has also failed to become a regional leader, although there are some recent developments that might change the perceptions of the actors in the region and their willingness to co-operate in the future. First, the EU was again a spectator to another Gaza war during the summer of 2014. The latest Gaza war followed a similar pattern to previous conflicts: Israel claimed that Hamas had started it by firing rockets over its territory, while Hamas argued that Israel was to blame for arresting hundreds of people in the West Bank and firing air strikes against Hamas members. The conflict left over 2,000 Palestinians dead, most of them

© 2015 The Author(s) JCMS: Journal of Common Market Studies © 2015 John Wiley & Sons Ltd

(around 70 per cent) civilians, including over 400 children. Israel also used this offensive as an opportunity to dismantle underground tunnels in Gaza. The EU did not play a role in the negotiation of the ceasefire, which was brokered once again by Egypt.

However, positions in Europe vis-à-vis Israel hardened throughout 2014, and especially after the conflict in the summer. Member States and EU institutions have become increasingly frustrated by Israel's settlement policy, with some Member State governments more inclined to use the recognition tool as a way to influence Israel's policies. As a result, 2014 witnessed a series of non-binding votes in key Member State parliaments recommending the recognition of Palestine, including the British, French, Irish, Portuguese and Spanish parliaments. The European Parliament also held a vote on a non-binding motion at the end of 2014 supporting the recognition of Palestine. Moreover, Sweden was the first EU Member State to formally recognize the Palestinian state, in October. France was also very active within the UN context, trying to table a UNSC resolution to re-launch the MEPP (Middle East peace process) with a new international conference on the matter, including a threat to recognize Palestine if Israel did not co-operate and retreat to the 1967 borders by 2016. However, although some EU diplomats suggested the possibility of threatening Israel with sanctions,[2] this possibility continued to be rejected by some Member States which preferred the use of incentives, fearing that a tougher line on Israel might actually boost the far right in the upcoming Israeli elections. Another issue that might challenge existing EU policy towards the Arab–Israeli conflict has to do with the European Court of Justice's decision to declare void 'on procedural grounds' a 2003 Council decision to impose an asset freeze on Hamas.[3] While it is likely that the decision will be appealed in 2015, this puts more pressure on the EU to negotiate with the Palestinian militant group to find a solution to the conflict.

While the EU has a long history of involvement in the MEPP, the fight against the Islamic State in Iraq and al-Sham (ISIS) emerged as a new and pressing security issue in the Southern neighbourhood for the Union in 2014. Although many European countries did not consider ISIS to be a direct security threat, there were growing concerns about EU nationals travelling to the Middle East to join ISIS and coming back to their home countries as radicalized jihadists. The EU, however, was not expected to and did not take a leadership role in military efforts to counter the threat posed by ISIS in Syria, Iraq and the wider region. Instead, the US led the fight against ISIS through an international coalition which carried out air strikes in Syria and Iraq, with most EU countries pledging support to the US's global coalition.

III. The EU's Response to the Crisis in Ukraine

Throughout 2014, the EU's activities on Ukraine were undertaken through three main strands. First, with the recognition of Ukraine's new government and providing political support for its consolidation. Second, pursuing a 'rebooted' Association Agreement through the pressing ahead with the signing and preliminary implementation process with

---

[2] *EUobserver.com*, 18 November 2014.
[3] *EUobserver.com*, 17 December 2014.

© 2015 The Author(s) JCMS: Journal of Common Market Studies © 2015 John Wiley & Sons Ltd

Ukraine. Third, diplomatic and sanctions responses to Russia as a result of its invasion of Crimea and its military role in eastern Ukraine.

Supporting the Revolution

The year opened with the hangover from the November 2013 Eastern Partnership summit in Vilnius still dominating the EU's Eastern European agenda. The domestic political consequences in Ukraine of the decision not to sign the Association Agreement continued, with the Euromaidan – Euro Square protestors – still in occupation of central Kyiv. At its December 2013 summit, the EU's Heads of State and Government made clear their sympathy for the protestors and that the departure of President Yanukovych from power was the key to reviving the Association Agreement that he declined to sign at the end of 2013 (European Council, 2013).

The Euromaidan protests were visited by the High Representative/Vice-President (HR/VP) Baroness Ashton on several occasions, together with a steady stream of foreign ministers of EU Member States and members of the European Parliament. The Foreign Affairs Council made clear in its conclusions of 10 February that it was monitoring abuses of human rights and cases of violence, intimidation and missing persons, expressing its readiness to react quickly (although the manner was unspecified) to any deterioration of the situation on the ground (Council of the European Union, 2014a).

The peaceful protests first turned violent in January, after the Ukrainian Parliament legislated to repress the protests. EU condemnation and the imposition of sanctions on Ukrainian officials who were deemed to have ordered the violence against the protestors swiftly followed. A more violent turn of events took place from 18 to 22 February 2014, which witnessed clashes between protestors and riot police and killings by unknown snipers as demonstrators occupied government buildings in Kyiv. At the Foreign Affairs Council meeting on 20 February, the EU's Member States maintained their vocal support for the demonstrators, called for political dialogue and agreed on targeted sanctions, but were in disagreement as to who should be sanctioned and from when sanctions should commence (Council of the European Union, 2014b). Events moved quickly over the next few days. The HR/VP visited Kyiv on 23 February as President Yanukovych was relocated to Crimea (and then departed for Russia) via helicopters supplied by the Russian Federation and while the formation of a new interim government was in progress. The crisis situation in Ukraine was marginally lightened by the leaking of recordings of US and EU diplomatic telephone conversations in which US State Department officials were less than flattering about EU diplomacy. [4]

An extraordinary meeting of the Council on 3 March 2014 used strong words, condemning the 'clear violation of Ukrainian sovereignty and territorial integrity by acts of aggression by the Russian armed forces as well as the authorisation given by the Federation Council of Russia on 1 March for the use of the armed forces on the territory of Ukraine' (Council of the European Union, 2014c). The EU called on Russia to immediately withdraw its armed forces to the areas of their permanent stationing, in accordance with the Agreement on the Status and Conditions of the Black Sea Fleet stationing on the territory of Ukraine of 1997. With political power and state control in

---

[4] *EUobserver.com*, 6 February 2014; *EUobserver.com*, 7 February 2014.

© 2015 The Author(s) JCMS: Journal of Common Market Studies © 2015 John Wiley & Sons Ltd

a condition of flux in Ukraine on 5 March, the Foreign Affairs Council also adopted sanctions focused on the freezing and recovery of misappropriated Ukrainian state funds. In a statement of the Heads of State or Government following an extraordinary meeting on 6 March, the EU underlined that a solution to the crisis must be found through negotiations between the governments of Ukraine and the Russian Federation, including through potential multilateral mechanisms. Having first suspended bilateral talks with the Russian Federation on visa matters and discussions on the New (EU–Russia) Agreement, as well as preparations for participation in the G8 Summit in Sochi, in the absence of de-escalatory steps the EU set out a second stage of further measures and additional far-reaching consequences for EU–Russia relations in case of further destabilization of the situation in Ukraine.

In Ukraine the new interim government faced formidable problems in establishing its authority across the country, including the outbreak of secessionist demonstrations in eastern Ukraine. Russia's response to the political events in Kyiv was both hostile and belligerent and is examined below. In contrast, the EU continued to lend its political support to the interim government in Ukraine, and subsequently to the presidential elections held on 25 May and the parliamentary elections held on 26 October 2014. It gave rather shorter shrift to the presidential and parliamentary elections in Donetsk and Luhansk 'People's Republics' on 2 November, describing these as illegal and illegitimate.[5]

Rebooting the Association Agreement

Following the change of regime in Ukraine, the EU moved swiftly to re-establish the momentum of EU–Ukraine relations with the signing of the political provisions of the Association Agreement on 21 March. The remaining parts of the agreement, following technical preparations, were signed in Brussels on 27 June. While awaiting the completion of the ratification process on both sides, parts of the agreement came into force on 1 November 2014 covering respect for human rights, fundamental freedoms and rule of law; political dialogue and reform; justice, freedom and security; and economic and financial co-operation. On 15 December 2014 the EU and Ukraine held the first meeting of the Association Council under the new Association Agreement. Work progressed on an updated version of the EU–Ukraine Association Agenda to guide the process of reforms and economic modernization in Ukraine, with a view to securing its endorsement by the EU–Ukraine Association Council on March 2015. The EU continued to apply autonomous trade measures granting Ukrainian exporters continued preferential access to EU markets without awaiting the entry into force of the trade provisions under the Association Agreement. Provisional application of the Deep and Comprehensive Free Trade Area (DCFTA) part of the Agreement was delayed until 1 January 2016. This was intended to allow for consultations on its implementation with the Russian Federation and with both Ukraine and Russia in a trilateral format. The EU also acted as moderator in discussions on energy security between Ukraine and Russia in bilateral

---

[5] «http://www.consilium.europa.eu/uedocs/cms_Data/docs/pressdata/en/cfsp/145644.pdf»

© 2015 The Author(s) JCMS: Journal of Common Market Studies © 2015 John Wiley & Sons Ltd

gas talks, leading to an agreement on 30 October 2014 on outstanding energy debt issues and an interim solution that enabled gas supplies to continue throughout the winter.

Just as important as the Association Agreement process were the financial support measures intended to support the new government in Kyiv. On 5 March 2014 the European Commission announced that €11 billion could be available over the next years, both from the EU budget and international financial institutions, for economic and financial support measures as part of the support for Ukraine's economic and political reforms.[6] In the short term these funds were intended to stabilize the economic and financial situation in Ukraine, assist with the transition and encourage political and economic reform. One component of this support was to temporarily remove customs duties on Ukrainian exports to the EU (the legislation adopted on 14 April and entering into force on 23 April) and anticipating the tariffs-related section of the Association Agreement's provisions on a Deep and Comprehensive Free Trade Area without waiting for its entry into force. The temporary tariff cuts entered into force on 23 April. On 9 April the Commission also decided to create a support group to ensure that the Ukrainian authorities had all the assistance they needed in undertaking the political and economic reforms necessary to stabilize the country.

The Russian Reaction and the EU's Response

Russia's response to the events in Ukraine was to invade, occupy and annex Crimea to the Russian Federation and to pursue military intervention in eastern Ukraine through proxy forces. Following the annexation of Crimea by the Russian Federation, on 18 March, demonstrations by pro-Russian groups in the Donbass area of Ukraine escalated into an armed conflict between the separatist forces of the self-declared Donetsk and Lugansk People's Republics and the Ukrainian government.

The Russian Federation's military intervention in eastern Ukraine was both direct and indirect, with military personnel and equipment entering the region without insignia and with Russian government denials that its forces were present. Russian intervention in men and materiel increased markedly in August; Russia also massed significant forces near the Ukrainian forces. These interventions were seen as responsible for the defeat of Ukrainian forces in the region in early September. Despite the best efforts of the German-led peace initiatives, Russian military involvement in eastern Ukraine increased through the final months of 2014.

Throughout this period, the EU sought to respond to this situation via diplomatic initiatives, as it quickly became clear that that there was no appetite for direct military intervention in support of the Ukrainian government by the United States, NATO or Ukraine's western neighbours. The EU's diplomatic response to Russia's involvement in Ukraine was led by Germany. For many commentators this represented a marked departure for Germany's post-second world war diplomacy in that it sought to take a high profile leading role on a major issue of international security (Pond and Kundnani, 2015).

The main goal of the Berlin-led EU policy over Ukraine was to move the situation with Russia away from military intervention and to establish a diplomatic process. This effort resulted in the Minsk Agreement of September 2014. The agreement was reached through

[6] «http://europa.eu/rapid/press-release_MEMO-14-159_en.htm»

© 2015 The Author(s) JCMS: Journal of Common Market Studies © 2015 John Wiley & Sons Ltd

considerable efforts on the part of Merkel, through her personal communications and meetings with President Putin, and considerable diplomatic efforts with Ukraine, Russia, the US and EU Member States by Walter Steinmeier, Germany's foreign minister. This provided a framework through which the EU sought to contain and dampen down the conflict in eastern Ukraine. The HR/VP and the EEAS were bystanders to this diplomacy as the Member States, via Germany, drove the EU's diplomatic response.

A key component of the EU's response to Russia's intervention was sanctions. A first set of sanctions was agreed by the EU following Russia's annexation of Crimea on 17 March 2014. These adopted 'measures against persons responsible for actions which undermine or threaten the territorial integrity, sovereignty and independence of Ukraine as well as persons and entities associated with them'.[7] These measures were further strengthened on four separate occasions over the following two months, expanding the number of individuals covered by the sanctions.

A second set of comprehensive 'tier-three' sanctions was agreed by the Member States on 25 and 30 July 2014. These followed the downing of the Malaysian Airlines Flight MH17 in Donetsk on 17 July. The Foreign Affairs Council of 22 July concluded that that those directly and indirectly responsible for the incident must be held accountable and brought to justice, calling on all states and parties to co-operate fully to achieve this end (Council of the European Union, 2014d). The EU urged Russia to use its influence over illegally armed groups to allow full access to the site and co-operation to recover remains and possessions and with the independent investigation. The EU also adopted further trade and investment restrictions for Crimea and Sevastopol, as part of the EU's policy of not recognizing the illegal annexation. The EU announced on 29 July that it had agreed on a package of significant additional restrictive measures targeting sectoral co-operation and exchanges with Russia. Following a request by the European Council, the Commission and EEAS proposed further steps to be taken against Russia, which entered into force on 12 September, concerning access to EU capital markets, defence, dual use goods and sensitive technologies.

The agreement on these different rounds of sanctions between the Member States required considerable discussions to broker a common position that was acceptable to all Member States. Maintaining consensus between the Member States, with a divergent set of views on how to respond to Russia, was a major achievement for the EU. It was also a strong signal to Russia of the willingness of Member States to subsume their differences to allow for an unambiguous position on the annexation of Crimea and Russia's military involvement in eastern Ukraine.

Newly appointed High Representative Federica Mogherini, who had been perceived in some quarters as pro-Russian, chaired her first Foreign Affairs Council on 17 November 2014.[8] Against the backdrop of heavy shelling and reports of heavy weapons convoys in separatist held areas with, the Council urged all parties to implement fully the Minsk Protocol and Memorandum without further delay. On 28 November the EU reinforced its sanctions targeting separatists in eastern Ukraine.

Beyond sanctions, the EU's Member States were more cautious in their interventions. In July 2014 the Council established a Common Security and Defence Policy mission to assist Ukraine in this field. The EU Advisory Mission for Civilian Security Sector Reform

---

[7] «http://www.consilium.europa.eu/uedocs/cms_data/docs/pressdata/EN/foraff/141603.pdf»

[8] See also Dinan's contribution and Pomorska and Vanhoonacker's contribution to this volume.

© 2015 The Author(s) JCMS: Journal of Common Market Studies © 2015 John Wiley & Sons Ltd

(EUAM) was intended to provide strategic advice for the development of sustainable, accountable and efficient security services that contribute to strengthening the rule of law in Ukraine. EUAM Ukraine, headquartered in Kyiv, is an unarmed, non-executive civilian mission with a budget of €13.1 million launched on 1 December 2014. The EU and its Member States were also the biggest contributor to the OSCE Special Monitoring Mission (SMM), contributing about two thirds of both the mission's budget and monitors; the EU contributed €7 million to the SMM budget through the instrument contributing to Stability and Peace.

There is recognition in a number of quarters that the EU demonstrated a major systemic failing in its lack of comprehension of Russia's thinking and willingness to take direct action against the deepening of the Eastern Partnership, and most especially on the direction in which EU policy was developing on Ukraine (House of Lords, 2014). Russia's active contestation of the EU's role in its Eastern neighbourhood will require a major policy recalibration by the Member States and the EU's institutions. It also fits into a more general pattern of the EU's international relations that Menon characterized in last year's *Annual Review* as 'hard powerlessness' with 'normative delusions' (Menon, 2014, p. 14).

III. Regional Actorness and Enlargement

2014 marked the tenth anniversary of the so-called 'big bang' enlargement of 1 May 2004, which saw the accession of ten new Member States to the EU. This momentous date provided a unique opportunity to reflect on the achievements and failures of the EU's enlargement policy in this part of the continent and lessons learned for future enlargements (Grabbe, 2014). According to the Commission, '[a]ccession benefited both those countries joining the EU and the established Member States. Trade and investment have increased. The quality of life of citizens has improved as EU environmental, consumer and other standards apply more widely' (European Commission, 2014, p. 1). In their assessment of the EU's enlargements to central and eastern European countries, the volume edited by Rachel Epstein and Wade Jacoby concluded that

> on balance the EU has had stronger economic effects since eastern enlargement than political, and that all NMS [New Member States] have had significant problems with aspects of democratic consolidation. Moreover, although the EU gained 100 million new citizens and consumers through its eastern enlargements and has claimed a number of achievements through its enlargement policy, it is not clear the EU's power has grown in global politics. (Epstein and Jacoby, 2014, p. 3)

There have been important lessons learned from previous waves of enlargement that have led to changes in the enlargement strategy over the years, in particular after the accession of Romania and Bulgaria in 2007. While the importance of the meritocratic nature of the process remains, recent enlargement strategies have placed more emphasis on the rule of law (see Whitman and Juncos, 2013) and more recently on economic governance and public administration reform as three key inter-related pillars (European Commission, 2014, p. 1). The changes introduced into the enlargement strategy reflect the different nature of the challenges that the EU faces in the new candidate and potential candidates of the Western Balkans and Turkey, which have generally weaker rule-of-law and administrative structures and poorer economies than those of central and east European countries. It also reflects a different opportunity structure than that of the

© 2015 The Author(s) JCMS: Journal of Common Market Studies © 2015 John Wiley & Sons Ltd

1990s and early 2000s. The 2004 enlargement took place in a permissive international context, with Russia still debilitated by the end of the Cold War and where liberal democracy and western economic models were seen as a panacea for progress. The current international climate is a rather different one. While Russia did not openly oppose enlargement to the CEE countries, as its economy has strengthened, it has become politically more assertive and it has become increasingly wary of the EU's enlargement agenda. This is particularly the case in the EU's Eastern neighbourhood, as discussed in the previous section, but Russian geopolitical influence can also be felt in the Western Balkans (Bechev, 2012). For example, Russia abstained from a UN Security Council vote on the extension of the mandate of EUFOR Althea (Merdzanovic, 2014). Because of traditional political ties but also economic and energy dependence, some governments in the region increasingly began to turn to Russia (Bechev, 2012). The war in Ukraine also meant that countries in the region were being forced to take sides, for instance when it came to sanctions against Russia, which Serbia did not adopt (Bechev, 2014). The close relation between Serbia and Russia is also illustrated by the fact that Vladimir Putin was the guest of honour at Serbia's military parade marking 70 years since liberation from Nazi occupation, with Serbian President Tomislav Nikolić stating that Russia was his country's 'big ally'.[9]

It is also important to note that western sanctions against Russia might also have a negative effect in the Balkans given the level of Russian investment in the region. The decision to stop the construction of the South Stream Pipeline will also have serious implications. Hence, if the EU wants to balance Russian influence, it needs to start thinking about how to better use economic incentives and the promise of membership in the Western Balkans. According to Grabbe (2014, p. 54), 'the EU faces a major strategic choice now: preserve the current Union by continuing to prioritize internal consensus over external effectiveness, or respond to the new external challenge by exerting its transformative power across the European continent to strengthen its neighbours and counter Russian influence'. It is interesting, for instance, that in the Commission's 2014 Enlargement Strategy, there is mention of the need to address earlier in the accession process the negotiating chapter on Foreign, Security and Defence Policy (Chapter 31), with a view to strengthening foreign policy co-operation between the EU and the candidate countries (Fouéré, 2014, p. 8).

The opportunity structure has also changed because of the international financial crisis and its impact on the eurozone countries (Whitman and Juncos, 2012, 2013). This has had an impact on the EU's willingness and capacity to act as a regional leader and how the EU is perceived by the candidate countries. Although there are signs of recovery in some EU countries, the recovery is likely to be a slow one and the effects of the eurozone crisis will still be felt in the medium and long term, in particular in terms of the erosion of the EU's transformative power in the neighbourhood. The Greek crisis, in particular, has had a very negative effect in the Western Balkans, and not just because of the economic ramifications of the crisis given Greek investments in the region and the reduction in diaspora remittances (O'Brennan, 2013, p. 40; Panagiotou, 2013). The Greek crisis has also had two other crucial impacts on the region. First, it has damaged the role of Greece as a champion of the Western Balkan countries' accession,[10] as the country is absorbed by

[9] BBC News, 16 October 2014.
[10] Note, for instance, that it was at the Thessaloniki European Council that the EU first referred to the countries' potential EU membership.

how to solve its economic and political crisis. Second, it has damaged the image of the EU as promoter of prosperity. If, after three decades of EU membership, Greece is still struggling to achieve economic growth and modernization and fighting corruption, how can the western Balkan countries expect to overcome similar challenges? As summarized by Panagiotou (2013, p. 89), 'the EU's hitherto undisputable symbolic role as an 'anchor' of stability, as a one way path to prosperity and as a goal to be aspired to, may be losing its credibility and appeal for some of these countries'. The eurozone crisis has thus damaged the EU's presence in the Western Balkans and Turkey, and possibly their acceptance of the EU's regional leadership.

In terms of capabilities, the EU's enlargement process relies on one of its strongest tools: the promise of membership. However, as argued before, this incentive might have been somewhat eroded by the effects of the economic crisis and the increasing competition from other structural powers in the EU's periphery. The main elements of the EU's enlargement strategy (conditionality and a meritocratic approach) have remained unchanged over the past decade. As summarized by the Commission in its most recent enlargement strategy: 'The accession process is rigorous, built on strict but fair conditionality, established criteria and the principle of own merit. This is crucial for the credibility of enlargement policy, for providing incentives to enlargement countries to pursue far-reaching reforms and for ensuring the support of EU citizens' (European Commission, 2014, p. 1). This strategy is supported by the screening processes and progress monitoring of candidate countries carried out by the Commission. However, this reporting mechanism is also not without faults. For some observers, the Commission needs to change its way of reporting to incentivize reforms, following the model of the visa liberalization process: with precise roadmaps (clear criteria and similar criteria for all the countries), benchmarks, fair assessments with experts' visits to the countries and clear (public-friendly) reports. This would facilitate regional competition by providing comparable data about the achievement of different benchmarks by each country (Knaus, 2014). Monitoring prior to accession is all the more important given that the EU lacks effective monitoring and implementation mechanisms after accession and that the Cooperation and Verification Mechanism set up in the cases of Romania and Bulgaria has not proven to be an effective one. The EU has been unable to prevent democratic backsliding in new Member States, as illustrated by the case of Hungary (Sedelmeier, 2014) or the deterioration of the rule of law in Romania and Bulgaria. As far as financial instruments are concerned, the bulk of the assistance is delivered through the Instrument for Pre-Accession (IPA). In 2014, the EU launched IPA II, which will provide €11.7 billion for the period 2014–20. According to the Commission strategy report, IPA II 'increases focus on priorities for EU accession in the areas of democracy and rule of law as well as competitiveness and growth, IPA II also introduces a sector approach, incentives for delivery on results, increased budget support and prioritisation of projects' (European Commission, 2014, p. 3). Although this is an important incentive for candidate countries, it still remains insufficient in view of the economic challenges affecting most countries of the region, such as high unemployment and fiscal deficits.

Another aspect to consider in terms of the EU's actorness and leadership in the region refers to the EU's willingness to act as a regional power and a regional leader. While the EU remains officially committed to further enlargement, in recent years there is however evidence of 'enlargement fatigue' eroding support for expansion on the part of the

Member States. Support for enlargement within the EU remains low. For example, according to a recent survey, a higher percentage of respondents within the EU is now against further enlargement (49 per cent) than those supporting enlargement (37 per cent) (Eurobarometer, 2014, p. 143). In the past, 'enlargement fatigue' signified the view that the increasing widening of the EU would have a negative impact on deepening, undermining the functioning of the EU. The notion of 'absorption capacity' was coined to capture the need to take into account the later objective when proceeding with future enlargements. Today, it would seem that both widening and deepening are seen with suspicion among some policy-makers and the public. These dynamics have been accentuated with the rise of eurosceptic parties in the majority of EU Member States, as illustrated by the results of the elections to the European Parliament in May 2014,[11] and debates about migration coming from new Member States and candidate countries (Grabbe, 2014, pp. 51–3). To paraphrase Hooghe and Marks (2009), this symbolizes the end of a 'permissive consensus' on enlargement, with domestic politics expected to have more of an impact in the making of the policy in the coming years (Grabbe, 2014). It is arguably in response to these domestic pressures that enlargement has disappeared from the new Commission's list of priorities. In his opening speech to the European Parliament in July 2014, the newly designated President of the Commission, Jean-Claude Juncker, stated that the EU 'needs to take a break from enlargement' and that 'no further enlargement will take place over the next five years' (Juncker, 2014, p. 11). There were even rumours that the new Commission would not have an Enlargement portfolio.[12] Although such reports were proven wrong – Johannes Hahn was appointed as the Commissioner for European Neighbourhood Policy and Enlargement Negotiations in the autumn 2014 – these developments could undermine the credibility of enlargement by putting into question the EU's long-standing commitment to further enlargement.

This enlargement fatigue is also likely to have an impact on the transformational power of the EU (O'Brennan, 2013; Grabbe, 2014) and undermine its leadership role in the region. Enlargement fatigue has an impact in candidate and potential candidate countries, reducing their willingness to implement conditionality-related reforms as uncertainty about the process increases. While Croatian accession might have provided some needed stimulus to the process, problems remain. An illustration of this is the declining support for EU membership among the candidate countries. While Macedonian citizens are still largely pro-EU membership (56 per cent considered EU membership a 'good thing'), support for membership has continued to decline in Turkey, where only 38 per cent considered accession to the EU a 'good thing'; in Iceland, too, only a minority of respondents (24 per cent) consider membership to be positive (Eurobarometer, 2013, pp. 67–8), which explains why the new eurosceptic coalition government decided to put negotiations on hold after coming to power in 2013.[13]

Candidate countries will only be willing to adopt painful reforms if the EU offers credible and sizeable rewards which outweigh the costs of adaptation. The credibility of the enlargement process becomes even more significant in the case of the Western Balkans and Turkey, given the set of domestic political challenges faced by these countries. This is

---

[11] See Hobolt's contribution to this volume.
[12] *Euractiv.com*, 5 September 2014.
[13] Iceland officially withdrew its candidacy in March 2015, after six years of negotiations.

© 2015 The Author(s) JCMS: Journal of Common Market Studies © 2015 John Wiley & Sons Ltd

compounded by the fact that new 'hurdles' have been erected in order to reassure the Member States that conditionality is being applied strictly and that the problems encountered during the 2007 enlargement will not happen again. According to O'Brennan (2013, p. 42), '[a]n excess of enlargement fatigue has led to an excess of "accession fatigue": transposition and implementation of EU laws in the Western Balkans has slowed to a standstill'. The 2014 Commission's report on enlargement paints a bleak picture of the situation in the region. While there has been some modest progress in the cases of Albania, Serbia and Kosovo, in other cases, such as FYROM, Turkey and Bosnia and Herzegovina, there remain serious concerns. In general, the Commission found that that public administration 'remains weak in most enlargement countries, with limited administrative capacity, high levels of politicisation and a lack of transparency' (European Commission, 2014, p. 2). There are still problems affecting the functioning of democratic institutions, in particular national parliaments, a need for more constructive and sustainable exchanges among competing political forces, strengthening the role of civil society organizations and freedom of the media. Regarding the rule of law, the main challenges still relate to the need to improve the functioning and independence of the judiciary and fighting corruption and organized crime. Finally, in the area of economic governance, the Commission concluded that

> There remain significant challenges in all enlargement countries in terms of economic reform, competitiveness, job creation and fiscal consolidation. Weaknesses with the rule of law and public financial management exacerbate the risk of corruption, negatively impacting on the investment climate. To date, none of the countries have produced a comprehensive and convincing domestic reform agenda (European Commission, 2014, pp. 5–6).

The most positive development in 2014 was the granting of candidate status for Albania at the European Council in June. The initialling of a Stabilisation and Association Agreement with Kosovo in July was also hailed as a 'milestone on Kosovo's European integration path' (European Commission, 2014, p. 25). By contrast, it was another year of stagnation in Bosnia, with no progress being achieved regarding the key conditions of membership, which refer to the implementation of the so-called Seidic and Finci verdict of the European Court of Human Rights.[14] For its part, FYROM seems to be backsliding, with the European Commission warning that failure to address the growing politicization and independence of the judiciary and to address the deterioration of freedom of expression could lead to the recommendation for the opening of accession negotiations to be withdrawn.

The latter case also highlights the significance of bilateral disputes in the enlargement process. In the case of the Greek/Macedonian dispute, 2014 saw no progress on the resolution of the 'name issue', with the Commission's report recalling '[t]he failure of the parties to this dispute to reach a compromise after 19 years of UN-mediated talks' (European Commission, 2014, p. 23). The report acknowledges that this bilateral dispute is having a negative impact on FYROM's accession process. However, as with other disputes, the Commission considers this to be a bilateral matter and hence it has been

---

[14] The verdict refers to the violation of rights of national minorities, other than the three 'constituent peoples' (Bosniaks, Serbs and Croats), under the current Bosnian constitution.

© 2015 The Author(s) JCMS: Journal of Common Market Studies © 2015 John Wiley & Sons Ltd

reluctant to intervene directly in the negotiations (Geddes and Taylor, 2013), calling instead for 'resolute action' from the parties involved and for EU leaders to show proactive support.

The current candidates have also seen how the Member States have become more involved in enlargement politics, with the process becoming increasingly intergovernmental in recent years. While the Commission still plays a central role, the Member States have been more closely involved in the opening and closing of negotiating chapters and in each stage of the process sometimes blocking progress because of bilateral disputes as in the case above or because of specific concerns. However, their role has not always been obstructive. In other cases, they have sought to move the process forward, with or without the support of the Commission. In 2014, it is worth mentioning two Member State initiatives, both of them led by Germany, which has become the new leader in enlargement (if only by default) (see also Whitman and Juncos, 2014). In August, Chancellor Merkel convened a Balkan summit in Berlin to reiterate the EU's commitment to the European future of the region and to keep the pressure on these countries to implement EU-related reforms. The 'Berlin process' is to be followed by another summit in 2015 being hosted by Austria. Germany was also in the driving seat, this time in co-operation with the UK, for another initiative regarding Bosnia. The German–British proposal aimed to revitalize Bosnia's accession process by removing the 'Sejdic and Finci' question and focusing on a broad reform agenda, including economic issues, good governance, rule of law and some institutional questions, to make Bosnia a functioning state. According to this initiative, the EU would unblock the implementation of the Stabilisation and Association Agreement if Bosnian politicians signed a written commitment to this reform agenda (Merdzanovic, 2014). This initiative can be said to be problematic, however, not least because it might be seen as yet another illustration of the EU 'giving up' in the face of recalcitrant domestic elites (de Borja Lasheras, 2014). While these are two welcome initiatives that show some much-needed re-engagement with the region, it is still not clear whether they will be able to mobilize support from other Member States towards the Balkans and the enlargement process more generally. In the absence of this political support, the EU will continue to struggle to become a full-fledged actor and regional leader in a less favourable context characterized by a re-emergence of geopolitics and increasing enlargement fatigue.

Conclusion

Despite this being the one region where one would expect the EU to have some clout, the EU's political and economic influence in its neighbourhood was marginal in 2014. Furthermore, the foundations of the post-Cold War regional order within which the EU is embedded were called into question by the Russian Federation's use of force to seize Crimea from Ukraine, its increasing meddling in enlargement politics and the emergence of non-state actors such as ISIS with the capacity to overturn the authority and rule of existing nation-states. The EU's milieu-shaping goals and instruments are not equipped for these challenges. An EU response equivalent to the magnitude of these challenges did not take shape during the course of the year.

The EU's capacity for crisis management, and most especially the institutions created by the Lisbon Treaty, proved to be insufficiently capable of responding in spirit or

© 2015 The Author(s) JCMS: Journal of Common Market Studies © 2015 John Wiley & Sons Ltd

substance to a neighbourhood which is being remade largely without the influence of the EU. The events in Ukraine have also demonstrated that Germany is willing to take an active and leading role in EU diplomacy towards Russia, eastern Europe and the Western Balkans, and one which eclipses that of the other large Member States and especially France and the UK.

The EU's absence of a strategy for Russia, beyond hoping for indigenous economic and political reform, proved to be a major weakness in the EU's approach towards its neighbourhood. Consequently a new divide has been consolidated in eastern Europe, with EU and Russian spheres of predominant influence. On the one side of the divide lie those states that are willing, and able, to deepen their relationship with the EU; on the other are EaP states with a restricted relationship with the EU due to economic and political pressure being exercised by the Russian Federation, and that are resistant to domestic political reform processes.

In the Southern neighbourhood the states affected by the Arab Spring, excepting Tunisia, have not looked to the EU for assistance in political and economic transition processes. Rather, the EU is a bystander to the civil wars in Libya and Syria, and is not mitigating the political and economic fragility of the majority of its southern neighbours.

In the past decades, the EU was able to shape its neighbourhood through its enlargement policy, promoting democratization and fostering economic reform. However, ten years after the 'big bang' enlargement to central and eastern Europe, there are significant lessons learned as to the challenges faced by EU conditionality to promote deeper political and economic domestic reforms. In the context of a resurgent Russia and increasing enlargement fatigue within and outside the EU, the power of conditionality seems even more limited than was previously the case. The stagnation of the enlargement process in the Western Balkans and Turkey constitutes a case in point.

The new regional context for the EU is dislocation and instability, and a challenge to which the EU has not yet created a diplomatic or economic strategy sufficient to contribute to security and stability. While it appeared the EU was edging out of its own economic and eurozone crises in 2014, the challenges in its neighbourhood were broadening and deepening.

References

Bechev, D. (2012) 'The Periphery of the Periphery: The Western Balkans and the Euro Crisis'. ECFR Policy Brief (London: European Council on Foreign Relations).

Bechev, D. (2014) 'Russia Sanctions: Balkan Countries React'. Available at «http://blogs.lse.ac. uk/lsee/2014/07/31/russia-sanctions-balkan-countries-react/».

Council of the European Union (2014a) Council conclusions on Ukraine, Foreign Affairs Council Meeting, Brussels, 10 February 2014. Available at «http://www.consilium.europa.eu/uedocs/ cms_data/docs/pressdata/EN/foraff/140960.pdf».

Council of the European Union (2014b) Council conclusions on Ukraine, Foreign Affairs Council Meeting, Brussels, 20 February 2014. Available at «http://www.consilium.europa.eu/uedocs/ cms_data/docs/pressdata/EN/foraff/140960.pdf».

Council of the European Union (2014c) Council conclusions on Ukraine, Foreign Affairs Council Meeting, Brussels, 3 March 2014. Available at «http://www.consilium.europa.eu/uedocs/ cms_data/docs/pressdata/EN/foraff/141291.pdf».

Council of the European Union (2014d) Council conclusions on Ukraine, Foreign Affairs Council Meeting, Brussels, 22 July 2014. Available at «http://www.consilium.europa.eu/uedocs/cms_data/docs/pressdata/EN/foraff/144090.pdf».

De Borja Lasheras, F. (2014) 'Can Steinmeier and Hammond reset Bosnia?' ECFR Commentary. Available at «http://www.ecfr.eu/article/commentary_can_steinmeier_and_hammond_reset_bosnia371».

Epstein, R. and Jacoby, W. (2014) 'Eastern Enlargement Ten Years On: Transcending the East–West Divide?' *JCMS*, Vol. 52, No. 1, pp. 1–16.

Eurobarometer (2013) 'Eurobarometer 79: Public Opinion in the European Union'. Available at «http://ec.europa.eu/public_opinion/archives/eb/eb79/eb79_publ_en.pdf».

Eurobarometer (2014) 'Eurobarometer 81: Public Opinion in the European Union'. Available at «http://ec.europa.eu/public_opinion/archives/eb/eb81/eb81_publ_en.pdf».

European Commission (2014) 'Communication from the Commission to the European Parliament and the Council on enlargement strategy and main challenges, 2014–2015'. *COM*(2014) 700 final, 8 October.

European Council (2013) 'Conclusions: European Council 19–20 December, 2013'. Brussels, 20 December. Available at «http://www.consilium.europa.eu/uedocs/cms_Data/docs/pressdata/en/ec/140245.pdf».

Fouéré, E. (2014) 'The EU's Enlargement Agenda – Credibility at Stake?' CEPS Policy Brief No. 324, 31 October.

Geddes, A. and Taylor, A. (2013) 'Those Who Knock on Europe's Door Must Repent? Bilateral Border Disputes and EU Enlargement', KFG Working Paper Series No. 54, November 2013.

Grabbe, H. (2014) 'Six Lessons of Enlargement Ten Years On: The EU's Transformative Power in Retrospect and Prospect'. *JCMS*, Vol. 52, No. s1, pp. 40–56.

Hooghe, L. and Marks, G. (2009) 'A Postfunctionalist Theory of European Integration: From Permissive Consensus to Constraining Dissensus'. *British Journal of Political Science*, Vol. 39, No. 1, pp. 1–23.

House of Lords (2014) European Union Committee - Sixth Report, 'The EU and Russia: Before and Beyond the Crisis in Ukraine', 6th Report of Session 2014–15, HL Paper 115. Available at «http://www.publications.parliament.uk/pa/ld201415/ldselect/ldeucom/115/115.pdf».

Juncker, J.C. (2014) 'A New Start for Europe: My Agenda for Jobs, Growth, Fairness and Democratic Change Political Guidelines for the next European Commission'. Opening Statement in the European Parliament Plenary Session. Available at «http://ec.europa.eu/priorities/docs/pg_en.pdf».

Knaus, G. (2014) 'Enlargement until 2020'. European Stability Initiative, January 2014. Available at «http://www.esiweb.org/pdf/news_id_561_2014%20February%20ROME%20-%20Knaus%20-%20The%20future%20of%20enlargement%20as%20transformation.pdf».

Kostanyan, H. and Blockmans, S. (2014) 'Saving Libya from Itself: What the EU Should Do Now'. CEPS Commentary, 1 December 2014.

Merdzanovic, A. (2014) 'Bosnia: A New Opportunity for Getting Closer to the EU?' *euobserver.com*, 4 December 2014.

O'Brennan, J. (2013) 'Enlargement Fatigue and Its Impact on the Enlargement Process in the Western Balkans'. IDEAS Special Report 18. Available at «http://www.lse.ac.uk/IDEAS/publications/reports/pdf/SR018/OBrennan.pdf».

Panagiotou, R. (2013) 'The Greek Crisis as a Crisis of EU Enlargement: How will the Western Balkans be Affected?'. *Southeast European and Black Sea Studies*, Vol. 13, No. 1, pp. 89–104.

Pond, E. and Kundnani, H. (2015) 'Germany's Real Role in the Ukraine Crisis: Caught between East and West'. *Foreign Affairs*, March–April. Available at «https://www.foreignaffairs.com/articles/eastern-europe-caucasus/germany-s-real-role-ukraine-crisis».

© 2015 The Author(s) JCMS: Journal of Common Market Studies © 2015 John Wiley & Sons Ltd

Menon, A. (2014) 'The JCMS Annual Review Lecture: Divided and Declining? Europe in a Changing World'. *JCMS*, Vol. 52, No. s1, pp. 5–24.

Rehn, O. (2006) 'Europe's Next Frontiers'. Speech at the European Policy Center, Brussels, 10 October.

Sedelmeier, U. (2014) 'Anchoring Democracy from Above? The European Union and Democratic Backsliding in Hungary and Romania after Accession'. *JCMS*, Vol. 52, No. 1, pp. 105–21.

Vachudova, M.A. (2014) 'EU Leverage and National Interests in the Balkans: The Puzzles of Enlargement Ten Years On'. *JCMS*, Vol. 52, No. 1, pp. 122–38.

Whitman, R.G. and Juncos, A.E. (2011) 'Relations with the Wider Europe'. *JCMS*, Vol. 49, No. s1, pp. 187–208.

Whitman, R.G. and Juncos, A.E. (2012) 'The Arab Spring, the Eurozone Crisis and the Neighbourhood: A Region in Flux'. *JCMS*, Vol. 50, No. s2, pp. 147–61.

Whitman, R.G. and Juncos, A.E. (2013) 'Stasis in Status: Relations with the Wider Europe'. *JCMS*, Vol. 51, No. s1, pp. 155–67.

Whitman, R.G. and Juncos, A.E. (2014) 'Challenging Events, Diminishing Influence? Relations with the Wider Europe', *JCMS*, Vol. 52, No. s1, pp. 157–69.

© 2015 The Author(s) JCMS: Journal of Common Market Studies © 2015 John Wiley & Sons Ltd

JCMS 2015 Volume 53 Annual Review pp. 216–229   DOI: 10.1111/jcms.12272

Europe as a Global Actor: the (Un)Holy Trinity of Economy, Diplomacy and Security

KAROLINA POMORSKA and SOPHIE VANHOONACKER
Maastricht University

Introduction

It has become customary in recent years to start the *JCMS Annual Review* articles on the EU as a global actor by signalling the omnipresence of crises. The year 2014 is no different. In his contribution to this volume, Desmond Dinan even coins the expression of a more 'fractious' year than ever before. Both the international as well as the European context have indeed proven to be challenging in various respects. On the global level, the difficult transformation is ongoing and there is no consensus on the norms and rules that could govern a shared international order (Kissinger, 2014). In Europe, the annexation of the Crimean peninsula and the war in Ukraine triggered the most serious security crisis since the end of the Cold War, exposing deep dividing lines between the Member States.[1] Domestically, economic recovery has been slow and the 2014 elections for the European Parliament showed an increasingly disenchanted European public giving a considerable number of votes to eurosceptic parties.[2] In the world of EU external relations we observed a 'change of guard', with newcomers in the positions of Presidents of the European Council and the European Commission and High Representative/Vice President (HR/VP) from autumn 2014. For this reason, we start our contribution with a short evaluation of Ashton's term of office (December 2009 to November 2014), followed by an initial discussion on the significance of the changes in leadership for the Union's policy in the world.

As a second step, we examine three major areas in which the EU traditionally has pledged to make an 'international difference': playing the role of market actor, security actor, and diplomatic actor. We borrow this typology from Mike Smith (2012), who, reflecting on the hybridity of EU external relations, also included a fourth role of normative actor. In our view, the normative dimension pervades all three external roles performed by the EU, so we do not distinguish it here as a separate category. The concept of roles is attractive as it allows for an analysis that combines both material factors (such as institutions, procedures and resources) as well as ideational factors (images, expectations and discourses) (Smith, 2012, p. 705).

As the EU continues to be the world's biggest trading power, we begin by looking into the major developments in the field of the Common Commercial Policy (CCP), with special attention given to the negotiations of the Transatlantic Trade and Investment

---

[1] See Juncos and Whitman's contribution to this volume.

[2] See the contributions by Hodson, Hobolt and Benczes and Szent-Ivanyi to this volume.

© 2015 The Author(s) JCMS: Journal of Common Market Studies © 2015 John Wiley & Sons Ltd, 9600 Garsington Road, Oxford OX4 2DQ, UK and 350 Main Street, Malden, MA 02148, USA

Partnership (TTIP) and the Bilateral Investment Treaty with China. Second, we analyse the EU's role in the field of the Common Security and Defence Policy (CSDP) by looking at the question of defence as well as civilian and military crisis management. In 2014, the EU was involved in 15 crisis management operations, of which the majority were mostly taking place in Africa. Third, we look into the role of the EU as a diplomatic actor and an international broker by focusing on the case of Iran, where, in 2014, the HR/VP Ashton played a key co-ordinating role in the negotiations on Teheran's controversial nuclear programme.

I. Five Years of Catherine Ashton and the European External Action Service

The year 2014 was the last of the five-year tenure of the first High Representative for Foreign Affairs and Security Policy, Catherine Ashton. Even though she received considerable praise in the year before her departure, largely due to perceived success in negotiations with Iran (see below), her leadership and management of the EEAS was met with harsh criticism both from the press[3] and from academia (Howorth, 2011; Spence, 2012; Vanhoonacker and Pomorska, 2015). In spite of the extenuating circumstances of a challenging international context and having to build up a new service from scratch, there were also considerable inherent weaknesses in the ways in which the HR/VP and the EEAS functioned.

Five years ago, in their contribution to the *Annual Review*, Allen and Smith (2010, p. 205) wondered whether the changes introduced by the Lisbon Treaty would provide the basis for a new role of the EU in the world arena. Their previous assessments had shown that there was often much to report in terms of institutional structures but little on real policy substance. Looking back at the first years of the HR/VP and the EEAS, we see that not much has changed. The reasons for this are mixed but the attitude and actions by the Member States stand out as key. When the EU Heads of State and Government decided to give the job to Ashton in December 2009, it was clear that they did not have the ambition of nominating a strong foreign policy chief with considerable experience in foreign policy and diplomacy. Ashton confirmed this minimalist interpretation in her first public speeches, when she contrasted her own approach to that of Javier Solana, claiming she would concentrate on 'quiet diplomacy'. This, in turn, sparked a debate among practitioners and observers with the central question: 'why did she take this huge job, when her instinct seems to be to make it as low key as possible?'[4] At the time of writing in 2015, we may be closer to an answer – because this is what the Member States, especially the larger ones, wanted her to do (Balfour and Raik, 2013). The benchmark was set low as far as independence from the Member States was concerned; no 'competence creep' would be tolerated (Edwards, 2013, p. 285) and competition with national diplomatic services was 'unacceptable' (Wright, 2013, p. 9; Adler-Nissen, 2013).[5]

The first priority that Ashton turned to was capacity-building: establishing the EEAS and having it operational. Her negotiation skills and determination led to relatively smooth and fast negotiations with the Member States and to the agreement on the Council

[3] *The Economist*, 5 February 2011; *European Voice*, 5 January 2012.
[4] *The Economist*, 26 January 2010.
[5] On Ashton's appointment, see Barber (2010). For more on Member States and EU foreign policy see last year's Annual Review lecture: Menon (2014).

© 2015 The Author(s) JCMS: Journal of Common Market Studies © 2015 John Wiley & Sons Ltd

framework decision outlining the EEAS organizational structure (Council of the EU, 2010). This was followed by a deal on budget and staff regulations. In the subsequent months, even years, the internal structures needed to be tried and verified, alongside the establishment of the operating procedures. Once the EEAS was set up, the HR/VP prioritized the external EU presence and her diplomatic role, such as in, for example, the negotiations with Iran or Kosovo. This prioritization, however, came at the detriment of 'putting her own house in order' and fostering the creation of an *esprit de corps* in the EEAS or focusing on internal agenda-setting in the Council (Vanhoonacker and Pomorska, 2013). Even in the field of external affairs, where Ashton invested more of her time and effort, there has not been any major improvement in the internal and external leadership (Vanhoonacker and Pomorska, 2015) – an opinion voiced in the Special Report of the European Court of Auditors (Court, 2014, p. 26). The document also established that the EEAS chairing the Working Groups and Committees in the Council had not shown any improvement in providing a more strategic approach in comparison with the pre-Lisbon situation, when the rotating presidency was in the chair.

A more positive side of the institutional transformation took place in the EU delegations around the world. The Member States' attitudes toward the delegations proved to be, in general, more positive than those toward the HQ in Brussels (Novotna, 2014, p. 30). Even here, however, the study of delegations in Washington DC and in Moscow has shown that the Member States were 'protective of their own turf', especially in situations when they felt the delegation was trying to either push its own particular view or to speak on matters where no single position had yet been agreed upon (Maurer and Raik, 2014, p. 9).

The area where we had seen a notable improvement for the better since the establishment of the EEAS is continuity (Vanhoonacker and Pomorska, 2015). The replacement of the rotating presidency by new institutional players put an end to the six-monthly stop–go process with sudden priority changes. The increased capacity through the availability of a permanent administration, both in Brussels and abroad, able to invest in developing expertise and long-term approaches to foreign policy is unquestionably an important step forward. The enduring presence of actors both at the political and administrative levels brought added value in terms of external representation and the development of long-term relations with external interlocutors.

Even though many hoped for the appointment of a more experienced successor, the post of HR/VP went again to a politician without considerable experience in the world of international politics, the Italian foreign minister Federica Mogherini. Her strongest rival, then Poland's foreign minister, Radek Sikorski, was out of the race once there was an agreement to appoint Donald Tusk as the new President of the European Council. Following the start of the Juncker Commission, it soon turned out that the new Commission president, who was very experienced in EU affairs, would try to do something about Ashton's legacy of prioritizing the position as chair of the Foreign Affairs Council over that of Commission Vice President. His expectations toward the new HR/VP were included in a mission letter addressed to Mogherini (European Commission, 2014c). Clearly, in the efforts to address the criticism toward the EEAS for not co-ordinating sufficiently its actions with the European Commission and, more broadly, to ensure the EEAS would not become a tool of the Member States, the new HR/VP, on the instructions of Commission president Juncker, decided to take a few significant steps. First, she left the EEAS building and relocated her office to the Berlaymont to join the other members of the College of Commissioners. Second, she appointed Stefano Marservisi, an experienced Commission official, as the head of her cabinet. Third, half of her cabinet had been recruited from the European Commission. Finally, she has, at the instigation of Juncker, reactivated the meetings of the Commissioners' Group on External Action. This task was previously very difficult to fulfil for Ashton, considering her busy agenda and the need to travel. Reacting to the calls for more coherence, the new HR/VP 'guides' the work of Commissioners responsible for European neighbourhood policy and enlargement negotiations; trade; international co-operation and development; and humanitarian aid and crisis management. It was envisaged that the group would meet once a month, which is an ambitious goal, considering the strained calendar of the High Representative (Blockmans, 2014). The task proved too difficult for the previous HR/VP, but Mogherini hoped to change that, which she also emphasized during her hearings in the European Parliament.

It is too early to tell what will be the outcomes of these decisions, but they will put to the test the relationship with the Member States, which are the driving force in foreign and security policies. Only a year after Catherine Ashton took office, it was clear that she would consolidate her activities within the Council and the EEAS (Allen and Smith, 2011), at the expense of the European Commission. Mogherini's different approach was also already clear early in her tenure. The appointment of an Italian national to the key post in foreign affairs, during a period of strained relations with Russia, proved controversial in many (especially central and eastern) European capitals. A product of a compromise, the choice of Mogherini did not ensure trust on the side of those Member States who now hope Donald Tusk will provide a 'counterbalance' with regard to the ongoing crisis beyond the EU's eastern border.

Some time ago, we pointed out considerable weaknesses in the use of the newly gained prerogative of agenda-setting (Vanhoonacker and Pomorska, 2013). This situation did not improve considerably in 2014. The HR/VP and the EEAS have been sidelined in the ongoing conflicts in EU's neighbourhood, especially the one in Ukraine. This, however, is because of the Member States' choices (sometimes resulting from accepting the preferences of their interlocutors such as Russia) to deal with the crises elsewhere. It proves once again that the EEAS for now can only be what the Member States 'make of it'. It has not developed into a strong institution, into anything akin to a foreign ministry.

There was also a change in other posts relevant to EU external relations: Donald Tusk took over the task of the President of the European Council. In his opening speech, given on 1 December 2014, Tusk said that 'Europe has to secure its borders and support those in the neighbourhood who share our values'. The first European Council summit over which he presided (18 December 2014) dealt with the new sanctions against Russia and Tusk used the opportunity to emphasize the need for a long-term strategy toward Russia.[6] His calendar during the first three days in the new job was filled with foreign policy items: calling the White House; making a pro-American statement; meeting the new Afghani leadership; and having discussions with the presidents of China, Ukraine and the Nato

---

[6] *The Telegraph*, 19 December 2014.

© 2015 The Author(s) JCMS: Journal of Common Market Studies © 2015 John Wiley & Sons Ltd

Secretary General.[7] A former speech writer to Herman van Rompuy, Luuk van Middelaar, suggested that Tusk might want to do for foreign affairs 'what van Rompuy did for the euro'.[8] It is certainly too early to make any judgment at this point, but we will return to this topic in next year's *Annual Review*.

II. The European Union as a Market Actor

As the world's largest trade power, the European Union undeniably continues to occupy a key place in the international trading system, and it is well known that it uses this position to export its regulatory practices and to promote its own values in third countries (Meunier and Nicolaidis, 2011). With the rise of the emerging powers, however, the EU's long-term position is expected to become increasingly challenged. Some have argued that as a result of the changing political and economic power relations the EU's capacity to use trade as an instrument of international influence will diminish over time (McGuire and Lindeque, 2010). It is, therefore, not surprising that the EU has been exploring ways to consolidate its position. Against the background of the changing geopolitical context and the stalled Doha negotiations, the EU has in recent years increasingly resorted to the conclusion of bilateral Free Trade Agreements (FTAs), trade and co-operation agreements and association agreements.[9]

Despite the well-known rhetoric about multilateralism (European Security Strategy, 2003; Van Schaik and Ter Haar, 2013), the EU has continued to invest heavily in bilateral deals. An important achievement in this respect was the conclusion in September 2014 of the negotiations on the EU–Canada Comprehensive Economic and Trade Agreement,[10] the first EU free trade agreement with a G8 economy. The 1500-page agreement was negotiated over a period of five years and includes, among other things, a gradual removal of customs for almost all goods, increased regulatory co-operation, the opening up of public procurement, improved protection of intellectual property rights, the streamlining of trade in services and the promotion of investment. The fully-fledged investment chapter also contains provisions on an investor-to-state dispute settlement (ISDS), which proved to be one of the more controversial stipulations of the treaty as it raised concerns that it may negatively affect governments' capacity to regulate in the public interest. The most important gains emerging from CETA are expected to come from the mutual recognition of regulations.

Following so-called 'legal scrubbing' and translation into the 24 EU official languages, the text will be presented to the Council for approval; it also requires the formal consent of the European Parliament. The entire process is expected to take two years, taking the ratification well into 2016 or even 2017 (Bierbrauer, 2014). In parallel with CETA, the EU and Canada have also concluded a Strategic Partnership Agreement (SPA), aimed at enhancing co-operation in foreign policy and crisis management as well as in sectoral policies such as energy, justice and home affairs and education and technology.

Although Canada is only the EU's 12th most important trading partner, the agreement is not unimportant, as it is expected to serve as a template for the Transatlantic Trade and

---

[7] *Bloomberg Business*, 12 December 2014.
[8] Cited in Carnegie Europe (2014).
[9] See for instance the bilateral free trade agreements (FTAs), including with South Korea (2011), Columbia (2013), Peru (2013), Singapore (2013) and several countries in Central America (2013).
[10] «http://trade.ec.europa.eu/doclib/docs/2014/september/tradoc_152806.pdf»

© 2015 The Author(s) JCMS: Journal of Common Market Studies © 2015 John Wiley & Sons Ltd

Investment Partnership (TTIP) with the United States. Following the launch of the negotiations in 2013, there were three major TTIP rounds in 2014. As levies on goods traded between both sides of the Atlantic are already very low, the negotiations mainly focused on regulatory co-operation and issues such as services, intellectual property rights and rules on investment and public procurement. Given the importance of the agreement, as the US is the EU's largest trading partner, the process received a lot of attention from trade unions, professional organizations and NGOs. Critical about the lack of transparency of the negotiations, opponents warned against the adoption of inferior American standards and a subordination of EU interests to US corporations. One of the most controversial provisions of the agreement is the earlier mentioned investor-to-state dispute settlement, allowing foreign companies to challenge governmental decisions that impact on their ability to make profits. With overall support of 58 per cent, a majority of European citizens in 2014 were still in favour of an extensive regional free trade agreement across the Atlantic (Eurobarometer, 2014); with, respectively, 53 and 41 per cent against, Austria and Germany were the most critical countries (Eurobarometer, 2015). However, it remains to be seen how these figures and concentration of criticism develop as the negotiations progress. In the US, at the time of writing (spring 2015), priority is being given to the Trans-Pacific Partnership Agreement (TTP), where the negotiations are reaching their final stage and where the big challenge for the Obama administration is to obtain fast-track authority from Congress.[11] Negotiated among 12 countries of the Asia-Pacific region, with the US and Japan as its key players and accounting for 40 per cent of the world's GDP,[12] it is one of the cornerstones of the Obama administration's economic policy.[13]

TTIP is a clear illustration of how trade agreements can also serve political purposes. In the light of the evolving geopolitical context and renewed tensions with Russia, the agreement is considered an instrument that can further strengthen the position of the west. The huge new market would serve as a pole of attraction for third countries, provide leverage in international trade negotiations and give a boost to the western economic model which, following the economic and financial crisis, is viewed more critically by emerging economies (Korteweg, 2015). The attraction of the agreement is well illustrated by the voices urging Brussels and Washington to become more open about possible accession or association of interested parties (Ulgen, 2014). An important concern for countries like Turkey and Norway, who heavily depend on the internal market, is that it will be difficult to 'multilateralize' the bilateral agreement once it has been concluded. It should also be an issue of further reflection for those in the UK advocating British exit from the EU.

Next to traditional partners such as Canada and the US, the EU has been investing heavily over recent years in the conclusion of trade agreements with Asia and Latin America. The obvious priority country is China, with whom the EU in November 2013 agreed upon a wide-ranging action plan for the period up to 2020 (EEAS, 2013). Although it also has a

---

[11] According to the fast-track negotiation authority or the Trade Promotion Authority (TPA), Congress can only validate international trade agreements as a package and not amend separate parts.
[12] The countries in question include Australia, Brunei, Canada, Chile, Japan, Malaysia, Mexico, New Zealand, Peru, Singapore, United States and Vietnam.
[13] Interview with European Parliament official, 23 April 2015.

© 2015 The Author(s) JCMS: Journal of Common Market Studies © 2015 John Wiley & Sons Ltd

political and civil society dimension, the economic pillar is clearly predominant (Smith, 2015). In 2014, the EU and China engaged in talks about a so-called bilateral investment treaty (BIT). An important objective is to provide investors with a secure legal framework and the abolition of restrictions on trade and investment. The current investment levels are very low, with only 2.1 per cent of EU Foreign Direct Investment (FDI) going to China. China only accounts for 1 per cent of EU FDI, but since 2008 the amounts that are invested have been growing rapidly, and are expected to surge further in the years to come (Meunier, 2014).

The ongoing negotiations over the EU–China BIT provide insights into both the strengths and weaknesses of EU external actorness (Meunier, 2014). The fact that, since the Lisbon Treaty, the EU has the exclusive competence to conclude international invest-ment treaties (Art. 207, TFEU) should in principle increase its leverage over third parties, positively affect its access to attractive international markets and enhance its capacity to impose its rules and values. In practice, however, it remains to be seen whether the European Commission, representing the 28 Member States, will be able to exploit its collective bargaining power and shape the international investment regime according to its own preferences. The long legacy whereby individual Member States were concluding their own BITs cannot be swept away overnight. In addition, countries such as Germany and France have expressed fears that an EU-level agreement may be more restrictive than one concluded on a national basis, and it is tempting for China to exploit EU internal differences. A final challenge is that the EU has the legal obligation to include clauses on sustainable development, human rights and environmental protection (Art. 205, TFEU). It is well known that China is extremely reluctant to have its hands tied by all kind of conditions and will therefore not hesitate to try to exploit its preferential relations with Member States such as Germany to limit the conditionality requirements to a minimum.

Summarizing, the year 2014 has shown a very active EU in terms of 'market power', not only in traditional fields of trade in goods and services but also in areas such as intel-lectual property rights, regulatory matters and investment policy. As is illustrated by the TTIP negotiations with the US and the BIT discussions with China, the trend of previous years whereby there is an increasing emphasis on the conclusion of bilateral agreements continues. As shown by the parallel negotiations with both the US and China, exerting influence in a world with multiple centres of gravity is complex and requires action at several fronts at the same time.

III. The European Union as a Security Actor

In the area of the Common Security and Defence Policy, the year 2014 was particularly challenging for the so far mainly silent 'D' in CSDP. The crisis in Ukraine more than ever brought the urgent need for a more articulated strategic direction and enhanced capabili-ties to the fore. It also gave a new impetus to the debate about defence spending in Europe and led some of the eastern Member States to reconsider their defence budgets. During the summer, Poland announced its plans to increase defence spending from the current 1.95 per cent to 2.0 per cent in 2016, while Latvia and Lithuania pledged to reach that level by 2020. The European Commission, through its Industry Commissioner, called for greater collaboration between Member States' defence industries, repeating the earlier appeal of the European Council, in December 2013, to develop a more integrated

© 2015 The Author(s) JCMS: Journal of Common Market Studies © 2015 John Wiley & Sons Ltd

European defence technological and industrial base (EDTIB) (European Council, 2013). The defence industry also came into the spotlight with discussion on the contracts between the Russian government and some Member States, in particular France, which, as a result of the situation in Ukraine, reluctantly postponed the delivery of two Mistral-class assault ships.

The limits of the CSDP are well illustrated when comparing the EU's timid response to the crisis on its eastern border to the response given by Nato. The latter, at its summit in Wales (September 2014), promptly raised the objective of collective defence again to the top of its agenda, immediately accompanying this strategic decision with concrete measures of operationalization (North Atlantic Council, 2014). This included the adoption of a Readiness Action Plan defining measures to respond to the security challenges along Nato's borders both in the east and the south and plans for the creation of a Very High Readiness Joint Task Force (VJTF) deployable within a couple of days. Nato also has taken much more seriously the concerns of the Baltic States and Black Sea Region by responding with military training exercises in the region (Duke and Vanhoonacker, forthcoming). For the EU, so far, this type of action is simply impossible.

Still, there were also some positive developments in the field of EU security and defence. Even though the overall impact of the 2013 December summit on CSDP has so far been limited, it nevertheless led to some follow-up initiatives in 2014. They mainly concerned striving for a strategic outlook, such as the adoption of an EU Strategy for Security at Sea, the EU Cyber Defence Policy Framework and a Policy Framework for Systematic and Long-Term Defence Cooperation (CEPS, 2015, p. 5). Another initiative was related to the adoption of a European Union Maritime Security Strategy (EUMSS), which was agreed upon in June. This welcome development took place in the complex environment of maritime security, where international co-operation had been quite difficult (European Parliament, 2013, p. 92), and can be understood as a 'litmus test' for the comprehensive approach to EU's external relations (Frontini, 2014). The long-awaited update of the 2003 European Security Strategy is, however, not to be expected before the end of 2017 or even early 2018. The revised strategy is supposed to be the result of a strategic reflection process to start after mid-June 2015 and will involve not only national governments but also representatives of civil society, think-tanks and academia.

With the ongoing crises in the EU's neighbourhood both in the east and south, crisis management is also back on the EU's agenda, in spite of the earlier signs that the EU's ambitions in this field might have been buried (Smith, 2013). In 2014, the EU launched two new missions: the Advisory Mission for Civilian Security Sector Reform in Ukraine (EUAM Ukraine, July 2014-)[14] and the civilian mission EUCAP Sahel Mali (April 2014-). The latter is aimed at restoring state authority in that country and complements the EU training mission for Malian armed forces (EUTM Mali, February 2013-). In addition, the EU continued to be engaged in various other countries and regions, especially in Africa.[15]

Within the realm of maritime security, for instance, the EU carried on with its EU NAVFOR Atalanta operation as a way to comprehensively tackle the piracy problem

---

[14] See Juncos and Whitman's contribution to this volume.

[15] Apart from Mali, other African countries in which the EU was involved include the Democratic Republic of Congo, Djibouti, Kenya, Libya, Niger, Seychelles, Somalia and Tanzania.

© 2015 The Author(s) JCMS: Journal of Common Market Studies © 2015 John Wiley & Sons Ltd

on the coast of Somalia, with Germany, Italy and Spain contributing ships. The mission, ongoing since 2008, is showing results: the piracy problem is diminishing and al-Shabaab is weakening (ECFR, 2015, p. 18). In November 2014, it was prolonged for another two years. Another new development was the relocation of the EU trainers of the Maritime Security Centre–Horn of Africa (MSC–HOA), providing 24-hour monitoring of vessels passing through the strategic Gulf of Aden. While previously working in Uganda, in February they were for the first time deployed to the capital of Somalia.

Due to the dramatic worsening of the security situation in Libya, the staff of the EU Integrated Border Assistance Mission in Libya (EUBAM) was relocated from Tripoli to Tunisia in August 2014 and was subsequently downsized to 17 members. The situation became too complex for the EU, but this, admittedly, can also be said about other international actors involved in the region who are also unable to stabilize the situation. Critics have pointed out that while the EU's efforts were geared toward achieving a long-term democratic transition and country reconstruction, not enough attention was given to short-term crisis-management planning and the possible use of military instruments. This, coupled with the fact that several Member States – such as Italy, France and the UK – undermined the collective action by the EU when they competed with each other to secure contracts for their defence industries, led to unsatisfactory results (Kostanyan and Blockmans, 2014, p. 2). The EEAS itself ascribed the lack of success in Libya to a lack of co-ordination between actors involved, leading to overlap, and to 'extremely low absorption capacity' resulting from the lack of political institutions and disagreements on political principles (EEAS, 2014b). The internal document also states that any EU re-involvement is only possible if there is a ceasefire.

The civilian mission EUCAP Sahel Niger launched in 2012 was extended in July for another two years. It was designed to collaborate with the CSDP Capacity Building Mission by providing training to the police, *Gendarmerie* and *Garde Nationale* in the country. When setting up the mission, the EU emphasized that it formed part of the comprehensive approach to security and development in the Sahel region.

Crisis management has always been considered a showcase for a comprehensive approach and it is certainly the case that the combination of approaches, including military missions with political and diplomatic actions and development and humanitarian aid, is an important asset. Still, as long as the EU is not willing to invest in its military capacities, it will remain condemned to small-scale and rather short-term missions. This has been all too clear in cases such as Syria and northern Iraq, where it was not the EU but the US taking the lead in the airstrikes against the Islamic State of Iraq and the ash-Sham (ISIS). As noted in a recent review of CSDP by a task force led by the former High Representative Javier Solana: 'without a strong military arm, the EU cannot live up to its self-imposed duty to protect security and development, or meet expectations of its citizens and international partners like the United Nations to provide added value by operationalizing its comprehensive approach to conflict prevention, crisis-management and peace-building' (CEPS, 2015, p. 3).

In sum, the increased international instability in 2014 has made the strengths and weaknesses of the EU as a security actor clearer than ever. Although it has over the years built up an important track record in crisis response and reached tangible results in cases such as Operation Atalanta, the EU finds it evidently more difficult to respond to hard security threats such as those posed by jihadi terrorist groups or territorial annexation. It is

© 2015 The Author(s) JCMS: Journal of Common Market Studies © 2015 John Wiley & Sons Ltd

therefore not surprising that in the above-mentioned CEPS report under the chairmanship of Solana (CEPS, 2015, p. 8), CSDP was called 'the weakest link in the European integration project'. When it comes to hard security, the EU continues to be more of a bystander rather than a security provider.

IV. The European Union as a Diplomatic Actor

The field of diplomacy provides the scene for the third role of the EU in the world. The historical record shows that we could expect some successes here in cases when there is no need for a 'European' army and where the EU's negotiators had been appreciated in the past. Of course, even in this role the EU faced some external limitations, one of which is the nature of international law, which is, in essence, traditional and focused on the role of states (Wessel and Van Vooren, 2013). Another limitation is of a practical nature. The EU may not always be wanted at the negotiation table, paradoxically, as a result of its growing international presence and involvement in the crisis situations. For example, after its initial engagement in the Ukrainian crisis (Ashton had a recognized presence in Kyiv, while the EU was actively involved in the Geneva negotiations in April 2014), from late spring 2014, Russia perceived the EU as a part of the 'problem' rather than an 'honest broker'. Consequently, the political negotiations proceeded in the so-called 'Normandy format' that consists of France, Germany, Russia and Ukraine – but without the EU, while a ceasefire would be negotiated with the engagement of the OSCE.

One of the EU's success stories is that of the negotiations on the Iranian nuclear programme. The outgoing HR/VP Catherine Ashton continued to chair the negotiations with Iran, which were initially scheduled to end in November, but continued for a further seven months (EEAS, 2014a). This created an unusual situation for the European Union, as it was uncertain who would continue fulfilling Ashton's role. Federica Mogherini was already busy in her new role, not least because of the evolving crisis to the east of the EU. Finally, at the end of the year, it was decided that Ashton would stay on as an EU special adviser on the Iranian nuclear talks. Her role was clearly appreciated by all stakeholders, as she kept the information flowing between the main actors involved. After months, even years, of extremely critical media coverage, the first HR/VP received praise in the international press, who called her the 'centre of the world diplomacy'.[16] She was reportedly greeted with a standing ovation from ambassadors on her return from the October round of negotiations.[17] This was due to her ability to build up a good relationship with Iranian foreign minister Mohammed Javad Zarif and bring the parties back to the negotiating table in October 2014. It was reportedly Ashton who convinced US secretary of state John Kerry to fly to Geneva in an unprecedented move. Notably, in pursuit of these efforts, the HR/VP even found the time to meet with Iranian women activists in March, spurring a wave of criticism from Iranian officials. Nevertheless, even though the EU was undoubtedly visible and the HR/VP played an important role in facilitating the talks, it was also understood that the crucial players are those outside Europe: the United States, China and Russia.

[16] *Der Spiegel*, 1 October 2013.
[17] *Financial Times*, 26 November 2014.

© 2015 The Author(s) JCMS: Journal of Common Market Studies © 2015 John Wiley & Sons Ltd

The success of the HR/VP personally in her role as a diplomatic actor may be related to the fact that she evidently prioritized this role over the others and that the style of negotiations played exactly into the style she announced at the start of her mandate as 'quiet diplomacy'. The success also resulted from long-term efforts into building personal trust and good relationships with all stakeholders involved. One limitation of this approach, however, is that people move on to different positions and there is no assurance of continuity.

Conclusions

Last year's *Annual Review* on the relations with the wider world spoke about the anticipated move from chaos to consolidation (Hadfield and Fiott, 2014). Unfortunately, as 2014 showed, this consolidation never happened and the EU was still facing major challenges both in its neighbourhood as well as globally. The year 2014 was the last in the five-year term of the first HR/VP, so we started our contribution with an evaluation of Ashton's legacy. While she was able to set up the new service in a relatively short time span and succeeded in difficult cases such as Iran and the Kosovo–Serbia dossier, it is clear that Ashton did not bring the supranational leadership that many had hoped for. This is, however, only partly the result of her self-perception as a facilitator rather than a leader and the lack of substantial foreign policy background. It is also a result of the reticence on the part of the Member States to create a truly European system of diplomacy where leadership would come from the European level. Although the new HR/VP, by moving to the Commission premises, has given a clear signal that she wanted to tilt the balance in a supranational direction, it remains to be seen whether Mogherini will be able to create a truly collective European diplomacy. The ongoing crisis in the EU's periphery may provide a new chance, but it may also prove an important obstacle as the sense of urgency and the proposed solutions in the different Member States vary widely.

In this contribution, we also analysed the EU's evolving role as a market, security and diplomatic actor in 2014. The ongoing negotiations of a Transatlantic Trade and Investment Partnership with the US and a Bilateral Investment Treaty with China illustrate that the EU continues to be an attractive trading partner for key international players. These bilateral consultations, however, also show that in a changing geo-economic and political context, where power is dispersed, there are several centres, both in the west and the east, with whom the EU wants to develop preferential relations. As a highly integrated market actor, the EU continues to be in a relatively good position to diffuse its internal norms and regulatory rules. However, as the EU–China BIT negotiations illustrate, non-western countries often resist the EU normative standards on human rights and sustainability and we will observe in the future whether a crisis-ridden EU will prioritize values over its eagerness to conquer new markets.

The most important challenges for the EU appeared in its role of a security actor – not so much in the area of crisis management, where it is gradually becoming an established actor, but in the area of defence. The crisis in Ukraine brought home the message that territorial defence continues to matter, even in a post-modern EU. Notwithstanding recent initiatives such as the adoption of a Maritime Security Strategy and an EU Cyber Defence Policy Framework, the EU has not progressed much when it comes to defence issues. As a result of its incapacity to develop its own military capabilities, it remains heavily

© 2015 The Author(s) JCMS: Journal of Common Market Studies © 2015 John Wiley & Sons Ltd

dependent on Nato and more particularly on the US, where the real decisions on the security of the European continent continue to be taken (Techau, 2015). With the instability on the EU's eastern and southern borders, the future shape of the European security architecture, as first discussed in Maastricht in 1991, is fully back on the agenda. Despite more than 20 years of CFSP/CSDP, it still seems more likely that the Americans and Nato, rather than the EU Member States, will remain in charge of guaranteeing the security of the continent.

Finally, this contribution also looked into the question of the EU's capacity to exert diplomatic influence. Here, the signals from the events of 2014 are mixed. While in a crisis such as Ukraine it is still the big Member States, such as Germany and France, who are the key players, the EU's role in the negotiations with Iran showed a respected international interlocutor who is able to make a difference. This success, however, has largely been built on Ashton's persistence and personal skills, which were lost once she left office. Examples presented in this review show that it is still the Member States rather than Brussels who would pick up the phone if third parties were calling (see also Cameron, 2015).

Taking a step back and looking at the overall picture emerging from the EU's response to the numerous external events of 2014, we see, perhaps not surprisingly, that the centre of gravity varies substantively depending on the area of external relations. Despite the Lisbon rhetoric about the abolition of the pillar structure and the single objectives for all dimensions of external action, it is clear that only in the area of external commercial policy does Brussels operate as the real centre of decision-making. In the area of diplomacy and security, the tone is still set by the different national capitals, while in the area of defence it is Washington DC that remains the predominant actor.

References

Adler-Nissen, R. (2013) 'Symbolic Power in European Diplomacy: the Struggle between National Foreign Services and the EU's External Action Service'. *Review of International Studies*, Vol. 40, No. 4, pp. 657–81.

Allen, D. and Smith, M. (2010) 'Relations with the Rest of the World'. *JCMS*, Vol. 48, No. s1, pp. 205–23.

Allen, D. and Smith, M. (2011) 'Relations with the Rest of the World'. *JCMS*, Vol. 49, No. s1, pp. 209–30.

Balfour, R. and Raik, K. (eds) (2013) *The European External Action Service and National Diplomacies, EPC Issue paper No. 73*, 8 (Brussels: The EPC).

Barber, T. (2010) 'The Appointments of Herman van Rompuy and Catherine Ashton'. *JCMS*, Vol. 48, No. s1, pp. 55–67.

Bierbrauer, E. (2014) *Negotiations on the EU–Canada Comprehensive Economic and Trade Agreement (CETA) Concluded* (Brussels: Directorate for External Relations, European Parliament). Available at «http://www.europarl.europa.eu/thinktank/en/document.html?reference=EXPO_IDA(2014)536410» Accessed 4 June 2015.

Blockmans, S. (2014) *Priorities for the Next Legislature: EU External Action, CEPS Commentary* (Brussels: Centre for European Policy Studies).

Cameron, F. (2015) 'Concluding Remarks'. In Smith, M., Keukeleire, S. and Vanhoonacker, S. (eds) *The Diplomatic System of the European Union: Evolution, Change and Challenges* (London and New York: Routledge).

© 2015 The Author(s) JCMS: Journal of Common Market Studies © 2015 John Wiley & Sons Ltd

Carnegie Europe (2014) Judy Asks: Can Tusk Boost Europe's Foreign Policy? Available at «carnegieeurope.eu/strategiceurope/?fa=57368»

CEPS (2015) *Report of a CFSP Task Force: More Union in European Defence* (Brussels: CEPS).

Council of the EU (2003) A Secure Europe in a Better World. European Security Strategy Brussels.

Council of the EU (2010) 'Council decision of 26 July establishing the organization and functioning of the European External Action Service', 2010/427/EU, 2010, OJ L201/30-40.

Duke, S. and Vanhoonacker, S. (2016, forthcoming) 'EU–NATO Relations: Top-down Strategic Paralysis, Bottom-up Cooperation'. In Chappell, L., Mawdsley, J. and Petrov, P. (eds) *The EU, Strategy and Security Policy* (London and New York: Routledge).

Edwards, G. (2013) 'The EU Foreign Policy in the Search for Effect'. *International Relations*, Vol. 27, No. 3, pp. 276–91.

EEAS (2013) *EU–China 2020 Strategic Agenda for cooperation* (Brussels: EEAS). Available at «http://eeas.europa.eu/china/docs/20131123_agenda_2020__en.pdf» Accessed 4 June 2015.

EEAS (2014a) Joint Statement by Catherine Ashton and Iranian Foreign Minister Mohammad Javad Zarif following the talks in Vienna, 24 November 2014. Available at «http://eeas.europa.eu/statements-eeas/2014/141124_02_en.htm» Accessed 4 June 2015.

EEAS (2014b) Libya, a Political Framework for a Crisis Approach. Cover Note, Brussels 1 October 2014, 13829/14.

European Commission (2013) Joint Communication to the European Parliament and the Council; The EU's Comprehensive approach to external conflicts and crises. Available at «http://www.eeas.europa.eu/statements/docs/2013/131211_03_en.pdf» Accessed 4 June 2015.

European Commission (2014a) *Trade and Investment 2014* (Luxembourg: Publications Office of the European Union).

European Commission (2014b) *Public Opinion in the European Union. First Results*. Standard Eurobarometer 82. Available at «http://ec.europa.eu/public_opinion/archives/eb/eb82/eb82_first_en.pdf» Accessed 4 June 2015.

European Commission (2014c) President Juncker's Mission Letter to Federica Mogherini, 1 November. Available at «http://ec.europa.eu/commission/sites/cwt/files/commissioner_mission_letters/mogherini_en.pdf» Accessed 4 June 2015.

European Council (2013) Conclusions, Brussels, 20 December 2013. Available at «http://www.eca.europa.eu/Lists/ECADocuments/SR14_11/SR14_11_EN.pdf» Accessed 4 June 2015.

European Council on Foreign Relations (2015) *European Foreign Policy Scoreboard 2015* (London: ECFR).

European Court of Auditors (2014) Special Report: The Establishment of the European External Action Service, No. 11, Luxembourg. Available at «http://www.eca.europa.eu/Lists/ECADocuments/SR14_11/SR14_11_EN.pdf» Accessed 4 June 2015.

European Parliament (2013) The Maritime Dimension of CSDP: Geostrategic Maritime Challenges and Their Implications for the European Union, Directorate-General for External Policies of the European Union. Available at «http://www.europarl.europa.eu/RegData/etudes/etudes/join/2013/433839/EXPO-SEDE_ET(2013)433839_EN.pdf» Accessed 4 June 2015.

Frontini, A. (2014) The European Union Maritime Security Strategy: Sailing Uncharted Waters? CEPS. Available at «http://www.epc.eu/pub_details.php?pub_id=4569» Accessed 4 June 2015.

Hadfield, A. and Fiott, D. (2014) 'Relations with the Rest of the World: From Chaos to Consolidation?'. *JCMS*, Vol. 52, No. s1, pp. 170–85.

Howorth, J. (2011) 'The "New Faces" of Lisbon: Assessing the Performance of Catherine Ashton and Herman van Rompuy on the Global Stage'. *European Foreign Affairs Review*, Vol. 16, No. 3, pp. 303–23.

Kissinger, H. (2014) *World Order* (London: The Penguin Press).

Korteweg, R. (2015) 'It's the Geopolitics Stupid: Why TTIP Matters'. *Centre for European Reform*, 2 April 2015. Available at «http://www.cer.org.uk/insights/it's-geopolitics-stupid-why-ttip-matters»

Kostanyan, G. and Blockmans, S. (2014) *Saving Libya from Itself: What the EU Should Do Now*. CEPS Commentary, 1 December 2014.

Maurer, H. and Raik, K. (2014) *Pioneers of a European Diplomatic System*, FIIA Analysis no. 1.

McGuire, S. and Lindeque, J. (2010) 'The Diminishing Returns to Trade Policy in the European Union'. *Journal of European Public Policy*, Vol. 17, No. 5, pp. 1329–49.

Menon, A. (2014) 'The JCMS Annual Review Lecture: Divided and Declining? Europe in a Changing World'. *JCMS*, Vol. 52, No. s1, pp. 5–24.

Meunier, S. (2014) 'Divide and Conquer? China and the Cacophony of Foreign Investment Rules in the EU'. *Journal of European Public Policy*, Vol. 21, No. 7, pp. 996–1016.

Meunier, S. and Nicolaidis, K. (2011) 'The European Union as a Trade Power'. In Hill, C. and Smith, M. (eds) *International Relations and the European Union* (Oxford: Oxford University Press).

North Atlantic Council (2014) Wales Summit Declaration Issued by the Heads of State and Government participating in the meeting of the North Atlantic Council in Wales, 5 September. Available at «http://www.nato.int/cps/ic/natohq/official texts_112964.htm» Accessed 4 June 2015.

Novotna, T. (2014) 'The EU's Voice in Third Countries. The EU Delegations around the World'. *Studia Diplomatica*, Vol. 67, No. 1, pp. 29–45.

Smith, M. (2012) 'Still Rooted in Maastricht: EU External Relations as a "Third-generation Hybrid"'. *Journal of European Integration*, Vol. 34, No. 7, pp. 699–715.

Smith, M.E. (2013) 'The European External Action Service and the Security–Development Nexus: Organizing for Effectiveness or Incoherence?' *Journal of European Public Policy*, Vol. 20, No. 9, pp. 1299–315.

Smith, M. (2015) 'The EU and China: The Politics and Economics of Strategic Diplomacy'. In Smith, M., Keukeleire, S. and Vanhoonacker, S. (eds) *The Diplomatic System of the European Union: Evolution, Change and Challenges* (London and New York: Routledge).

Spence, D. (2012) 'The Early Days of the European External Action Service: A Practitioners' View'. *The Hague Journal of Diplomacy*, Vol. 7, No. 1, pp. 115–34.

Techau, J. (2015) European Security After Ukraine. Carnegie Europe. Available at «http://carnegieeurope.eu/strategiceurope/?fa=59025» Accessed 4 June 2015.

Ulgen, S. (2014) Locked in or Left out? Transatlantic trade beyond Brussels and Washington, Carnegie Europe. Available at: «http://carnegieeurope.eu/2014/06/03/locked-in-or-left-out-transatlantic-trade-beyond-brussels-and-washington/hcf1» Accessed 4 June 2015.

Vanhoonacker, S. and Pomorska, K. (2015) 'EU Diplomacy Post-Lisbon: The Legacy of the Ashton Era'. In Smith, M., Keukeleire, S. and Vanhoonacker, S. (eds) *The Diplomatic System of the European Union: Evolution, Change and Challenges* (London and New York: Routledge).

Vanhoonacker, S. and Pomorska, K. (2013) 'The European External Action Service and agenda-setting in European Foreign Policy'. *Journal of European Public Policy*, Vol. 20, No. 9, pp. 1316–31.

Van Schaik, L. and Ter Haar, B. (2013) 'Why the EU is Not Promoting Effective Multilateralism. On a Fundamental Flaw in the European Security Strategy', *Clingendael Policy Brief*, No. 21, June.

Wessel, R. and Van Vooren, B. (2013) 'The EEAS' Diplomatic Dreams and the Reality of European and International Law'. *Journal of European Public Policy*, Vol. 20, No. 9, pp. 1350–67.

Wright, N. (2013) 'Co-operation, Co-optation, Competition? How do Britain and Germany Interact with the European External Action Service?' Paper presented at the 43rd UACES Annual Conference, University of Leeds, UK, 2–4 September.

© 2015 The Author(s) JCMS: Journal of Common Market Studies © 2015 John Wiley & Sons Ltd

JCMS 2015 Volume 53 Annual Review pp. 230–236   DOI: 10.1111/jcms.12258

Chronology: The European Union in 2014

CHARLOTTE GALPIN
University of Bath

At a Glance

Presidencies of the EU Council: Greece (1 January–30 June) and Italy (1 July–31 December)

January

1	Latvia adopts the euro, bringing the number of eurozone members to 18.
1	The last restrictions on the free movement of workers from Bulgaria and Romania are lifted.
1	The European Youth Initiative comes into force.
15	The Commission proposes measures to tackle radicalization and violent extremism in the EU.
16	The Ukrainian Parliament passes anti-protest laws which lead to violent clashes in western Ukraine. The laws are subsequently overturned on 28 January with the resignation of Prime Minister Mykola Azarov.
16	The European Parliament launches an investigation into the democratic legitimacy of the Troika's role in the debt crisis.
20	The Commission announces its plan to develop Europe's renewable ocean energy sector.
20	At the Foreign Affairs Council, the EU suspends a number of economic sanctions against Iran as part of the Joint Plan of Action on Iran's nuclear programme. It also approves a military operation in the Central African Republic.
21	Serbia's EU accession negotiations begin.
28	The EU–Russia summit takes place in Brussels.
29	Bohuslav Sobotka of the centre-left Social Democrats is appointed Prime Minister of the Czech Republic, taking over from Jiří Rusnok, following elections in October.

February

5	The EU and Ecowas (Economic Community of West African States) reach a deal on the Economic Partnership Agreement.
9	Switzerland votes to limit immigration under EU freedom of movement rules in a referendum.
11	Greek and Turkish Cypriot leaders agree to the resumption of negotiations between the two sides.
17	EU suspends sanctions against top Zimbabwean officials.
22	Ukrainian Parliament votes to relieve President Viktor Yanukovych of his office following deadly clashes in Kyiv; he flees to Russia.

© 2015 The Author(s) JCMS: Journal of Common Market Studies © 2015 John Wiley & Sons Ltd, 9600 Garsington Road, Oxford OX4 2DQ, UK and 350 Main Street, Malden, MA 02148, USA

22	Matteo Renzi of the Democratic Party becomes Prime Minister of Italy following the resignation of Enrico Letta.
24	The EU–Brazil summit takes place in Brussels.
25	The European Parliament backs new rules on CO_2 emissions for new cars.
27	The Cypriot Parliament rejects the privatization plan required under the country's bailout terms.
27	Arseniy Yatsenyuk becomes Ukrainian Prime Minister.
27–28	Pro-Russian gunmen occupy the regional parliament and airport in Simferopol, the capital of the Crimean peninsula in Ukraine.

March

6	Following an extraordinary European Council meeting on Ukraine, EU leaders call for the immediate withdrawal of Russian forces from Crimea.
11	The Commission adopts a new mechanism for safeguarding the rule of law in EU Member States.
11	The European Parliament votes in favour of draft anti-money laundering rules, which would introduce a public register of company and trust owners.
16	97 per cent of voters back secession from Ukraine in an informal and unrecognised referendum held in Crimea. Two days later the peninsula is incorporated into the Russian Federation.
16	In parliamentary elections in Serbia, the Progressive Party (SNS) wins the most votes. Its leader Aleksandar Vučić subsequently becomes Prime Minister.
20–21	At the European Council, EU leaders discuss the Ukraine crisis and extend the first sanctions against Russia, which include travel bans and asset freezes for Russian officials. Other topics discussed include the European Semester, taxation and climate and energy policy.
21	The political part of the EU–Ukraine Association Agreement is signed by EU leaders and the Ukrainian Prime Minister.
24–25	53 countries, including the US, South Korea and the UK, take part in the third world Nuclear Security Summit in The Hague.
26	The EU–US summit takes place in Brussels.
26	Taavi Rõivas of the Reform Party becomes Prime Minister of Estonia, taking over from the chairman of the party, Andrus Ansip.
29	In a second-round run-off election, Andrej Kiska is elected President of Slovakia, beating Prime Minister Robert Fico.

April

1	Manuel Valls of the Socialist Party becomes French Prime Minister following the resignation of Prime Minister Jean-Marc Ayrault.
2–3	The EU–Africa summit takes place in Brussels.
6	In parliamentary elections in Hungary, Viktor Orbán is re-elected Prime Minister after his Fidesz party, in alliance with the small Christian Democratic People's Party, wins a constitutional two-thirds majority in Parliament.
6	Pro-Russian rebels take control of government buildings in the eastern Ukrainian cities of Kharkiv, Donetsk and Luhansk.

© 2015 The Author(s) JCMS: Journal of Common Market Studies © 2015 John Wiley & Sons Ltd

15	The Ukrainian government launches a military operation to regain control of eastern territories captured by pro-Russian separatists.
15	The European Parliament approves Commission proposals for a single resolution mechanism to complement the single supervisory mechanism, together comprising the EU's banking union.
16	The European Parliament votes to strengthen the transparency register for lobbyists.
16	The European Parliament votes to cut use of lightweight plastic bags by 50 per cent by 2015 and 80 per cent by 2019.
27	In presidential and parliamentary elections held in the Republic of Macedonia, the incumbent right-wing party VMRO-DPMNE wins the most votes, returning Nikola Gruevski as Prime Minister and Gjorge Ivanov as President.
28	The EU allows visa-free travel to the Schengen zone for Moldovan citizens.
30	The European Court of Justice rejects the UK's challenge to financial transactions tax plans as premature.

May

5	The Slovenian government collapses and Prime Minister Alenka Bratušek resigns after losing the leadership of the Positive Slovenia party.
7	The EU–Japan summit takes place in Brussels.
11	Separatists in the eastern Ukrainian cities of Donetsk and Luhansk declare independence following referendums.
13	In a test case against Google, the European Court of Justice backs the 'right to be forgotten' under EU privacy law.
17	Portugal becomes the second country to exit its bailout package.
22–25	Elections to the European Parliament are held across the EU. Winning 221 seats, the centre-right European People's Party (EPP) becomes the largest party. The Progressive Alliance of Socialists and Democrats (S&D) wins 191 seats, the European Conservatives and Reformists (ECR) wins 70, and the Alliance of Liberals and Democrats for Europe (ALDE) wins 67. The Greens/European Free Alliance (Green/EFA) takes 50 seats and the European United Left/Nordic Green Left (GUE/NGL) takes 52.
25	Belgian federal elections take place after three people are shot dead at the Jewish Museum in Brussels the previous day. The nationalist party New Flemish Alliance (N-VA) wins the most votes.
25	Dalia Grybauskaitė is re-elected President of Lithuania in a run-off election.
25	Petro Poroshenko is elected President of Ukraine with 54.7 per cent of the vote, an absolute majority which makes a second-round election unnecessary.
27	At a special meeting in Brussels, EU leaders discuss the presidential election in Ukraine and call on Russia to co-operate with Poroshenko.

June

| 2 | The Commission tables proposals for tackling global poverty and sustainable development, to contribute to the UN sustainable development goals. |
| 4 | The Commission announces that Lithuania has met the criteria for adopting the euro, confirming its accession on 1 January 2015. |

© 2015 The Author(s) JCMS: Journal of Common Market Studies © 2015 John Wiley & Sons Ltd

4–5	A G7 meeting takes place in Brussels, reduced from a G8 amid tensions with Russia over the crisis in Ukraine.
5	The European Central Bank (ECB) announces funding for new long-term loans for eurozone banks, known as targeted longer-term refinancing operations (TLTROs).
10	The Islamic State of Iraq and Syria (ISIS) seizes the Iraqi city of Mosul, followed by Tikrit a day later.
16	The Finnish government resigns and Prime Minister Jyrki Katainen of the National Coalition party steps down. Foreign Minister Alexander Stubb becomes Prime Minister.
18	Spanish King Juan Carlos formally abdicates, passing the throne to his son, Prince Felipe.
20	The Council votes to close a loophole under the Parent-Subsidiary Directive which allows multinational companies to avoid tax.
26–27	At the European Council, EU leaders agree to propose EPP candidate Jean-Claude Juncker as President of the European Commission. They also sign association agreements with Georgia and the Republic of Moldova and grant Albania EU candidate status. Ukraine also completes an association agreement with the EU.
30	A referendum proposing a ban on foreign ownership of land in Lithuania fails.

July

1	EU roaming charges are reduced, cutting the cost of web browsing by 55 per cent.
1	Martin Schulz is re-elected President of the European Parliament at the first session of the newly elected European Parliament.
13	The new centre-left party, the Party of Miro Cerar (SMC), comes first in parliamentary elections in Slovenia, ahead of the centre-right party, the Slovenian Democratic Party (SDS).
15	The European Parliament elects Jean-Claude Juncker as President of the European Commission.
16	At a special meeting, the European Council discusses key appointments in the EU, the Ukraine crisis and the situation in Gaza.
17	298 people die when Malaysian Airlines flight MH17 is shot down over rebel-held territory in eastern Ukraine.
17	EU agrees trade and development agreement with Ecuador.
22	The EU announces initiatives to increase funding for small and medium-sized businesses through the European Investment Fund's COSME programme and the Horizon 2020 programme.
23	Bulgaria's minority government resigns in light of controversies surrounding the South Stream pipeline, sparking new elections on 5 October.
30	New economic sanctions against Russia are announced, including restrictions on Russian access to EU capital markets and an arms embargo.

August

1	The eurozone's single euro payment area (SEPA) is completed.
5	The EU and Canada complete a draft text of the Comprehensive Economic and Trade Agreement (CETA) initiated in 2013.

© 2015 The Author(s) JCMS: Journal of Common Market Studies © 2015 John Wiley & Sons Ltd

6	The EU launches its Pan-African Programme, pledging €415 million to support continental African integration until 2017.
10	In the first direct election of a Turkish president, Prime Minister Recep Tayyip Erdoğan of the Justice and Development Party (AKP) wins with an outright majority.
12	At an extraordinary meeting of the Council's political and security committee, the EU agrees to Member States supplying arms to Iraqi Kurds fighting Islamic State insurgents.
18	The European Commission announces €125 million financial support for EU farmers affected by Russia's ban on Western food products.
21	The Commission adopts a strategy and action plan for customs risk management.
25	French President François Hollande asks Prime Minister Manuel Valls to form a new cabinet following the government's resignation in the wake of disputes over economic policy.
30	At a special European Council meeting, EU leaders appoint Polish Prime Minister Donald Tusk as President of the European Council and Italian Foreign Minister Federica Mogherini as High Representative for Foreign Affairs and Security Policy. Both take up their new roles on 1 December.

September

4–5	NATO summit is held in Wales.
12	The EU imposes new sanctions on Russia, including new asset freezes and travel bans and restrictions on the gas, oil and arms sector.
14	Altogether, the left-wing parties, which includes the Social Democrats, the Green Party and the Left Party, gain the most votes in general elections in Sweden but fail to achieve a parliamentary majority. The nationalist Swedish Democrats more than double their share of the vote. Social Democrat leader Stefan Löfven is confirmed as Swedish Prime Minister on 2 October.
16	EU–Ukraine association agreement ratified by European Parliament and the Ukrainian Parliament.
16	Start of 69th United Nations General Assembly in New York.
18	Scotland rejects independence from the United Kingdom in a referendum.
18	A new centre-left coalition government, headed by Prime Minister Miro Cerar and his eponymously named party, is approved by the Slovenian parliament.
22	Ewa Kopacz of the Civic Platform party becomes Prime Minister of Poland following Donald Tusk's appointment as President of the European Council.
24	The European Parliament agrees to Commission proposals to give heavy industries free carbon allowances under the EU emissions trading system.
26	EU–Canada Summit takes place in Ottawa.

October

| 1 | Former Norwegian Prime Minister Jens Stoltenberg takes over as Secretary-General of NATO. |
| 4 | In parliamentary elections in Latvia, the centre-left party Concord wins the most votes, followed by the centre-right Unity party led by Prime Minister Laimdota Straujuma. The ruling coalition parties achieve a majority of the |

© 2015 The Author(s) JCMS: Journal of Common Market Studies © 2015 John Wiley & Sons Ltd

	votes and Straujuma remains as prime minister, becoming the first re-elected female prime minister in Central and Eastern Europe.
5	The centre-right party Citizens for European Development of Bulgaria (GERB), led by Boyko Borisov, wins the most seats in parliamentary elections in Bulgaria.
7	135 days after the Belgian federal elections, four centre-right parties, including the N-VA, agree to form a government. Charles Michel of the Reformist Movement (MR) becomes Prime Minister.
7	The EU announces a plan for a new Mediterranean border patrol mission, Operation Triton.
12	General elections are held in Bosnia and Herzegovina. In the tripartite Presidency election, Bakir Izetbegović of the Party of Democratic Action (SDA) is re-elected to the Bosniak seat. Mladen Ivanić of the Party of Democratic Progress (PDP) wins the Serb seat, and Dragan Čović of the Croation Democratic Union wins the Croat seat.
16–17	The 10th Asia-Europe Meeting (ASEM) takes place in Milan.
22	The European Parliament approves Jean-Claude Juncker's Commission with 423 votes in favour, 209 against and 67 abstentions. The approval follows hearings in the European Parliament with all designated Commissioners and the rejection by MEPs of Slovenia's nominee, former prime minister Alenka Bratušek, with 112 votes to 13.
23	The European Commission issues the UK with a request for an additional €2.1 billion contribution to the EU budget.
23–24	At the European Council, EU leaders agree on the 2030 climate and energy policy framework, including the agreement of targets for greenhouse gas emissions, renewable energy and energy efficiency. They also promise €1 billion aid for West African countries hit by Ebola.
26	In parliamentary elections in Ukraine, Prime Minister Arseniy Yatsenyuk's party the People's Front narrowly beats President Petro Poroshenko's Bloc.
26	The European Banking Authority announces the results of its EU-wide stress tests of 123 European banks.
31	The EU secures a deal with Russia on gas supplies to Ukraine, including a $4.6 billion EU/IMF aid package to assist with Ukrainian debt.

November

1	Jean-Claude Juncker takes over as Commission President.
4	The ECB becomes banking supervisor for the eurozone under the single supervisory mechanism.
6	A minority government is formed in Bulgaria between the centre-right Citizens for a European Development of Bulgaria (GERB) and the centre-right Reformist Bloc. GERB leader Boyko Borissov returns as Prime Minister, replacing the caretaker premier Georgi Bliznashki.
11	Catalonians vote for independence in an informal, non-binding referendum, after the Spanish Constitutional Court suspends a formal vote.
12	European Space Agency probe Philae, from the Rosetta spacecraft, lands on a comet after a 10-year journey.
15–16	G20 summit in Brisbane, Australia.

16	In a run-off election, Klaus Iohannis of the Christian Liberal Alliance is elected President of Romania, defeating Prime Minister Victor Ponta of the Social Democrat Party and succeeding Traian Băsescu.
17	Portuguese interior minister Miguel Macedo resigns following a corruption investigation.
19	The European Commission announces further measures to improve transparency in TTIP negotiations and lobbying.
28	British Prime Minister David Cameron sets out his position on EU migration, warning that Britain's membership of the EU is at risk if rules on EU freedom of movement are not reformed.
30	In parliamentary elections in Moldova, the pro-Russian Socialist party (PSRM) wins the most votes, followed by the pro-European Liberal Democratic Party. No party wins an outright majority.

December

1	Former Polish Prime Minister Donald Tusk takes over the European Council presidency, replacing Herman Van Rompuy.
9	EU Member States reach a deal on 2015 budget to the amount of €141.2 billion.
14	At the 20th Conference of the Parties, the UN Climate Change Conference, all countries agree to reduce greenhouse gas emissions.
15	The first EU–Ukraine Association Council takes place in Brussels under the new association agreement.
18	The European Council summit is chaired for the first time by new European Council President Donald Tusk. Discussion centres on investment in Europe and the Eastern neighbourhood. Leaders agree to the €315 billion investment plan proposed by Juncker to boost the eurozone economy and encourage cash flows to southern Europe.
18	The European Court of Justice rules that the draft agreement on the EU's accession to the ECHR is incompatible with EU law.
19	The Parliament and Council agree to a deal on capping credit and debit card payment fees to reduce transaction costs for businesses and consumers.
20	New EU sanctions against Crimea take effect. These measures include a ban on investment in Crimea by Europeans or EU-based companies, exports in the oil and gas sectors.
29	In the third round of a presidential vote in the Greek parliament, Stavros Dimas fails to get a majority and a snap general election is called for 25 January 2015.

© 2015 The Author(s) JCMS: Journal of Common Market Studies © 2015 John Wiley & Sons Ltd

Index

Note: Italicised page references indicate information contained in tables.

© 2015 The Author(s) JCMS: Journal of Common Market Studies © 2015 John Wiley & Sons Ltd, 9600 Garsington Road, Oxford OX4 2DQ, UK and 350 Main Street, Malden, MA 02148, USA

© 2015 The Author(s) JCMS: Journal of Common Market Studies © 2015 John Wiley & Sons Ltd

© 2015 The Author(s) JCMS: Journal of Common Market Studies © 2015 John Wiley & Sons Ltd

Anywhere Article.
Any format, any device, any time.

Today, more than ever, we need access to information that is immediate, clear and communicable. As a member of the community we serve, you will know how important it is to have access to that data, whenever you need it, and wherever you are.

What is Anywhere Article?

Anywhere Article is focused on making our online journal content on Wiley Online Library more readable and portable, whilst also allowing rich information to be brought to the surface. It achieves these goals in the following ways:

1. Readability

Clean design. Superfluous information and unnecessary distractions have been removed so that readers can focus on the article. Figures can be viewed in context or separately, and easily navigated, browsed or downloaded.

2. Functionality

The new layout and sidebar tray allow readers access to important information, ie; references, figures, publication history at any point in the reading experience, without losing their place on the main page.

3. Mobility

Whatever device you use - desktop, tablet, or mobile - the article will be presented to take best advantage of that device, always readable, always easy to use, wherever you are.

When Can I Start Using Anywhere Article?

📄 Enhanced Article (HTML) You can view an article in the new 'Anywhere Article' format wherever you see this link. You'll be able to view it easily on the device of your choice, at your convenience.

Visit **www.wileyonlinelibrary.com** today and look out for the new links underneath each journal article, try it, and see the difference for yourself.

WILEY

Wiley Online Library

⊛WILEY Job Network

WE MAKE YOUR RESEARCH EASY.
NOW WE MAKE JOB HUNTING EASY.

Let your partners in research energize your career.

Drawing on our expertise and relationships across the research and business communities, Wiley-Blackwell invites you to join Wiley Job Network, the definitive job site for professionals in the sciences, technology, business, finance, healthcare and the arts.

- **FIND** premium jobs from the most respected names in your industry
- **ATTRACT** hundreds of recruiters and employers in your field
- **CREATE** job alerts that match your criteria
- **OBTAIN** expert career advice and candidate resources

Register and upload your resume/CV now to begin your job search!

wileyjobnetwork.com